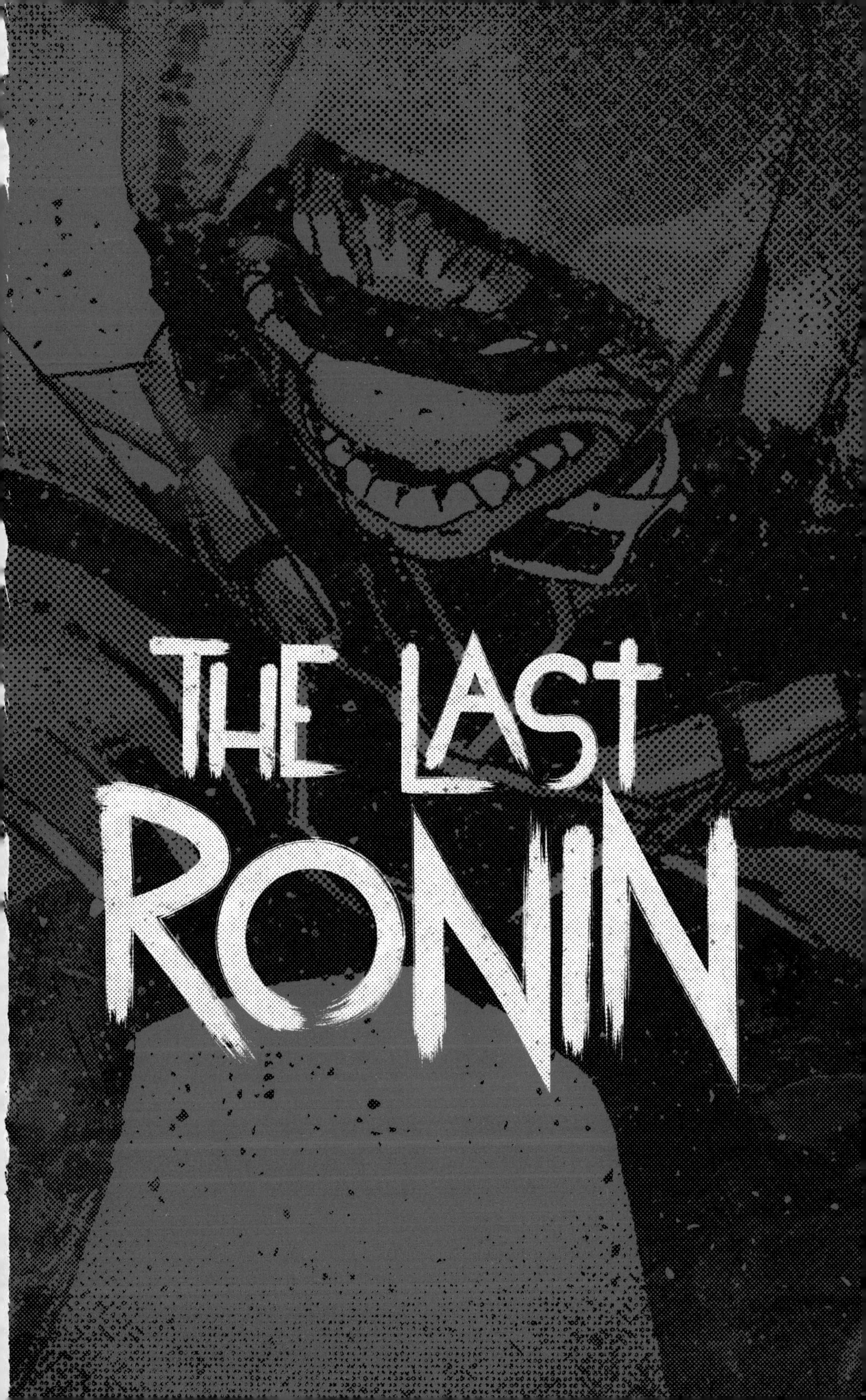
THE LAST
RONIN

Series Editor **Bobby Curnow**

Additional Editorial Coordination **R.G. Llarena**

Collection Editors **Alonzo Simon & Zac Boone**

IDW

TEENAGE MUTANT NINJA TURTLES: THE LAST RONIN. JANUARY 2023. SIXTH PRINTING. © 2022 Viacom International Inc. All Rights Reserved. Nickelodeon, TEENAGE MUTANT NINJA TURTLES, and all related titles, logos and characters are trademarks of Viacom International Inc. Based on characters created by Peter Laird and Kevin Eastman. The IDW Logo is registered in the U.S. Patent and Trademark Office. IDW Publishing, a division of Idea and Design Works, LLC. Editorial offices: 2355 Northside Drive, Suite 140, San Diego, CA 92108. Any similarities to persons living or dead are purely coincidental. With the exception of artwork used for review purposes, none of the contents of this publication may be reprinted without permission of Idea and Design Works, LLC. IDW Publishing does not read or accept unsolicited submissions of ideas, stories, or artwork. Printed in China.

Originally published as TEENAGE MUTANT NINJA TURTLES: THE LAST RONIN issues #1–5.

nickelodeon

Special thanks to Alexandra Maurer, Jeff Whitman, Linda Lee, James Salerno, and Joan Hilty for their invaluable assistance.

ISBN: 978-1-68405-841-9

26 25 24 23   6 7 8 9

@IDWpublishing
IDWpublishing.com

Story by

Kevin Eastman   **Peter Laird**   **Tom Waltz**

Script by

Kevin Eastman   **Tom Waltz**

Pencils/Inks by

Esau Escorza   **Ben Bishop**

Isaac Escorza   **Kevin Eastman**

Layouts by

Kevin Eastman

Colors by

Luis Antonio Delgado

Letters & Design by

Shawn Lee

Color Assistance by

Samuel Plata

Ronda Pattison

Cover Art by

Esau & **Isaac Escorza**

Cover Colors by

Luis Antonio Delgado

Introduction

I first discovered *Teenage Mutant Ninja Turtles* in the later '80s when I was in college.

The comics had been out a few years, the animated show had just begun, and it was the talk of the school because this phenomenon had been dreamed up in a kitchen over pizza by a couple of friends.

The original film came out a few years later, and I saw it in an advanced word-of-mouth preview screening.

I remember being blown away and inspired that this whole wild creation, that caught fire everywhere, was created independently and had started as an indie comic. It made us all feel like the sky was the limit and that maybe we too could come up with ideas that could mass entertain and have cultural impact. It was an exciting time, both as consumers and fans of comics, movies, and animation, and as budding creators.

Later, I again would get to experience just what a phenomenon of multi-generational fandom Ninja Turtles really was. I was able to turn all five of my kids onto it as each grew up through the many different eras and iterations of the property.

It was part of their rites of passage that they'd learn all about the lore and legacy of the Turtles and their world, through whatever medium was popular at the time.

And like a science project, I got to witness them argue passionately over which movies and animation versions were truer and more authentic (it always depended on which version each kid grew up with).

The only thing they seemed to agree on were the comics. They all loved the comics. We'd read them and draw from them.

I've gotten the privilege of being friends with Kevin Eastman over the past 12 years, and he's such an inspiration and the hardest working man in the business. I mean, this guy works hard. Hanging out in his studio while he cranked out a new run of *Ninja Turtle* comics was a life highlight for me.

It would blow my kids' minds that I knew Kevin Eastman. Whenever he was in Austin, he'd draw Turtles for my kids. He was the magic man. Them knowing the guy behind it all made them appreciate the property on a whole other level.

So, what a mind-blowing day it was when Kevin sent us a preview of *The Last Ronin* issue #1. Seeing their reaction as we read it together, it felt like a full circle in their growing up. Gut-wrenching and solemn at times, exciting...life-affirming and art affirming.

We all read it and were floored. It was yet another rite of passage for them going into the adult world.

We've now read the entire five-issue miniseries, and it's clear that *The Last Ronin* is a gritty, postapocalyptic, dramatic yarn that had us all riveted from start to finish. It was really something to see the series grow with them and get to this point at the right time of their lives. I can't think of another IP that has done that, that aligned with my and my kids' lives like that.

A true testament to the lasting and continuing impact this creation has had on our collective lives as a family.

So strap yourselves in, for this is serious fun. It's wildly imaginative and a full-senses assault that demonstrates the lasting power of the Turtles' inspired world, the independent spirit, and their collective lasting impact.

It's also a true testament to the passion and hard work of the treasure that is Kevin Eastman.

Robert Rodriguez

Filmmaker

Austin, Texas

March 3, 2022

Art by **Esau & Isaac Escorza**

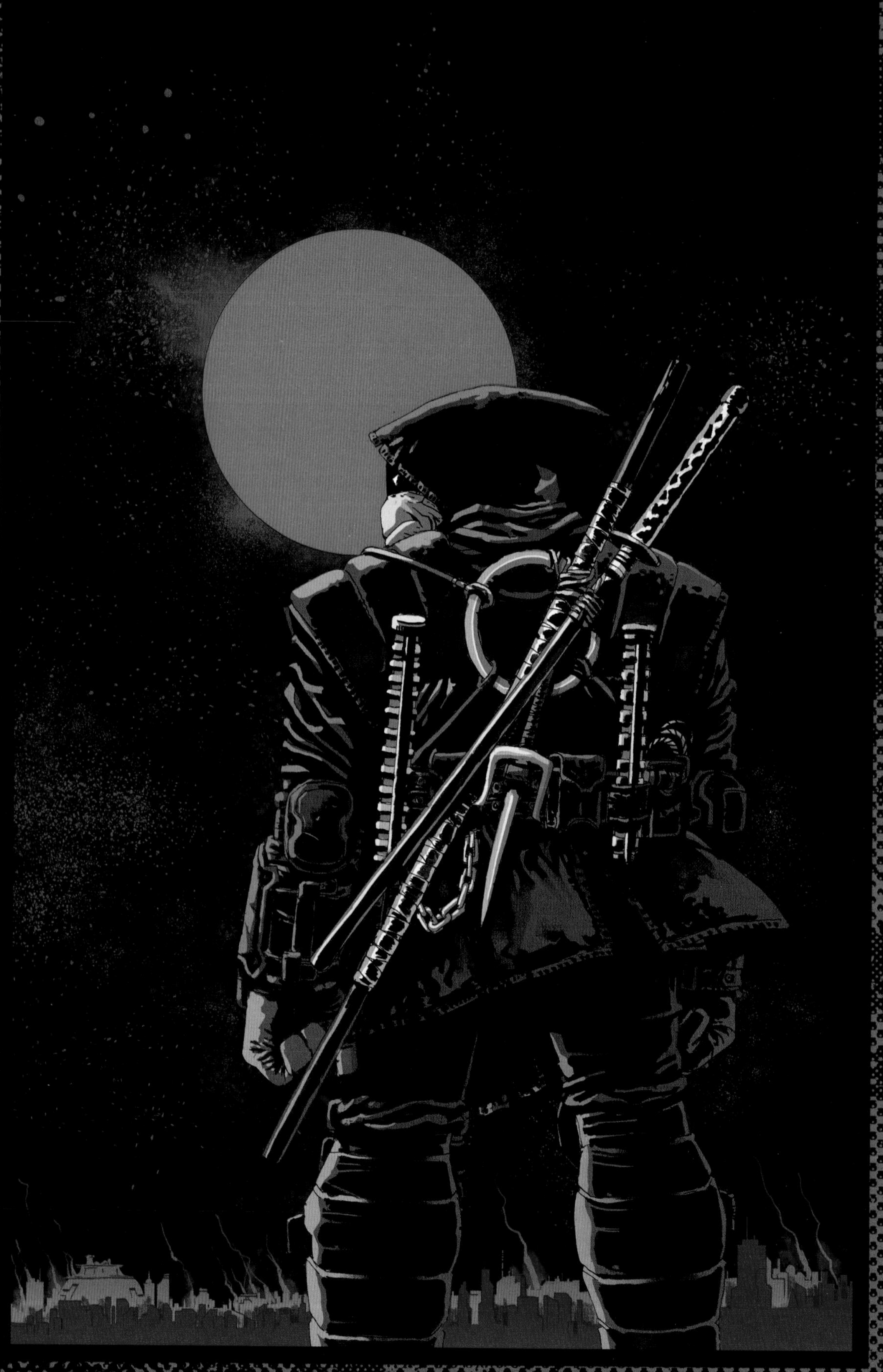

Colors by **Luis Antonio Delgado**

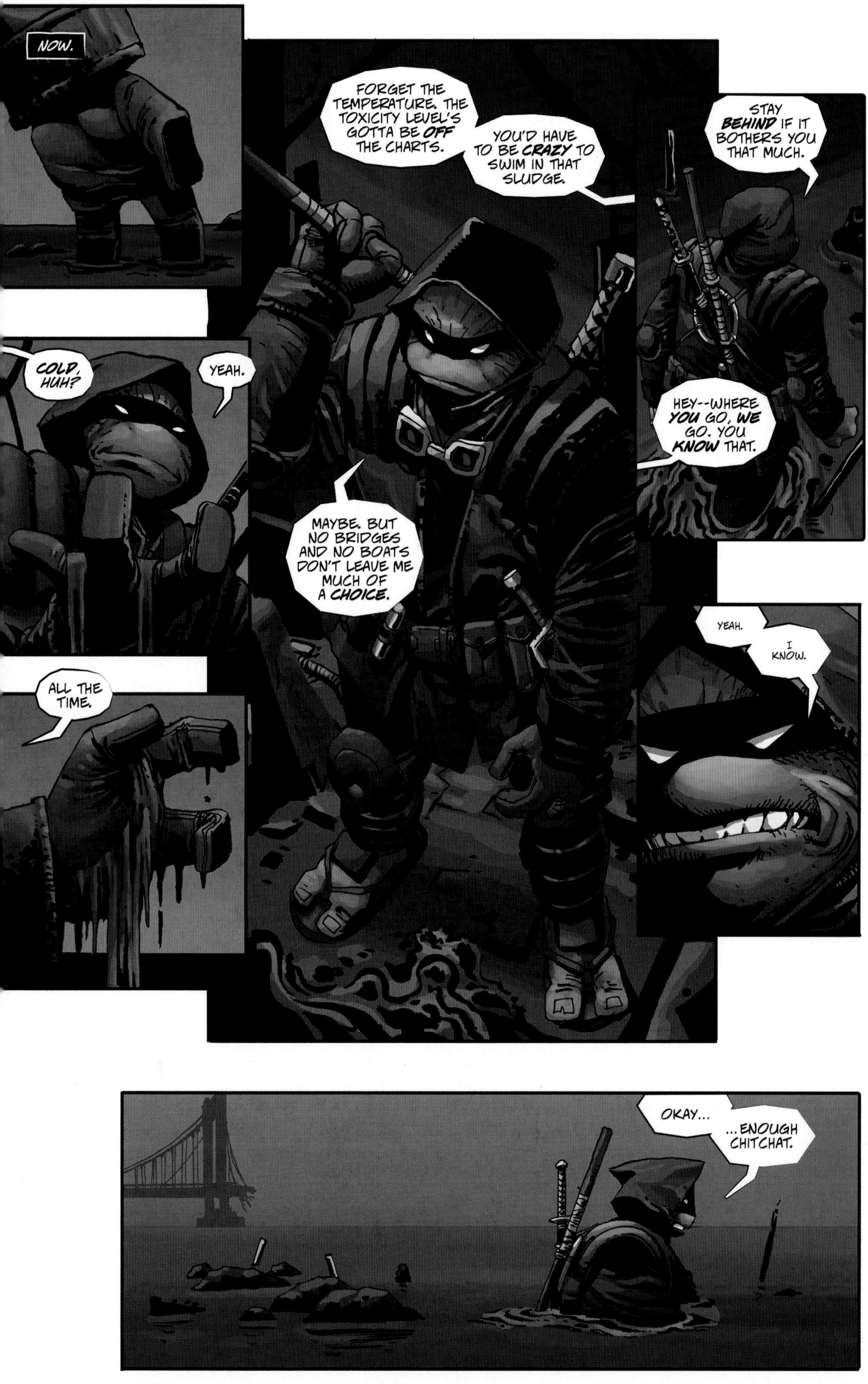
NOW.
COLD, HUH?
YEAH.
ALL THE TIME.
FORGET THE TEMPERATURE. THE TOXICITY LEVEL'S GOTTA BE OFF THE CHARTS.
YOU'D HAVE TO BE CRAZY TO SWIM IN THAT SLUDGE.
MAYBE. BUT NO BRIDGES AND NO BOATS DON'T LEAVE ME MUCH OF A CHOICE.
STAY BEHIND IF IT BOTHERS YOU THAT MUCH.
HEY--WHERE YOU GO, WE GO. YOU KNOW THAT.
YEAH.
I KNOW.
OKAY...
...ENOUGH CHITCHAT.

THE LAST RONIN PART 1

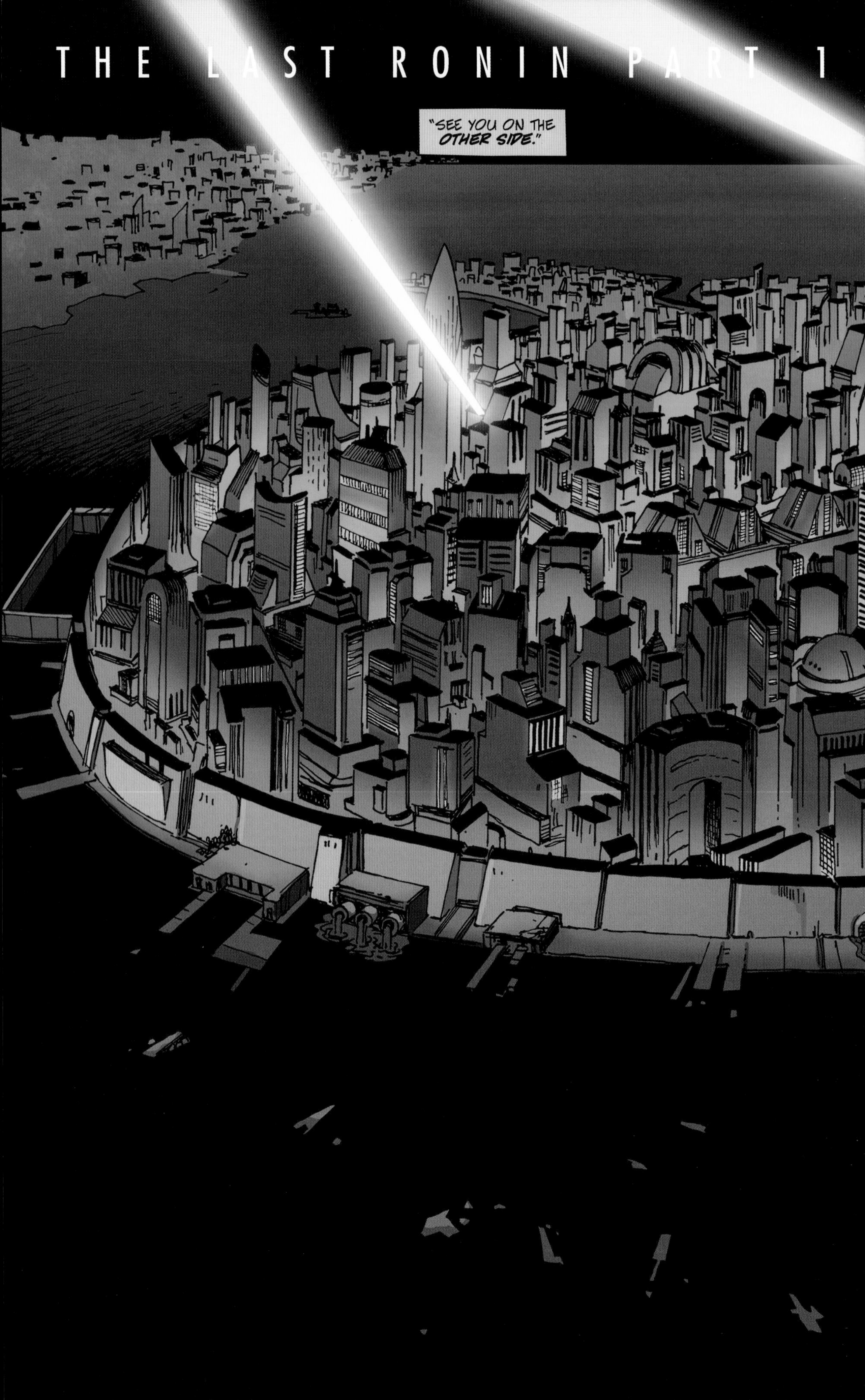
"SEE YOU ON THE OTHER SIDE."

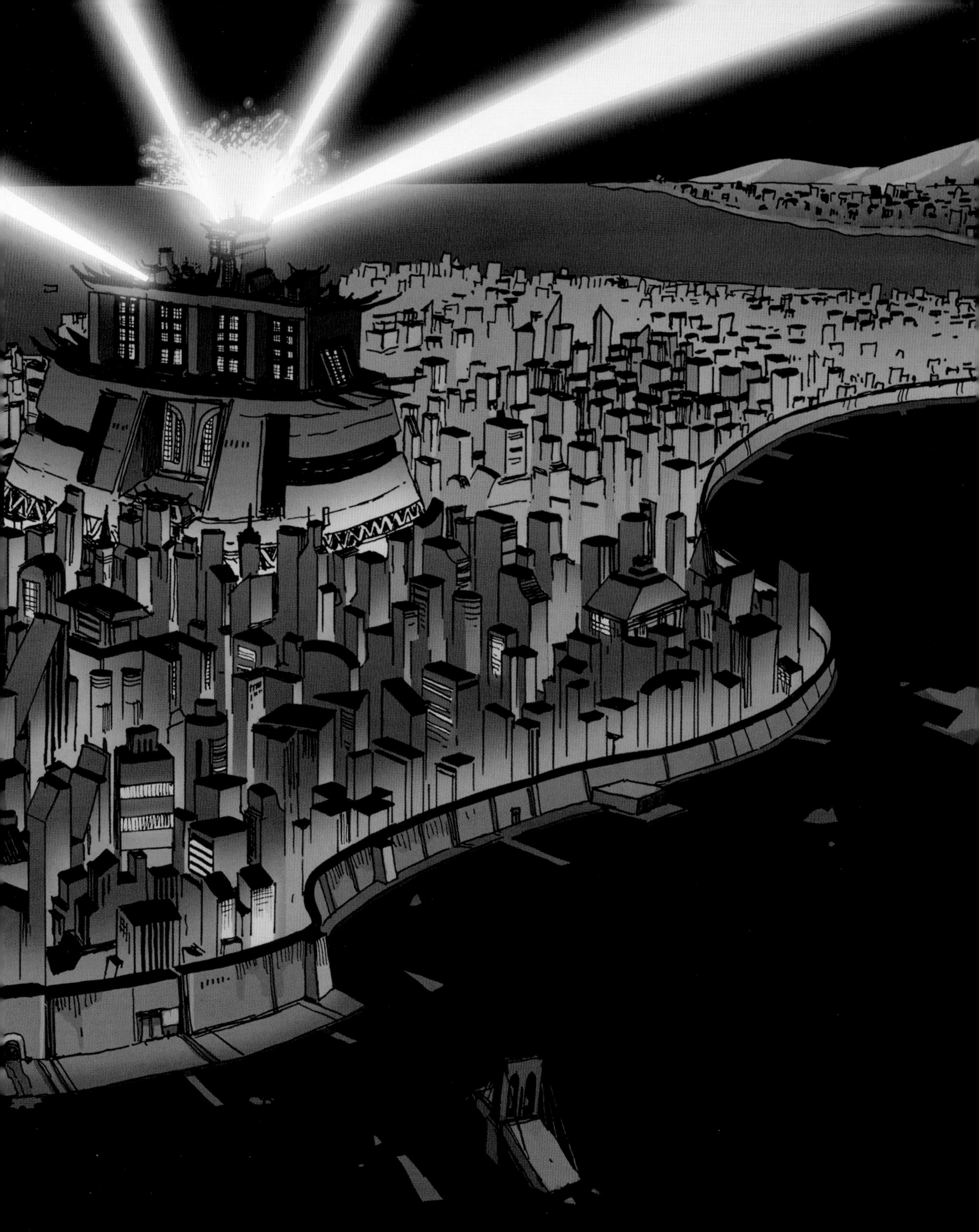

"WISH FOR DEATH"

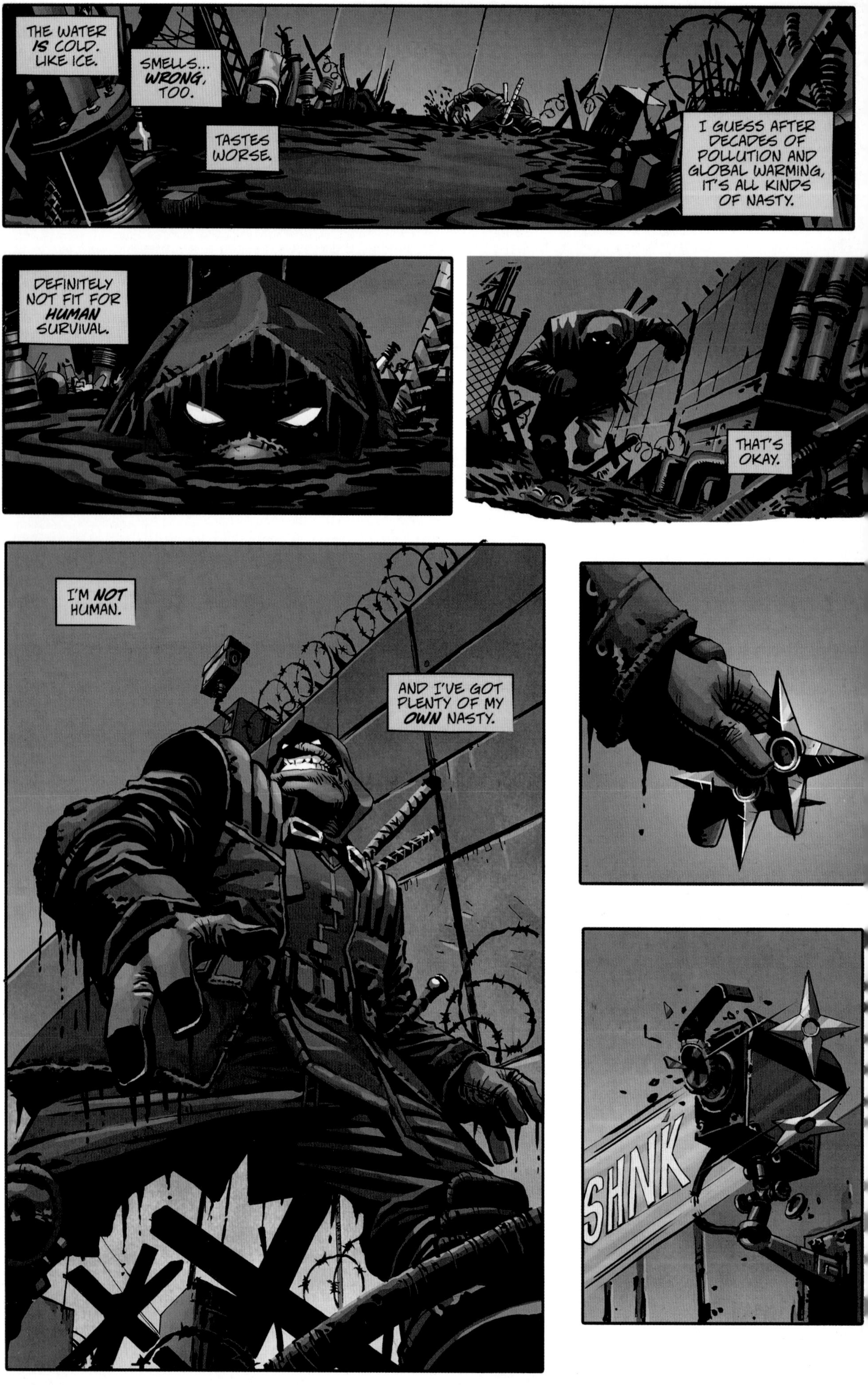
THE WATER IS COLD. LIKE ICE.
SMELLS... WRONG, TOO.
TASTES WORSE.
I GUESS AFTER DECADES OF POLLUTION AND GLOBAL WARMING, IT'S ALL KINDS OF NASTY.
DEFINITELY NOT FIT FOR HUMAN SURVIVAL.
THAT'S OKAY.
I'M NOT HUMAN.
AND I'VE GOT PLENTY OF MY OWN NASTY.
SHNK

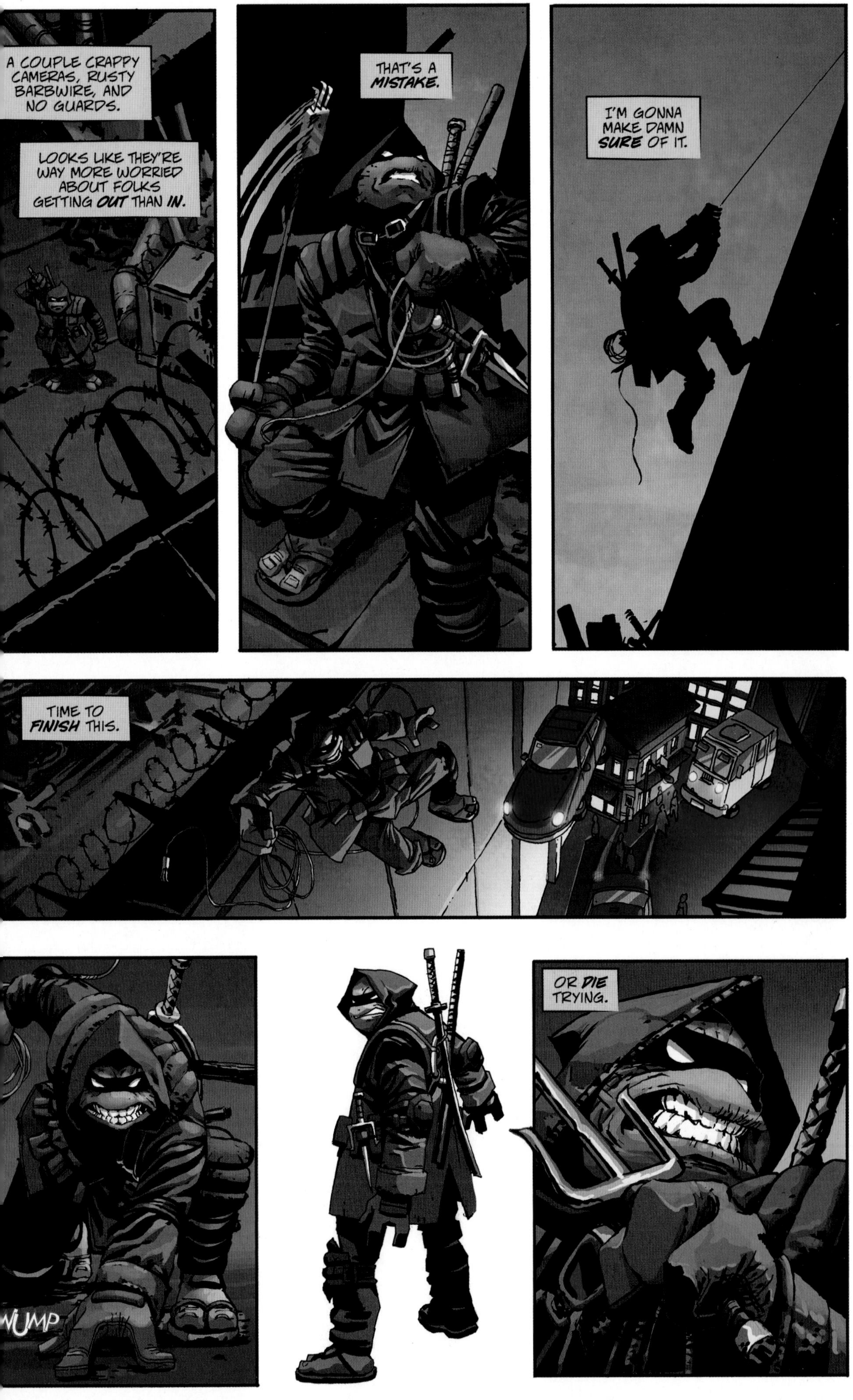
A COUPLE CRAPPY CAMERAS, RUSTY BARBWIRE, AND NO GUARDS.
LOOKS LIKE THEY'RE WAY MORE WORRIED ABOUT FOLKS GETTING OUT THAN IN.
THAT'S A MISTAKE.
I'M GONNA MAKE DAMN SURE OF IT.
TIME TO FINISH THIS.
WUMP
OR DIE TRYING.

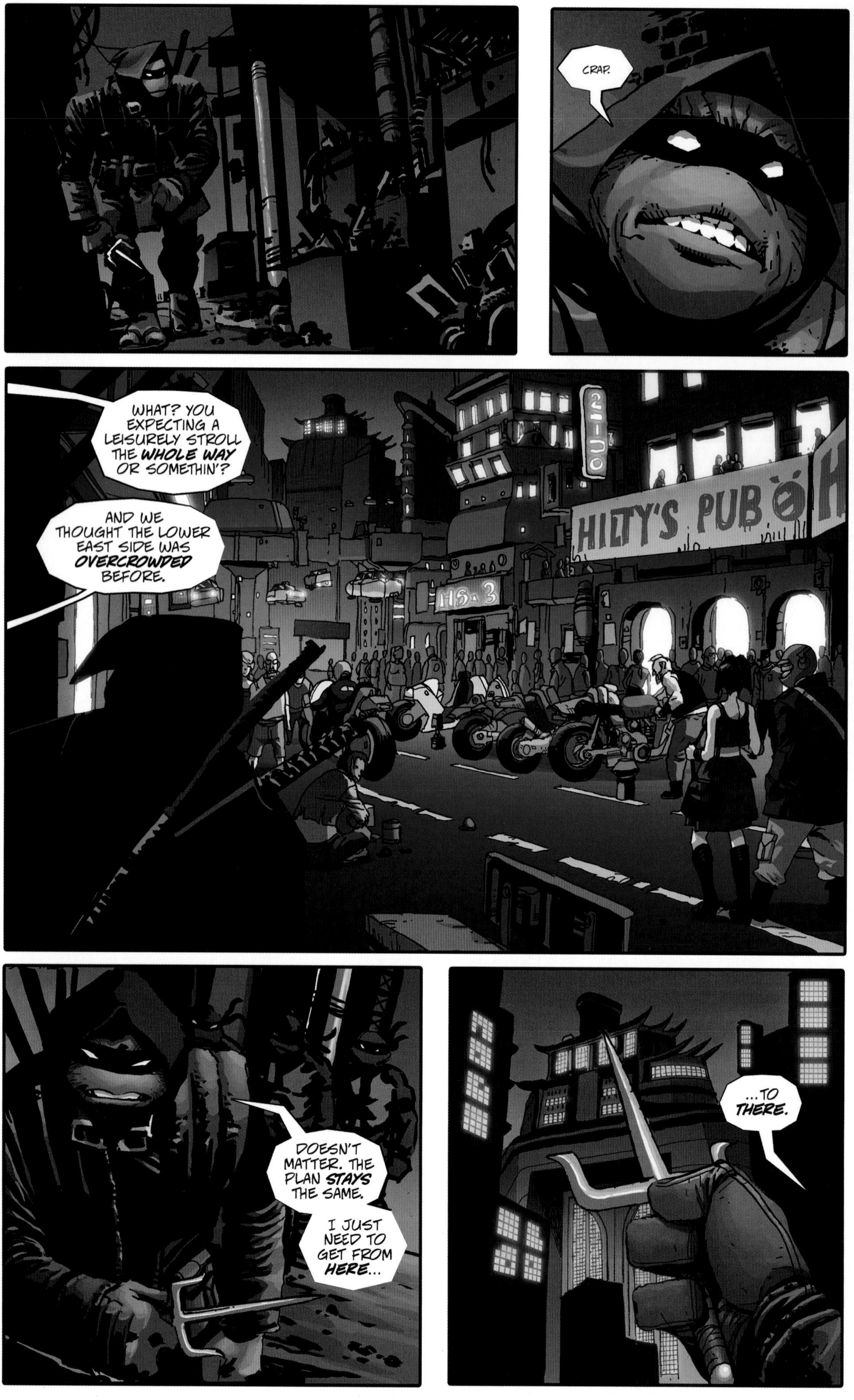
CRAP.
WHAT? YOU EXPECTING A LEISURELY STROLL THE WHOLE WAY OR SOMETHIN'?
AND WE THOUGHT THE LOWER EAST SIDE WAS OVERCROWDED BEFORE.
HILTY'S PUB
DOESN'T MATTER. THE PLAN STAYS THE SAME.
I JUST NEED TO GET FROM HERE...
...TO THERE.

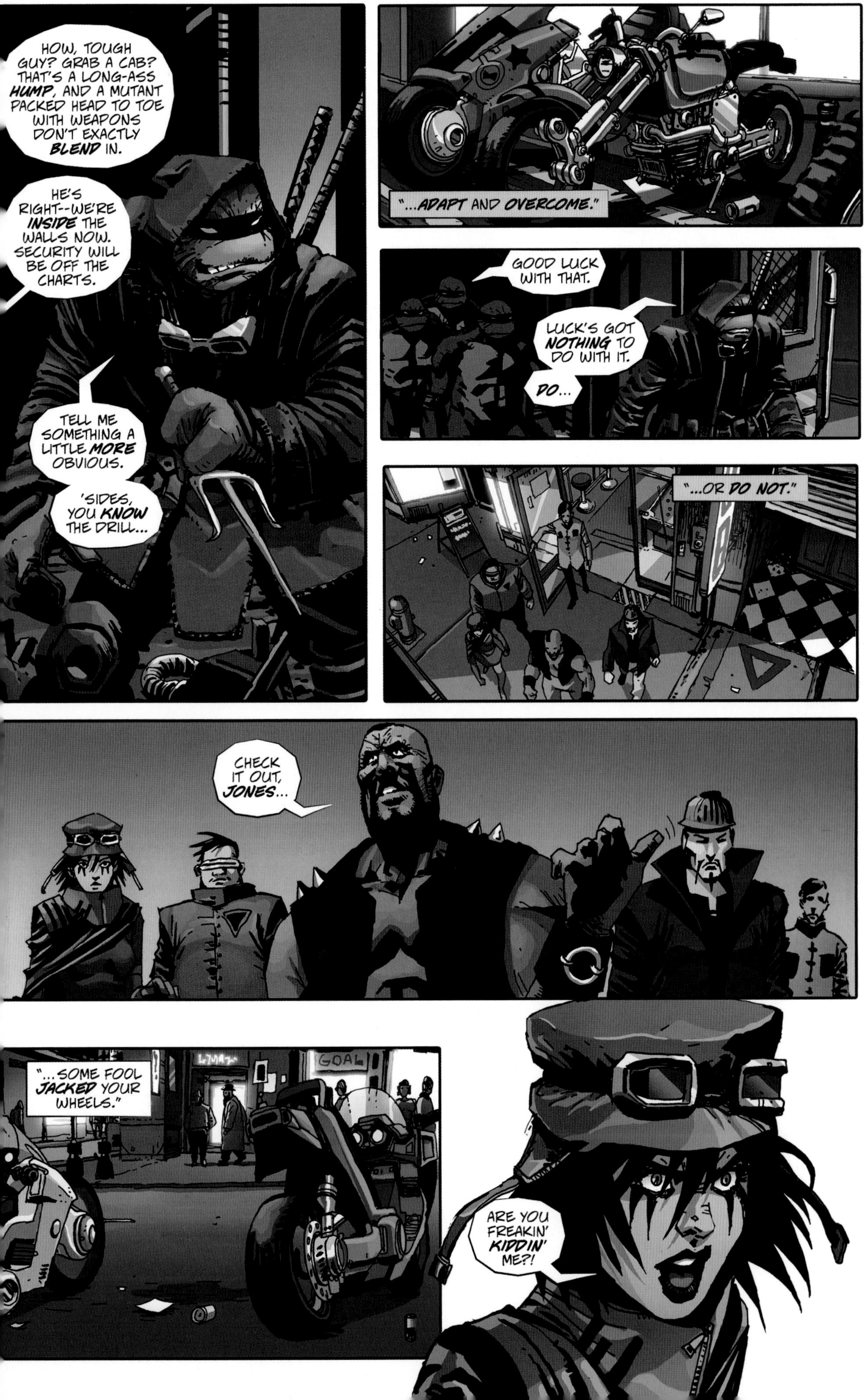
HOW, TOUGH GUY? GRAB A CAB? THAT'S A LONG-ASS HUMP, AND A MUTANT PACKED HEAD TO TOE WITH WEAPONS DON'T EXACTLY BLEND IN.
HE'S RIGHT--WE'RE INSIDE THE WALLS NOW. SECURITY WILL BE OFF THE CHARTS.
TELL ME SOMETHING A LITTLE MORE OBVIOUS.
'SIDES, YOU KNOW THE DRILL...
"...ADAPT AND OVERCOME."
GOOD LUCK WITH THAT.
LUCK'S GOT NOTHING TO DO WITH IT.
DO...
"...OR DO NOT."
CHECK IT OUT, JONES...
"...SOME FOOL JACKED YOUR WHEELS."
GOAL
ARE YOU FREAKIN' KIDDIN' ME?!

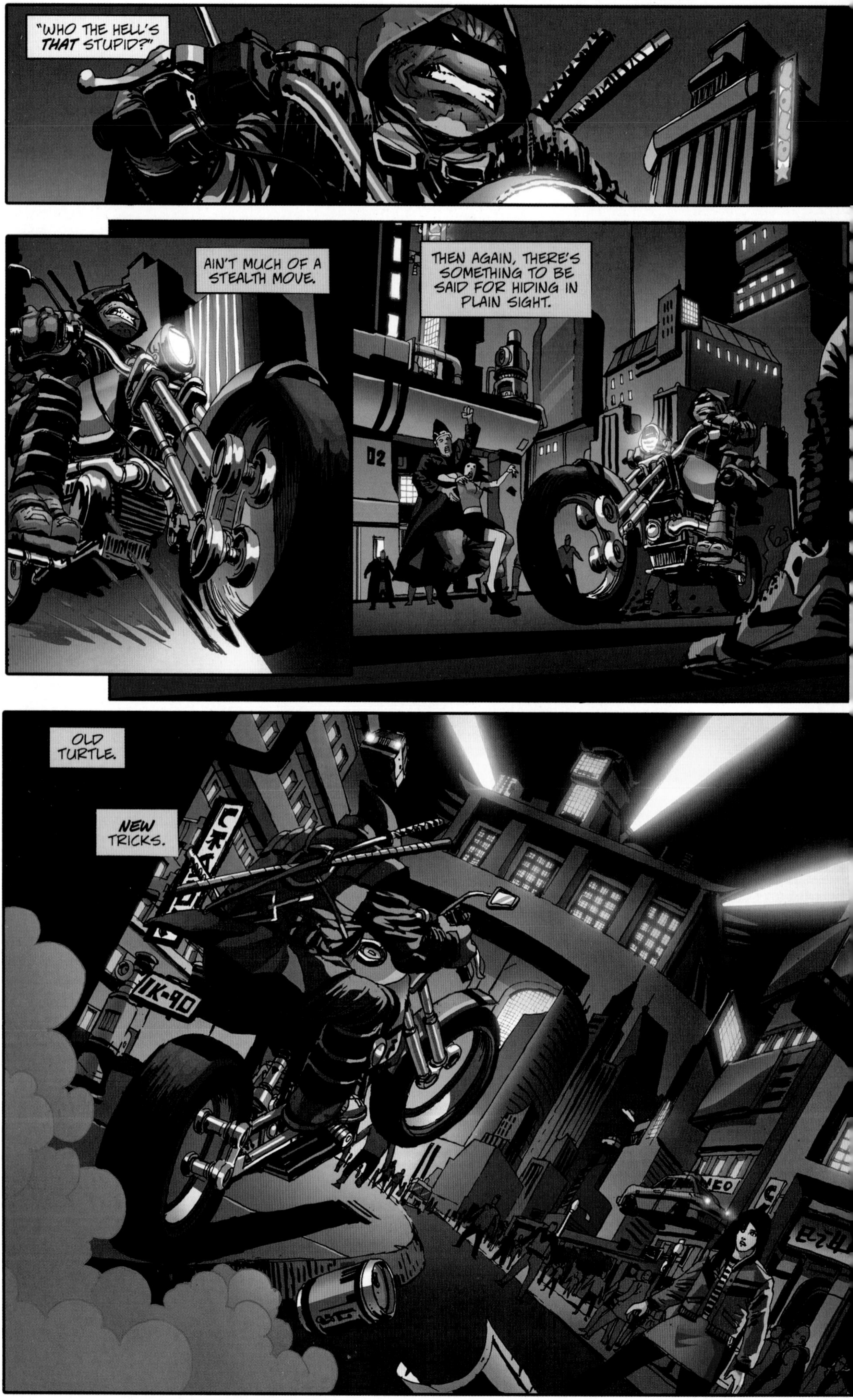
"WHO THE HELL'S *THAT* STUPID?"
AIN'T MUCH OF A STEALTH MOVE.
THEN AGAIN, THERE'S SOMETHING TO BE SAID FOR HIDING IN PLAIN SIGHT.
02
OLD TURTLE.
NEW TRICKS.
IK-90

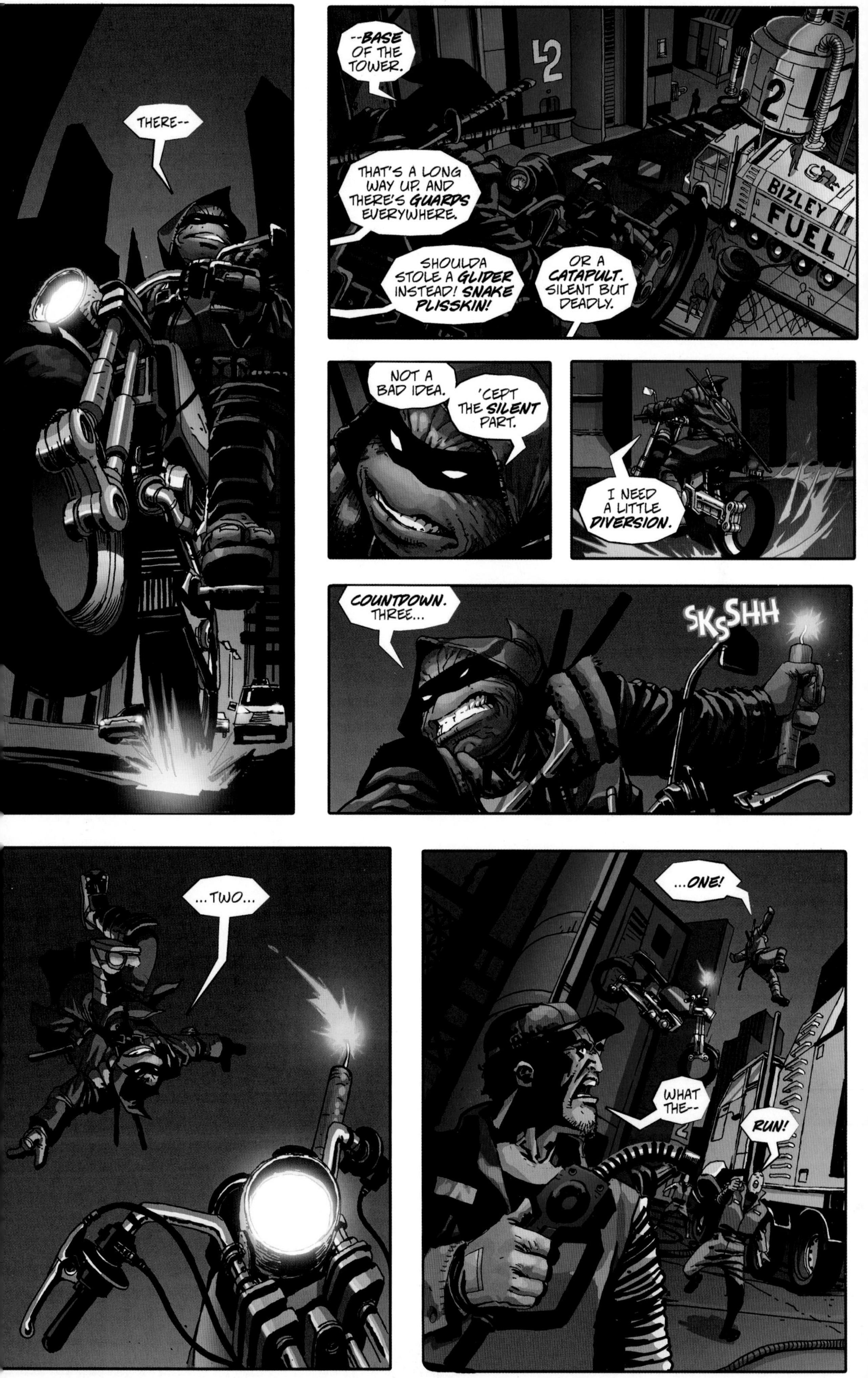
THERE--
--BASE OF THE TOWER.
THAT'S A LONG WAY UP. AND THERE'S GUARDS EVERYWHERE.
SHOULDA STOLE A GLIDER INSTEAD! SNAKE PLISSKIN!
OR A CATAPULT. SILENT BUT DEADLY.
BIZLEY FUEL
NOT A BAD IDEA.
'CEPT THE SILENT PART.
I NEED A LITTLE DIVERSION.
COUNTDOWN. THREE...
SKSSHH
...TWO...
...ONE!
WHAT THE--
RUN!

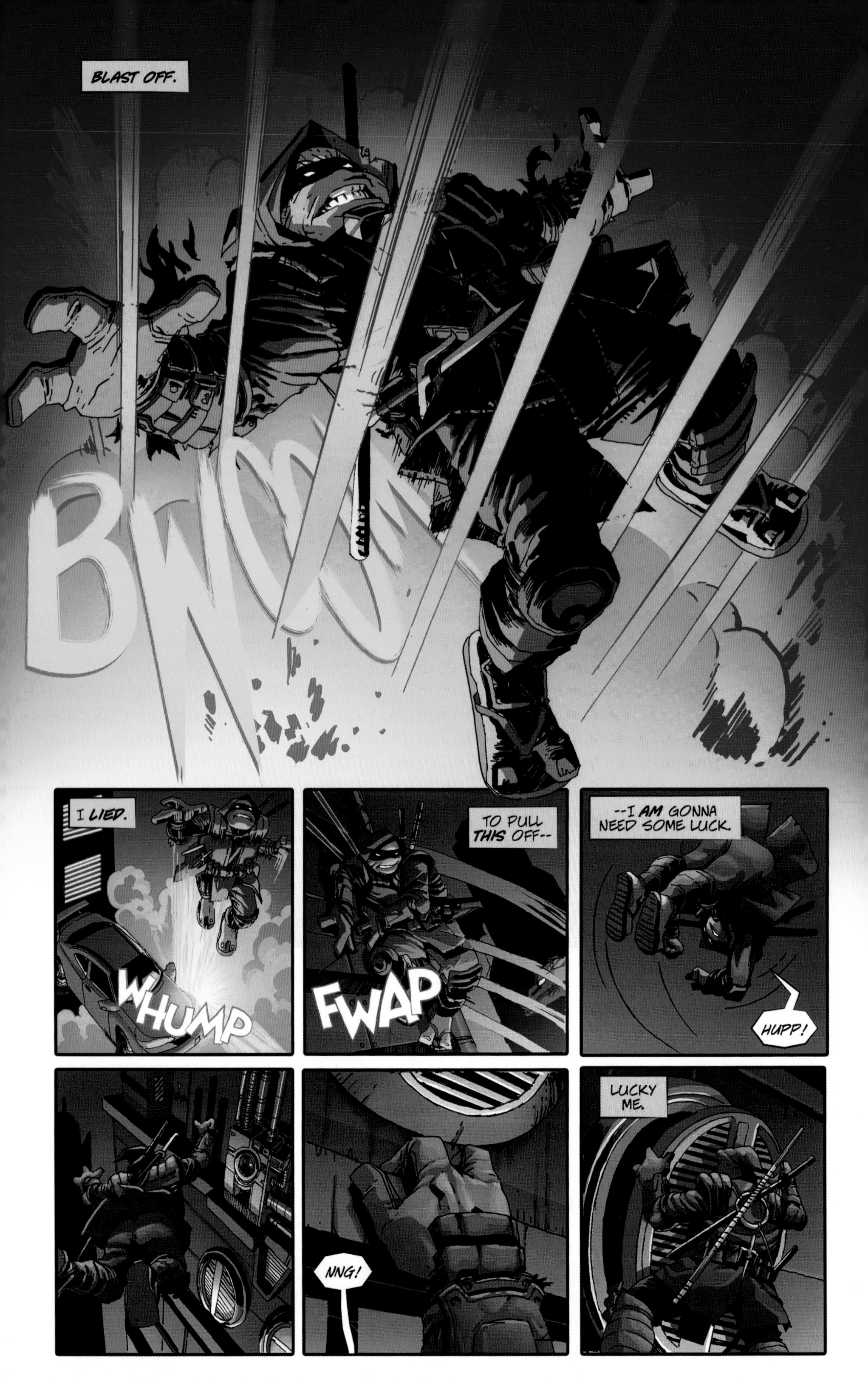
BLAST OFF.
BWOOM
I LIED.
WHUMP
TO PULL THIS OFF--
FWAP
--I AM GONNA NEED SOME LUCK.
HUPP!
NNG!
LUCKY ME.

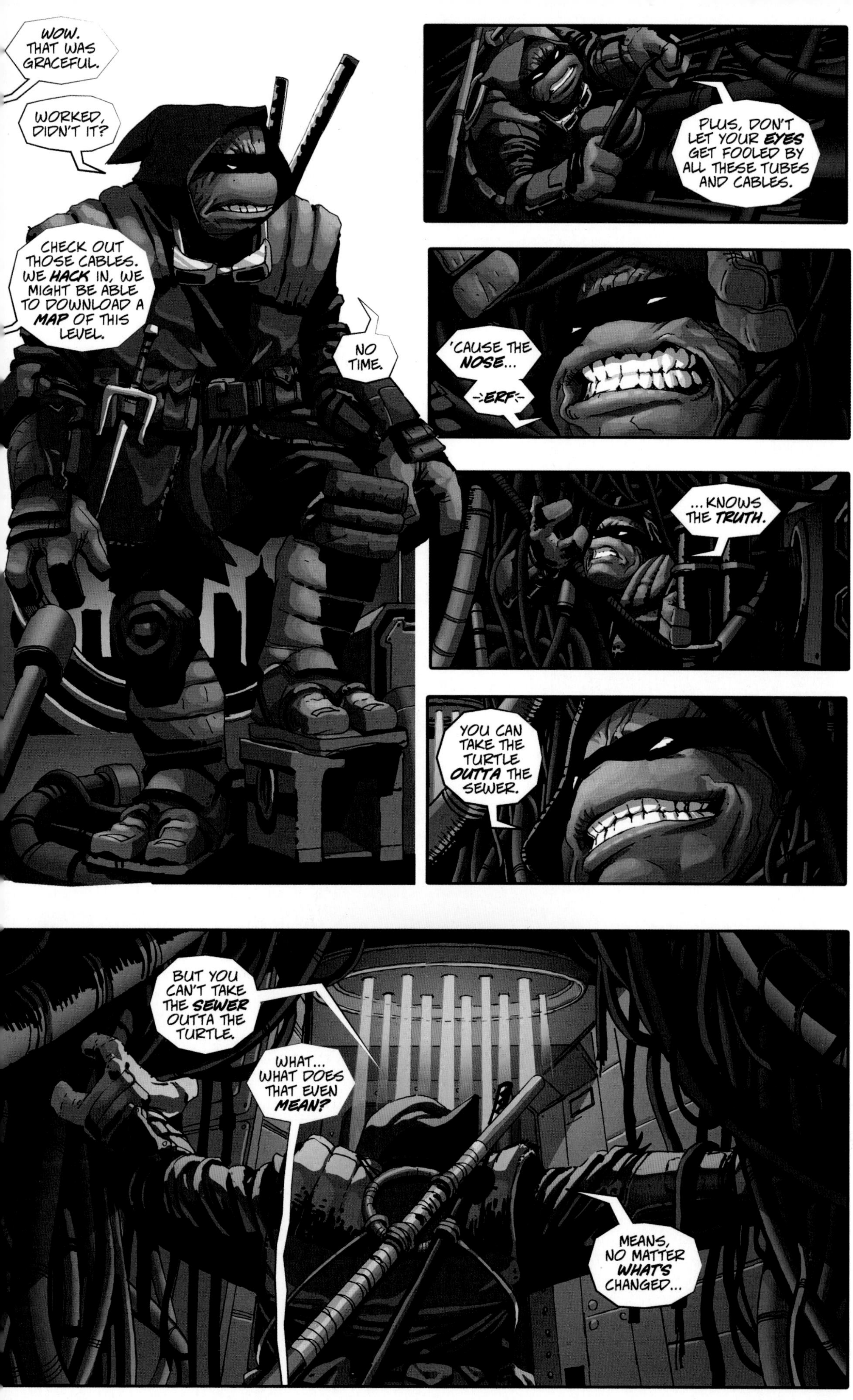
WOW. THAT WAS GRACEFUL.
WORKED, DIDN'T IT?
CHECK OUT THOSE CABLES. WE HACK IN, WE MIGHT BE ABLE TO DOWNLOAD A MAP OF THIS LEVEL.
NO TIME.
PLUS, DON'T LET YOUR EYES GET FOOLED BY ALL THESE TUBES AND CABLES.
'CAUSE THE NOSE...
ERF
...KNOWS THE TRUTH.
YOU CAN TAKE THE TURTLE OUTTA THE SEWER.
BUT YOU CAN'T TAKE THE SEWER OUTTA THE TURTLE.
WHAT... WHAT DOES THAT EVEN MEAN?
MEANS, NO MATTER WHAT'S CHANGED...

"...THIS IS **STILL** OUR HOME TURF."

BIP BIP BIP BIP BIP

DAMN.

I DON'T RECALL A LOT OF **MANHOLE ALARMS** BACK IN THE DAY.

ZIP IT!

BIP BIP BIP BIP BIP BIP BIP BIP BIP BIP

BIP BIP BIP BIP BIP BIP BIP BIP BIP BIP BIP BIP BIP BIP BI

HALT!

CRAP.

SECURITY. LIGHTLY ARMORED.

SOME KIND OF ROBO-COPS.

INTRUDER.

ROGER.

TIME FOR AN **OLD TRICK.**

P S S H

HALT! HALT!

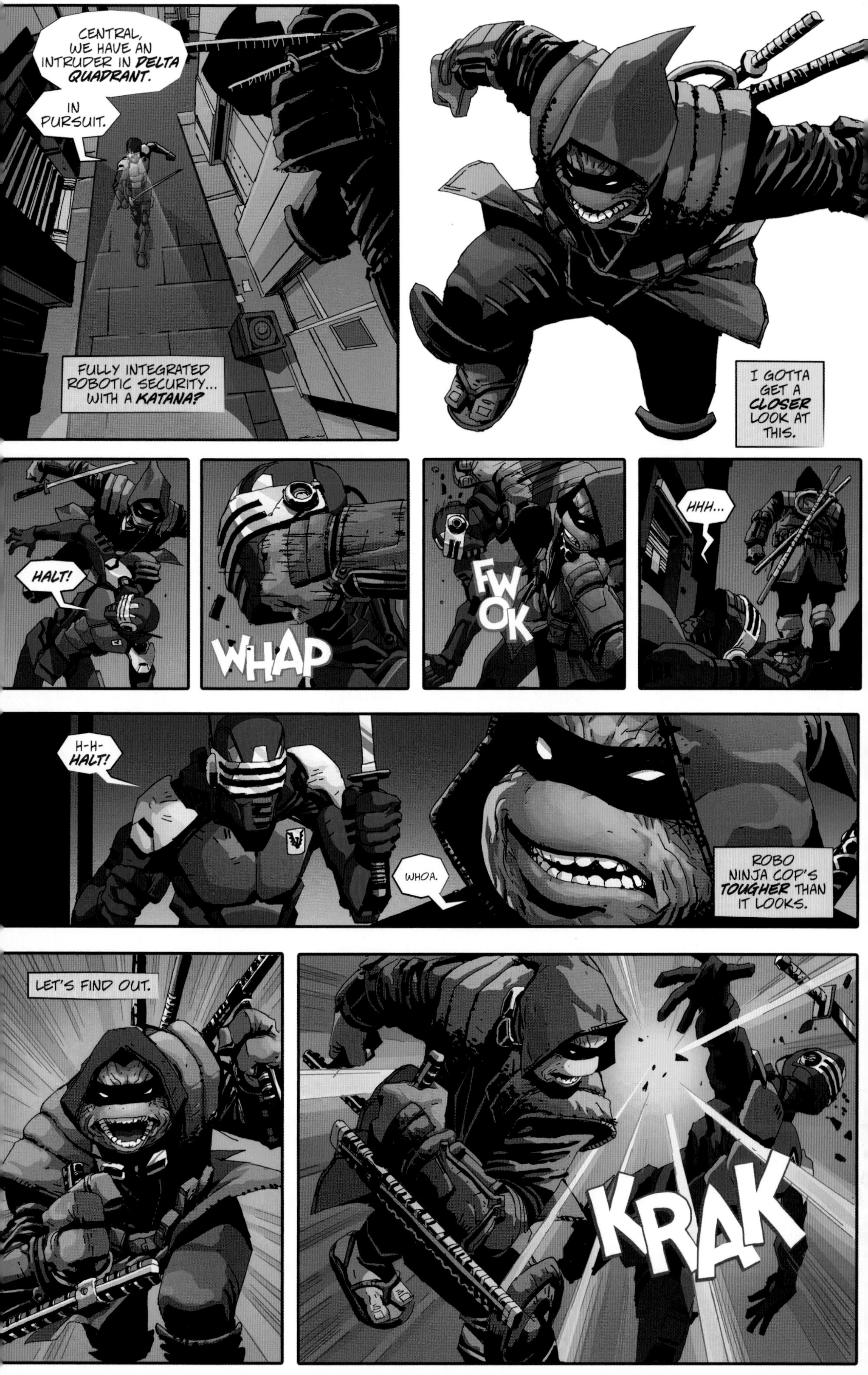
CENTRAL, WE HAVE AN INTRUDER IN DELTA QUADRANT.
IN PURSUIT.
FULLY INTEGRATED ROBOTIC SECURITY... WITH A KATANA?
I GOTTA GET A CLOSER LOOK AT THIS.
HALT!
WHAP
FWOK
HHH...
H-H-HALT!
WHOA.
ROBO NINJA COP'S TOUGHER THAN IT LOOKS.
LET'S FIND OUT.
KRAK

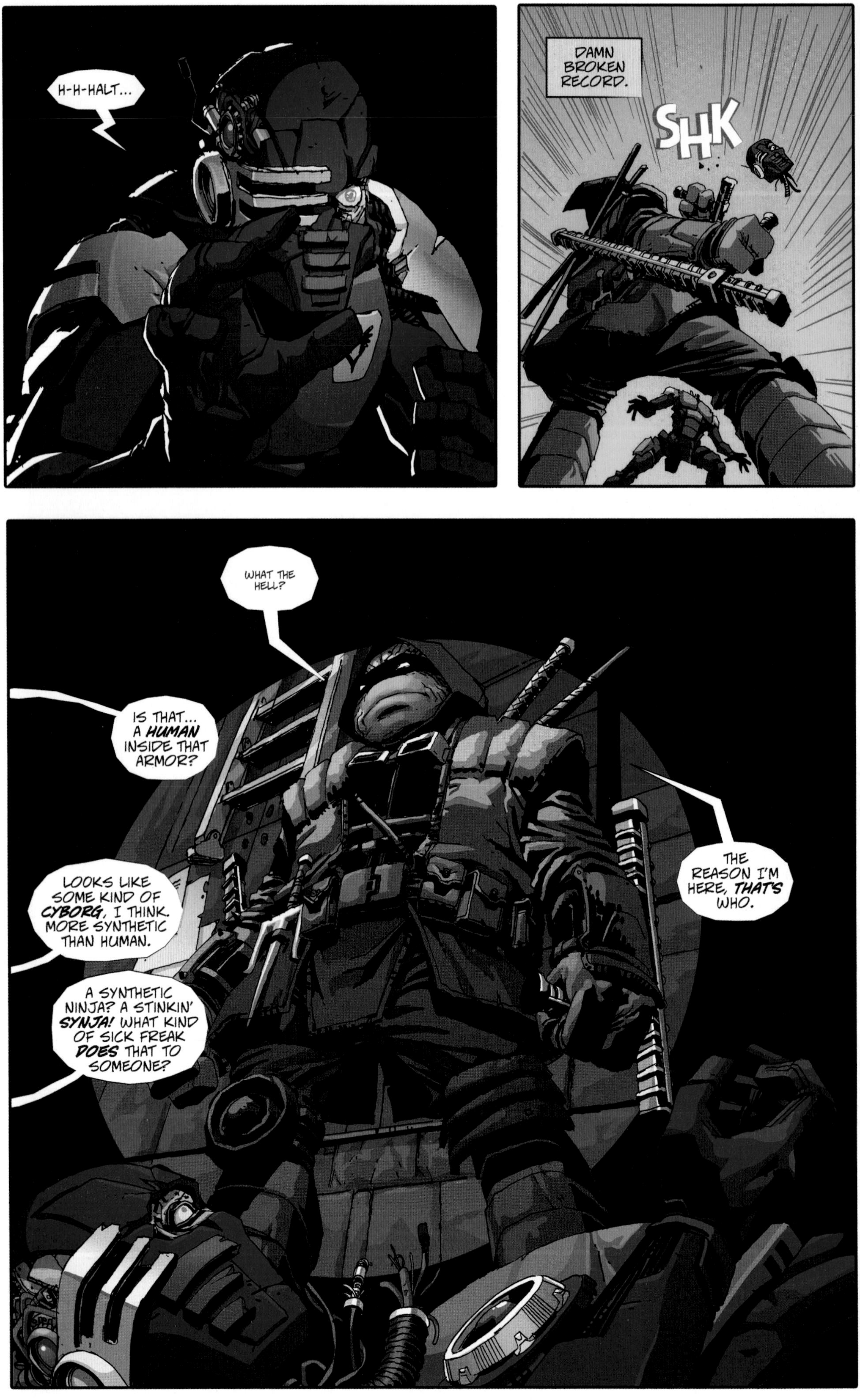
H-H-HALT...
DAMN BROKEN RECORD.
SHK
WHAT THE HELL?
IS THAT... A HUMAN INSIDE THAT ARMOR?
LOOKS LIKE SOME KIND OF CYBORG, I THINK. MORE SYNTHETIC THAN HUMAN.
A SYNTHETIC NINJA? A STINKIN' SYNJA! WHAT KIND OF SICK FREAK DOES THAT TO SOMEONE?
THE REASON I'M HERE, THAT'S WHO.

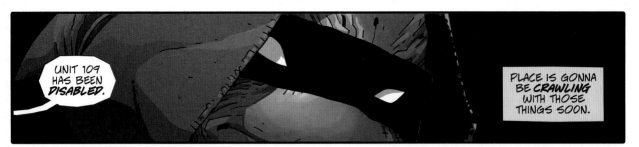

UNIT 109 HAS BEEN *DISABLED.*

PLACE IS GONNA BE *CRAWLING* WITH THOSE THINGS SOON.

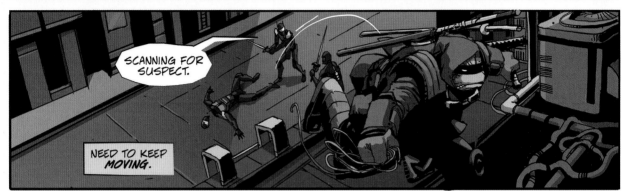

SCANNING FOR SUSPECT.

NEED TO KEEP *MOVING.*

TARGET ACQUIRED?

AFFIRMATIVE.

STAY ON MISSION.

AND REMEMBER THE *FIRST REAL LESSON* OUR FATHER EVER TAUGHT US.

STRIKE HARD.

FADE AWAY.

SHLIPP

NEVER LOSE FOCUS.

HALT!
SUSPECT LOCATED: RESIDENTIAL COMPLEX 661.
REQUESTING AIR SUPPORT.
PROCEED WITH CAUTION.
KRNCH
HALT!
THEY'RE FAST.
FZKK
PACKING MORE THAN SWORDS, TOO.

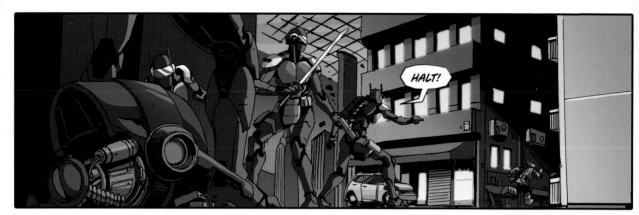

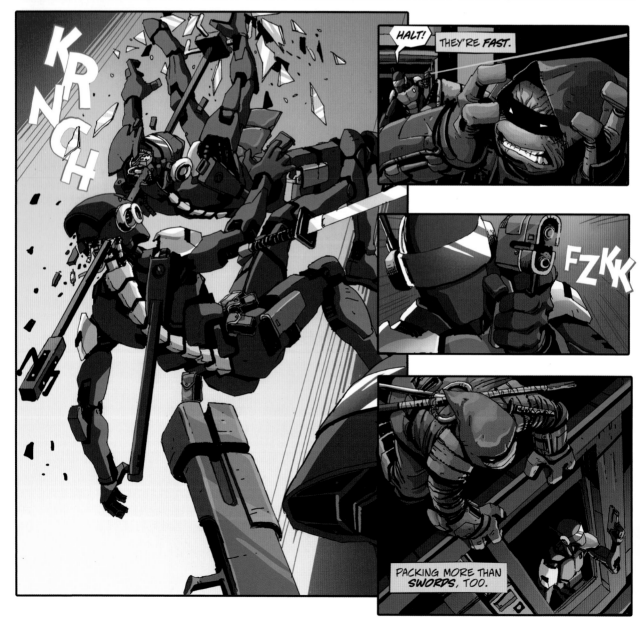

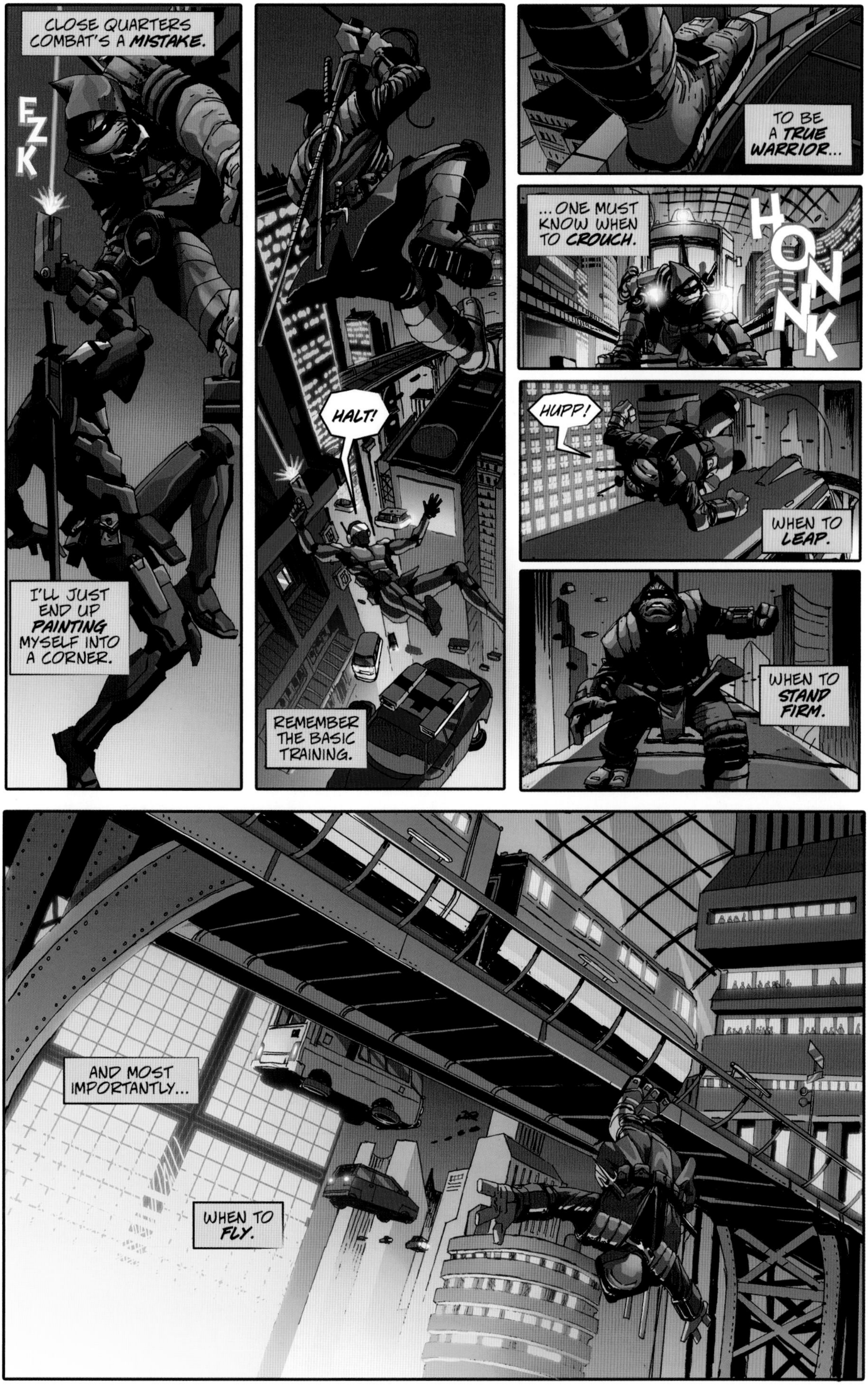
CLOSE QUARTERS COMBAT'S A MISTAKE.
FZK
I'LL JUST END UP PAINTING MYSELF INTO A CORNER.
HALT!
REMEMBER THE BASIC TRAINING.
TO BE A TRUE WARRIOR...
...ONE MUST KNOW WHEN TO CROUCH.
HONNK
HUPP!
WHEN TO LEAP.
WHEN TO STAND FIRM.
AND MOST IMPORTANTLY...
WHEN TO FLY.

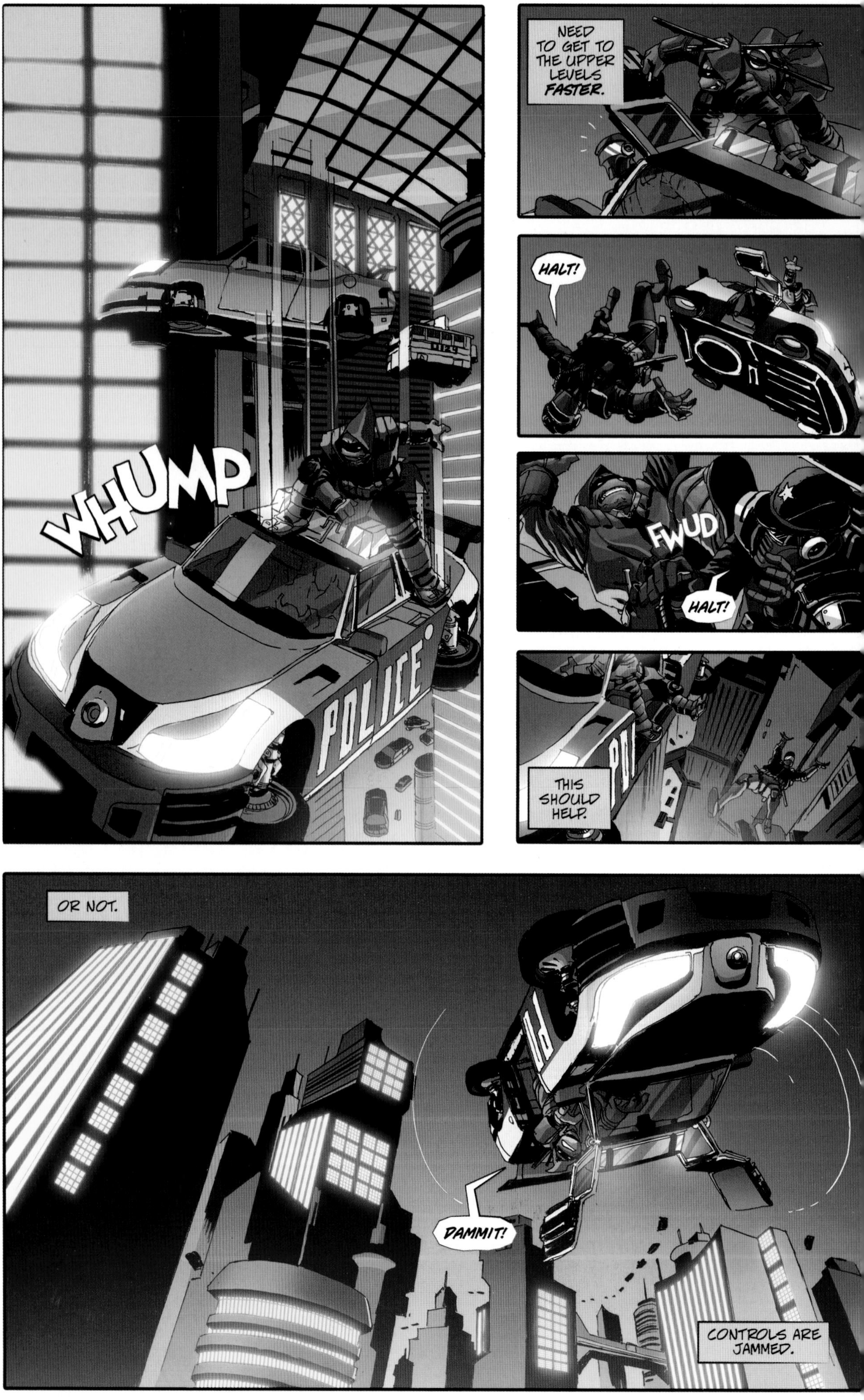
WHUMP
NEED TO GET TO THE UPPER LEVELS FASTER.
HALT!
FWUD
HALT!
THIS SHOULD HELP.
OR NOT.
DAMMIT!
CONTROLS ARE JAMMED.

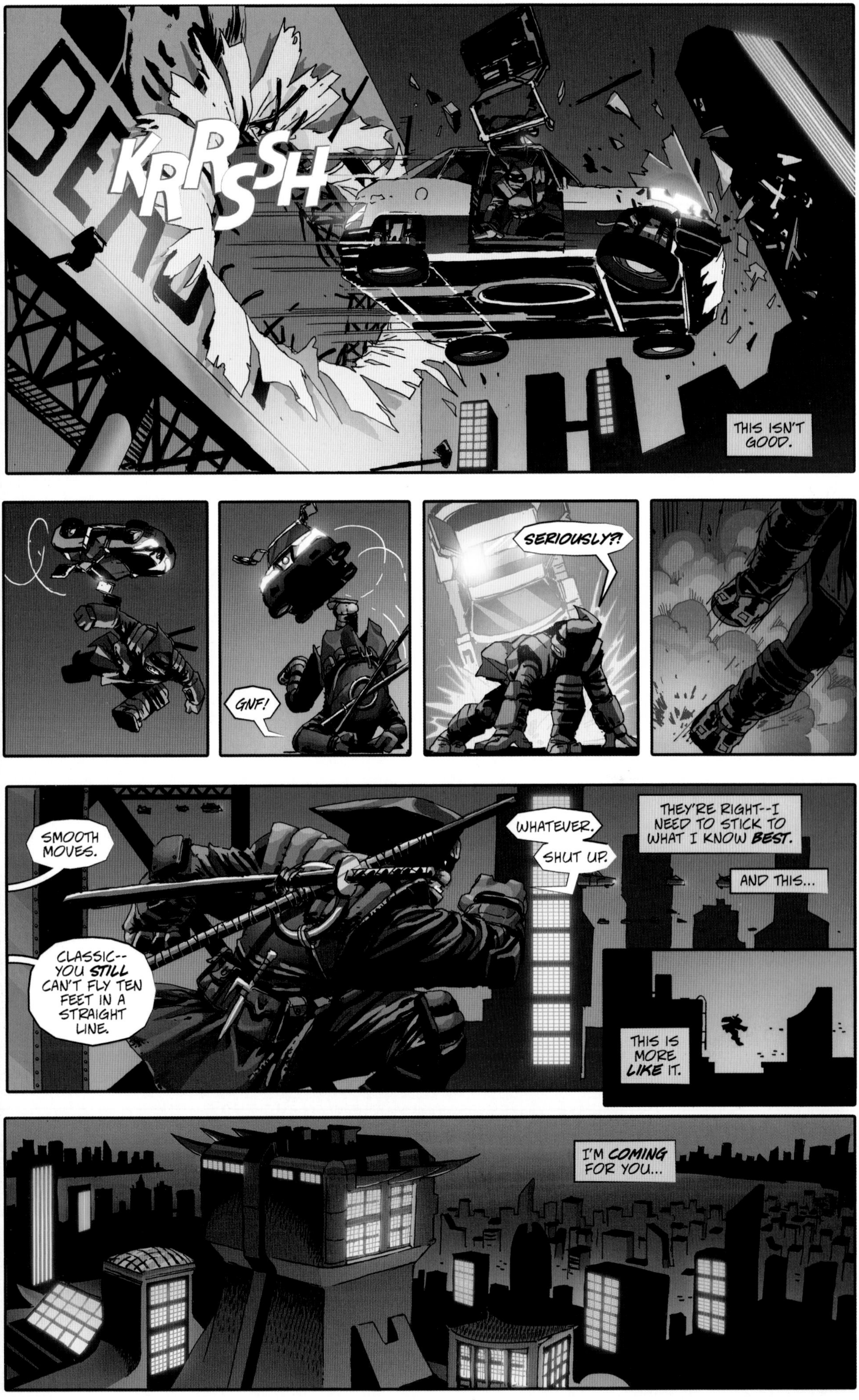
KRRSH
THIS ISN'T GOOD.
GNF!
SERIOUSLY?!
SMOOTH MOVES.
CLASSIC--YOU STILL CAN'T FLY TEN FEET IN A STRAIGHT LINE.
WHATEVER.
SHUT UP.
THEY'RE RIGHT--I NEED TO STICK TO WHAT I KNOW BEST.
AND THIS...
THIS IS MORE LIKE IT.
I'M COMING FOR YOU...

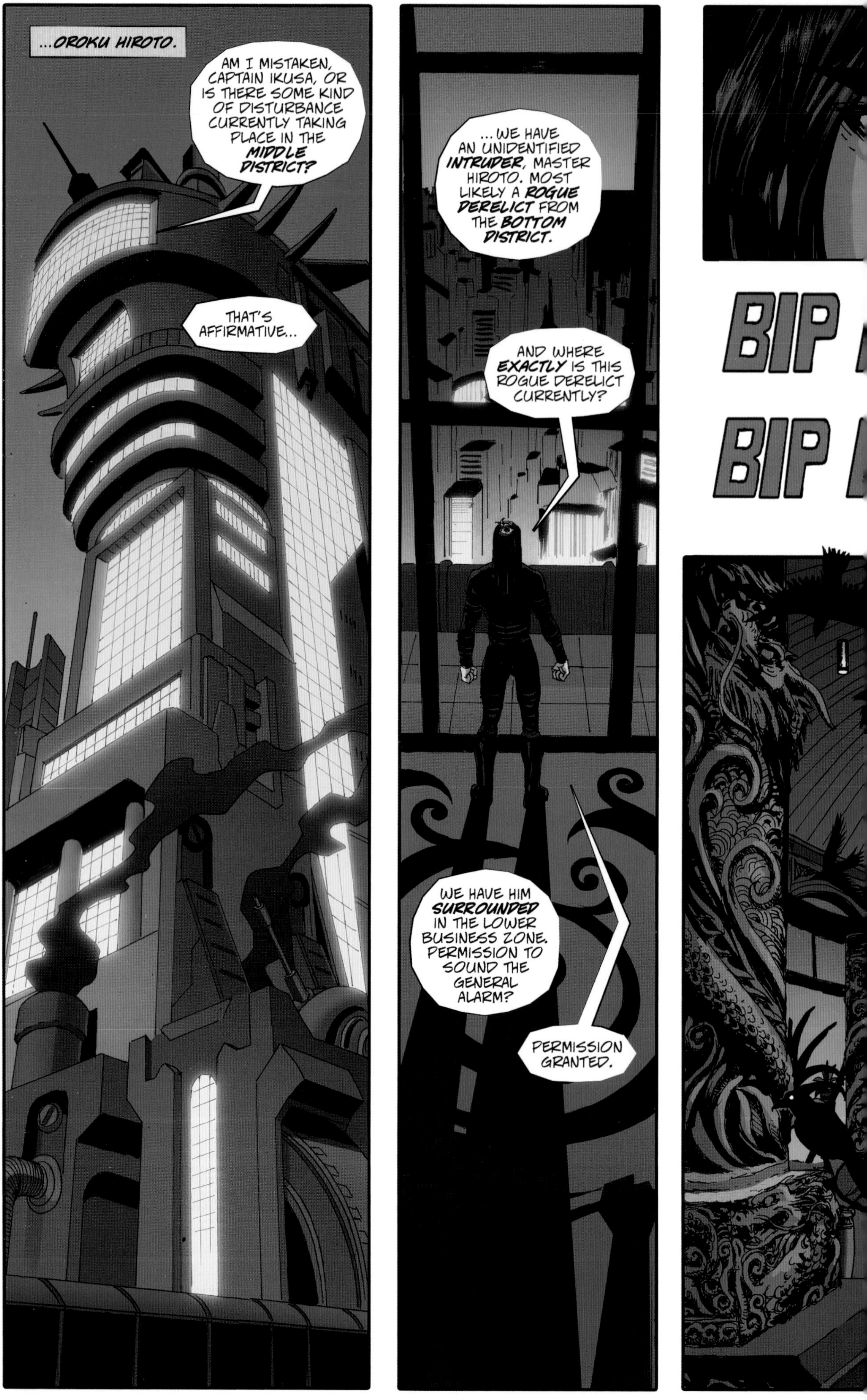
...OROKU HIROTO.
AM I MISTAKEN, CAPTAIN IKUSA, OR IS THERE SOME KIND OF DISTURBANCE CURRENTLY TAKING PLACE IN THE MIDDLE DISTRICT?
THAT'S AFFIRMATIVE...
...WE HAVE AN UNIDENTIFIED INTRUDER, MASTER HIROTO. MOST LIKELY A ROGUE DERELICT FROM THE BOTTOM DISTRICT.
AND WHERE EXACTLY IS THIS ROGUE DERELICT CURRENTLY?
WE HAVE HIM SURROUNDED IN THE LOWER BUSINESS ZONE. PERMISSION TO SOUND THE GENERAL ALARM?
PERMISSION GRANTED.
BIP
BIP

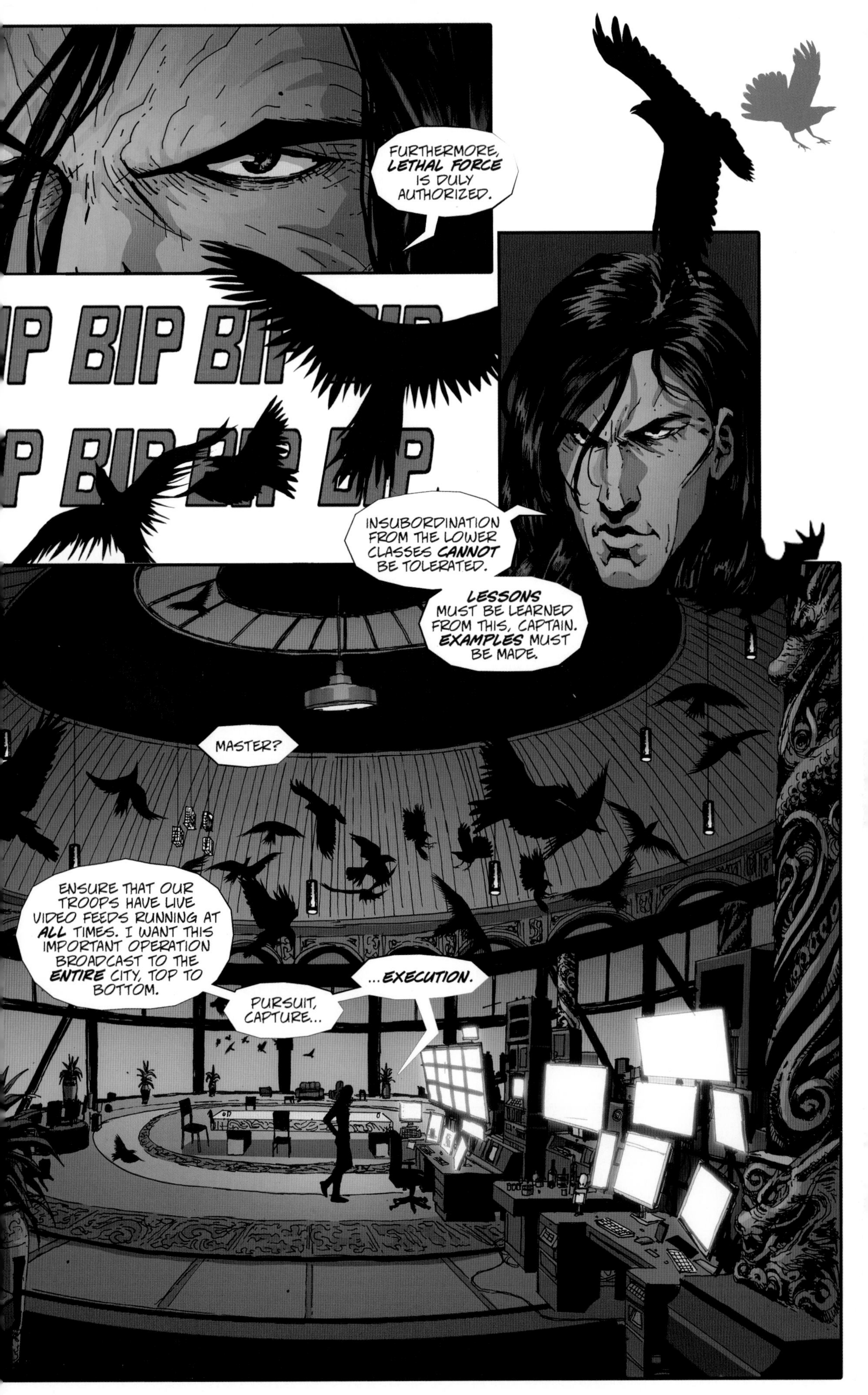
FURTHERMORE, LETHAL FORCE IS DULY AUTHORIZED.
INSUBORDINATION FROM THE LOWER CLASSES CANNOT BE TOLERATED.
LESSONS MUST BE LEARNED FROM THIS, CAPTAIN. EXAMPLES MUST BE MADE.
MASTER?
ENSURE THAT OUR TROOPS HAVE LIVE VIDEO FEEDS RUNNING AT ALL TIMES. I WANT THIS IMPORTANT OPERATION BROADCAST TO THE ENTIRE CITY, TOP TO BOTTOM.
PURSUIT, CAPTURE...
...EXECUTION.

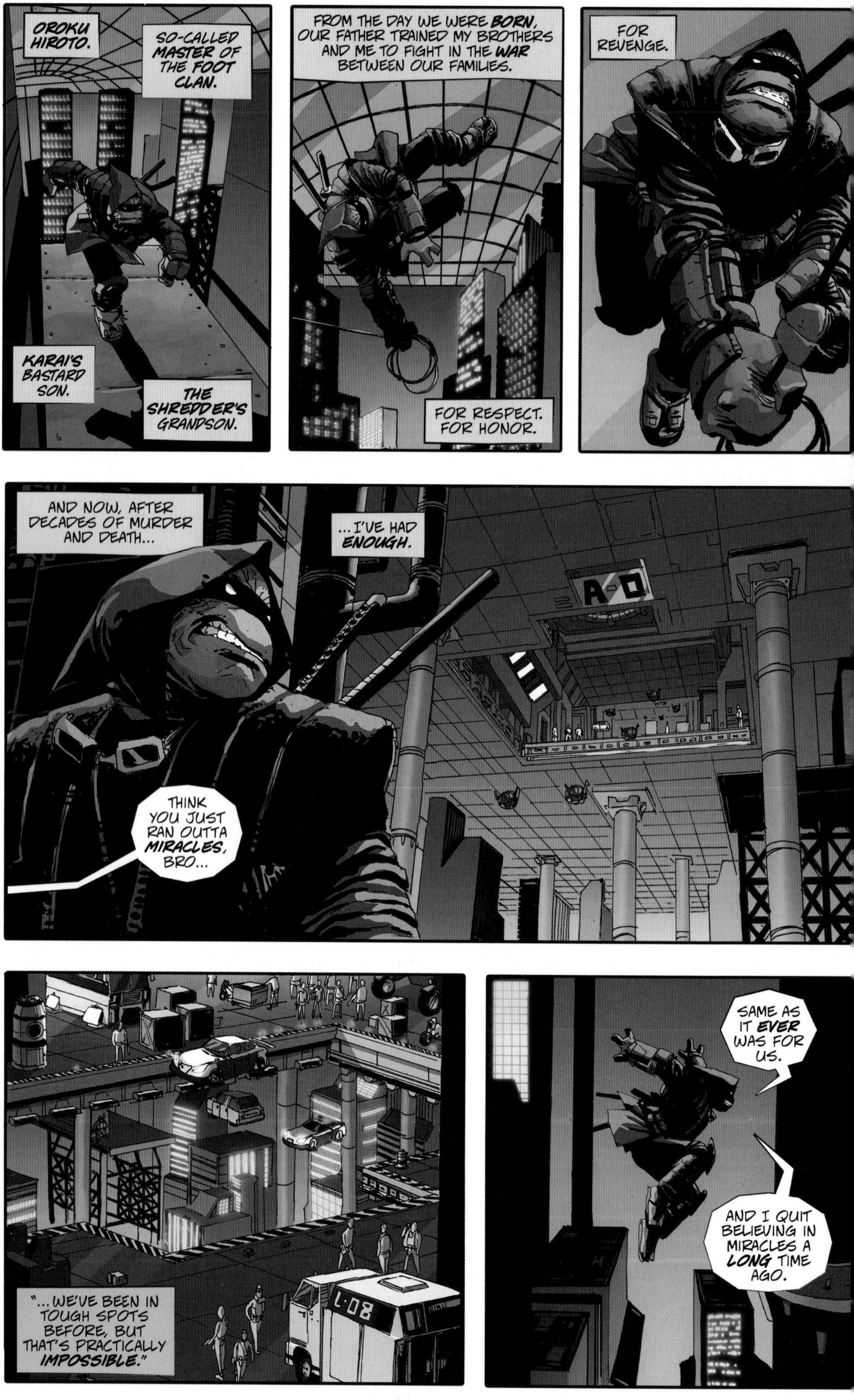
OROKU HIROTO.
SO-CALLED MASTER OF THE FOOT CLAN.
KARAI'S BASTARD SON.
THE SHREDDER'S GRANDSON.
FROM THE DAY WE WERE BORN, OUR FATHER TRAINED MY BROTHERS AND ME TO FIGHT IN THE WAR BETWEEN OUR FAMILIES.
FOR RESPECT. FOR HONOR.
FOR REVENGE.
AND NOW, AFTER DECADES OF MURDER AND DEATH...
...I'VE HAD ENOUGH.
THINK YOU JUST RAN OUTTA MIRACLES, BRO...
"...WE'VE BEEN IN TOUGH SPOTS BEFORE, BUT THAT'S PRACTICALLY IMPOSSIBLE."
SAME AS IT EVER WAS FOR US.
AND I QUIT BELIEVING IN MIRACLES A LONG TIME AGO.

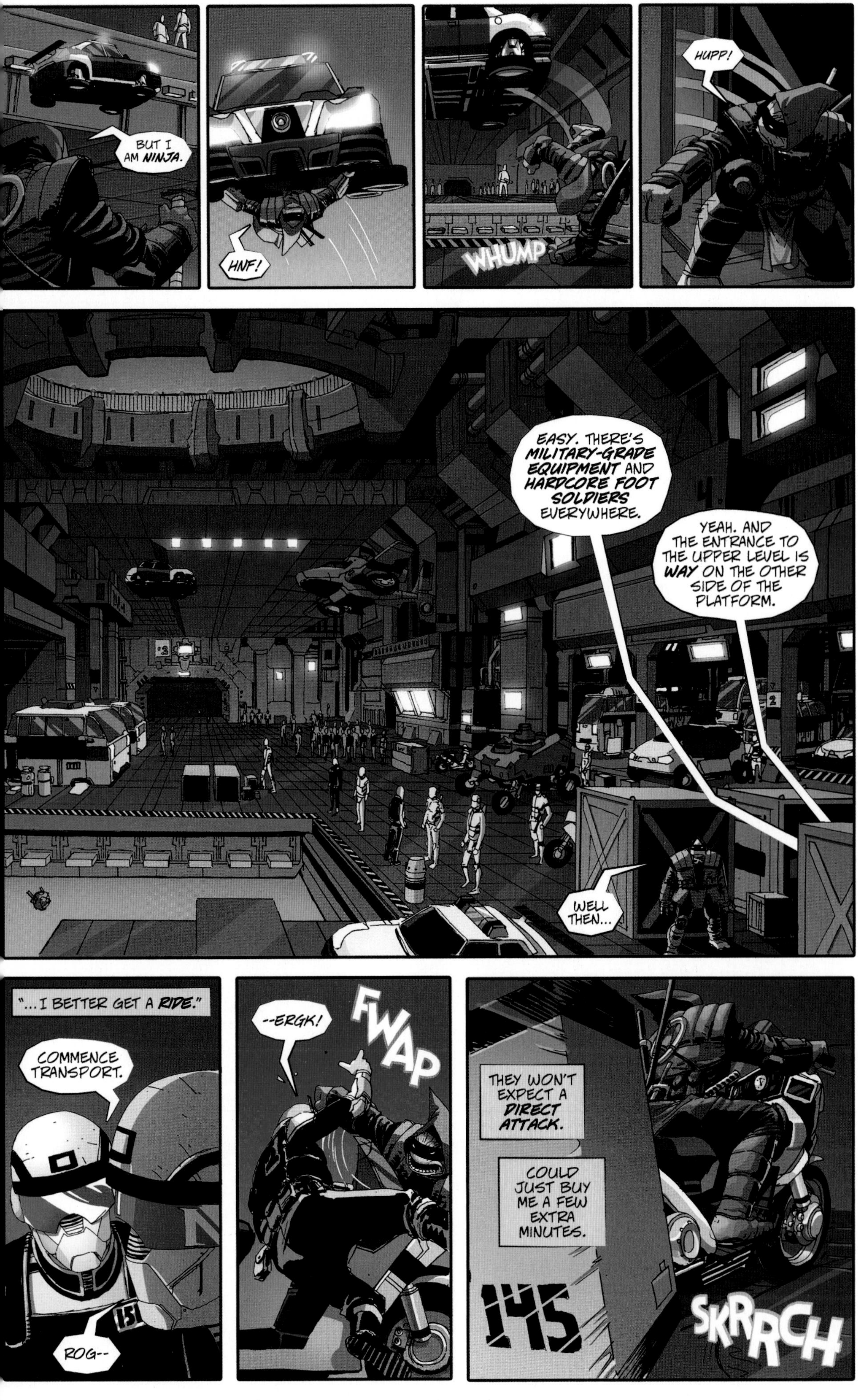
BUT I AM NINJA.
HNF!
WHUMP
HUPP!
EASY. THERE'S MILITARY-GRADE EQUIPMENT AND HARDCORE FOOT SOLDIERS EVERYWHERE.
YEAH. AND THE ENTRANCE TO THE UPPER LEVEL IS WAY ON THE OTHER SIDE OF THE PLATFORM.
WELL THEN...
"...I BETTER GET A RIDE."
COMMENCE TRANSPORT.
ROG--
--ERGK!
FWAP
THEY WON'T EXPECT A DIRECT ATTACK.
COULD JUST BUY ME A FEW EXTRA MINUTES.
145
SKRRCH

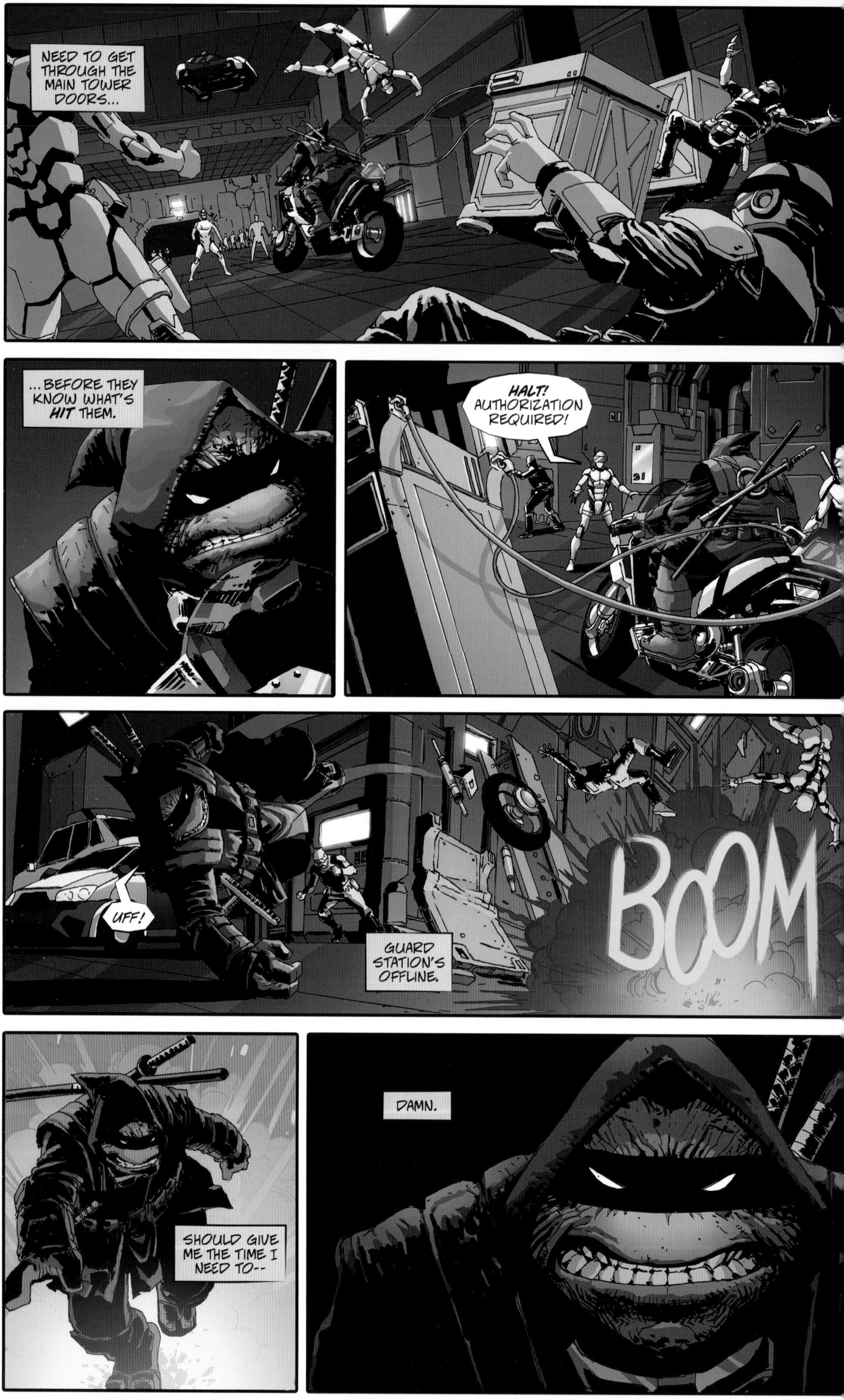
NEED TO GET THROUGH THE MAIN TOWER DOORS...
...BEFORE THEY KNOW WHAT'S HIT THEM.
HALT! AUTHORIZATION REQUIRED!
UFF!
BOOM
GUARD STATION'S OFFLINE.
SHOULD GIVE ME THE TIME I NEED TO--
DAMN.

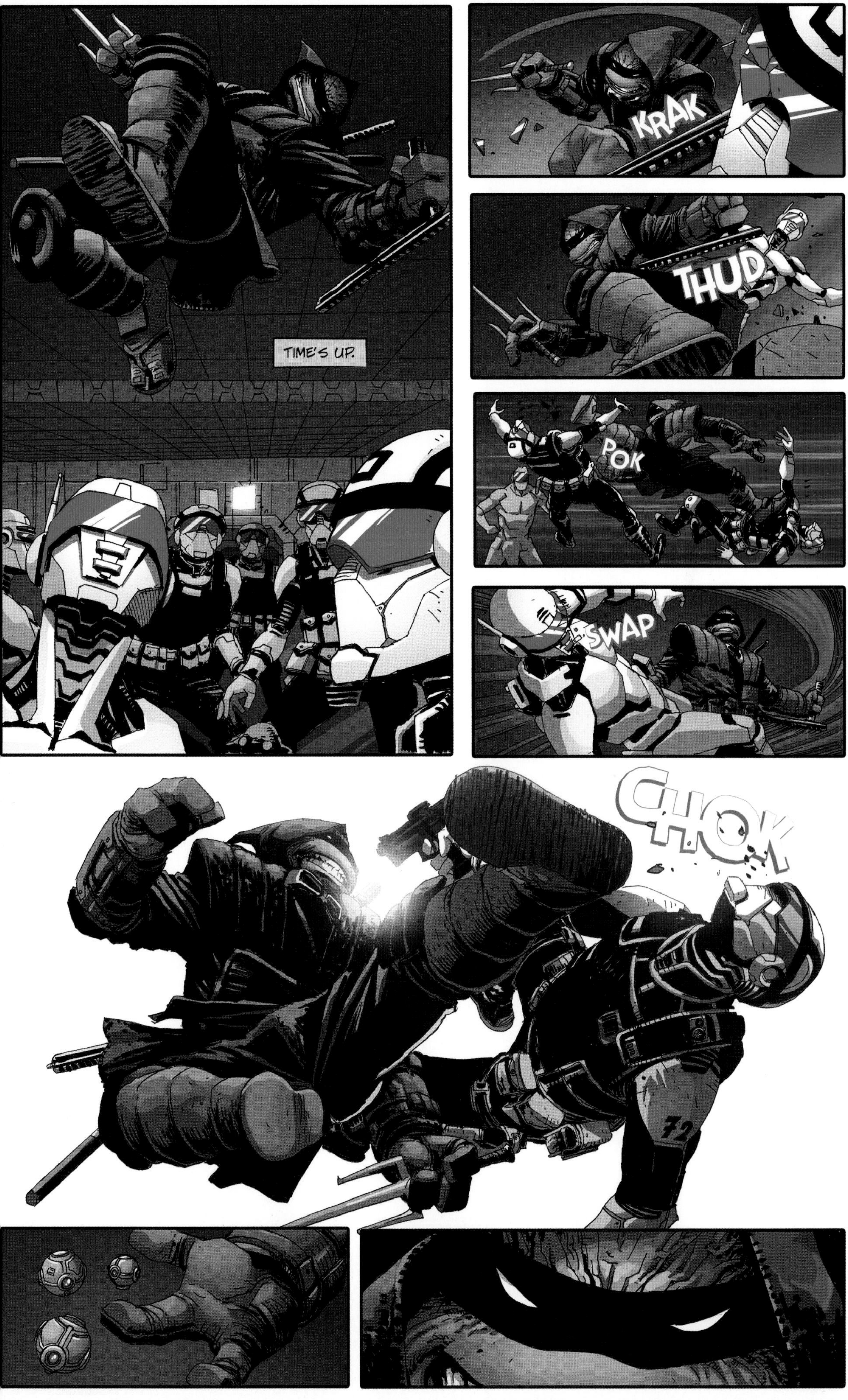
TIME'S UP.
KRAK
THUD
POK
SWAP
CHOK

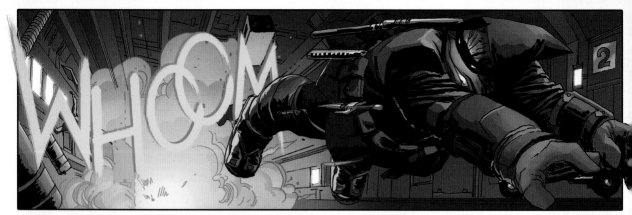

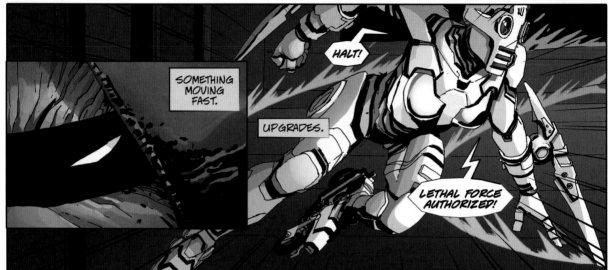

SOMETHING MOVING FAST.

UPGRADES.

HALT!

LETHAL FORCE AUTHORIZED!

I CAN DO THAT.

FWP

SHK SHK

HRGK!

MORE TOYS, HIROTO?

MACHINES DO *ALL* YOUR FIGHTING FOR YOU?

GUTLESS.

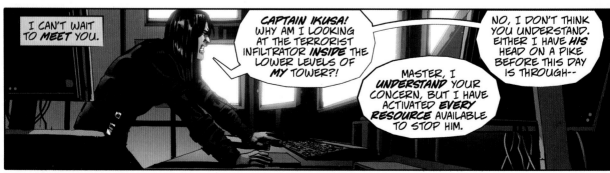

I CAN'T WAIT TO *MEET* YOU.

CAPTAIN IKUSA! WHY AM I LOOKING AT THE TERRORIST INFILTRATOR *INSIDE* THE LOWER LEVELS OF *MY* TOWER?!

MASTER, I *UNDERSTAND* YOUR CONCERN, BUT I HAVE ACTIVATED *EVERY RESOURCE* AVAILABLE TO STOP HIM.

NO, I DON'T THINK YOU UNDERSTAND. EITHER I HAVE *HIS* HEAD ON A PIKE BEFORE THIS DAY IS THROUGH--

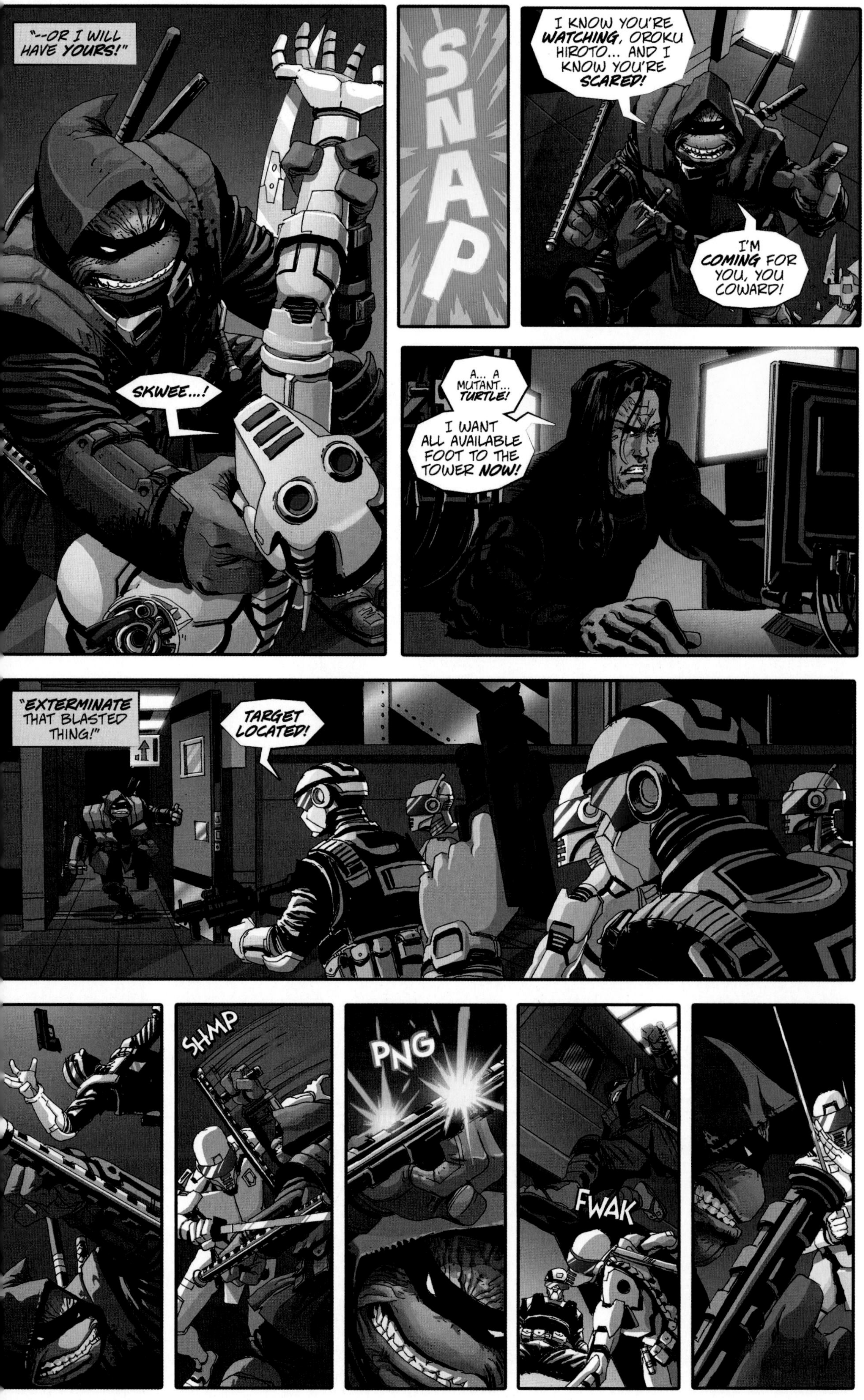
"--OR I WILL HAVE YOURS!"
SKWEE...!
SNAP
I KNOW YOU'RE WATCHING, OROKU HIROTO... AND I KNOW YOU'RE SCARED!
I'M COMING FOR YOU, YOU COWARD!
A... A MUTANT... TURTLE!
I WANT ALL AVAILABLE FOOT TO THE TOWER NOW!
"EXTERMINATE THAT BLASTED THING!"
TARGET LOCATED!
SHMP
PNG
FWAK

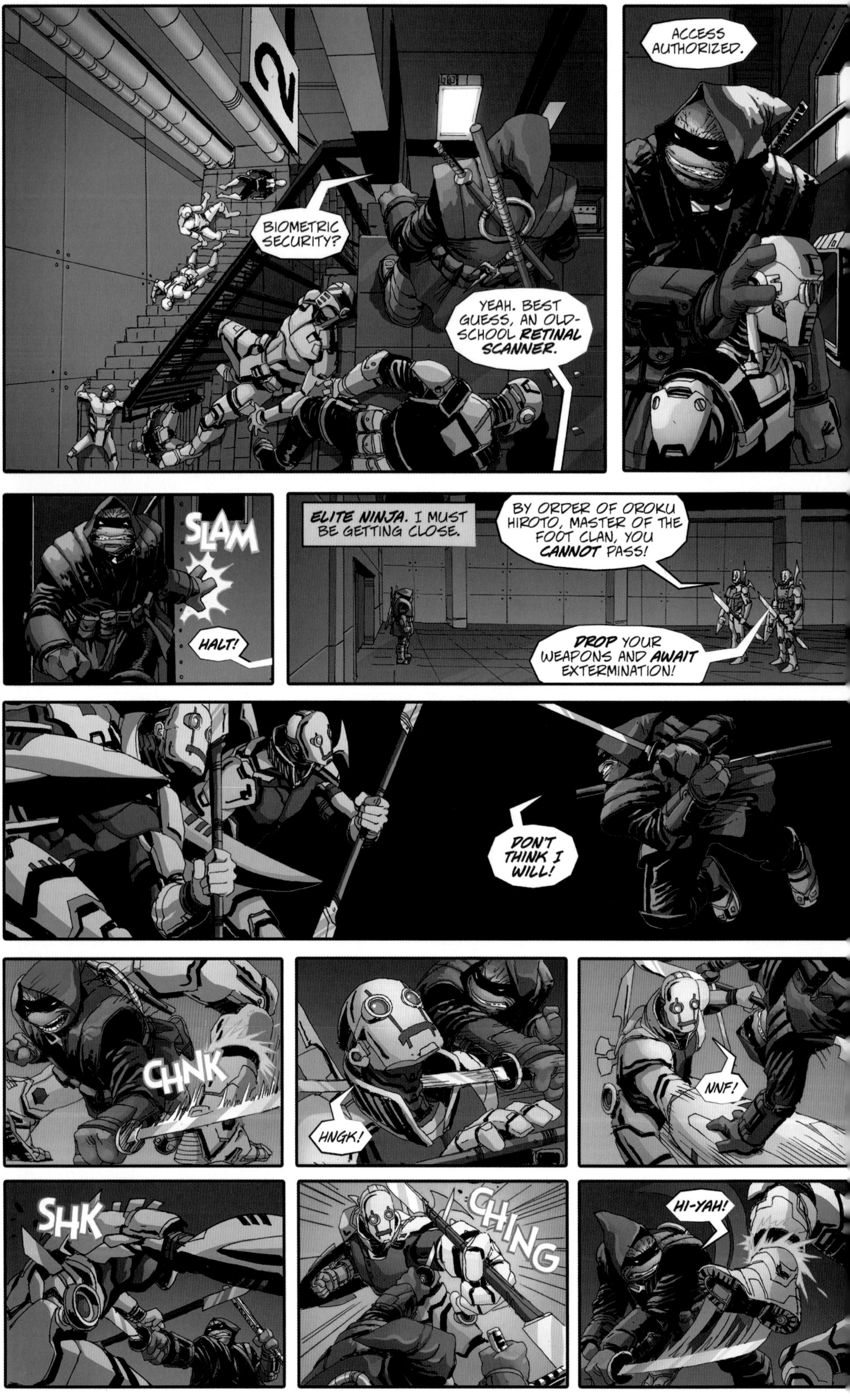
BIOMETRIC SECURITY?
YEAH. BEST GUESS, AN OLD-SCHOOL RETINAL SCANNER.
ACCESS AUTHORIZED.
SLAM
HALT!
ELITE NINJA. I MUST BE GETTING CLOSE.
BY ORDER OF OROKU HIROTO, MASTER OF THE FOOT CLAN, YOU CANNOT PASS!
DROP YOUR WEAPONS AND AWAIT EXTERMINATION!
DON'T THINK I WILL!
CHNK
HNGK!
NNF!
SHK
CHING
HI-YAH!

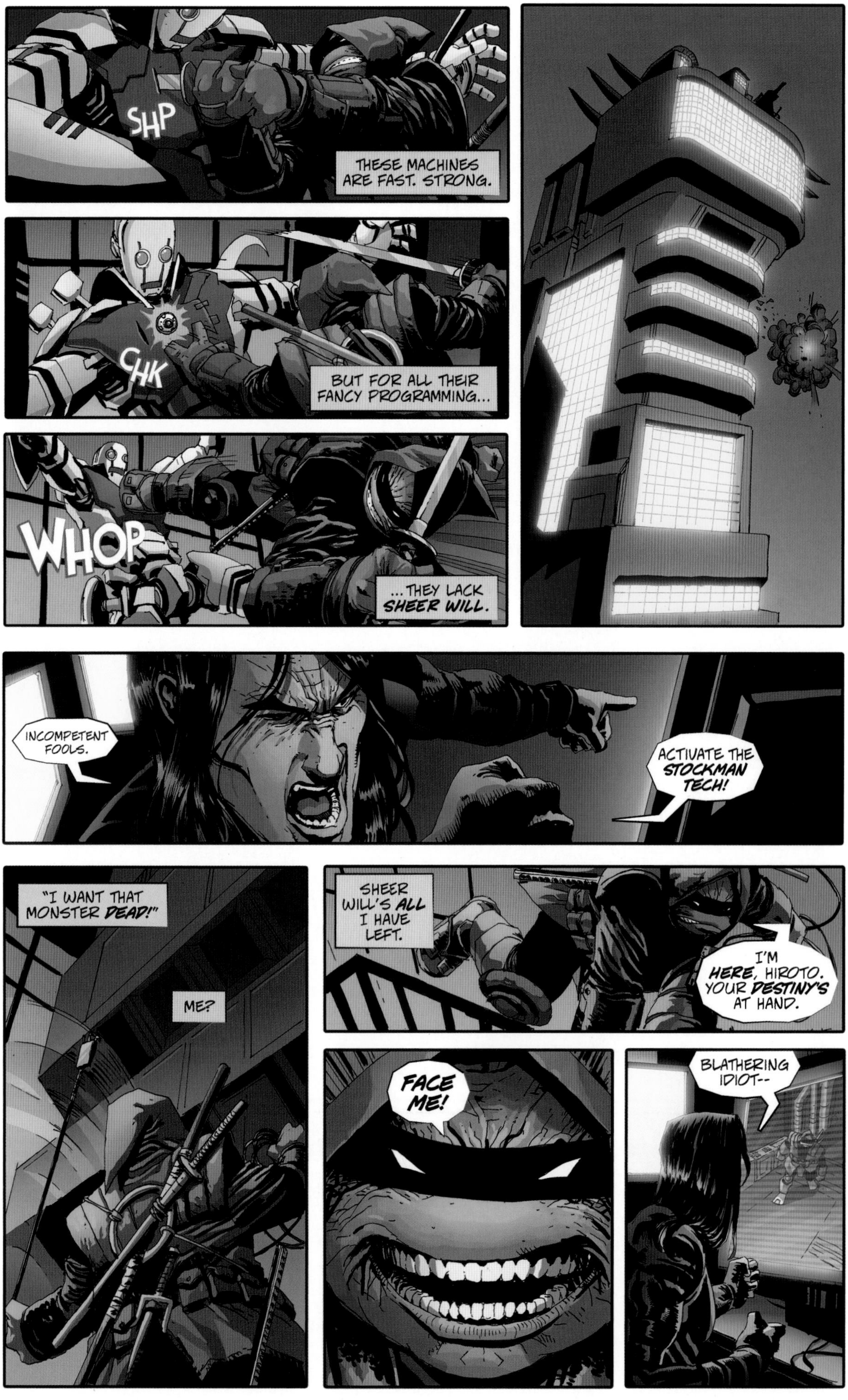
SHP
THESE MACHINES ARE FAST. STRONG.
CHK
BUT FOR ALL THEIR FANCY PROGRAMMING...
WHOP
...THEY LACK SHEER WILL.
INCOMPETENT FOOLS.
ACTIVATE THE STOCKMAN TECH!
"I WANT THAT MONSTER DEAD!"
ME?
SHEER WILL'S ALL I HAVE LEFT.
I'M HERE, HIROTO. YOUR DESTINY'S AT HAND.
FACE ME!
BLATHERING IDIOT--

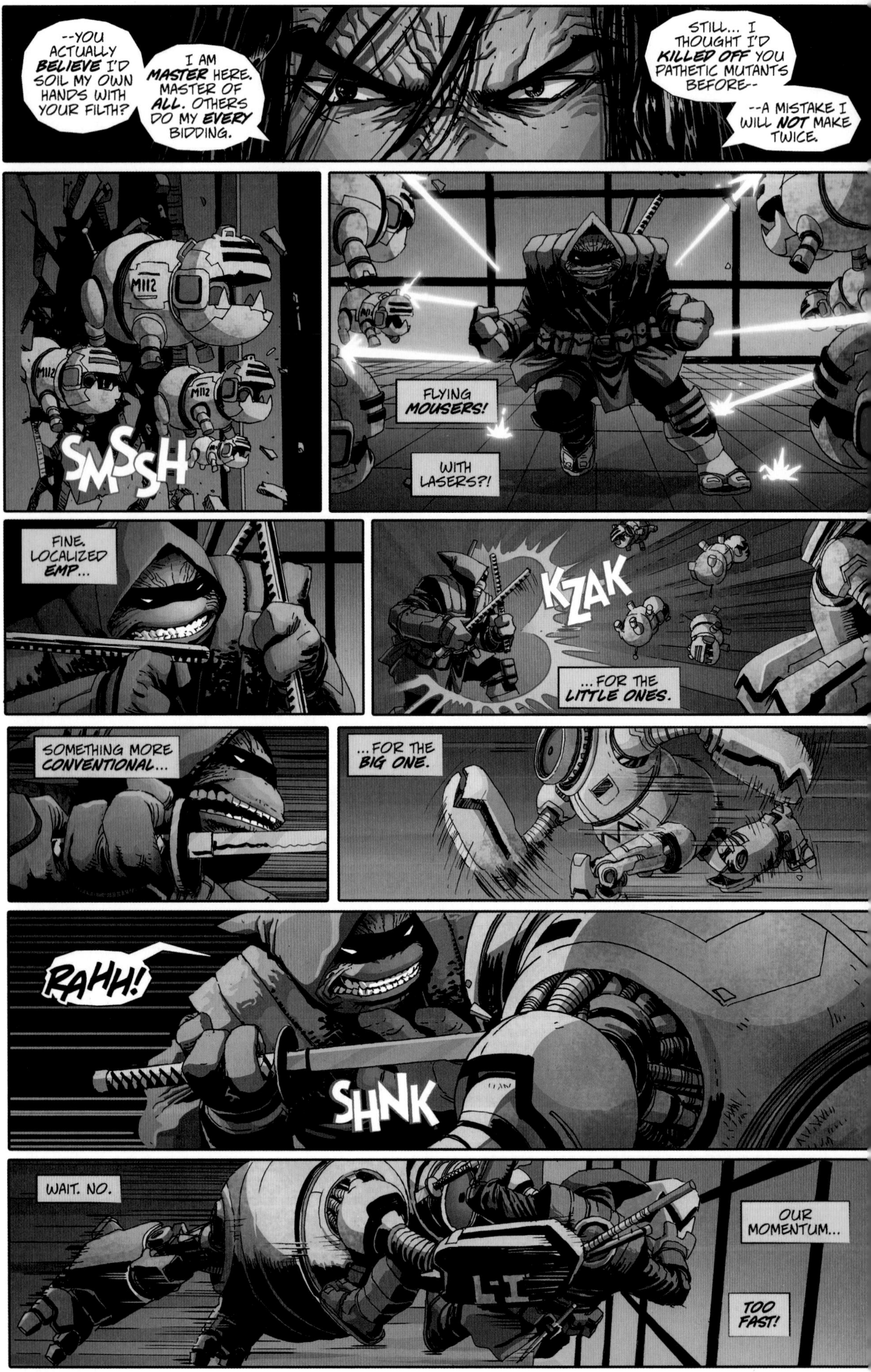
--YOU ACTUALLY BELIEVE I'D SOIL MY OWN HANDS WITH YOUR FILTH?
I AM MASTER HERE. MASTER OF ALL. OTHERS DO MY EVERY BIDDING.
STILL... I THOUGHT I'D KILLED OFF YOU PATHETIC MUTANTS BEFORE--
--A MISTAKE I WILL NOT MAKE TWICE.
M112
M112
M112
SMSSH
FLYING MOUSERS!
WITH LASERS?!
FINE. LOCALIZED EMP...
KZAK
...FOR THE LITTLE ONES.
SOMETHING MORE CONVENTIONAL...
...FOR THE BIG ONE.
RAHH!
SHNK
WAIT. NO.
OUR MOMENTUM...
TOO FAST!

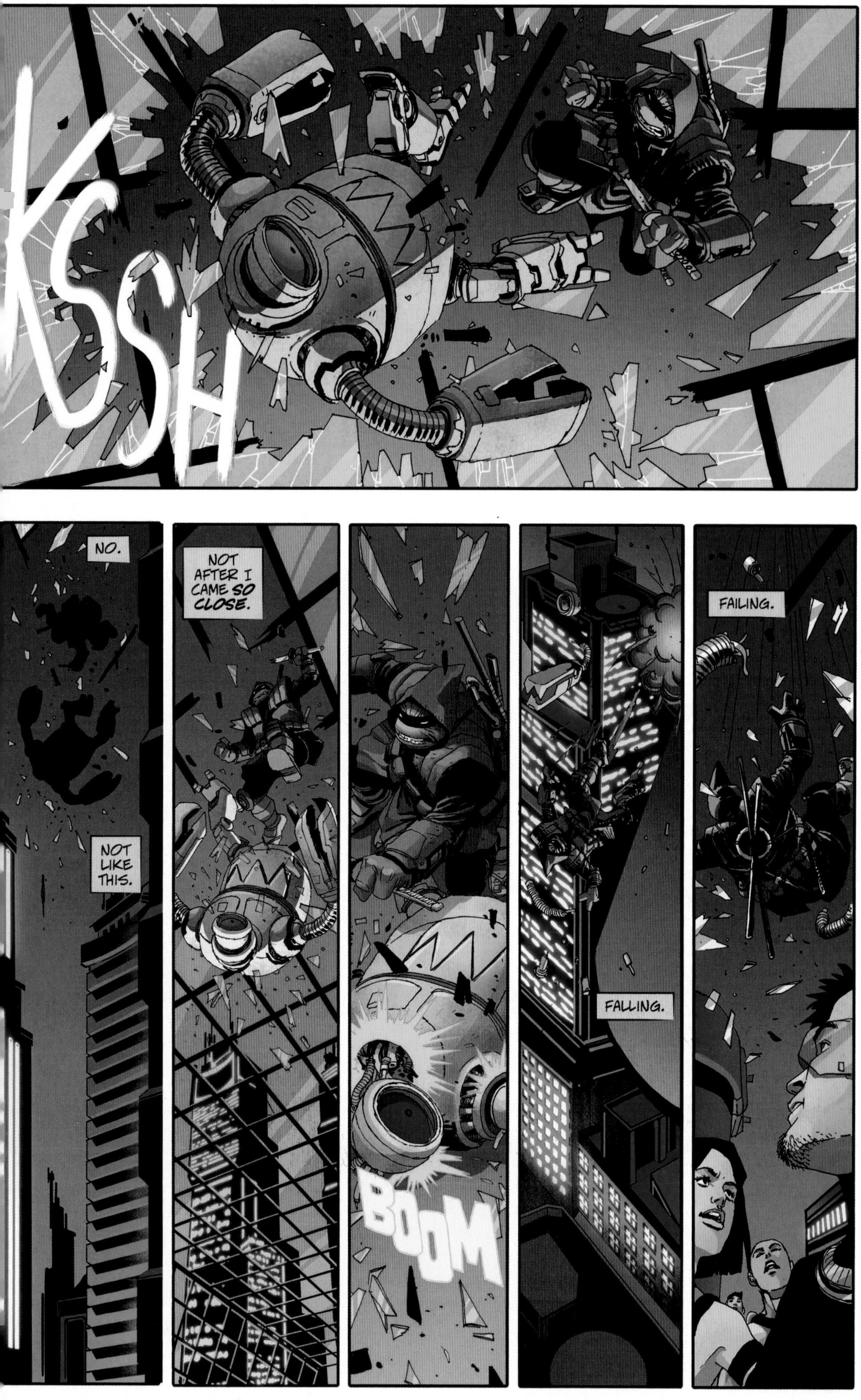
KSSH
NO.
NOT LIKE THIS.
NOT AFTER I CAME SO CLOSE.
BOOM
FALLING.
FAILING.

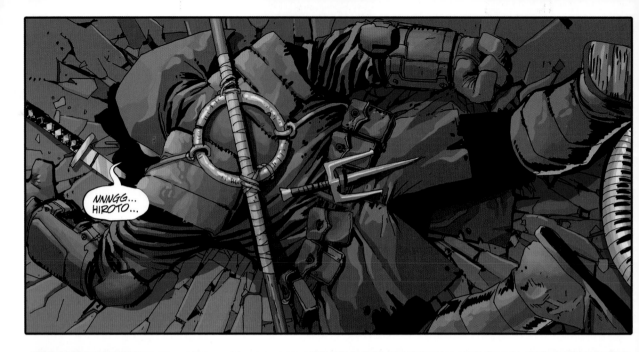

NNNGG...
HIROTO...

...COME FACE ME.

STILL ALIVE... SOMEHOW.

HIROTO... YOU... COWARD.

EVERYTHING FEELS... BROKEN.

ALL CITIZENS, DISPERSE IMMEDIATELY!

BY ORDER OF MASTER OROKU HIROTO!

NYAAGH...

I WON'T LET THEM FINISH ME THIS WAY.

I WON'T DISHONOR MY FAMILY.

DISPERSE IMMEDIATELY!

NOT ANYMORE.

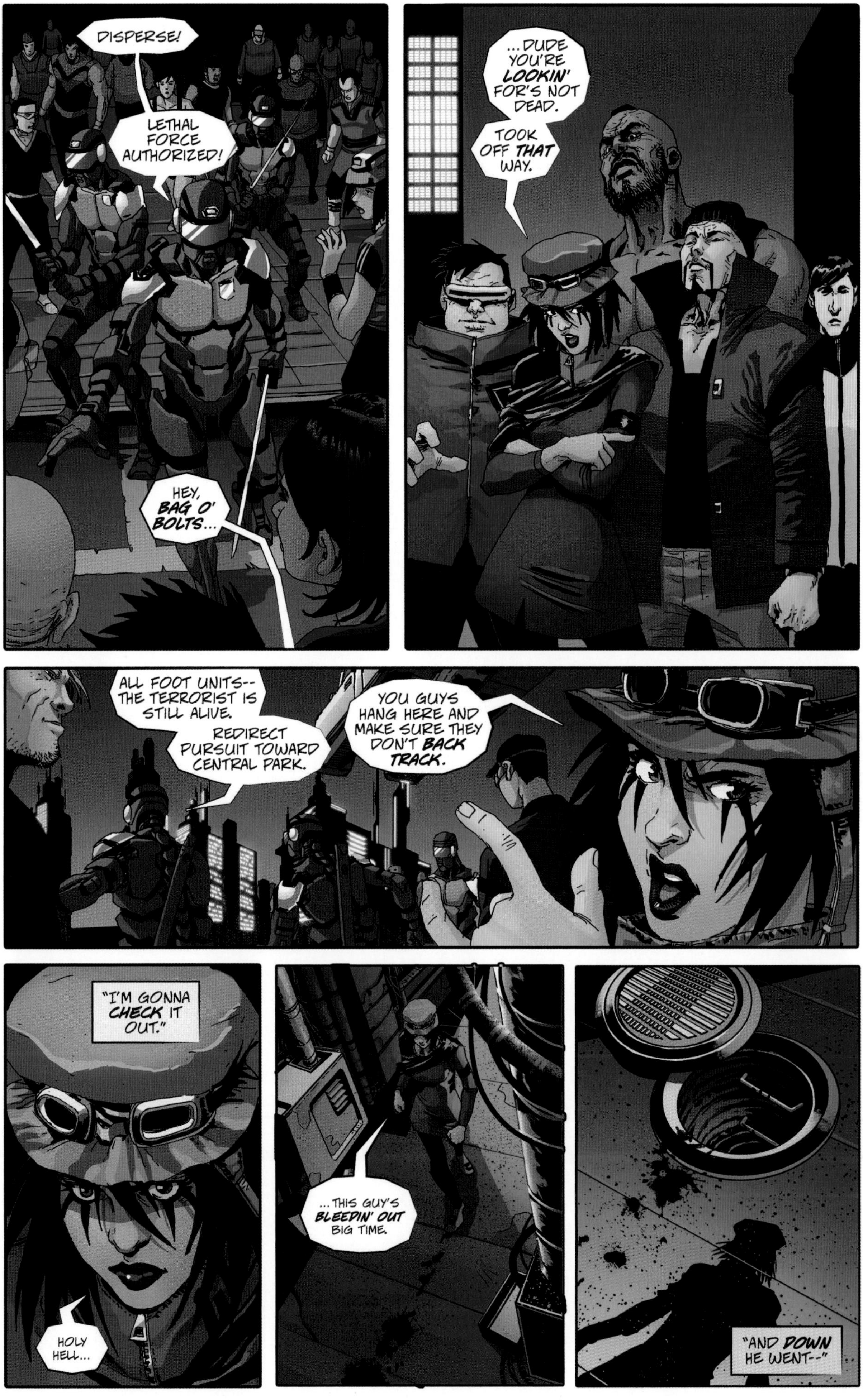
DISPERSE!
LETHAL FORCE AUTHORIZED!
HEY, BAG O' BOLTS...
...DUDE YOU'RE LOOKIN' FOR'S NOT DEAD.
TOOK OFF THAT WAY.
ALL FOOT UNITS-- THE TERRORIST IS STILL ALIVE.
REDIRECT PURSUIT TOWARD CENTRAL PARK.
YOU GUYS HANG HERE AND MAKE SURE THEY DON'T BACK TRACK.
"I'M GONNA CHECK IT OUT."
HOLY HELL...
...THIS GUY'S BLEEDIN' OUT BIG TIME.
"AND DOWN HE WENT--"

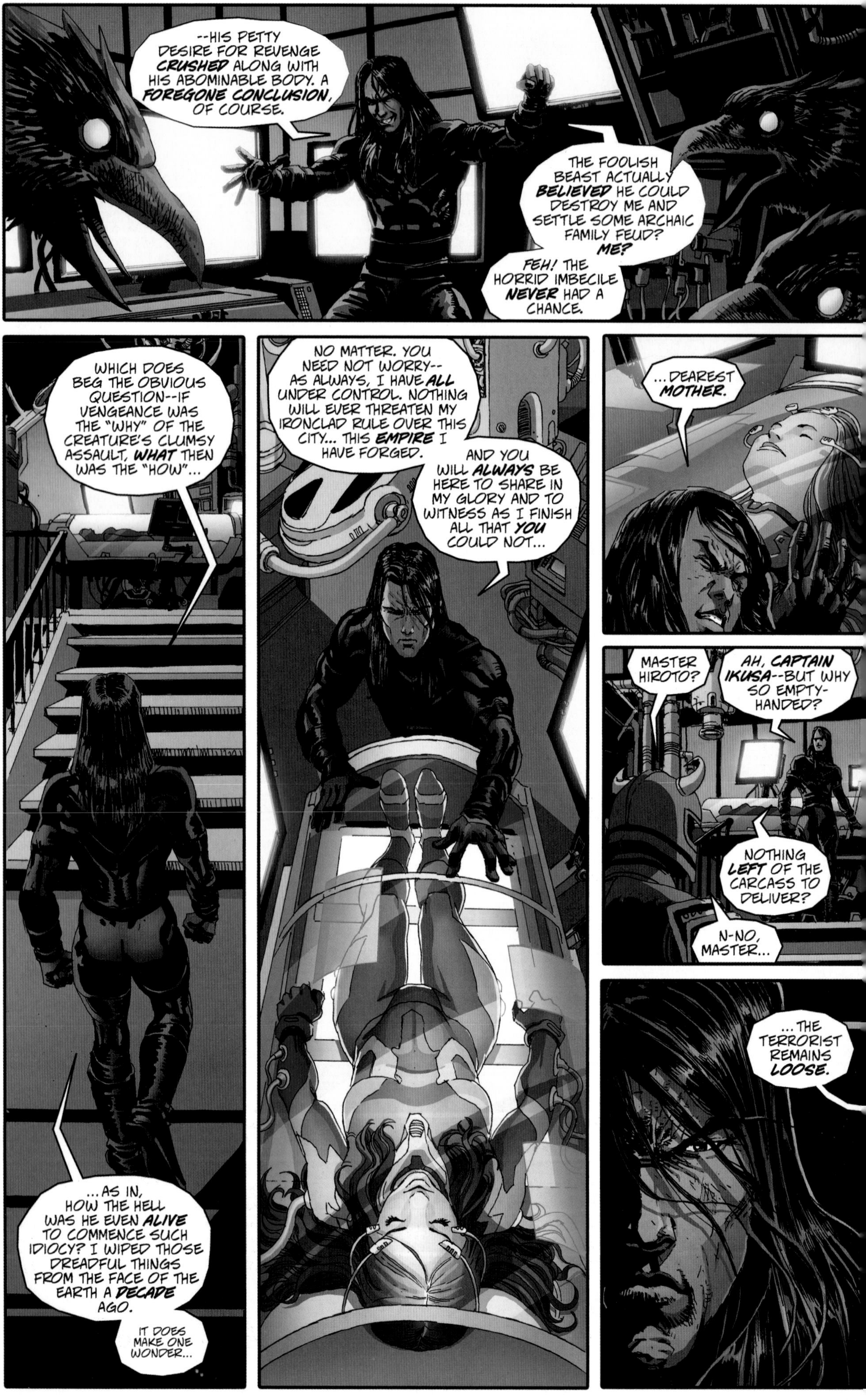
--HIS PETTY DESIRE FOR REVENGE CRUSHED ALONG WITH HIS ABOMINABLE BODY. A FOREGONE CONCLUSION, OF COURSE.
THE FOOLISH BEAST ACTUALLY BELIEVED HE COULD DESTROY ME AND SETTLE SOME ARCHAIC FAMILY FEUD? ME?
FEH! THE HORRID IMBECILE NEVER HAD A CHANCE.
WHICH DOES BEG THE OBVIOUS QUESTION--IF VENGEANCE WAS THE "WHY" OF THE CREATURE'S CLUMSY ASSAULT, WHAT THEN WAS THE "HOW"...
...AS IN, HOW THE HELL WAS HE EVEN ALIVE TO COMMENCE SUCH IDIOCY? I WIPED THOSE DREADFUL THINGS FROM THE FACE OF THE EARTH A DECADE AGO.
IT DOES MAKE ONE WONDER...
NO MATTER. YOU NEED NOT WORRY-- AS ALWAYS, I HAVE ALL UNDER CONTROL. NOTHING WILL EVER THREATEN MY IRONCLAD RULE OVER THIS CITY... THIS EMPIRE I HAVE FORGED.
AND YOU WILL ALWAYS BE HERE TO SHARE IN MY GLORY AND TO WITNESS AS I FINISH ALL THAT YOU COULD NOT...
...DEAREST MOTHER.
MASTER HIROTO?
AH, CAPTAIN IKUSA--BUT WHY SO EMPTY-HANDED?
NOTHING LEFT OF THE CARCASS TO DELIVER?
N-NO, MASTER...
...THE TERRORIST REMAINS LOOSE.

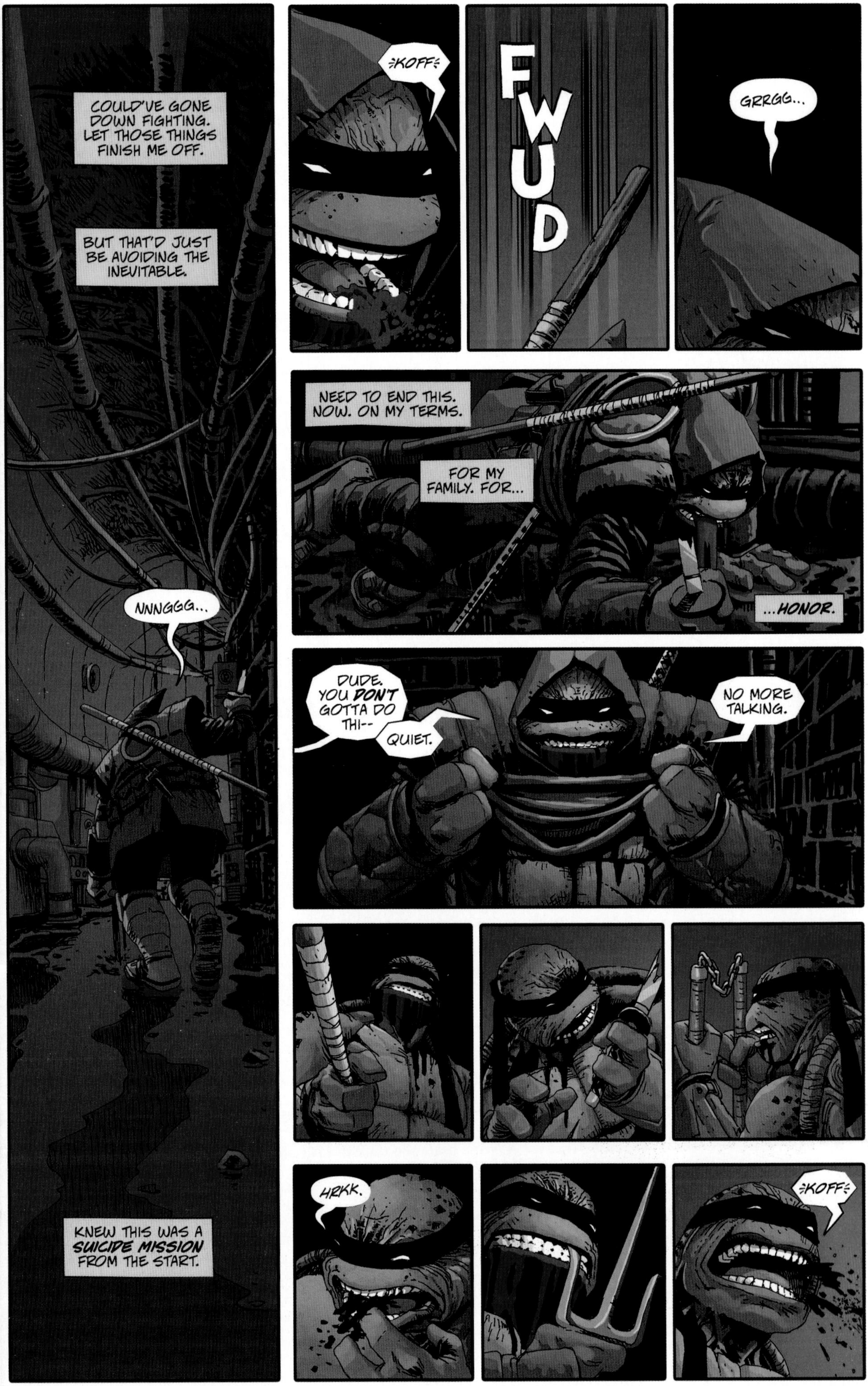
COULD'VE GONE DOWN FIGHTING. LET THOSE THINGS FINISH ME OFF.
BUT THAT'D JUST BE AVOIDING THE INEVITABLE.
NNNGGG...
KNEW THIS WAS A SUICIDE MISSION FROM THE START.
KOFF
FWUD
GRRGG...
NEED TO END THIS. NOW. ON MY TERMS.
FOR MY FAMILY. FOR...
...HONOR.
DUDE. YOU DON'T GOTTA DO THI--
QUIET.
NO MORE TALKING.
HRKK.
KOFF

WE WERE ALL ALWAYS SO DIFFERENT.

SO MUCH ALIKE.

ZZZP

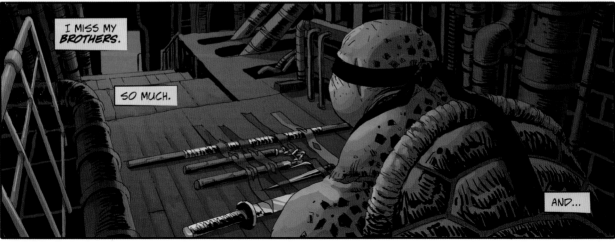

I MISS MY BROTHERS.

SO MUCH.

AND...

...I MISS MY *FATHER*.

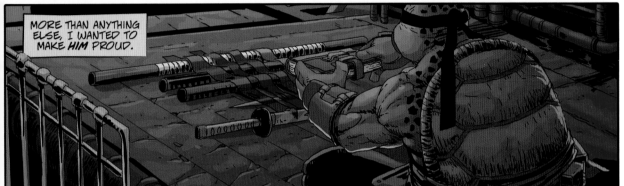

MORE THAN ANYTHING ELSE, I WANTED TO MAKE *HIM* PROUD.

IN THE END... TOO LITTLE, TOO LATE.

STORY OF MY LIFE.

I'M SORRY, FATHER. I FAILED.

PLEASE... *FORGIVE* ME.

TOO MUCH BLOOD.

NEVER LOSE... FOCUS.

≈KOFF≈ ≈KOFF≈

WHAT THE--

NO...

≈KOFF≈

NOT... YET...

...NOT LIKE... THIS...

KLANG

HOLY CRAP! IT'S... IT'S A...

...NO WAY.

YOU...

...YOU'RE A MUTANT TURTLE!

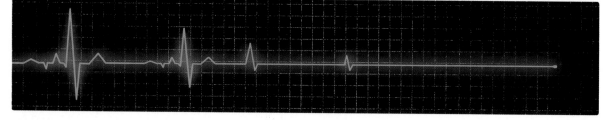

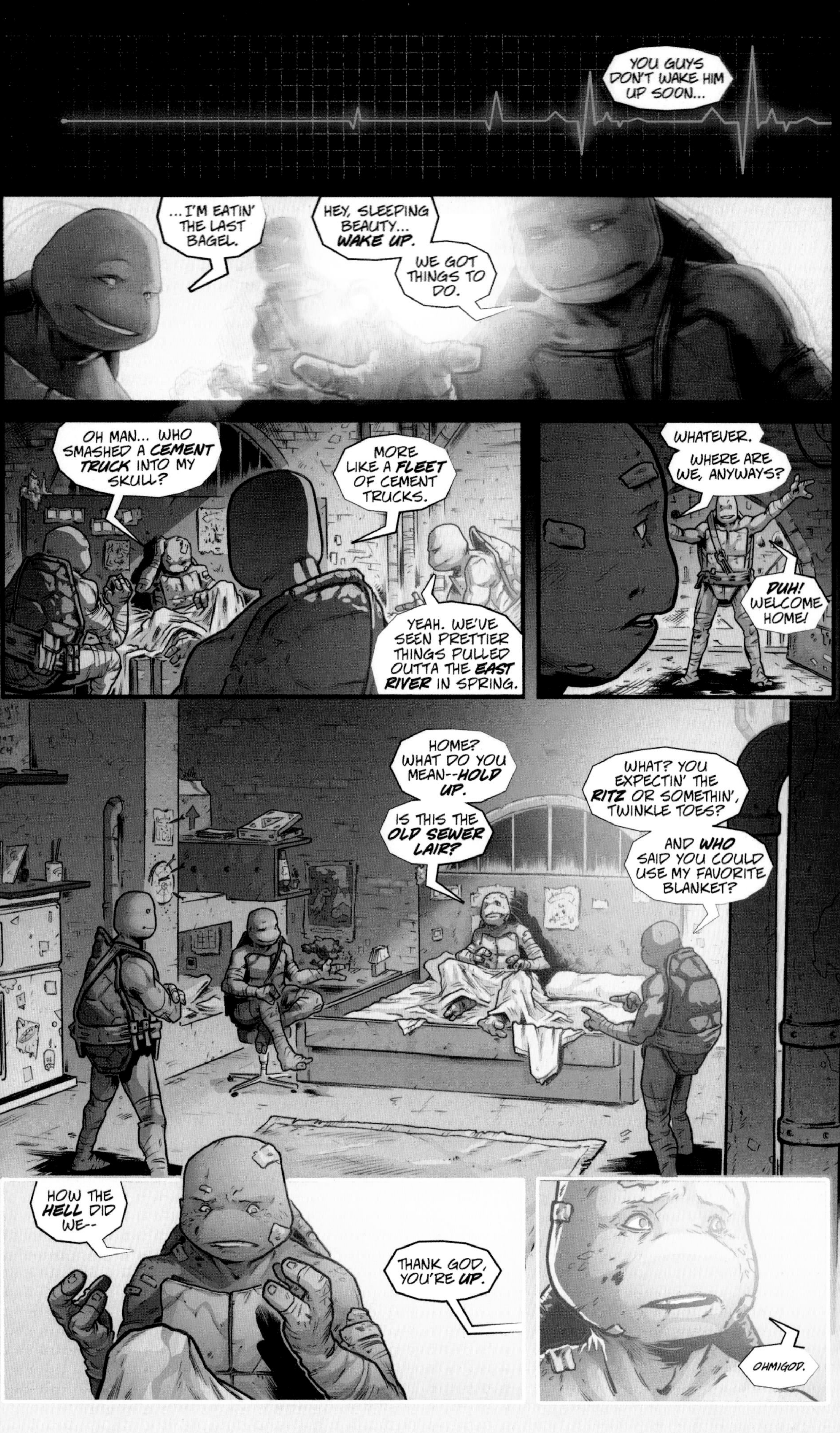
YOU GUYS DON'T WAKE HIM UP SOON...
...I'M EATIN' THE LAST BAGEL.
HEY, SLEEPING BEAUTY... WAKE UP.
WE GOT THINGS TO DO.
OH MAN... WHO SMASHED A CEMENT TRUCK INTO MY SKULL?
MORE LIKE A FLEET OF CEMENT TRUCKS.
YEAH. WE'VE SEEN PRETTIER THINGS PULLED OUTTA THE EAST RIVER IN SPRING.
WHATEVER.
WHERE ARE WE, ANYWAYS?
DUH! WELCOME HOME!
HOME? WHAT DO YOU MEAN--HOLD UP.
IS THIS THE OLD SEWER LAIR?
WHAT? YOU EXPECTIN' THE RITZ OR SOMETHIN', TWINKLE TOES?
AND WHO SAID YOU COULD USE MY FAVORITE BLANKET?
HOW THE HELL DID WE--
THANK GOD, YOU'RE UP.
OHMIGOD.

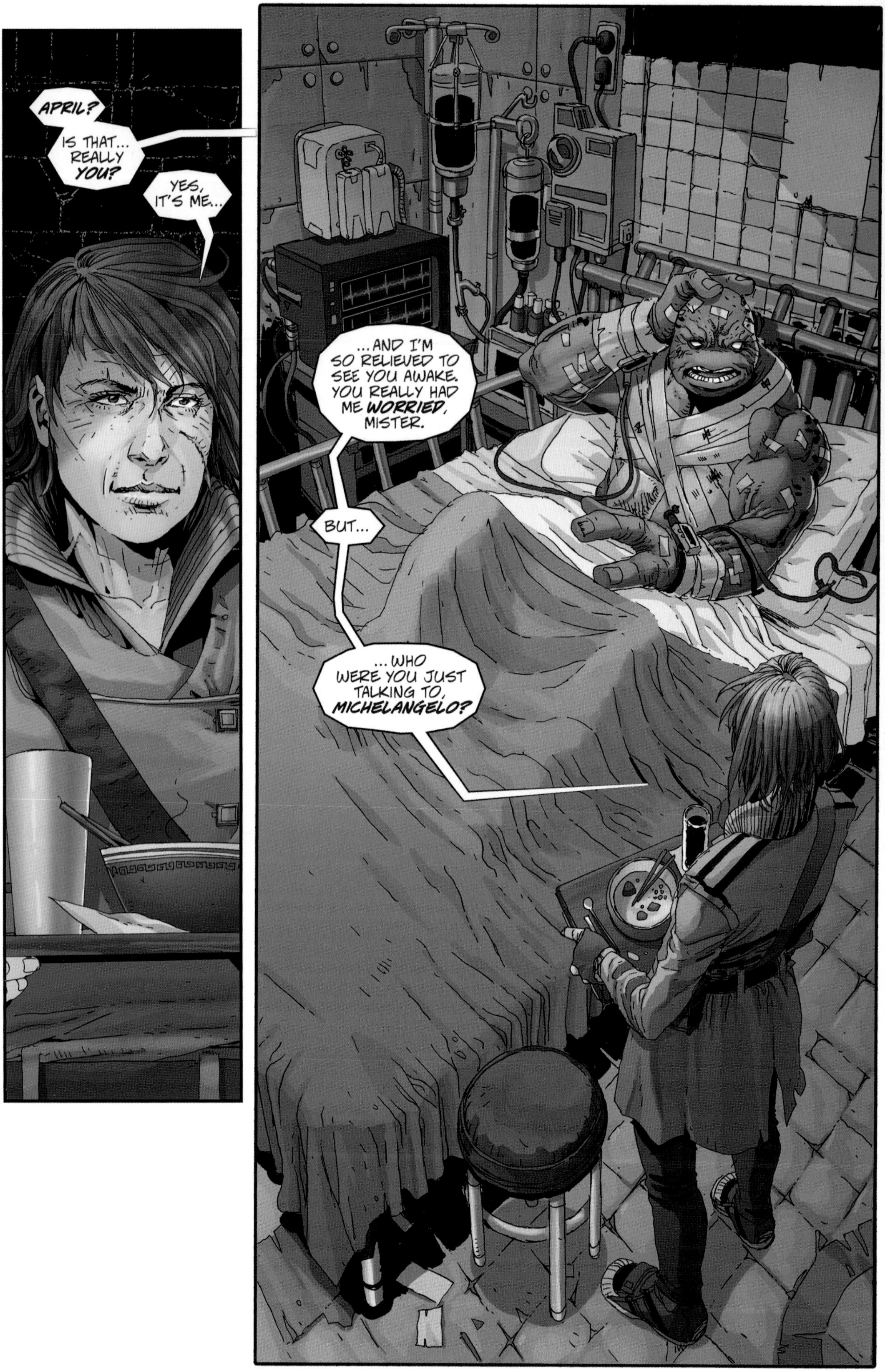
APRIL?
IS THAT... REALLY YOU?
YES, IT'S ME...
...AND I'M SO RELIEVED TO SEE YOU AWAKE. YOU REALLY HAD ME WORRIED, MISTER.
BUT...
...WHO WERE YOU JUST TALKING TO, MICHELANGELO?

THE LAST RONIN

PART 2

"FIRST TO FALL"

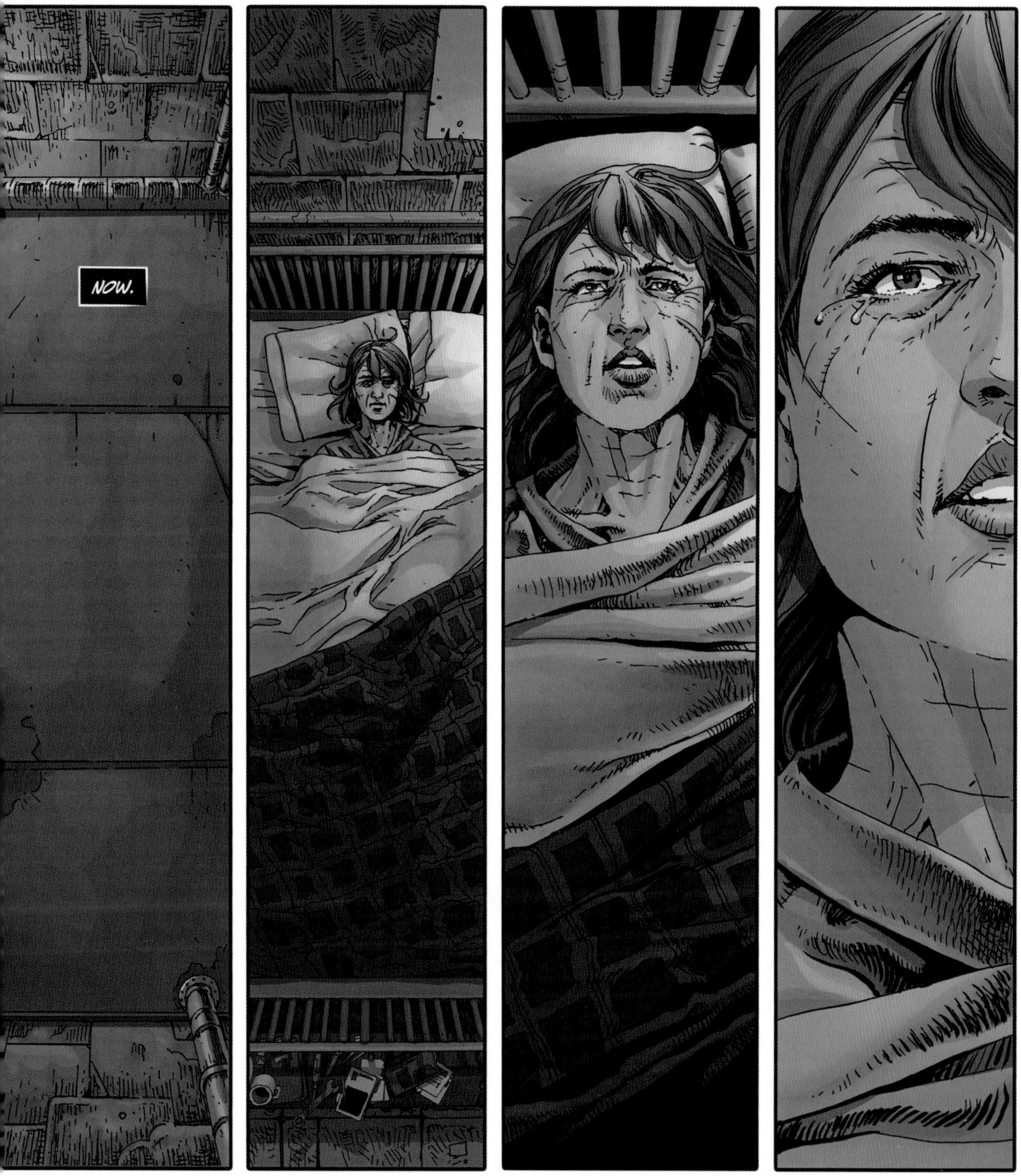
NOW.

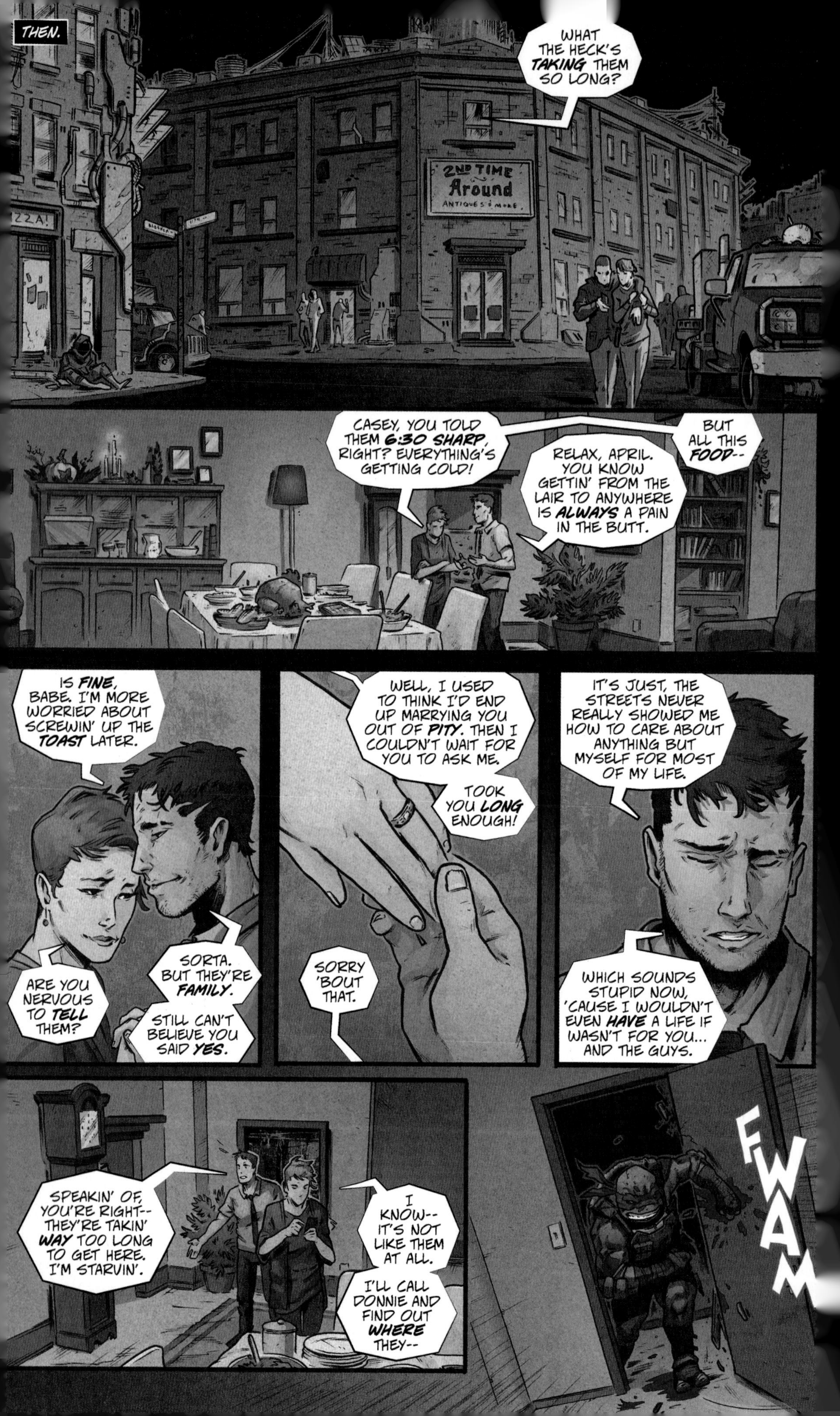
THEN.
WHAT THE HECK'S TAKING THEM SO LONG?
2ND TIME Around ANTIQUES & MORE
CASEY, YOU TOLD THEM 6:30 SHARP, RIGHT? EVERYTHING'S GETTING COLD!
BUT ALL THIS FOOD--
RELAX, APRIL. YOU KNOW GETTIN' FROM THE LAIR TO ANYWHERE IS ALWAYS A PAIN IN THE BUTT.
IS FINE, BABE. I'M MORE WORRIED ABOUT SCREWIN' UP THE TOAST LATER.
ARE YOU NERVOUS TO TELL THEM?
SORTA. BUT THEY'RE FAMILY.
STILL CAN'T BELIEVE YOU SAID YES.
WELL, I USED TO THINK I'D END UP MARRYING YOU OUT OF PITY. THEN I COULDN'T WAIT FOR YOU TO ASK ME.
TOOK YOU LONG ENOUGH!
SORRY 'BOUT THAT.
IT'S JUST, THE STREETS NEVER REALLY SHOWED ME HOW TO CARE ABOUT ANYTHING BUT MYSELF FOR MOST OF MY LIFE.
WHICH SOUNDS STUPID NOW, 'CAUSE I WOULDN'T EVEN HAVE A LIFE IF WASN'T FOR YOU... AND THE GUYS.
SPEAKIN' OF, YOU'RE RIGHT-- THEY'RE TAKIN' WAY TOO LONG TO GET HERE. I'M STARVIN'.
I KNOW-- IT'S NOT LIKE THEM AT ALL.
I'LL CALL DONNIE AND FIND OUT WHERE THEY--
FWAM

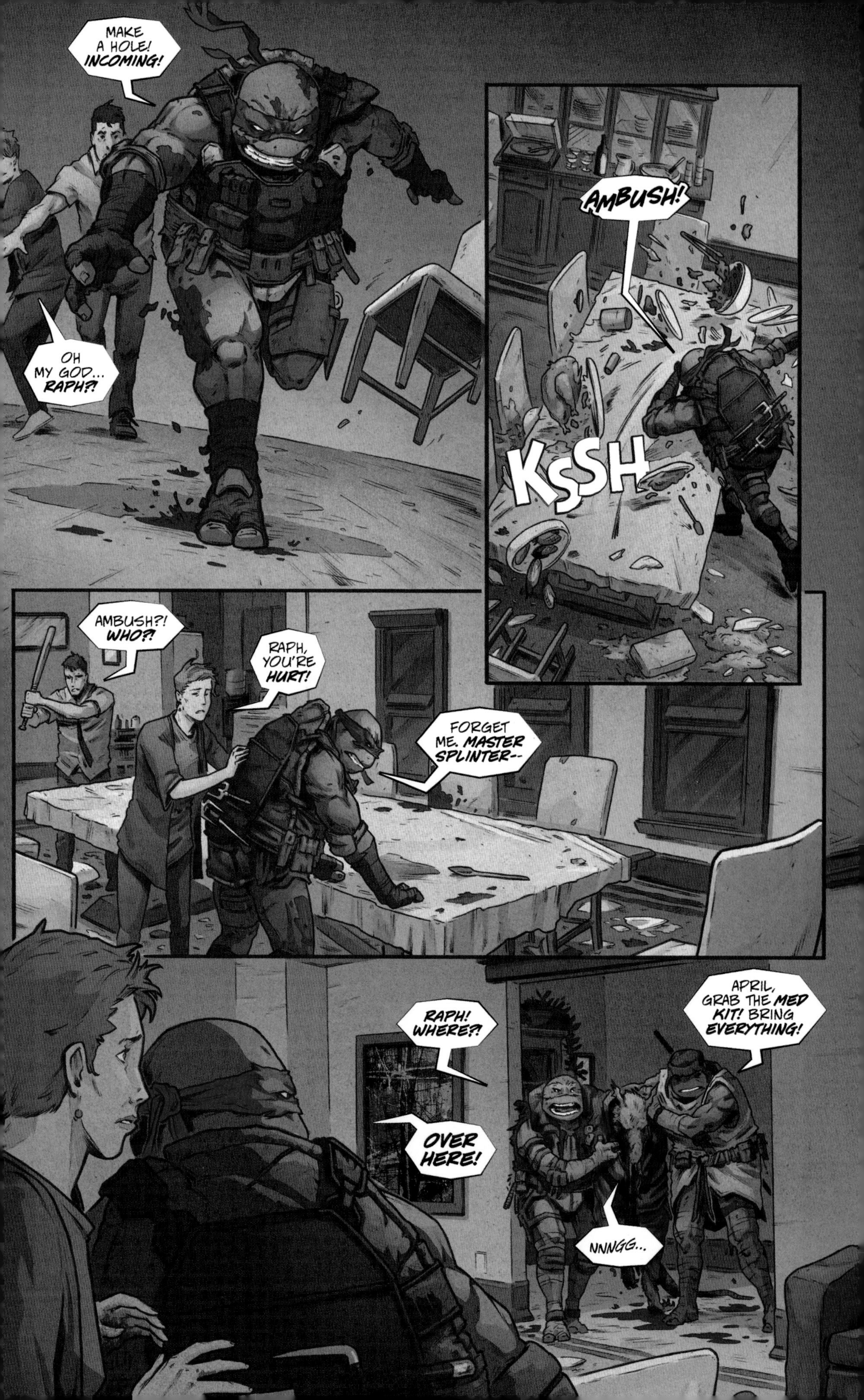
MAKE A HOLE! INCOMING!
OH MY GOD... RAPH?!
AMBUSH!
KSSH
AMBUSH?! WHO?!
RAPH, YOU'RE HURT!
FORGET ME. MASTER SPLINTER--
RAPH! WHERE?!
OVER HERE!
APRIL, GRAB THE MED KIT! BRING EVERYTHING!
NNNGG...

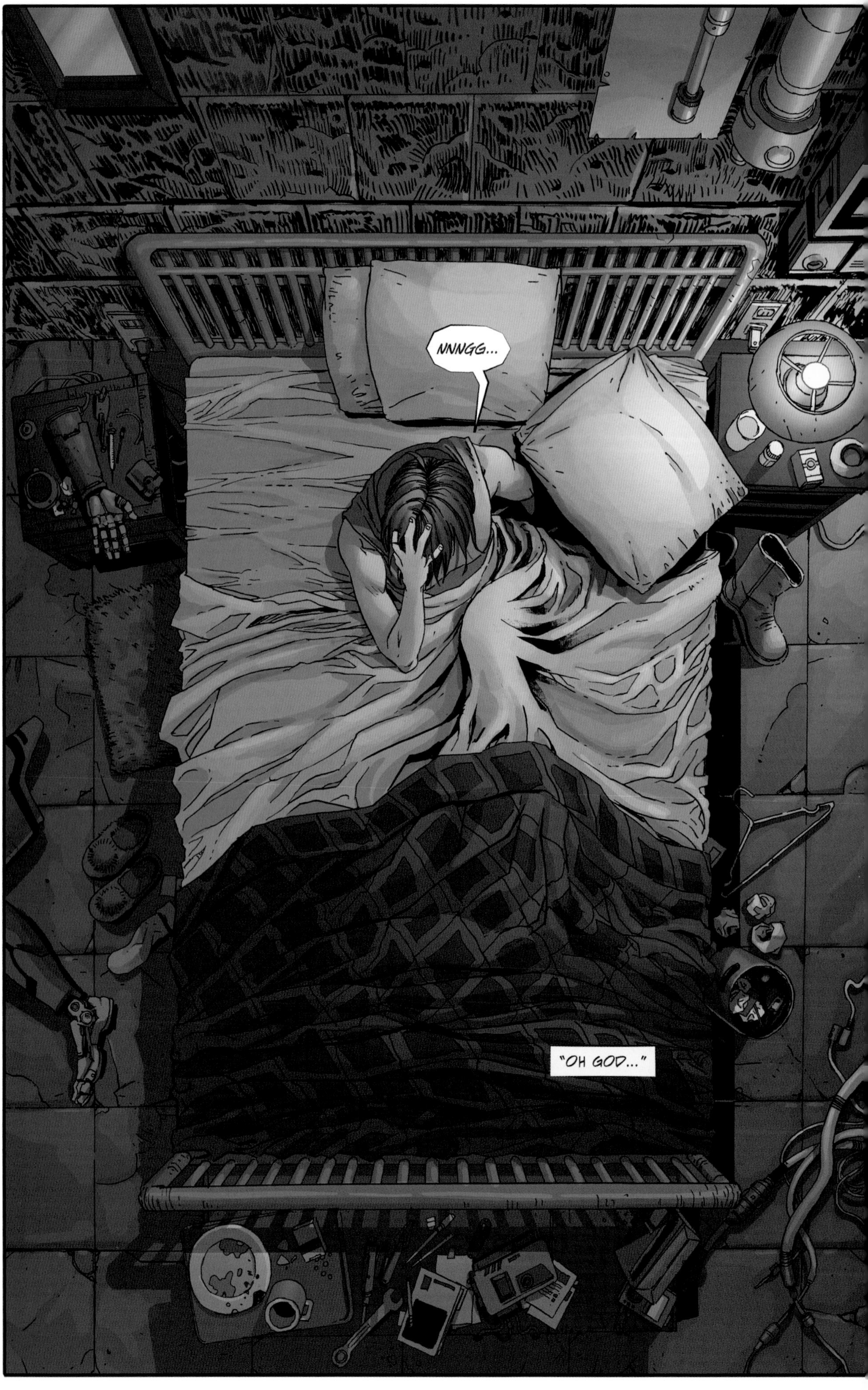
NNNGG...
"OH GOD..."

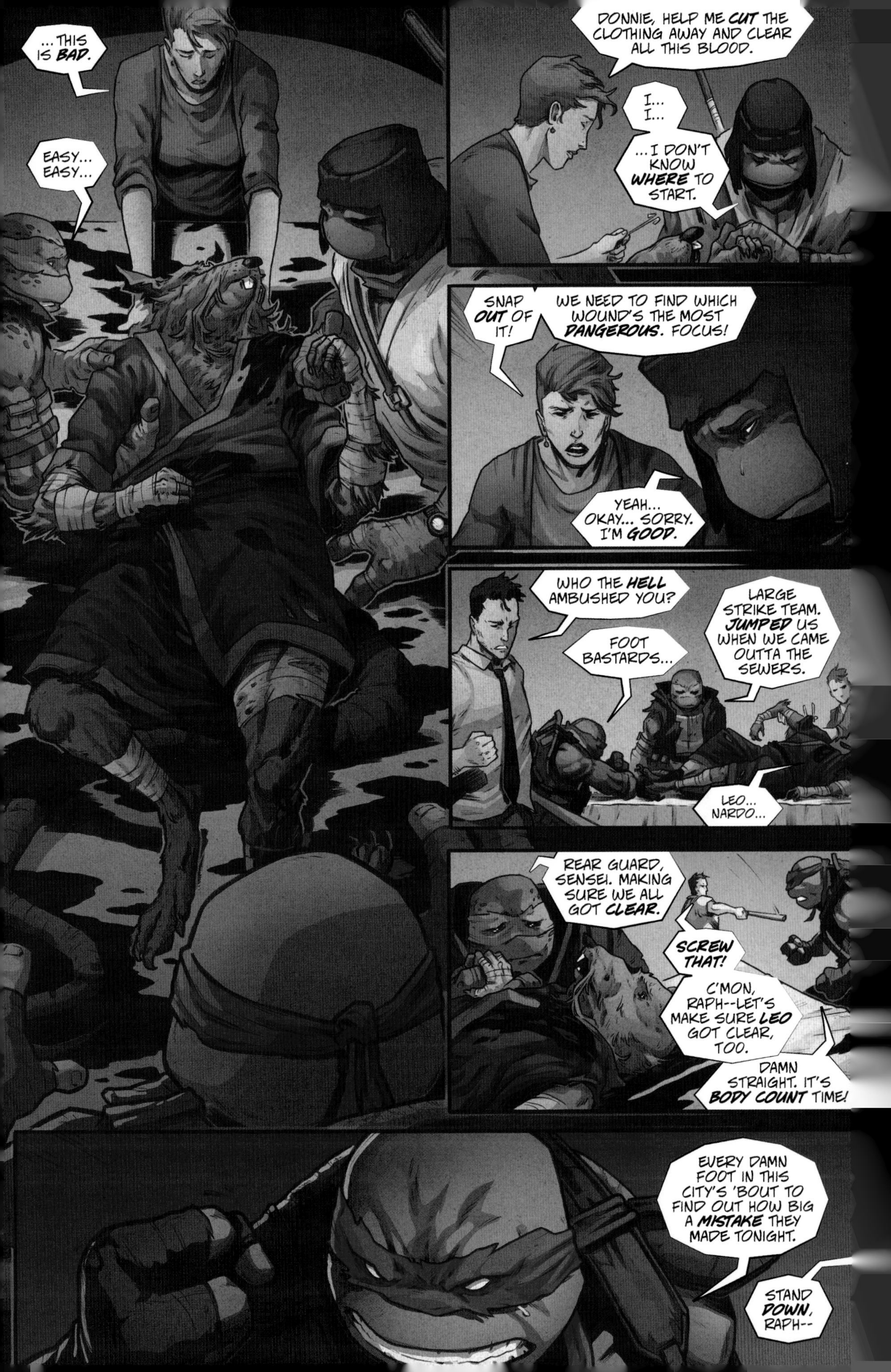

...THIS IS BAD.
EASY... EASY...
DONNIE, HELP ME CUT THE CLOTHING AWAY AND CLEAR ALL THIS BLOOD.
I... I...
...I DON'T KNOW WHERE TO START.
SNAP OUT OF IT!
WE NEED TO FIND WHICH WOUND'S THE MOST DANGEROUS. FOCUS!
YEAH... OKAY... SORRY. I'M GOOD.
WHO THE HELL AMBUSHED YOU?
FOOT BASTARDS...
LARGE STRIKE TEAM. JUMPED US WHEN WE CAME OUTTA THE SEWERS.
LEO... NARDO...
REAR GUARD, SENSEI. MAKING SURE WE ALL GOT CLEAR.
SCREW THAT!
C'MON, RAPH--LET'S MAKE SURE LEO GOT CLEAR, TOO.
DAMN STRAIGHT. IT'S BODY COUNT TIME!
EVERY DAMN FOOT IN THIS CITY'S 'BOUT TO FIND OUT HOW BIG A MISTAKE THEY MADE TONIGHT.
STAND DOWN, RAPH--

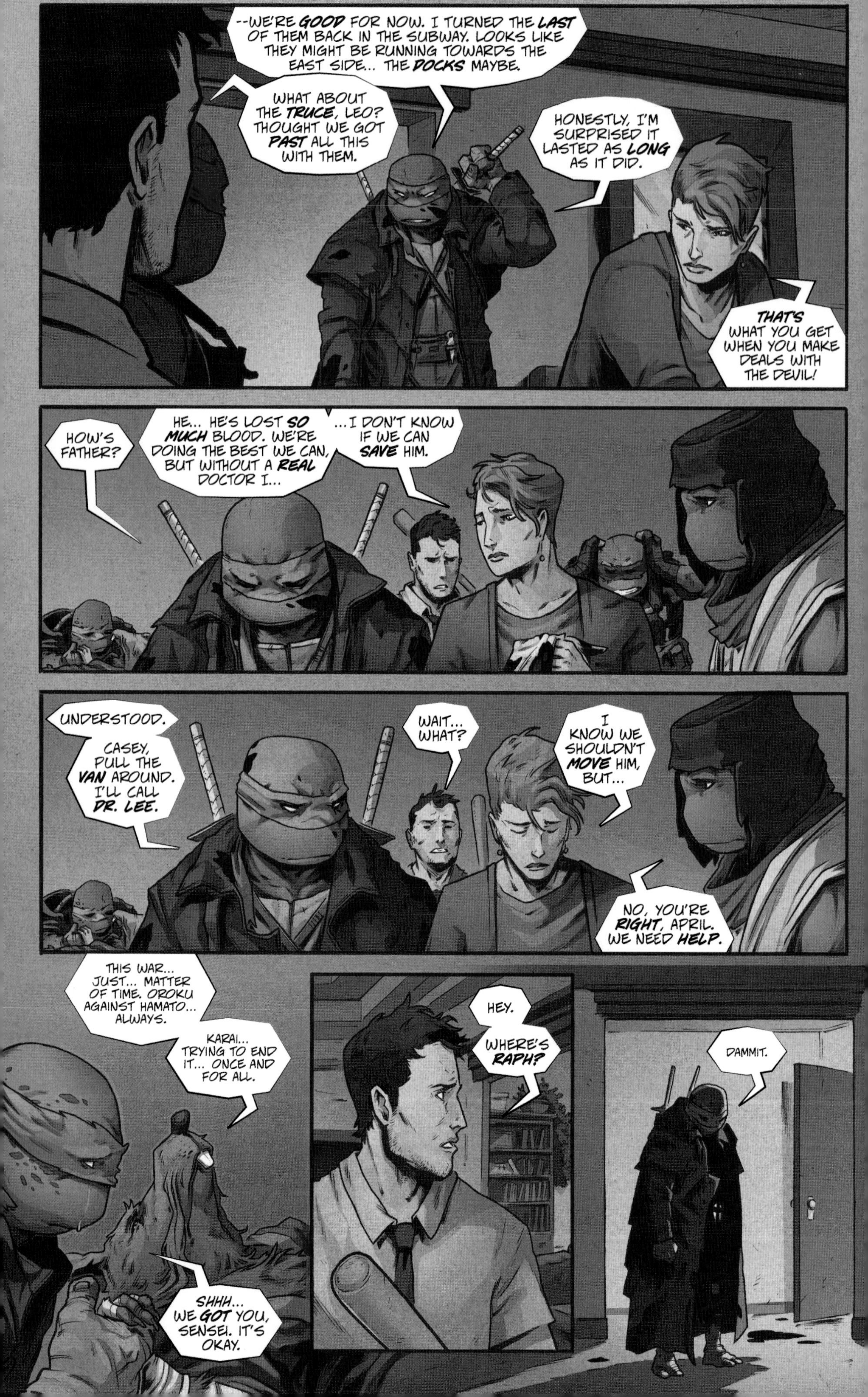
--WE'RE GOOD FOR NOW. I TURNED THE LAST OF THEM BACK IN THE SUBWAY. LOOKS LIKE THEY MIGHT BE RUNNING TOWARDS THE EAST SIDE... THE DOCKS MAYBE.
WHAT ABOUT THE TRUCE, LEO? THOUGHT WE GOT PAST ALL THIS WITH THEM.
HONESTLY, I'M SURPRISED IT LASTED AS LONG AS IT DID.
THAT'S WHAT YOU GET WHEN YOU MAKE DEALS WITH THE DEVIL!
HOW'S FATHER?
HE... HE'S LOST SO MUCH BLOOD. WE'RE DOING THE BEST WE CAN, BUT WITHOUT A REAL DOCTOR I...
...I DON'T KNOW IF WE CAN SAVE HIM.
UNDERSTOOD.
CASEY, PULL THE VAN AROUND. I'LL CALL DR. LEE.
WAIT... WHAT?
I KNOW WE SHOULDN'T MOVE HIM, BUT...
NO, YOU'RE RIGHT, APRIL. WE NEED HELP.
THIS WAR... JUST... MATTER OF TIME. OROKU AGAINST HAMATO... ALWAYS.
KARAI... TRYING TO END IT... ONCE AND FOR ALL.
SHHH... WE GOT YOU, SENSEI. IT'S OKAY.
HEY.
WHERE'S RAPH?
DAMMIT.

KLIK

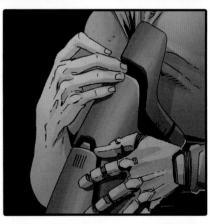

DAMN.

FUMP

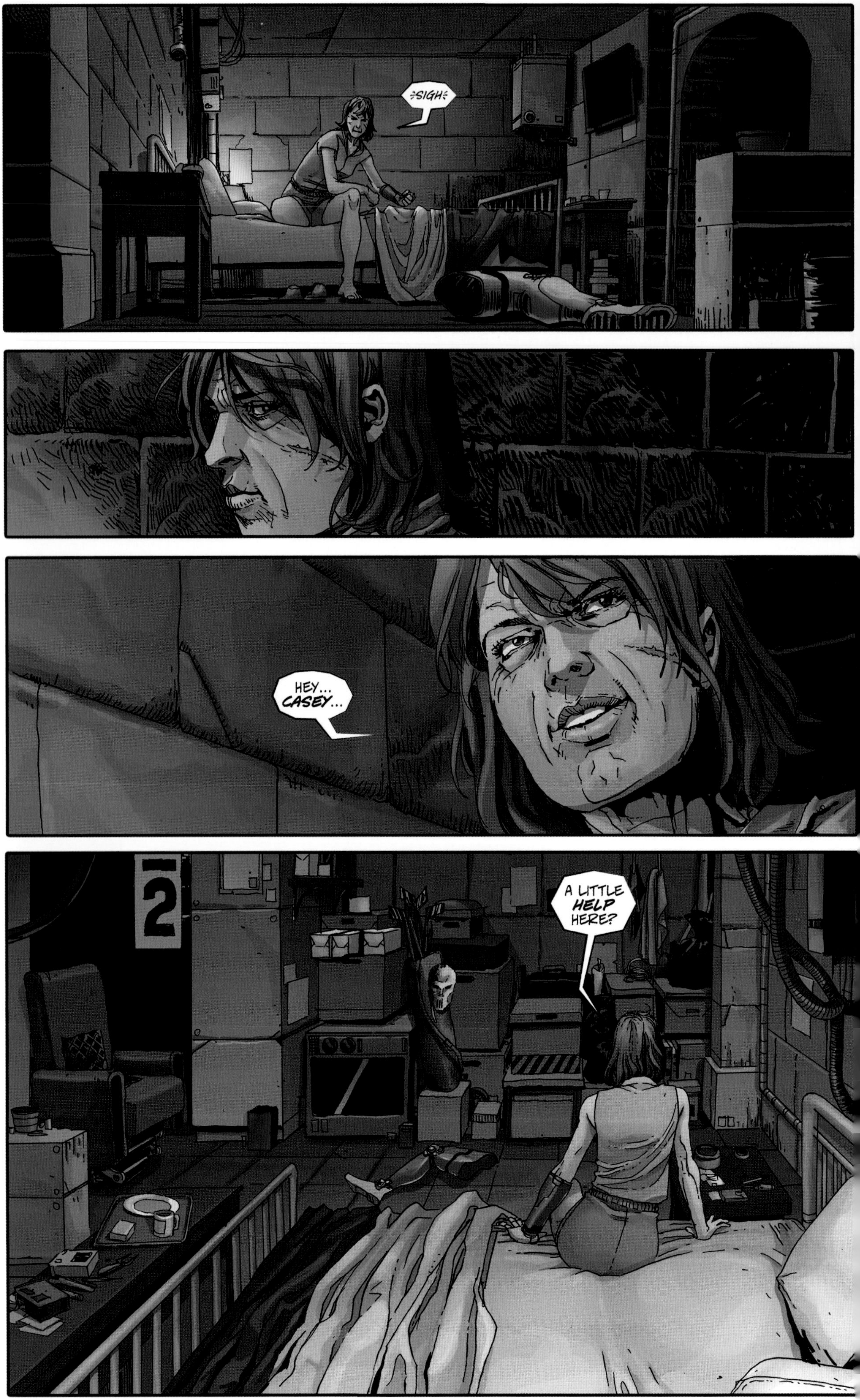
SIGH
HEY... CASEY...
A LITTLE HELP HERE?
2

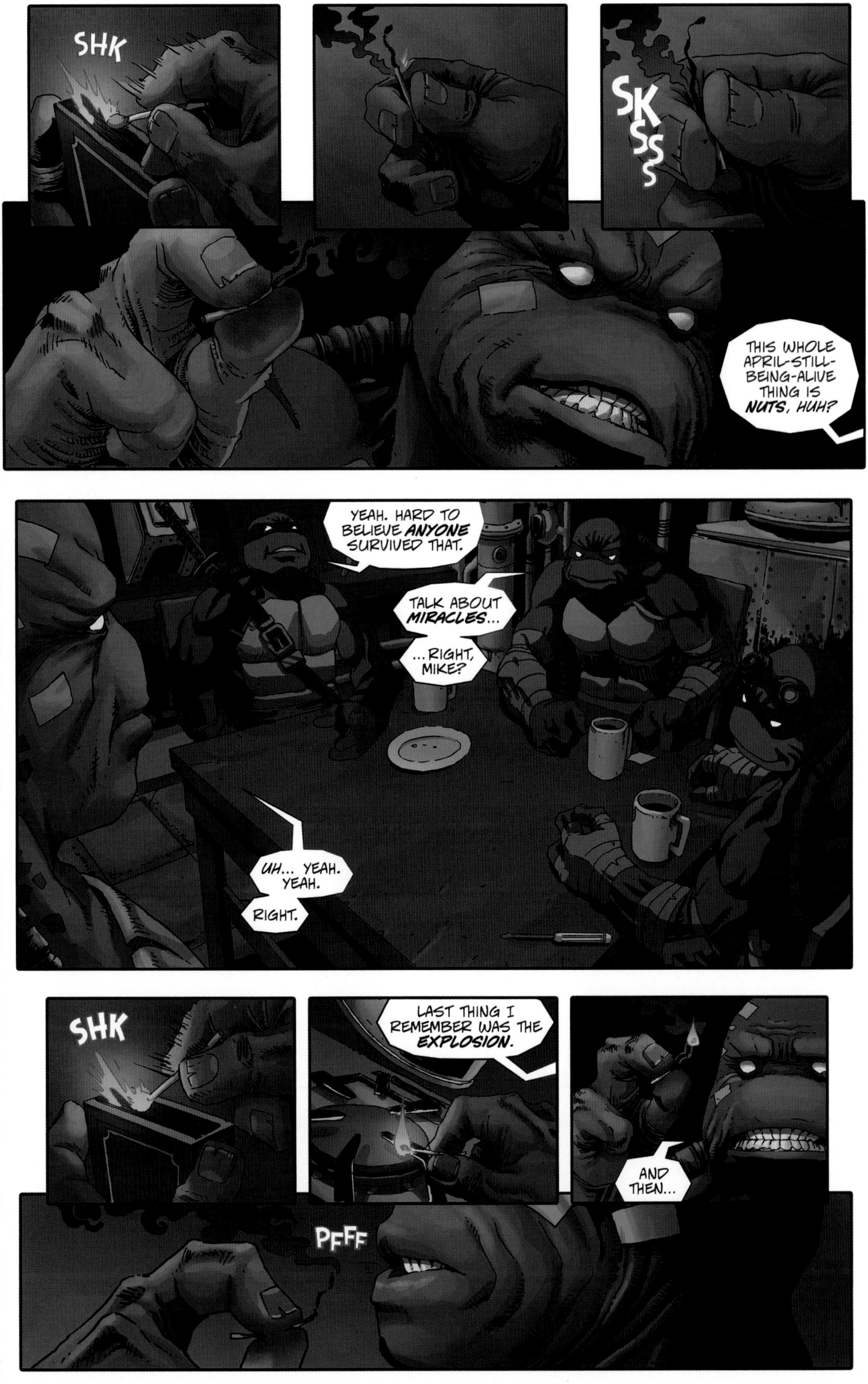
SHK
SKSSS
THIS WHOLE APRIL-STILL-BEING-ALIVE THING IS NUTS, HUH?
YEAH. HARD TO BELIEVE ANYONE SURVIVED THAT.
TALK ABOUT MIRACLES...
...RIGHT, MIKE?
UH... YEAH. YEAH.
RIGHT.
SHK
LAST THING I REMEMBER WAS THE EXPLOSION.
AND THEN...
PFFF

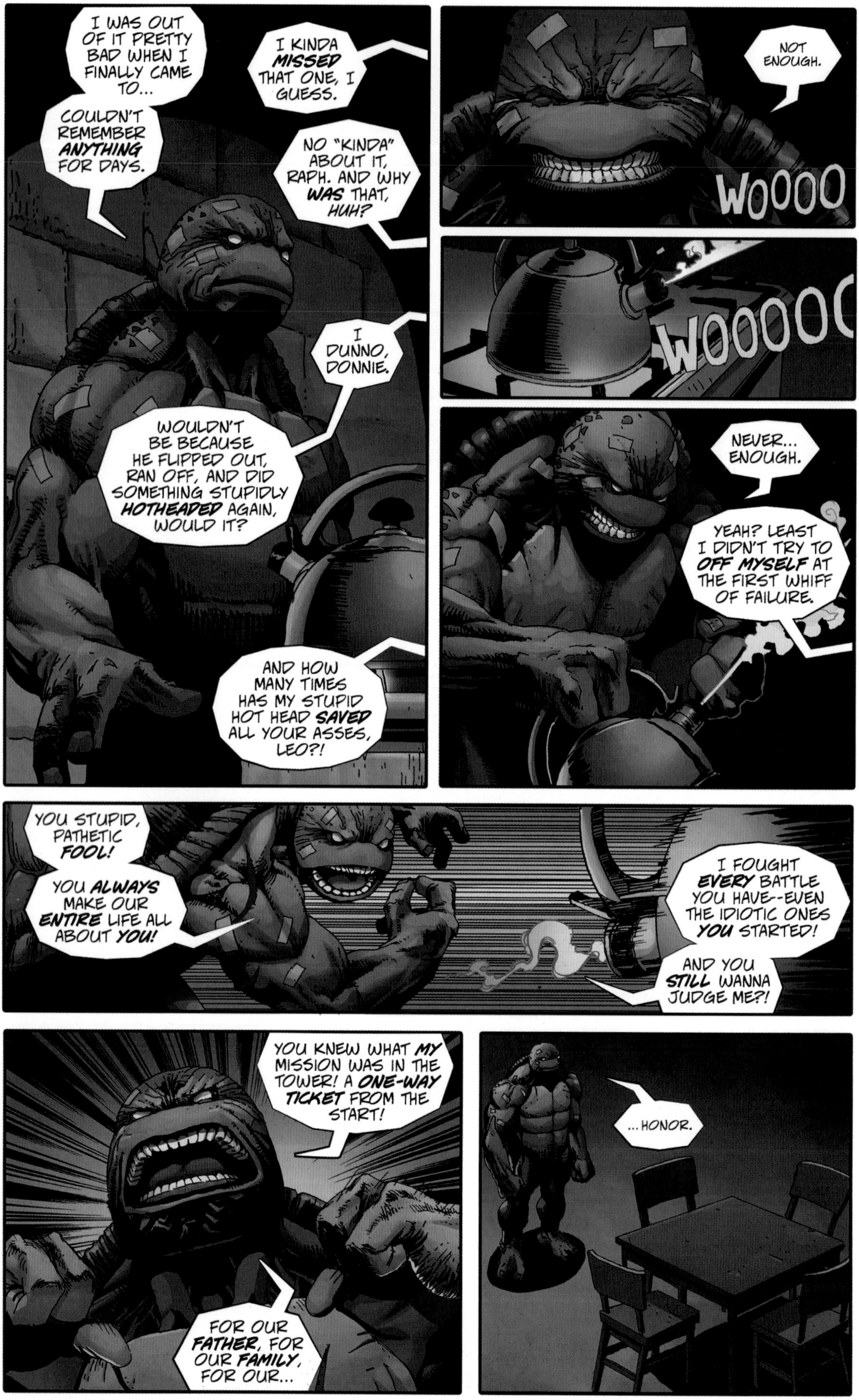
I WAS OUT OF IT PRETTY BAD WHEN I FINALLY CAME TO...
COULDN'T REMEMBER ANYTHING FOR DAYS.
I KINDA MISSED THAT ONE, I GUESS.
NO "KINDA" ABOUT IT, RAPH. AND WHY WAS THAT, HUH?
I DUNNO, DONNIE.
WOULDN'T BE BECAUSE HE FLIPPED OUT, RAN OFF, AND DID SOMETHING STUPIDLY HOTHEADED AGAIN, WOULD IT?
AND HOW MANY TIMES HAS MY STUPID HOT HEAD SAVED ALL YOUR ASSES, LEO?!
NOT ENOUGH.
WOOOO
WOOOOO
NEVER... ENOUGH.
YEAH? LEAST I DIDN'T TRY TO OFF MYSELF AT THE FIRST WHIFF OF FAILURE.
YOU STUPID, PATHETIC FOOL!
YOU ALWAYS MAKE OUR ENTIRE LIFE ALL ABOUT YOU!
I FOUGHT EVERY BATTLE YOU HAVE--EVEN THE IDIOTIC ONES YOU STARTED!
AND YOU STILL WANNA JUDGE ME?!
YOU KNEW WHAT MY MISSION WAS IN THE TOWER! A ONE-WAY TICKET FROM THE START!
FOR OUR FATHER, FOR OUR FAMILY, FOR OUR...
...HONOR.

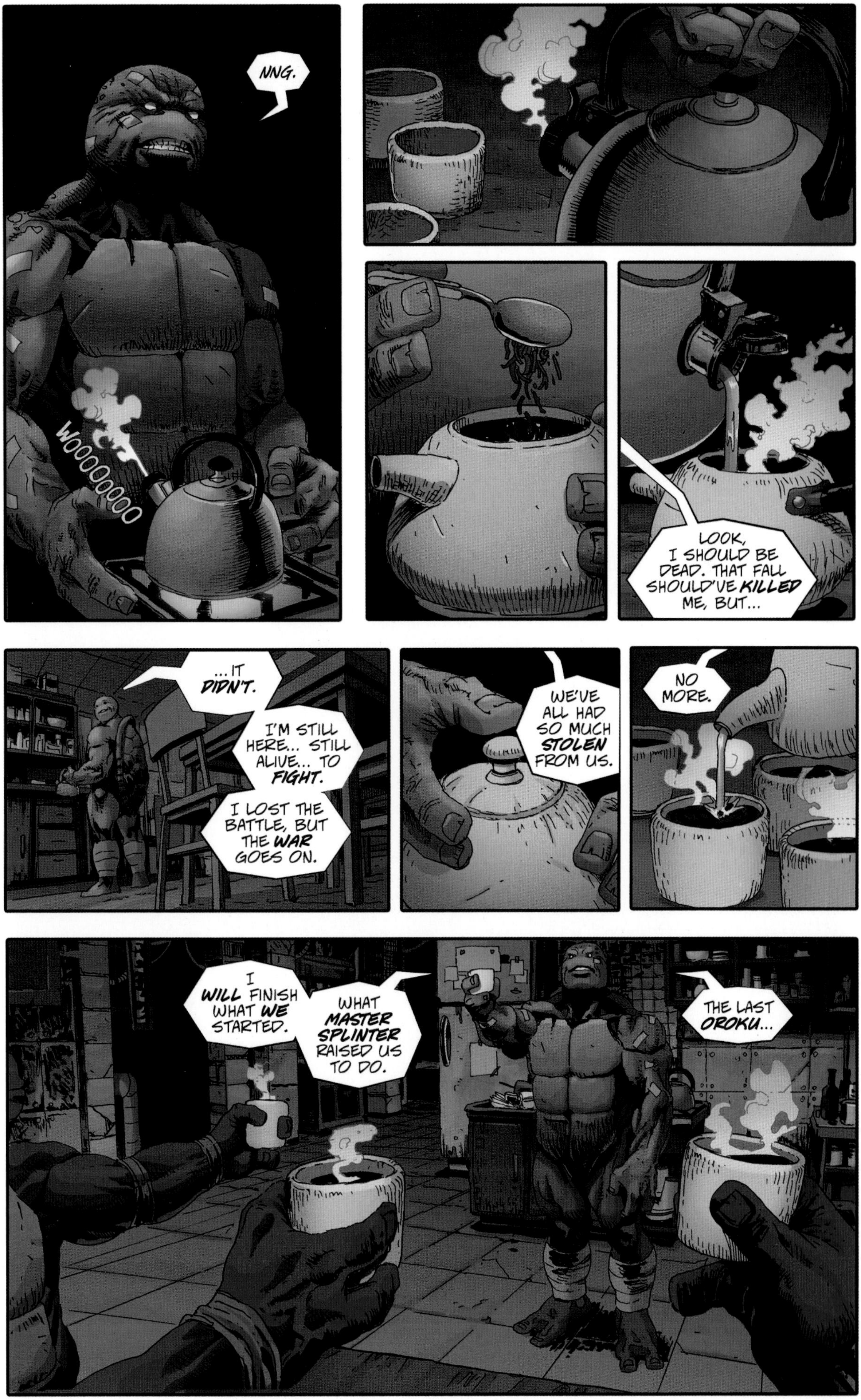
NNG.
WOOOOOOOO
LOOK, I SHOULD BE DEAD. THAT FALL SHOULD'VE KILLED ME, BUT...
...IT DIDN'T.
I'M STILL HERE... STILL ALIVE... TO FIGHT.
I LOST THE BATTLE, BUT THE WAR GOES ON.
WE'VE ALL HAD SO MUCH STOLEN FROM US.
NO MORE.
I WILL FINISH WHAT WE STARTED.
WHAT MASTER SPLINTER RAISED US TO DO.
THE LAST OROKU...

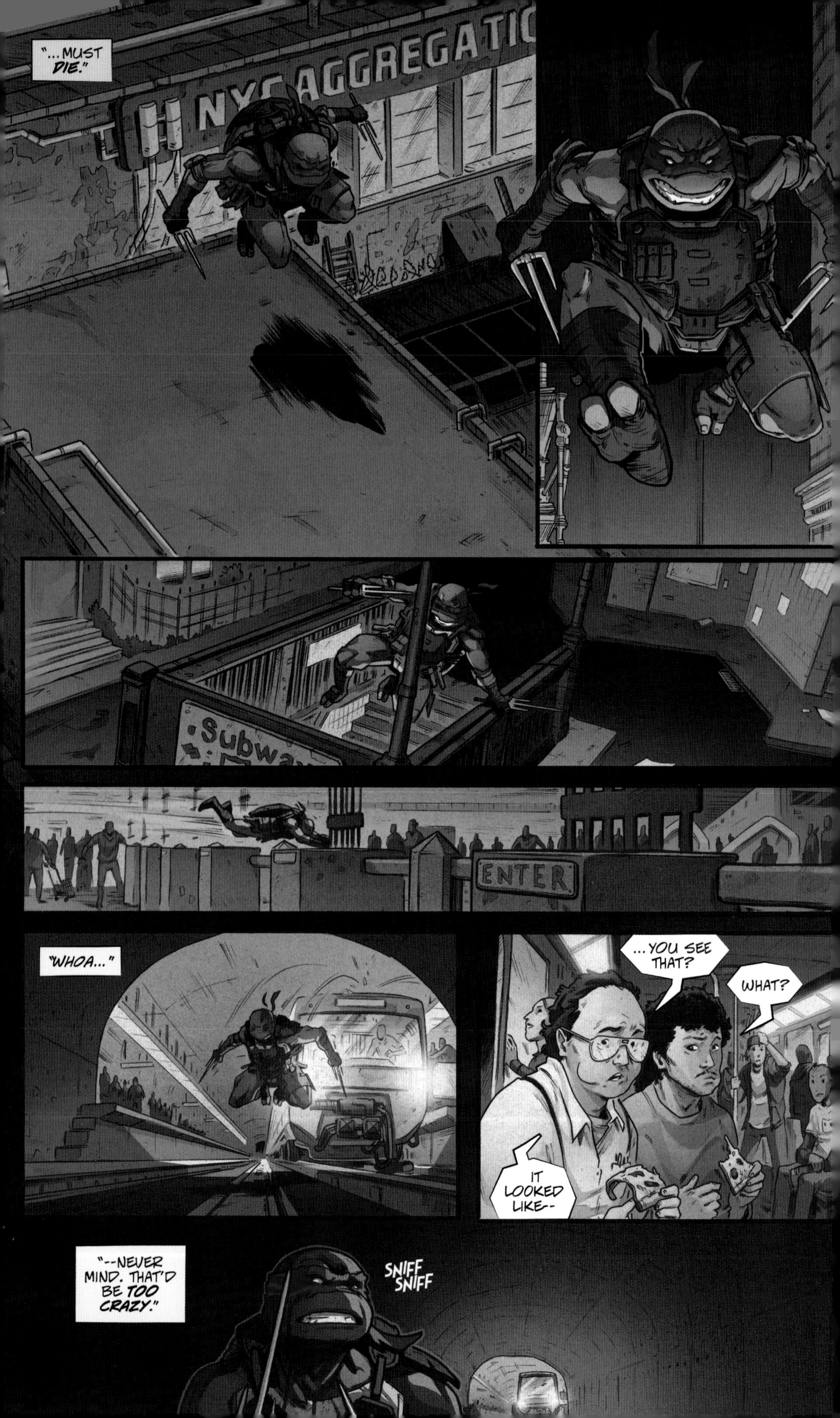
"...MUST DIE."
NYC AGGREGATIO
Subway
ENTER
"WHOA..."
...YOU SEE THAT?
WHAT?
IT LOOKED LIKE--
"--NEVER MIND. THAT'D BE TOO CRAZY."
SNIFF SNIFF

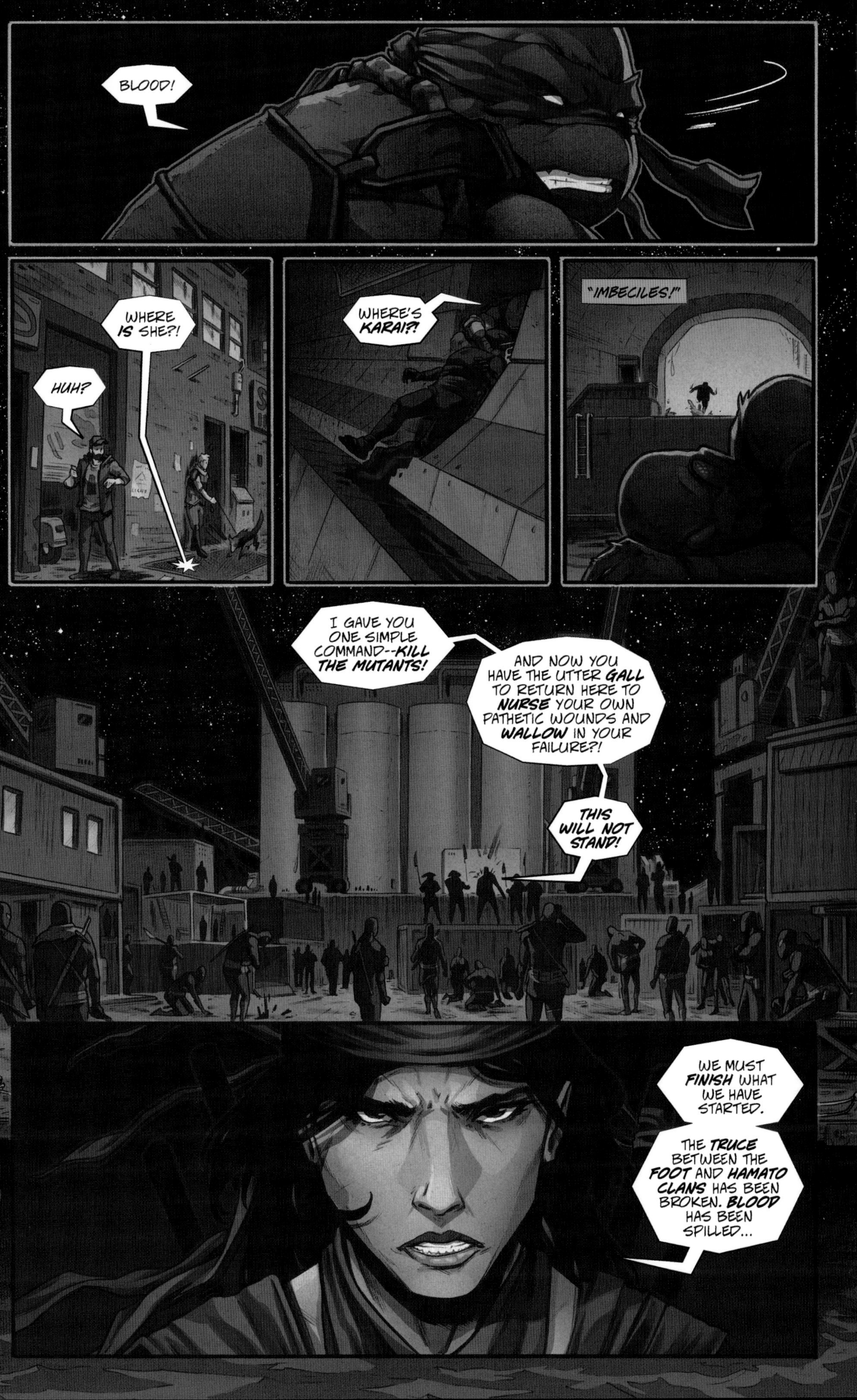
BLOOD!
HUH?
WHERE IS SHE?!
WHERE'S KARAI?!
"IMBECILES!"
I GAVE YOU ONE SIMPLE COMMAND--KILL THE MUTANTS!
AND NOW YOU HAVE THE UTTER GALL TO RETURN HERE TO NURSE YOUR OWN PATHETIC WOUNDS AND WALLOW IN YOUR FAILURE?!
THIS WILL NOT STAND!
WE MUST FINISH WHAT WE HAVE STARTED.
THE TRUCE BETWEEN THE FOOT AND HAMATO CLANS HAS BEEN BROKEN. BLOOD HAS BEEN SPILLED...

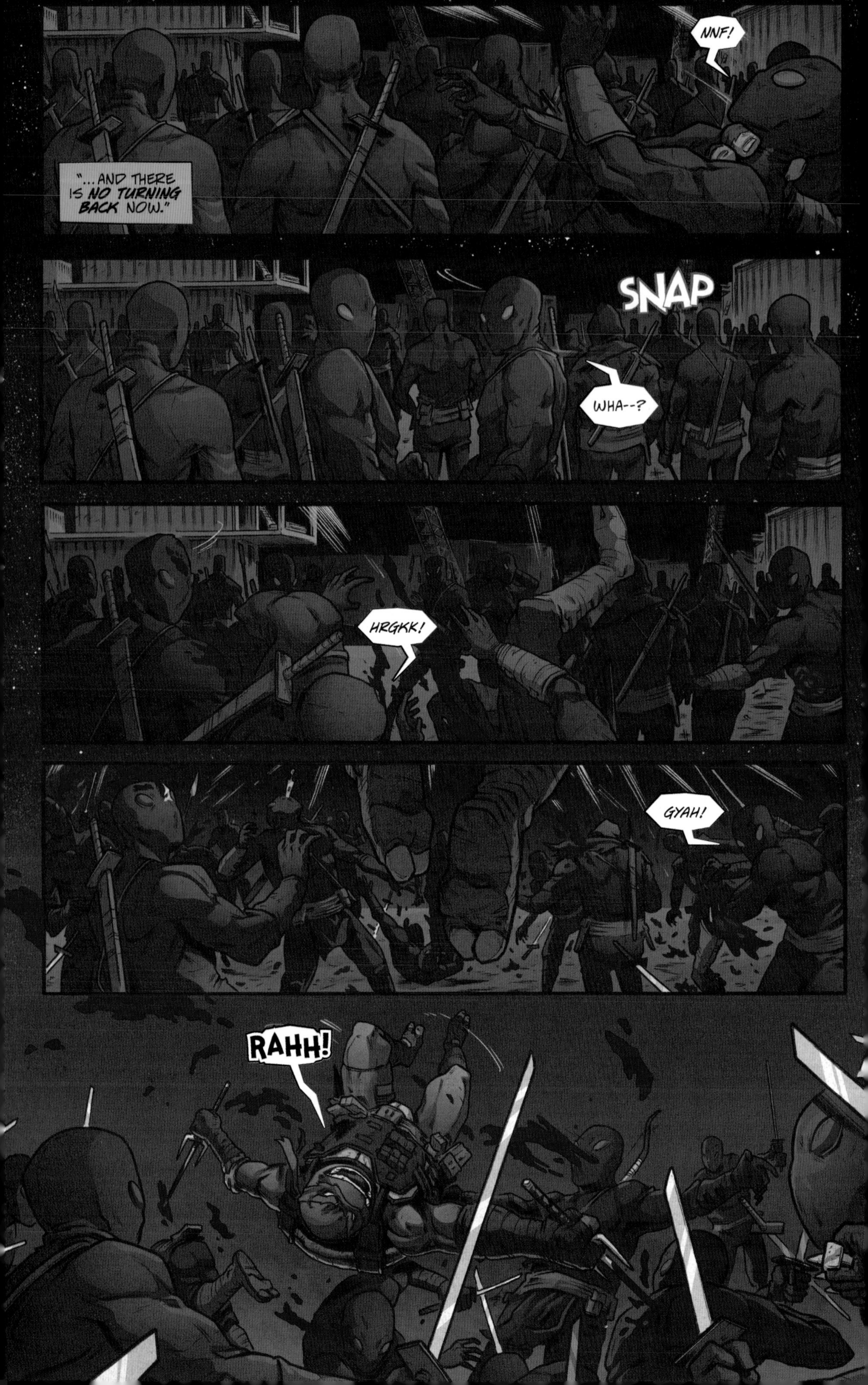
"...AND THERE IS NO TURNING BACK NOW."
NNF!
SNAP
WHA--?
HRGKK!
GYAH!
RAHH!

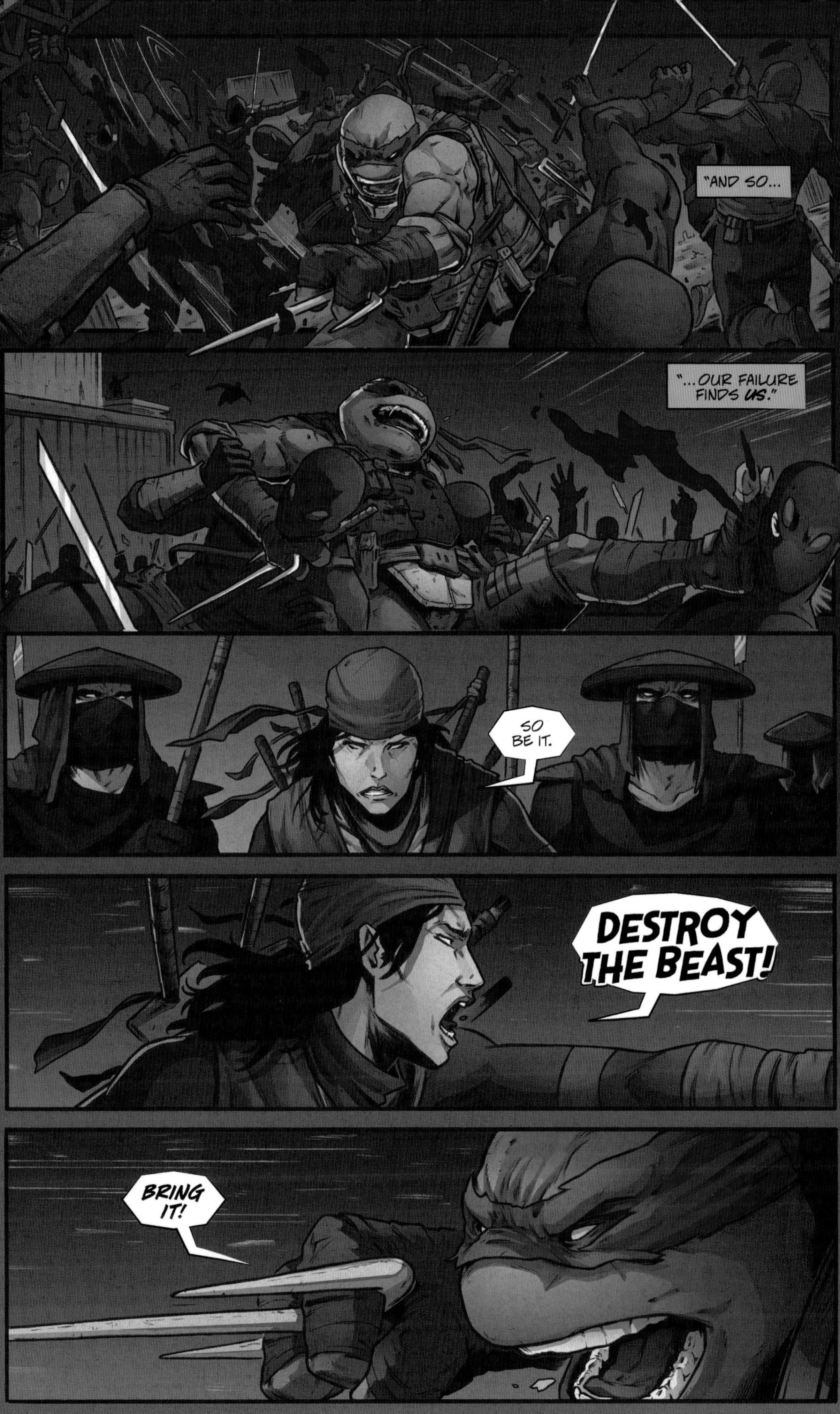
"AND SO...
"...OUR FAILURE FINDS US."
SO BE IT.
DESTROY THE BEAST!
BRING IT!

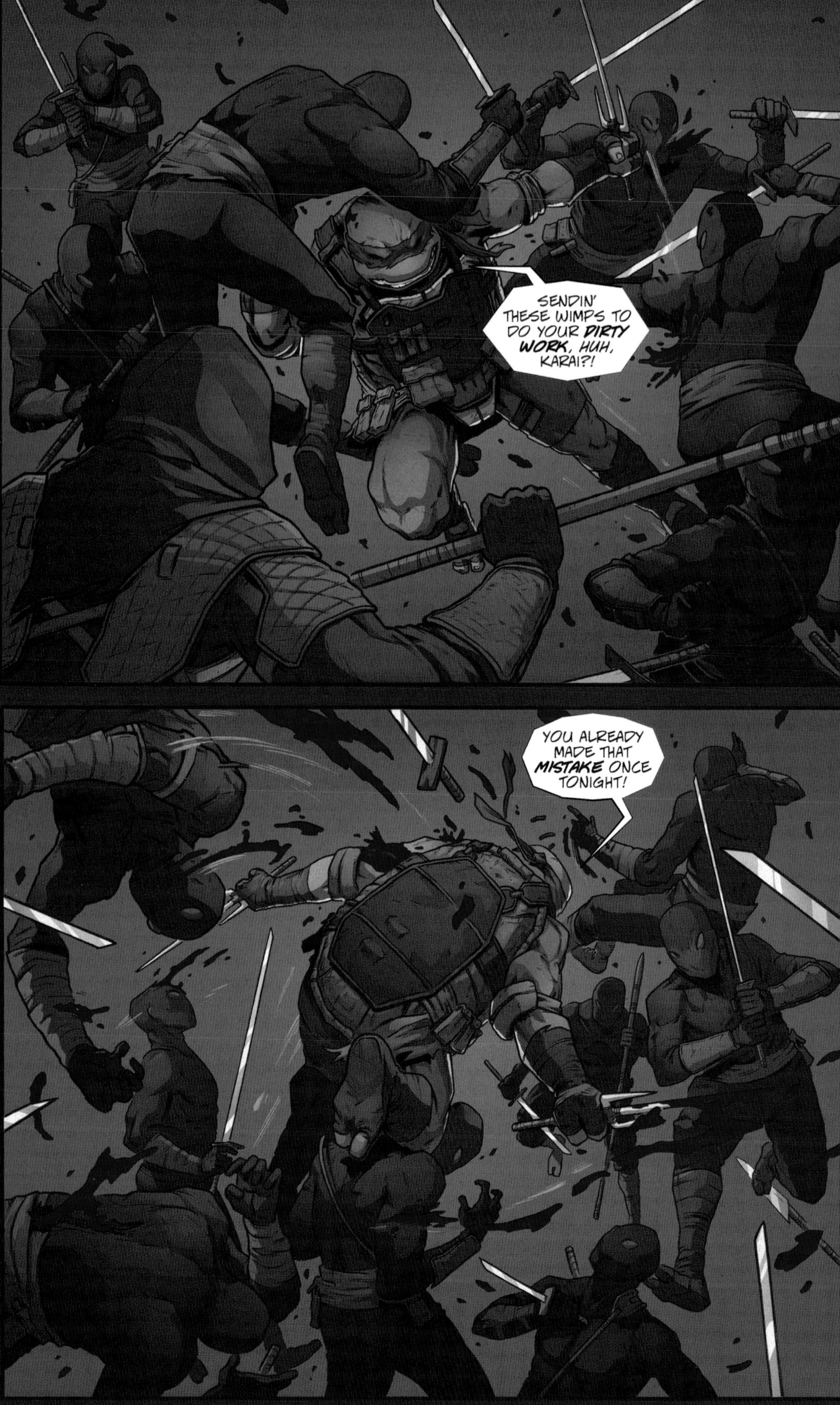
SENDIN' THESE WIMPS TO DO YOUR DIRTY WORK, HUH, KARAI?!
YOU ALREADY MADE THAT MISTAKE ONCE TONIGHT!

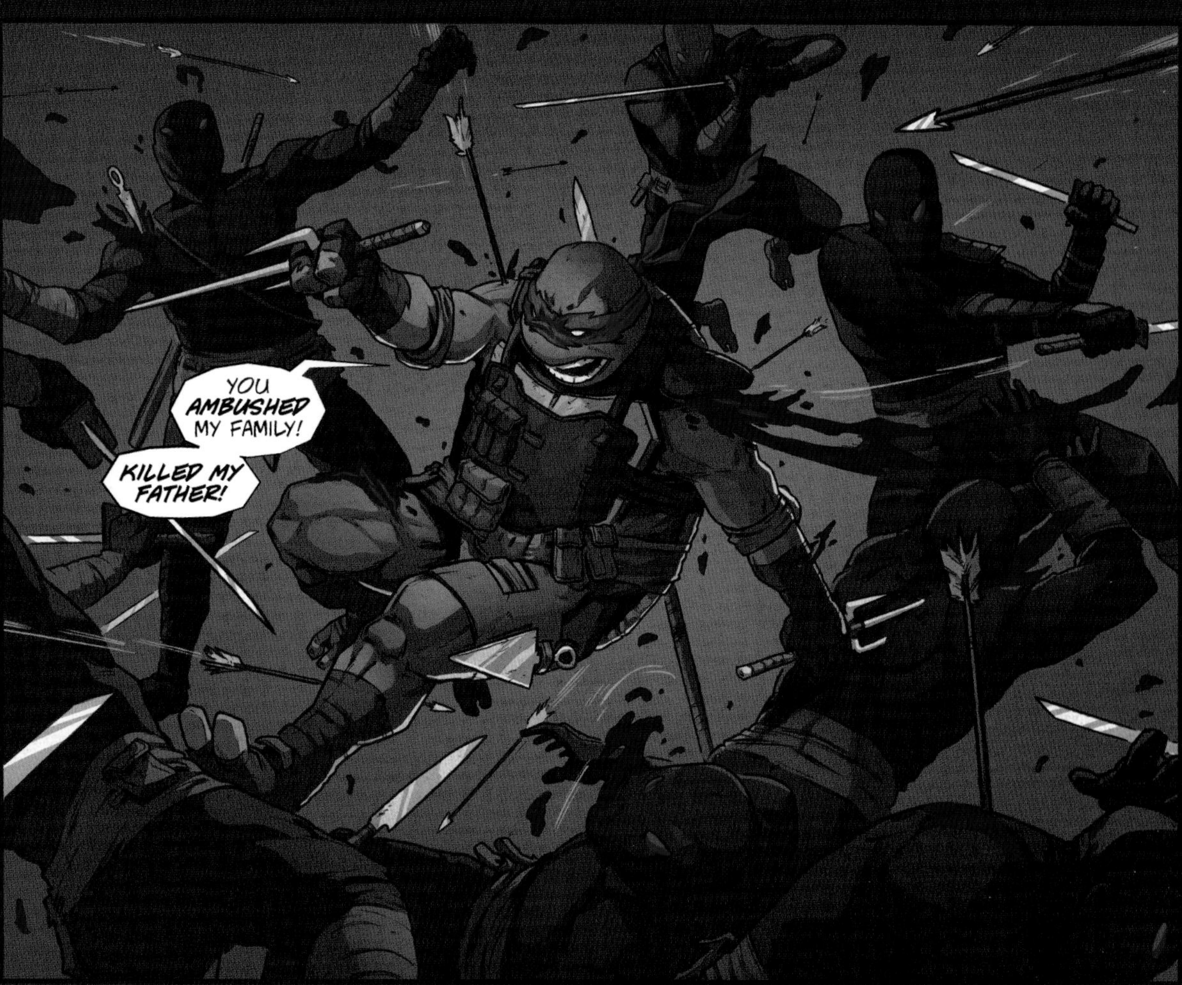
YOU AMBUSHED MY FAMILY!
KILLED MY FATHER!

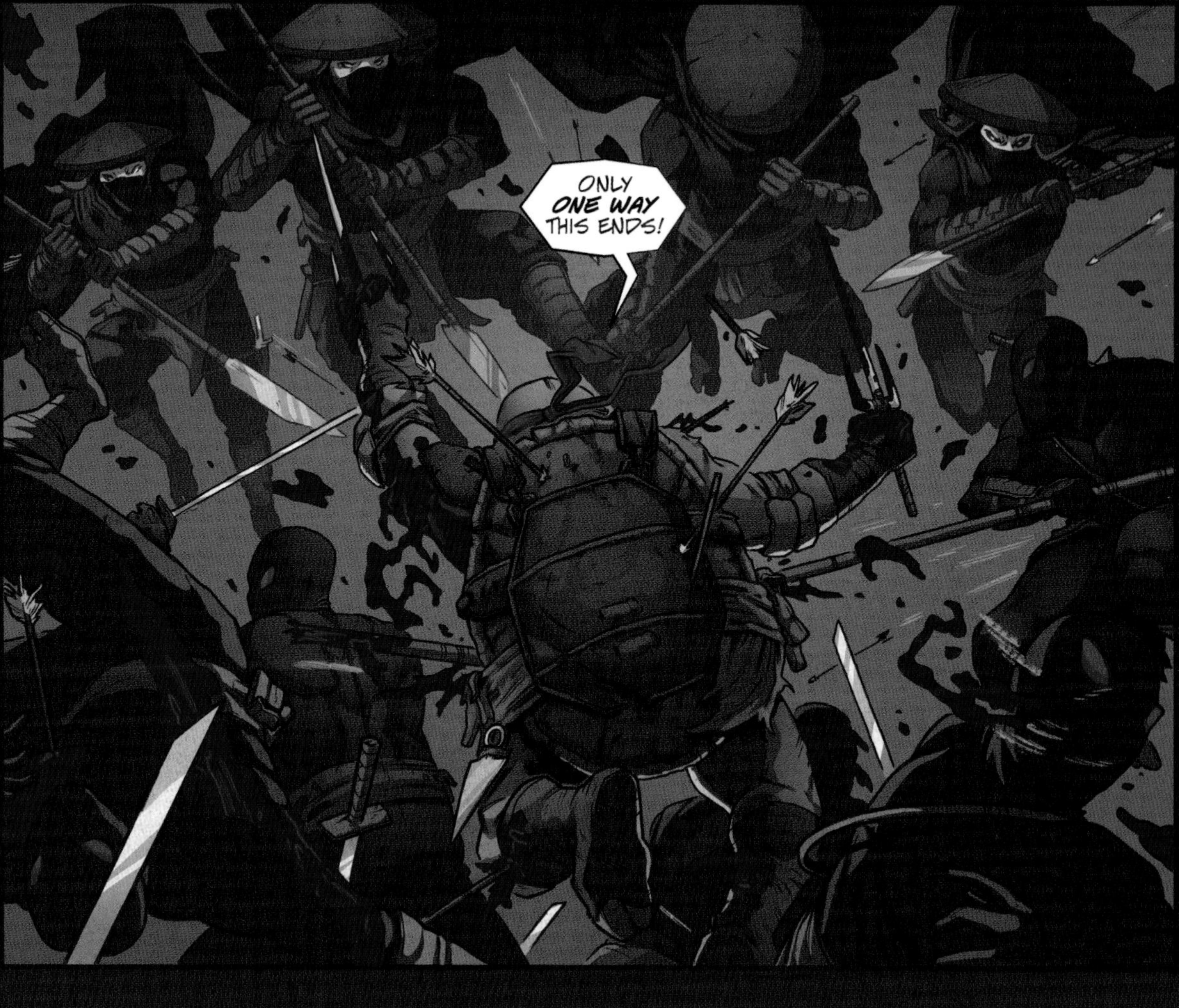
ONLY ONE WAY THIS ENDS!

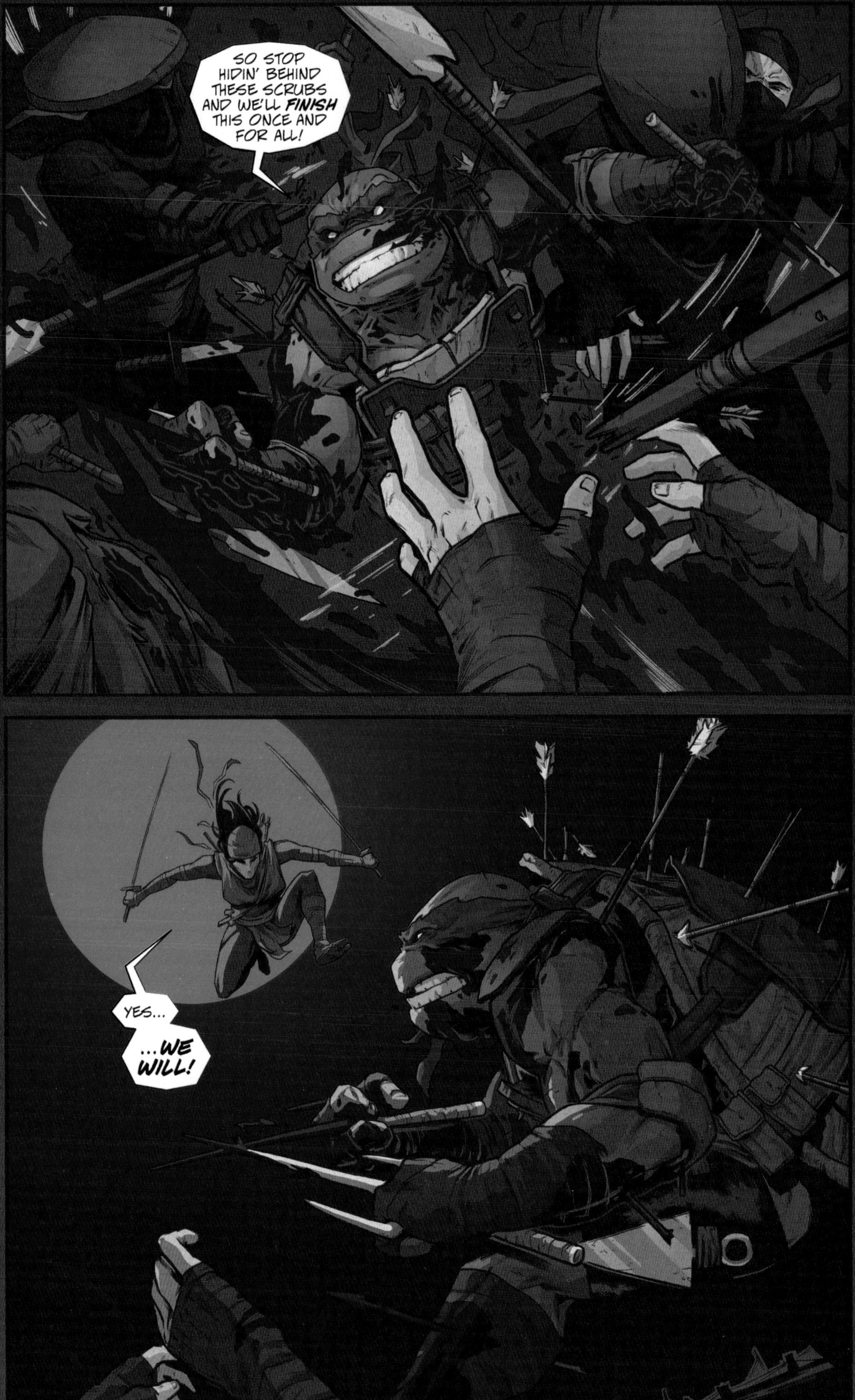
SO STOP HIDIN' BEHIND THESE SCRUBS AND WE'LL FINISH THIS ONCE AND FOR ALL!
YES...
...WE WILL!

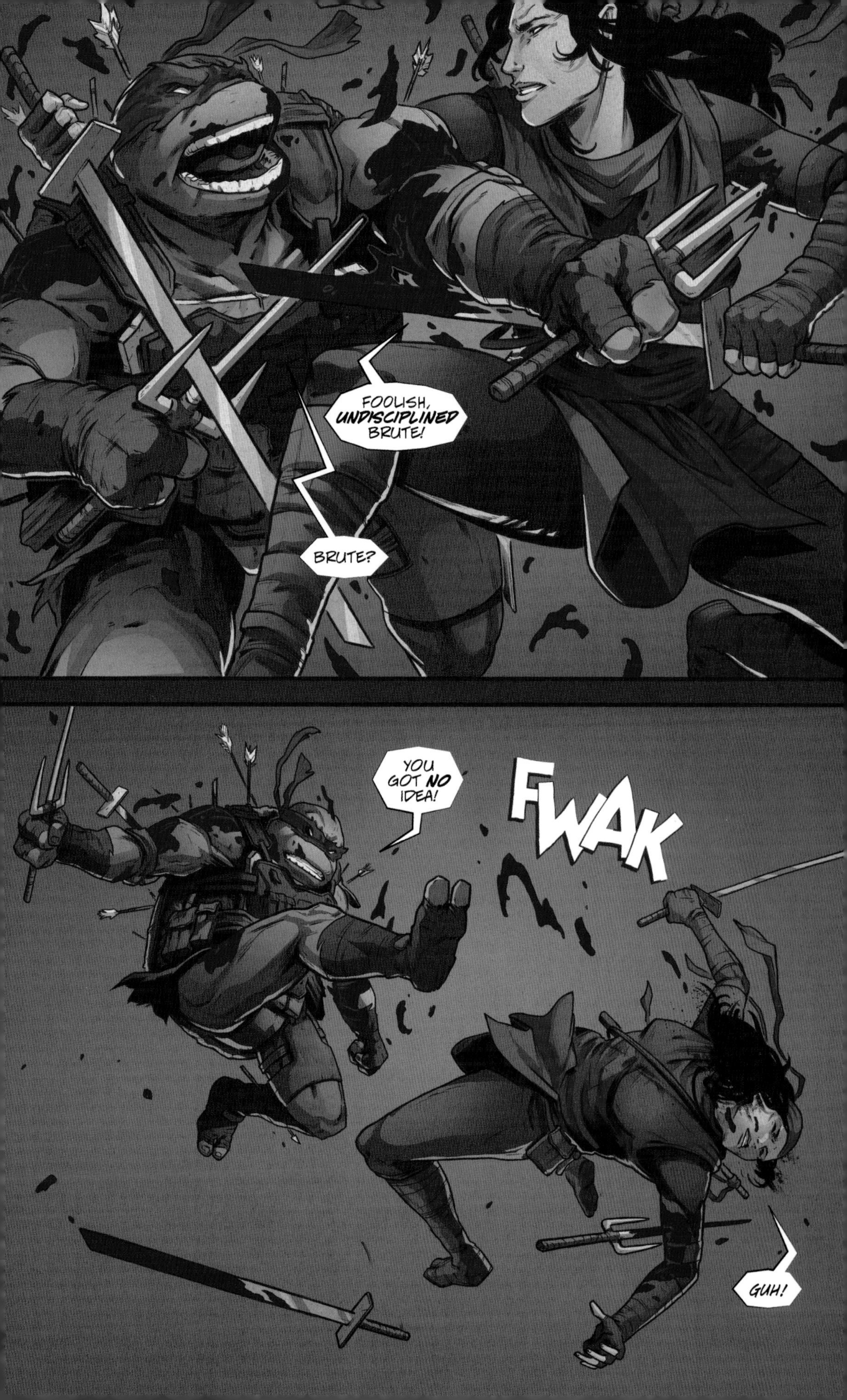
FOOLISH, UNDISCIPLINED BRUTE!
BRUTE?
YOU GOT NO IDEA!
FWAK
GUH!

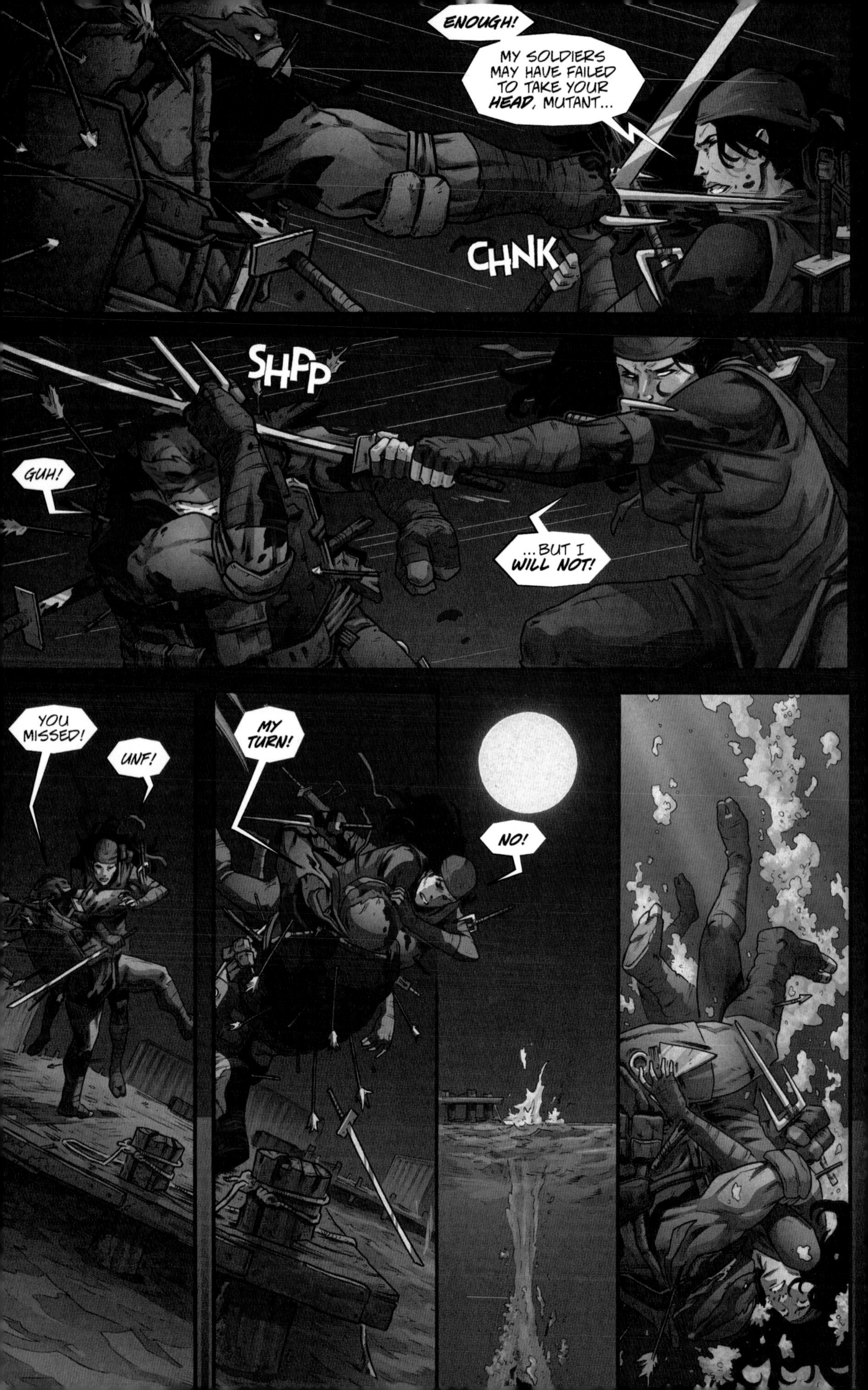
ENOUGH!
MY SOLDIERS MAY HAVE FAILED TO TAKE YOUR **HEAD**, MUTANT...
CHNK
SHFP
GUH!
...BUT I **WILL NOT!**
YOU MISSED!
UNF!
MY TURN!
NO!

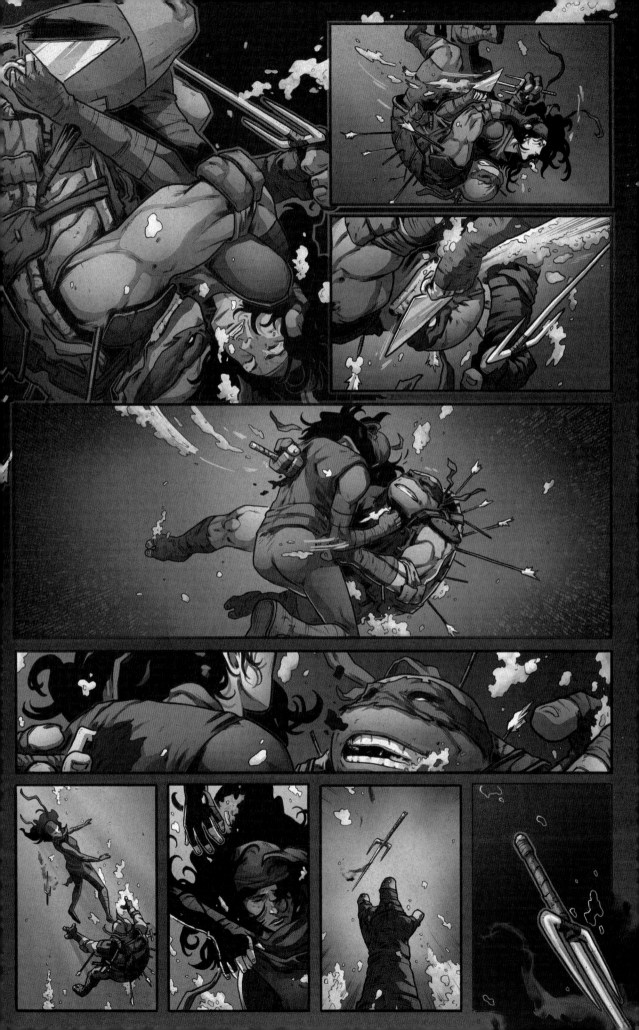

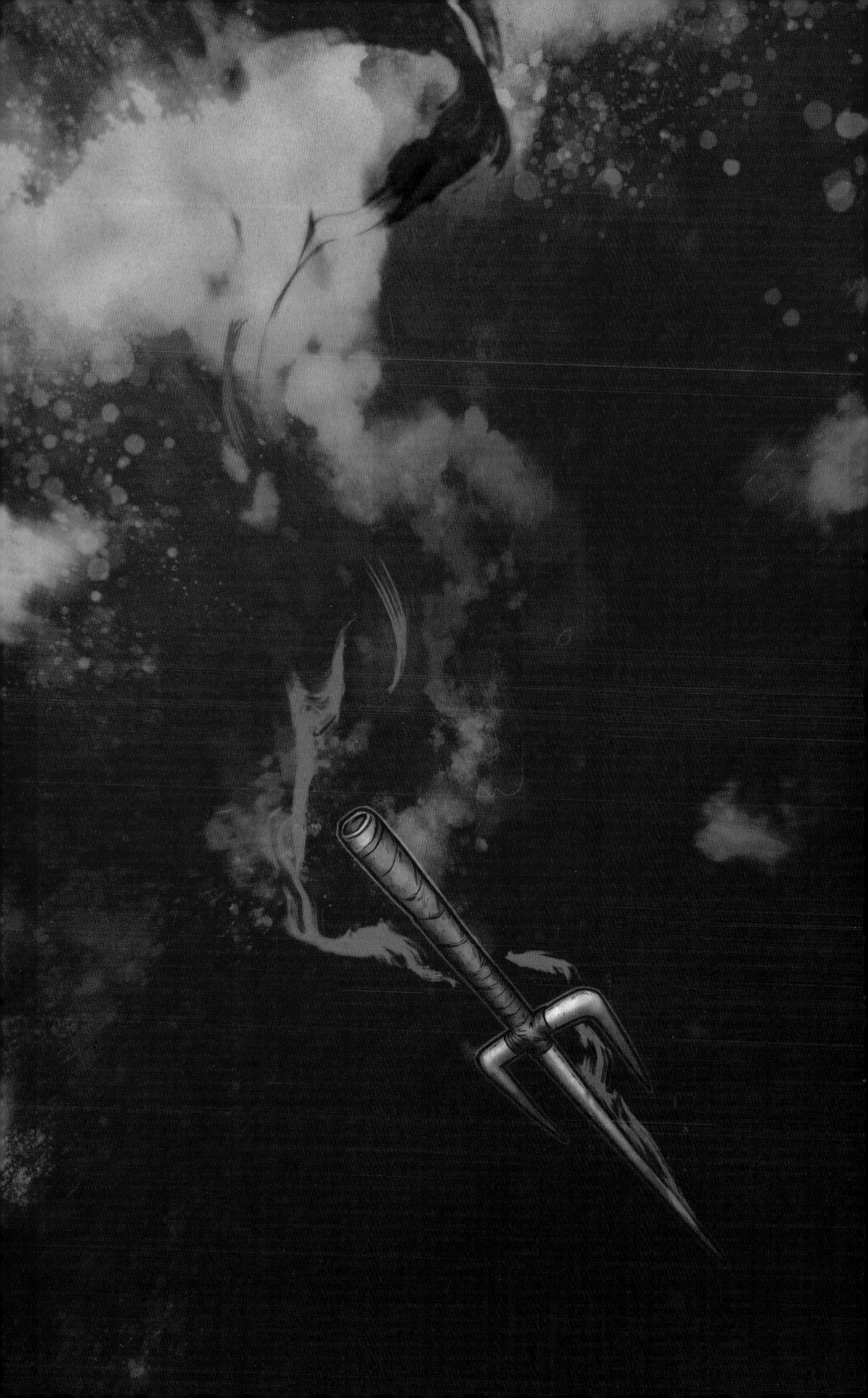

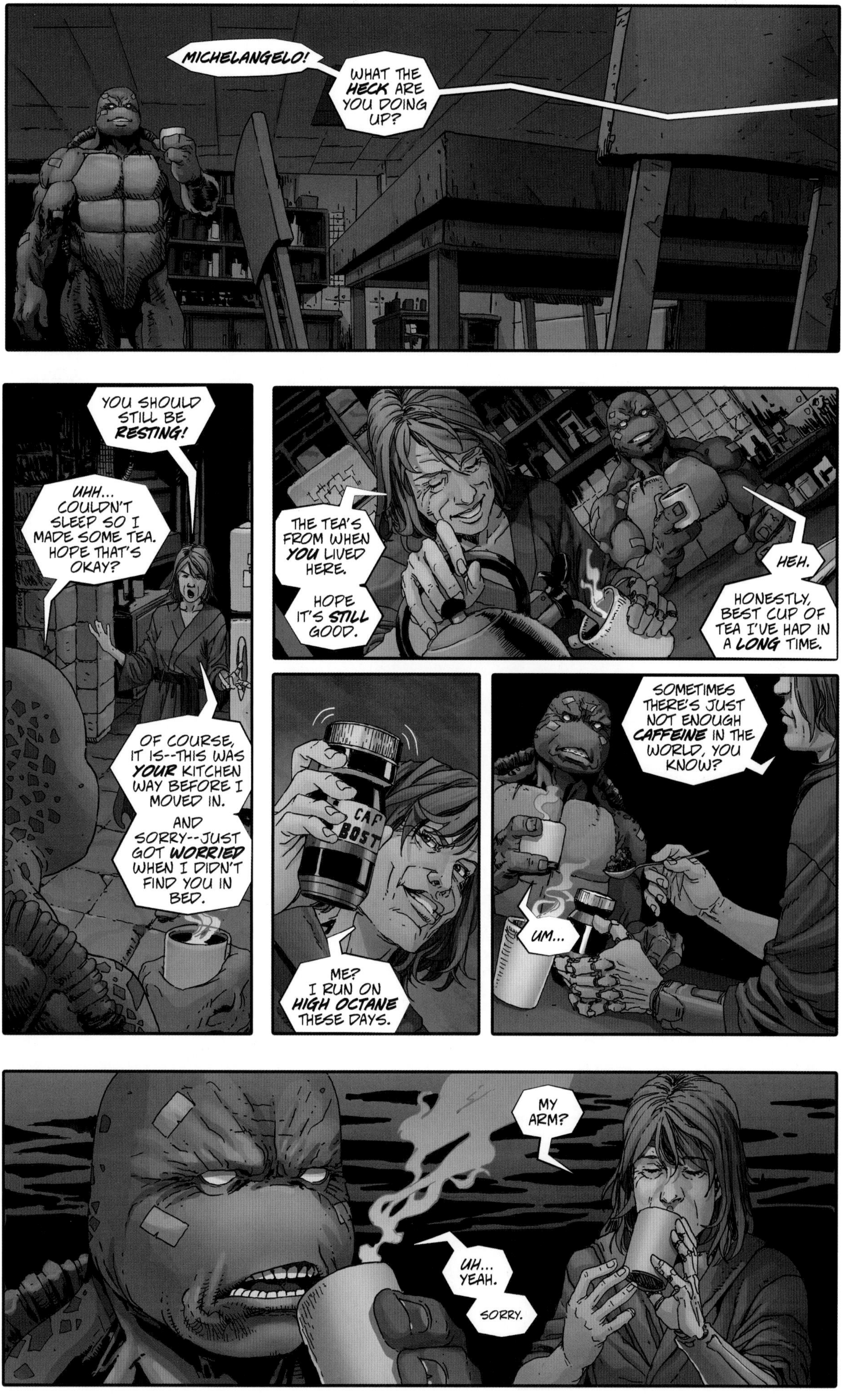
MICHELANGELO!
WHAT THE HECK ARE YOU DOING UP?
YOU SHOULD STILL BE RESTING!
UHH... COULDN'T SLEEP SO I MADE SOME TEA. HOPE THAT'S OKAY?
OF COURSE, IT IS--THIS WAS YOUR KITCHEN WAY BEFORE I MOVED IN.
AND SORRY--JUST GOT WORRIED WHEN I DIDN'T FIND YOU IN BED.
THE TEA'S FROM WHEN YOU LIVED HERE.
HOPE IT'S STILL GOOD.
HEH.
HONESTLY, BEST CUP OF TEA I'VE HAD IN A LONG TIME.
CAF
BOST
ME? I RUN ON HIGH OCTANE THESE DAYS.
SOMETIMES THERE'S JUST NOT ENOUGH CAFFEINE IN THE WORLD, YOU KNOW?
UM...
MY ARM?
UH... YEAH.
SORRY.

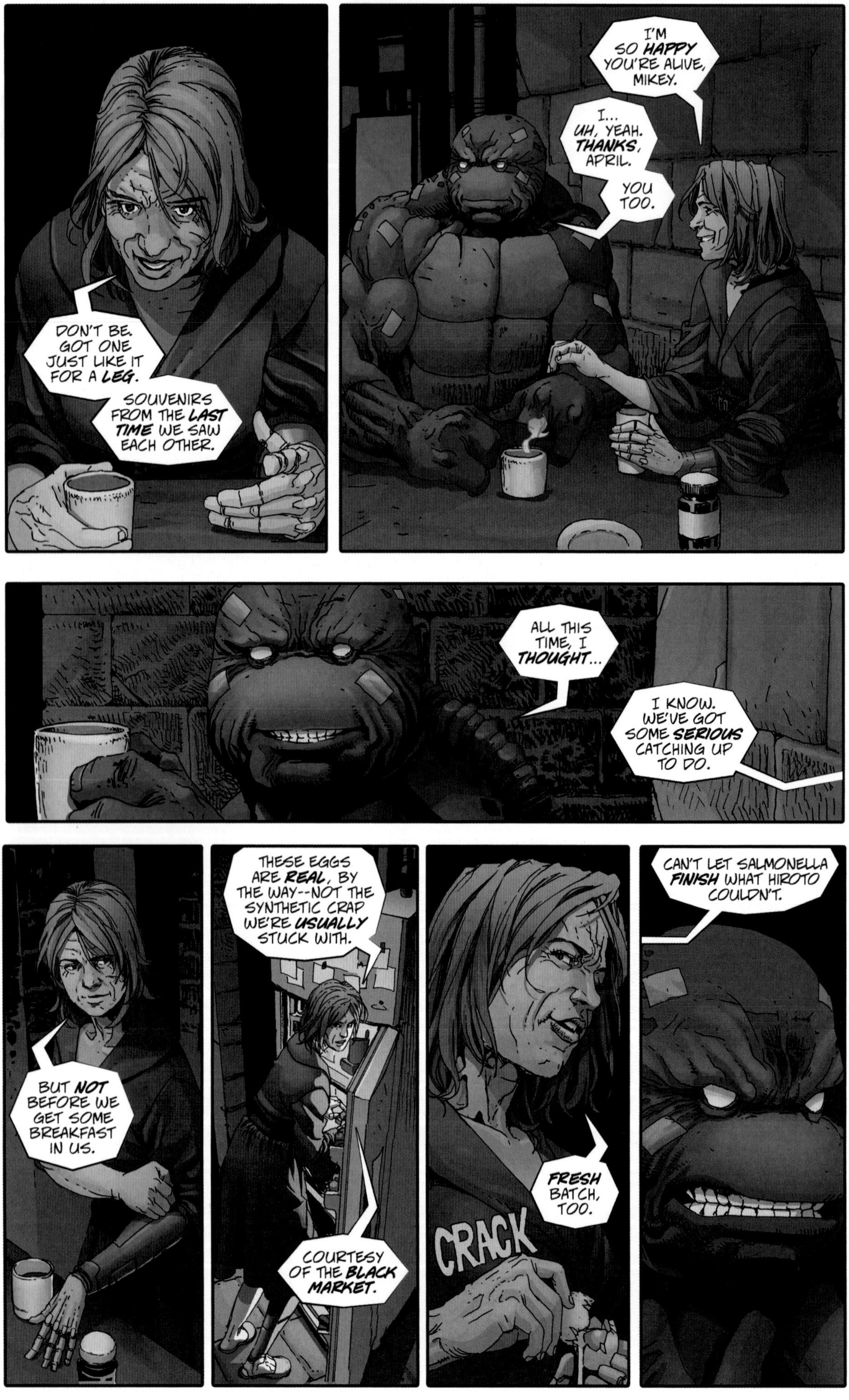
DON'T BE. GOT ONE JUST LIKE IT FOR A **LEG**.
SOUVENIRS FROM THE **LAST TIME** WE SAW EACH OTHER.
I'M SO **HAPPY** YOU'RE ALIVE, MIKEY.
I... UH, YEAH. **THANKS**, APRIL.
YOU TOO.
ALL THIS TIME, I **THOUGHT**...
I KNOW. WE'VE GOT SOME **SERIOUS** CATCHING UP TO DO.
BUT **NOT** BEFORE WE GET SOME BREAKFAST IN US.
THESE EGGS ARE **REAL**, BY THE WAY--NOT THE SYNTHETIC CRAP WE'RE **USUALLY** STUCK WITH.
COURTESY OF THE **BLACK MARKET**.
FRESH BATCH, TOO.
CRACK
CAN'T LET SALMONELLA **FINISH** WHAT HIROTO COULDN'T.

WORD ON THE STREET IS YOU REALLY **RATTLED** HIS CAGE.

MAYBE.

BUT RATTLING CAGES **WASN'T** THE PLAN.

I'M SURE IT WASN'T.

YOU KNOW, YOU'RE **LUCKY** TO BE ALIVE.

YEAH... STILL TRYING TO **PROCESS** IT ALL.

THAT FALL WOULD'VE **KILLED** ME WHEN I WAS YOUNGER.

INSTEAD...

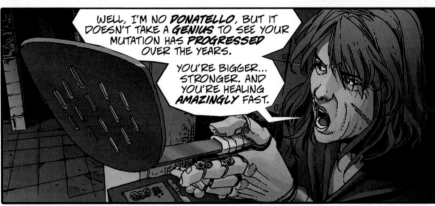

WELL, I'M NO **DONATELLO**, BUT IT DOESN'T TAKE A **GENIUS** TO SEE YOUR MUTATION HAS **PROGRESSED** OVER THE YEARS.

YOU'RE BIGGER... STRONGER. AND YOU'RE HEALING **AMAZINGLY** FAST.

NOT MY **HEAD.** EVERYTHING'S SO **FUZZY...**

STILL DON'T KNOW HOW I **GOT** HERE... **BACK** TO THE LAIR.

HOLD THAT THOUGHT.

CASEY!

BREAK-FAST!

WAIT-- **WHAT?**

CASEY'S STILL ALIVE, TOO?!

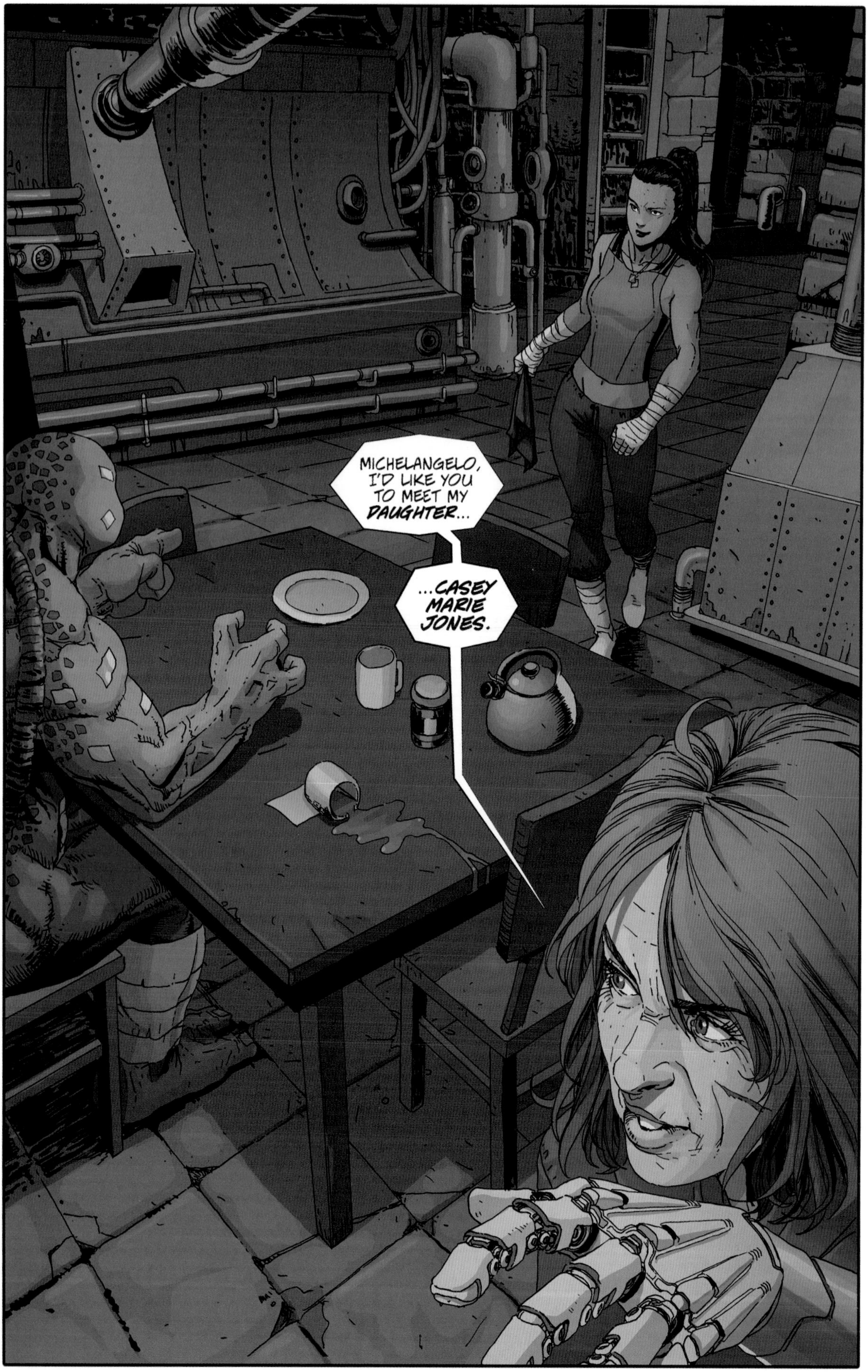
MICHELANGELO, I'D LIKE YOU TO MEET MY DAUGHTER...
...CASEY MARIE JONES.

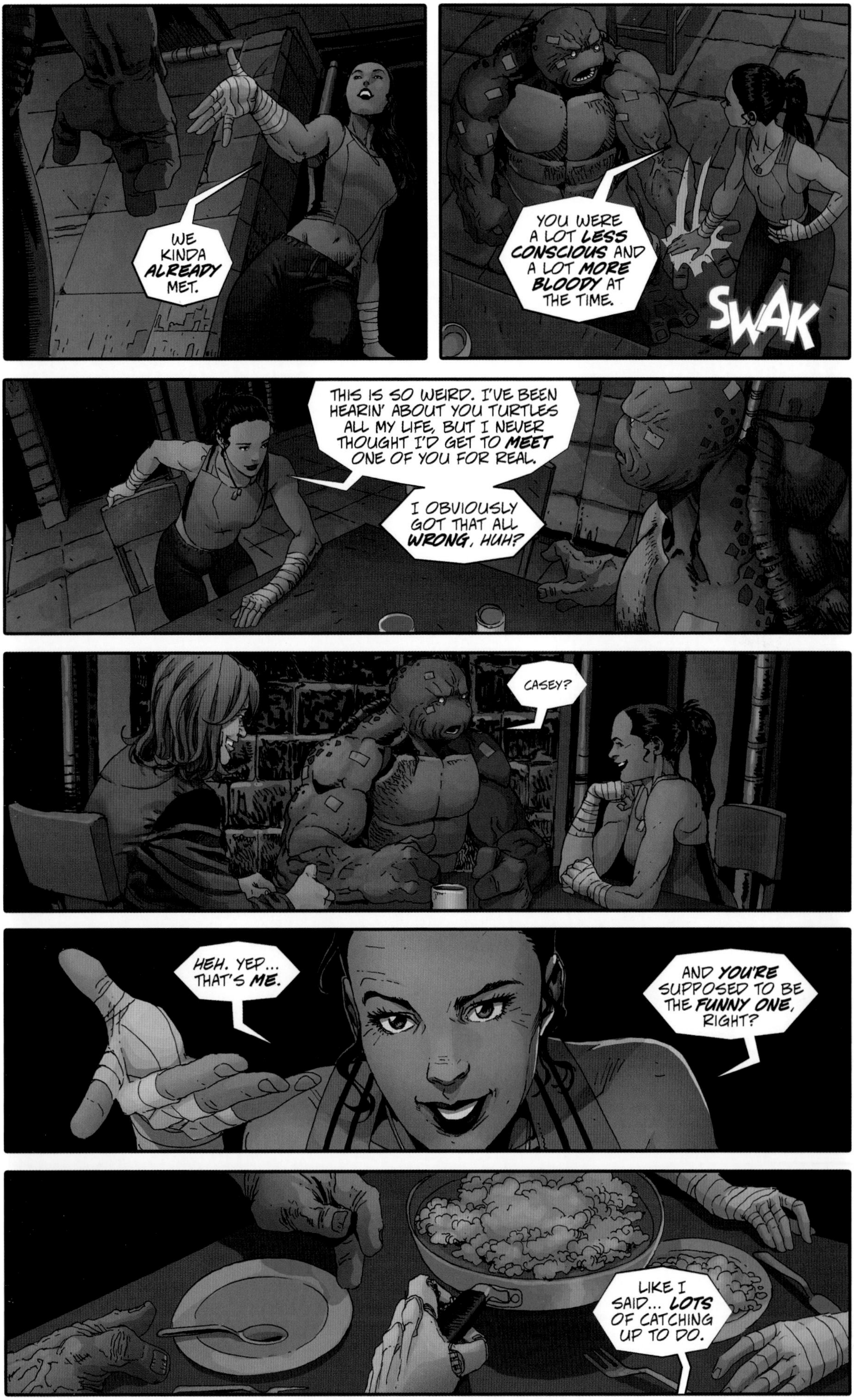
WE KINDA ALREADY MET.
YOU WERE A LOT LESS CONSCIOUS AND A LOT MORE BLOODY AT THE TIME.
SWAK
THIS IS SO WEIRD. I'VE BEEN HEARIN' ABOUT YOU TURTLES ALL MY LIFE, BUT I NEVER THOUGHT I'D GET TO MEET ONE OF YOU FOR REAL.
I OBVIOUSLY GOT THAT ALL WRONG, HUH?
CASEY?
HEH. YEP... THAT'S ME.
AND YOU'RE SUPPOSED TO BE THE FUNNY ONE, RIGHT?
LIKE I SAID... LOTS OF CATCHING UP TO DO.

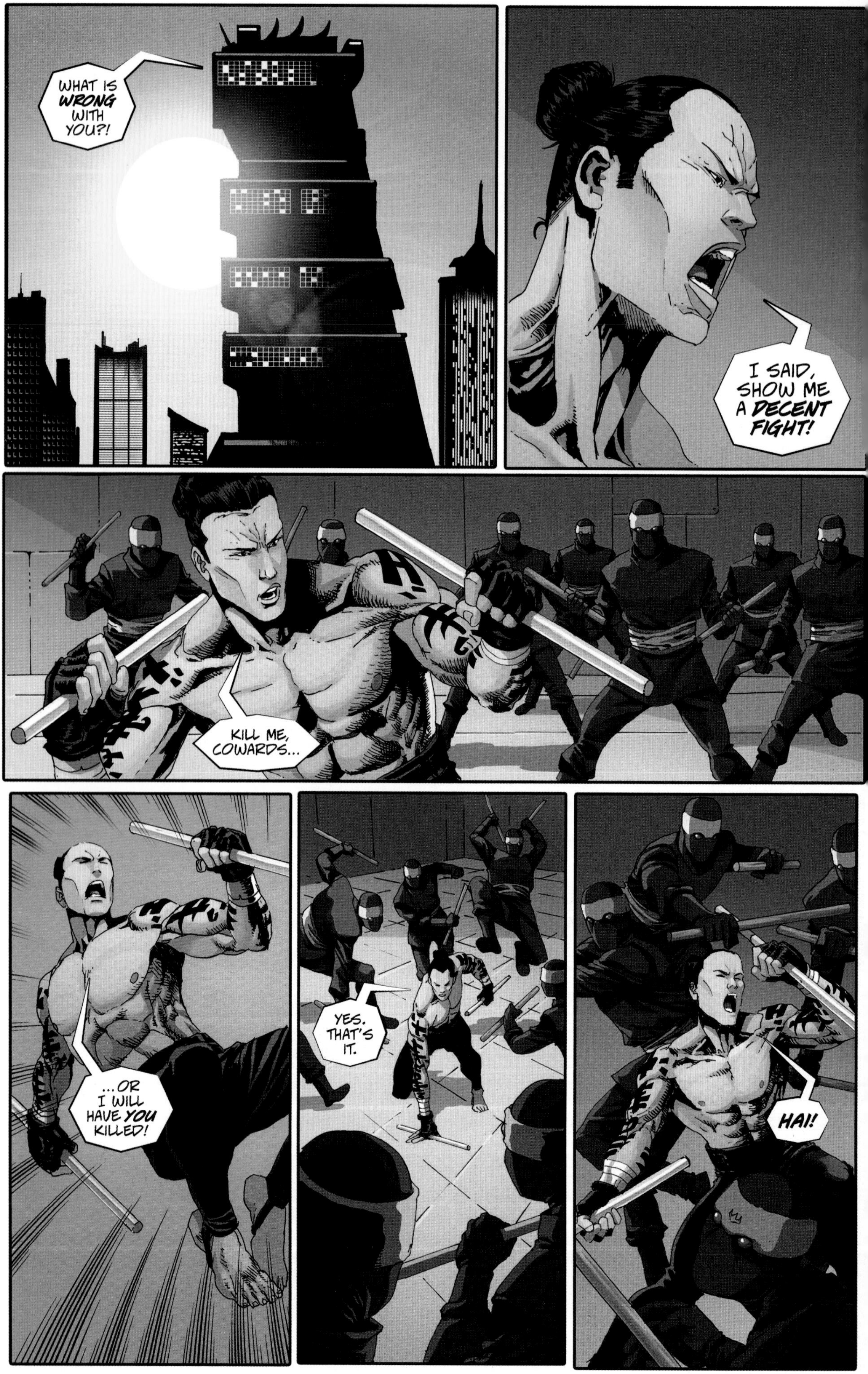
WHAT IS WRONG WITH YOU?!
I SAID, SHOW ME A DECENT FIGHT!
KILL ME, COWARDS...
...OR I WILL HAVE YOU KILLED!
YES. THAT'S IT.
HAI!

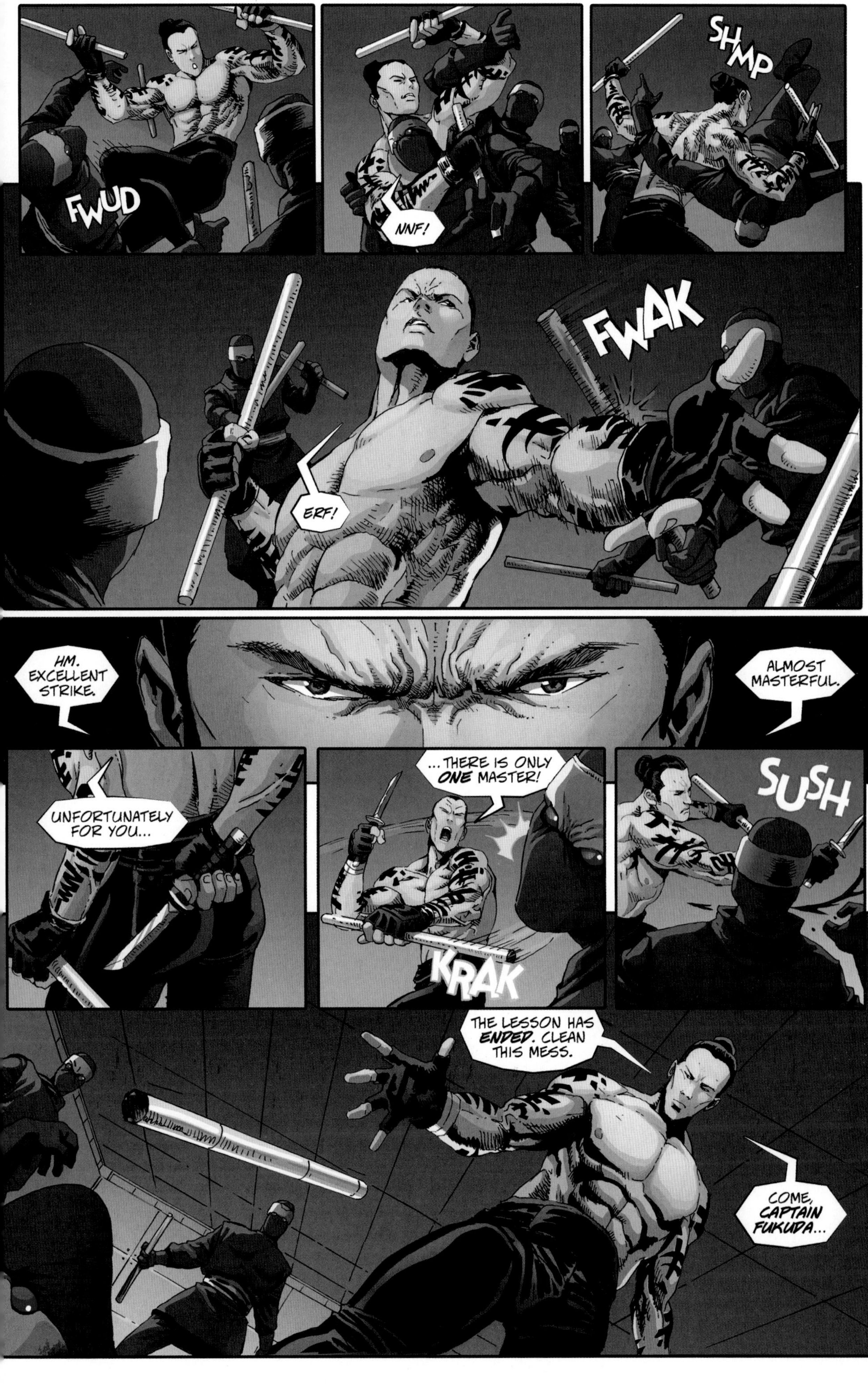
FWUD
NNF!
SHMP
FWAK
ERF!
HM. EXCELLENT STRIKE.
ALMOST MASTERFUL.
UNFORTUNATELY FOR YOU...
...THERE IS ONLY ONE MASTER!
KRAK
SUSH
THE LESSON HAS ENDED. CLEAN THIS MESS.
COME, CAPTAIN FUKUDA...

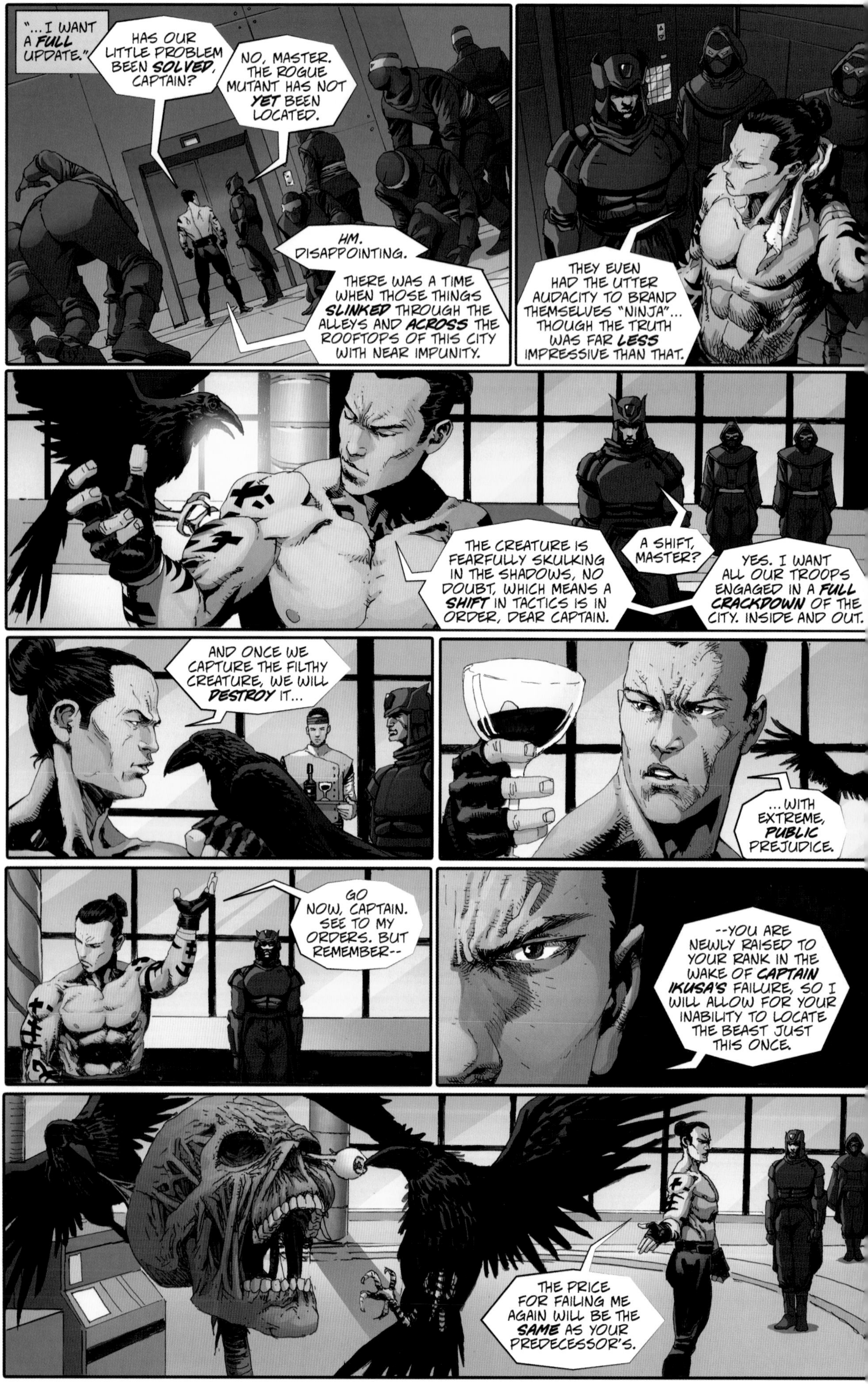
"...I WANT A FULL UPDATE."
HAS OUR LITTLE PROBLEM BEEN SOLVED, CAPTAIN?
NO, MASTER. THE ROGUE MUTANT HAS NOT YET BEEN LOCATED.
HM. DISAPPOINTING.
THERE WAS A TIME WHEN THOSE THINGS SLINKED THROUGH THE ALLEYS AND ACROSS THE ROOFTOPS OF THIS CITY WITH NEAR IMPUNITY.
THEY EVEN HAD THE UTTER AUDACITY TO BRAND THEMSELVES "NINJA"... THOUGH THE TRUTH WAS FAR LESS IMPRESSIVE THAN THAT.
THE CREATURE IS FEARFULLY SKULKING IN THE SHADOWS, NO DOUBT, WHICH MEANS A SHIFT IN TACTICS IS IN ORDER, DEAR CAPTAIN.
A SHIFT, MASTER?
YES. I WANT ALL OUR TROOPS ENGAGED IN A FULL CRACKDOWN OF THE CITY. INSIDE AND OUT.
AND ONCE WE CAPTURE THE FILTHY CREATURE, WE WILL DESTROY IT...
...WITH EXTREME, PUBLIC PREJUDICE.
GO NOW, CAPTAIN. SEE TO MY ORDERS. BUT REMEMBER--
--YOU ARE NEWLY RAISED TO YOUR RANK IN THE WAKE OF CAPTAIN IKUSA'S FAILURE, SO I WILL ALLOW FOR YOUR INABILITY TO LOCATE THE BEAST JUST THIS ONCE.
THE PRICE FOR FAILING ME AGAIN WILL BE THE SAME AS YOUR PREDECESSOR'S.

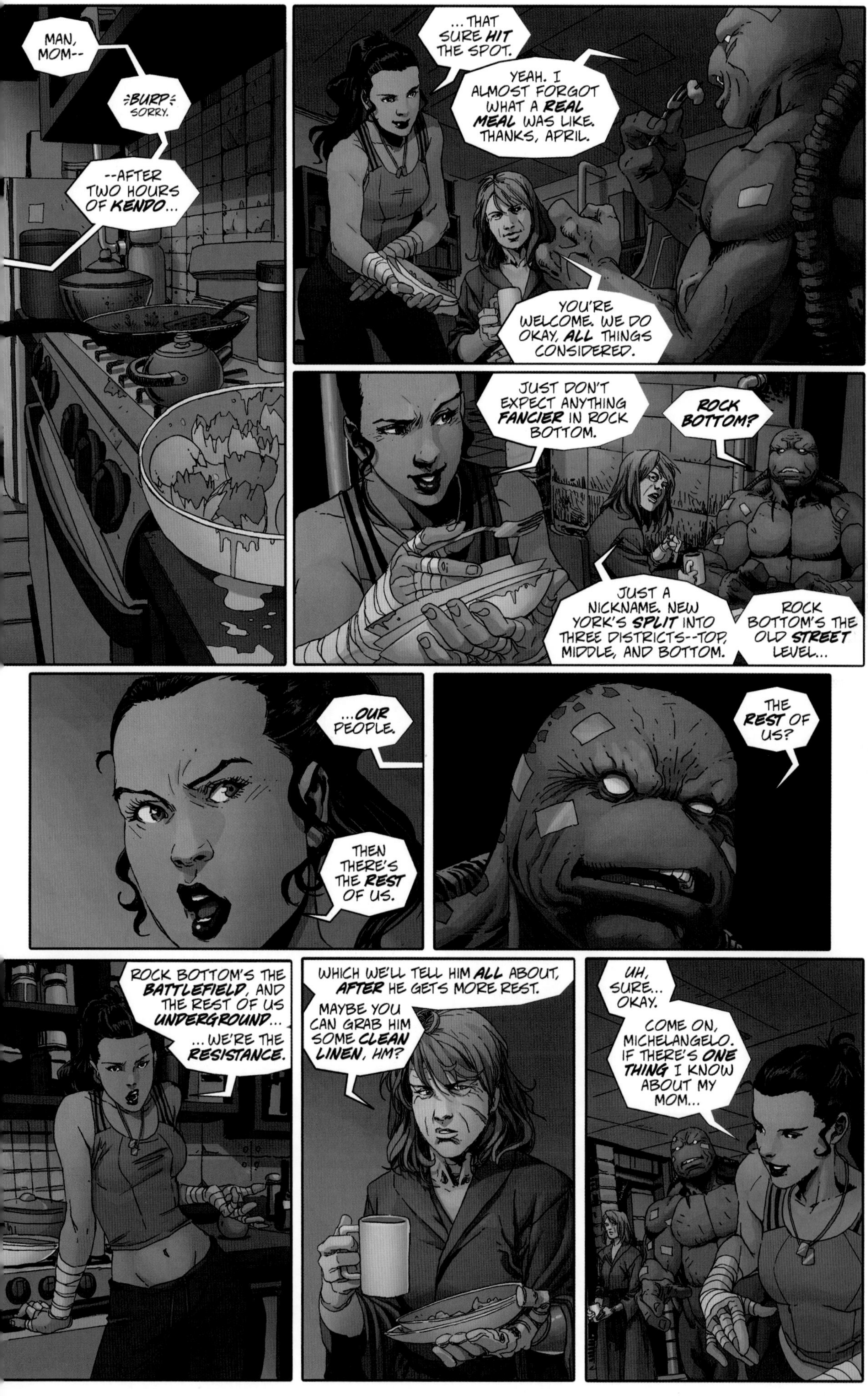

MAN, MOM--
BURP SORRY.
--AFTER TWO HOURS OF KENDO...
...THAT SURE HIT THE SPOT.
YEAH. I ALMOST FORGOT WHAT A REAL MEAL WAS LIKE. THANKS, APRIL.
YOU'RE WELCOME. WE DO OKAY, ALL THINGS CONSIDERED.
JUST DON'T EXPECT ANYTHING FANCIER IN ROCK BOTTOM.
ROCK BOTTOM?
JUST A NICKNAME. NEW YORK'S SPLIT INTO THREE DISTRICTS--TOP, MIDDLE, AND BOTTOM.
ROCK BOTTOM'S THE OLD STREET LEVEL...
...OUR PEOPLE.
THEN THERE'S THE REST OF US.
THE REST OF US?
ROCK BOTTOM'S THE BATTLEFIELD, AND THE REST OF US UNDERGROUND...
...WE'RE THE RESISTANCE.
WHICH WE'LL TELL HIM ALL ABOUT, AFTER HE GETS MORE REST.
MAYBE YOU CAN GRAB HIM SOME CLEAN LINEN, HM?
UH, SURE... OKAY.
COME ON, MICHELANGELO. IF THERE'S ONE THING I KNOW ABOUT MY MOM...

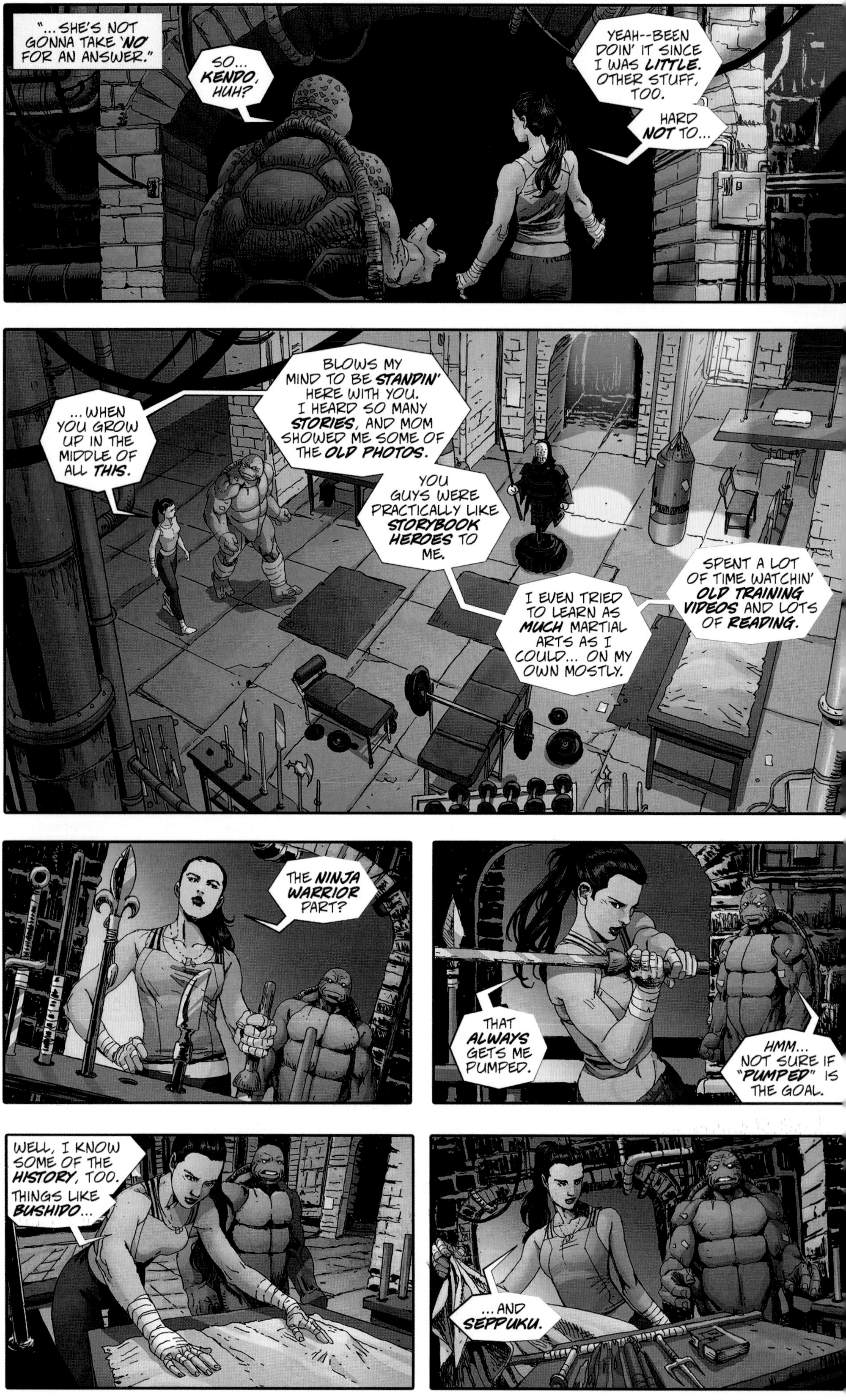
"...SHE'S NOT GONNA TAKE 'NO' FOR AN ANSWER."
SO... KENDO, HUH?
YEAH--BEEN DOIN' IT SINCE I WAS LITTLE. OTHER STUFF, TOO.
HARD NOT TO...
...WHEN YOU GROW UP IN THE MIDDLE OF ALL THIS.
BLOWS MY MIND TO BE STANDIN' HERE WITH YOU. I HEARD SO MANY STORIES, AND MOM SHOWED ME SOME OF THE OLD PHOTOS.
YOU GUYS WERE PRACTICALLY LIKE STORYBOOK HEROES TO ME.
I EVEN TRIED TO LEARN AS MUCH MARTIAL ARTS AS I COULD... ON MY OWN MOSTLY.
SPENT A LOT OF TIME WATCHIN' OLD TRAINING VIDEOS AND LOTS OF READING.
THE NINJA WARRIOR PART?
THAT ALWAYS GETS ME PUMPED.
HMM... NOT SURE IF "PUMPED" IS THE GOAL.
WELL, I KNOW SOME OF THE HISTORY, TOO.
THINGS LIKE BUSHIDO...
...AND SEPPUKU.

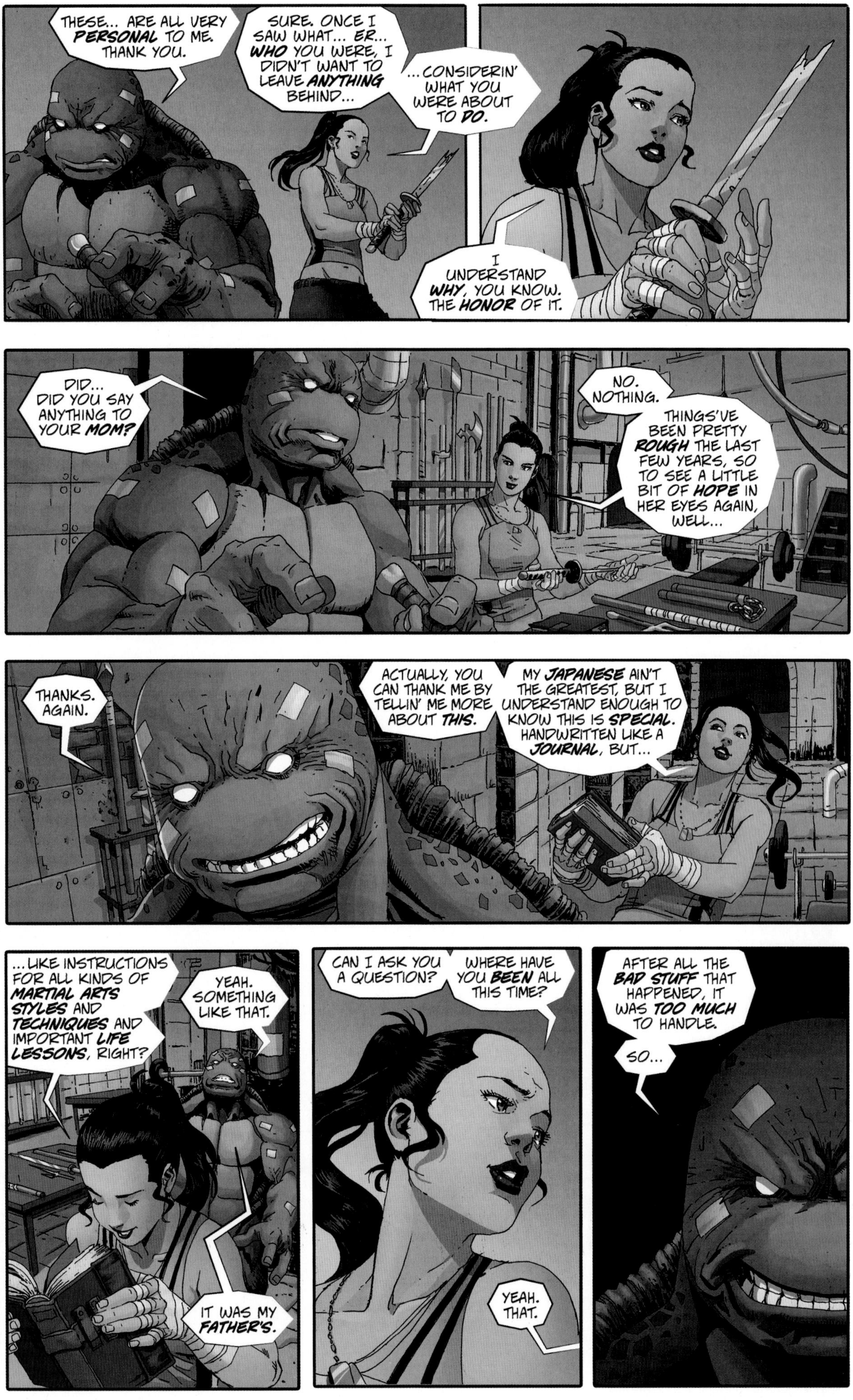
THESE... ARE ALL VERY **PERSONAL** TO ME. THANK YOU.
SURE. ONCE I SAW WHAT... ER... **WHO** YOU WERE, I DIDN'T WANT TO LEAVE **ANYTHING** BEHIND...
...CONSIDERIN' WHAT YOU WERE ABOUT TO **DO**.
I UNDERSTAND **WHY**, YOU KNOW. THE **HONOR** OF IT.
DID... DID YOU SAY ANYTHING TO YOUR **MOM?**
NO. NOTHING.
THINGS'VE BEEN PRETTY **ROUGH** THE LAST FEW YEARS, SO TO SEE A LITTLE BIT OF **HOPE** IN HER EYES AGAIN, WELL...
THANKS. AGAIN.
ACTUALLY, YOU CAN THANK ME BY TELLIN' ME MORE ABOUT **THIS**.
MY **JAPANESE** AIN'T THE GREATEST, BUT I UNDERSTAND ENOUGH TO KNOW THIS IS **SPECIAL**. HANDWRITTEN LIKE A **JOURNAL**, BUT...
...LIKE INSTRUCTIONS FOR ALL KINDS OF **MARTIAL ARTS STYLES** AND **TECHNIQUES** AND IMPORTANT **LIFE LESSONS**, RIGHT?
YEAH. SOMETHING LIKE THAT.
IT WAS MY **FATHER'S**.
CAN I ASK YOU A QUESTION?
WHERE HAVE YOU **BEEN** ALL THIS TIME?
YEAH. THAT.
AFTER ALL THE **BAD STUFF** THAT HAPPENED, IT WAS **TOO MUCH** TO HANDLE.
SO...

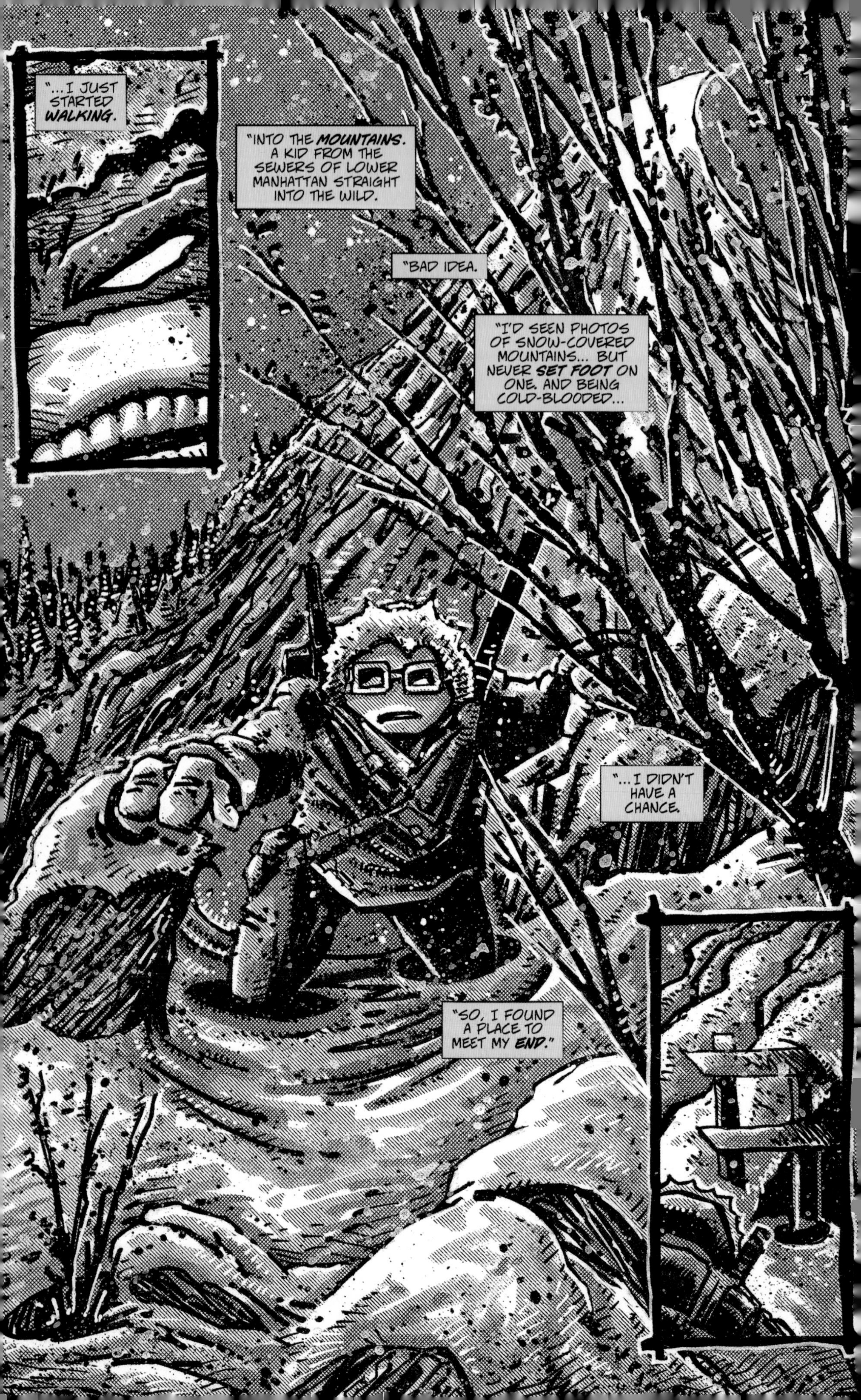
"...I JUST STARTED *WALKING*.
"INTO THE *MOUNTAINS*. A KID FROM THE SEWERS OF LOWER MANHATTAN STRAIGHT INTO THE WILD.
"BAD IDEA.
"I'D SEEN PHOTOS OF SNOW-COVERED MOUNTAINS... BUT NEVER *SET FOOT* ON ONE. AND BEING COLD-BLOODED...
"...I DIDN'T HAVE A CHANCE.
"SO, I FOUND A PLACE TO MEET MY *END*."

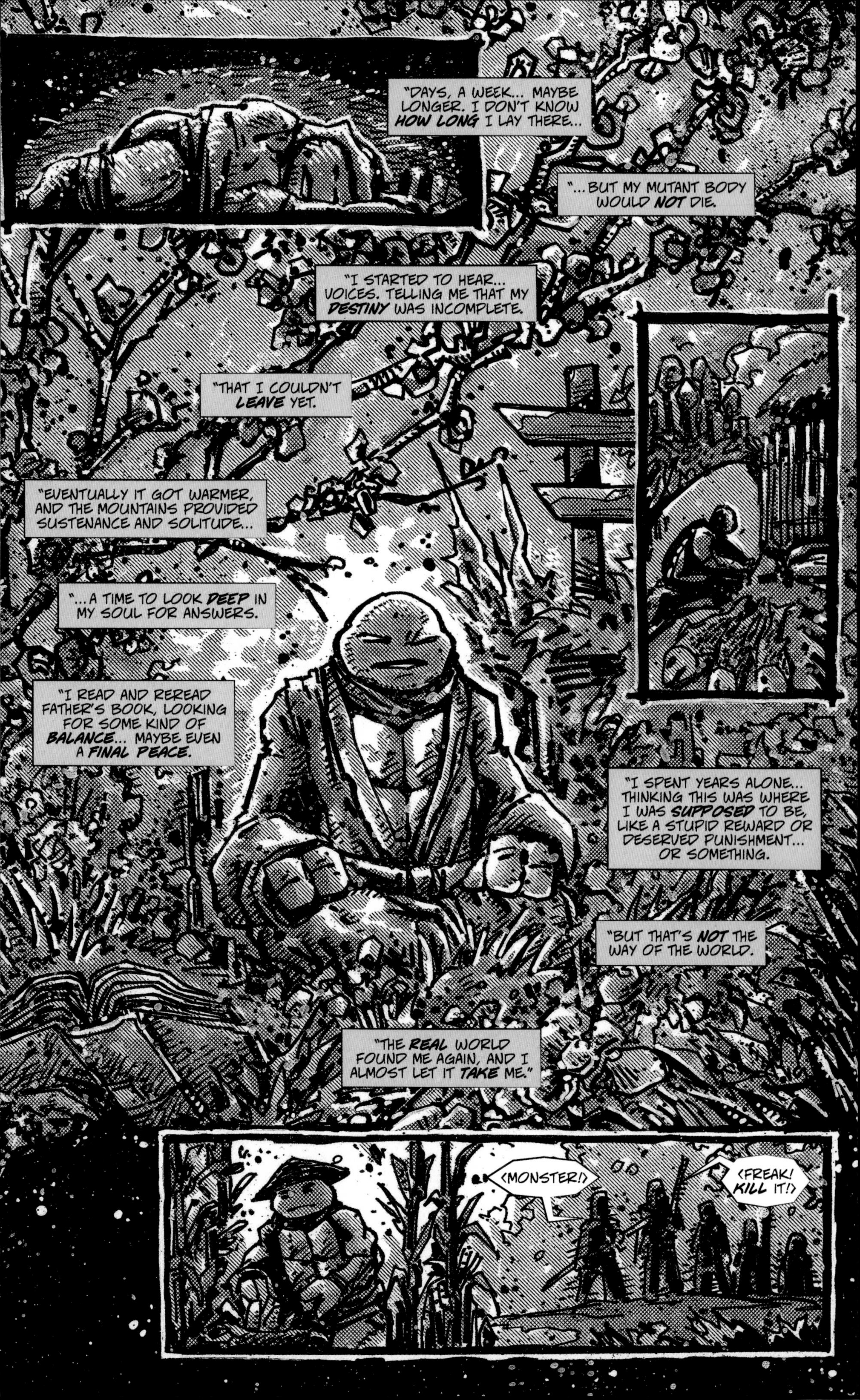

"DAYS, A WEEK... MAYBE LONGER. I DON'T KNOW HOW LONG I LAY THERE...
"...BUT MY MUTANT BODY WOULD NOT DIE.
"I STARTED TO HEAR... VOICES. TELLING ME THAT MY DESTINY WAS INCOMPLETE.
"THAT I COULDN'T LEAVE YET.
"EVENTUALLY IT GOT WARMER, AND THE MOUNTAINS PROVIDED SUSTENANCE AND SOLITUDE...
"...A TIME TO LOOK DEEP IN MY SOUL FOR ANSWERS.
"I READ AND REREAD FATHER'S BOOK, LOOKING FOR SOME KIND OF BALANCE... MAYBE EVEN A FINAL PEACE.
"I SPENT YEARS ALONE... THINKING THIS WAS WHERE I WAS SUPPOSED TO BE, LIKE A STUPID REWARD OR DESERVED PUNISHMENT... OR SOMETHING.
"BUT THAT'S NOT THE WAY OF THE WORLD.
"THE REAL WORLD FOUND ME AGAIN, AND I ALMOST LET IT TAKE ME."
‹MONSTER!›
‹FREAK! KILL IT!›

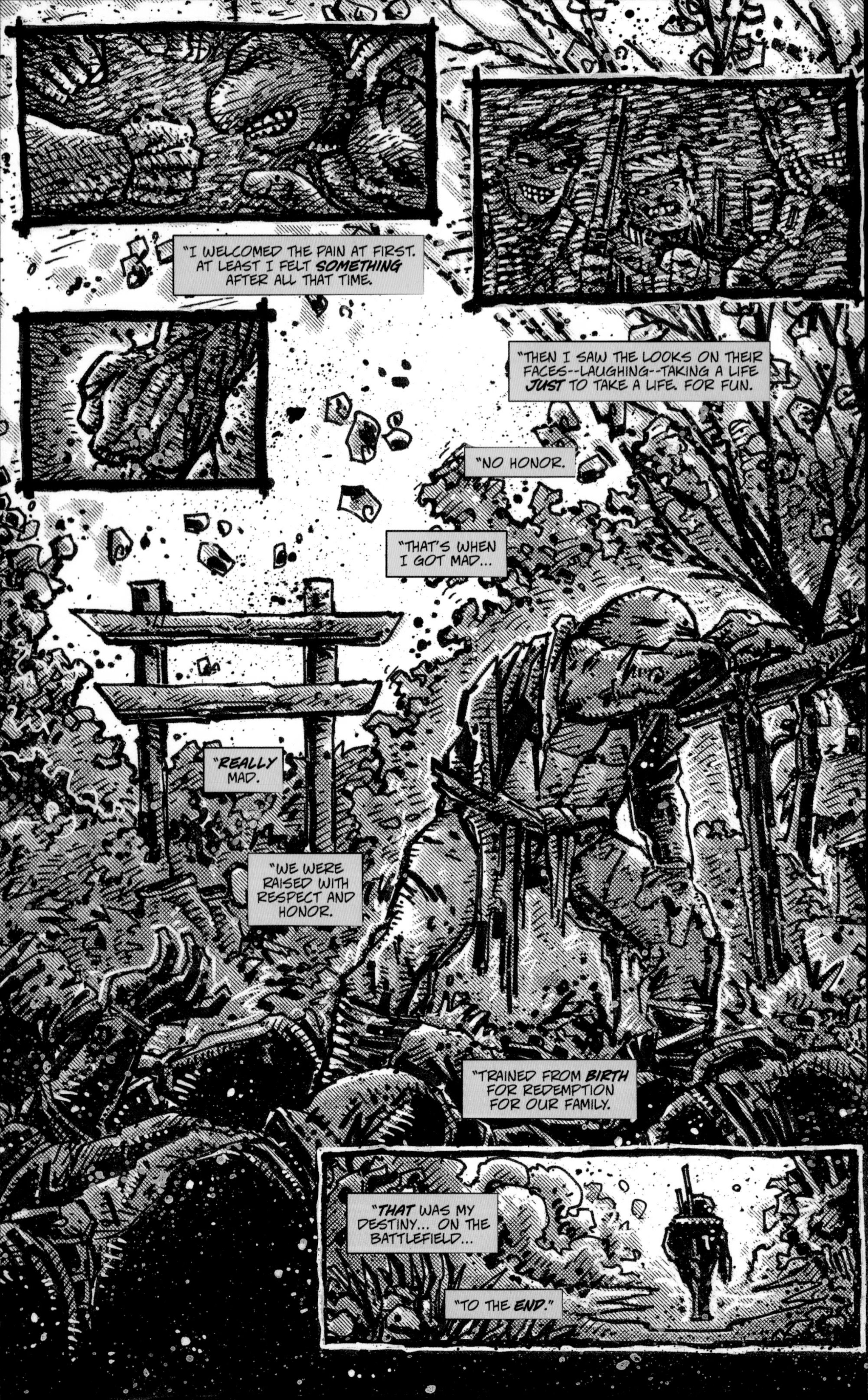
"I WELCOMED THE PAIN AT FIRST. AT LEAST I FELT SOMETHING AFTER ALL THAT TIME.
"THEN I SAW THE LOOKS ON THEIR FACES--LAUGHING--TAKING A LIFE JUST TO TAKE A LIFE. FOR FUN.
"NO HONOR.
"THAT'S WHEN I GOT MAD...
"REALLY MAD.
"WE WERE RAISED WITH RESPECT AND HONOR.
"TRAINED FROM BIRTH FOR REDEMPTION FOR OUR FAMILY.
"THAT WAS MY DESTINY... ON THE BATTLEFIELD...
"TO THE END."

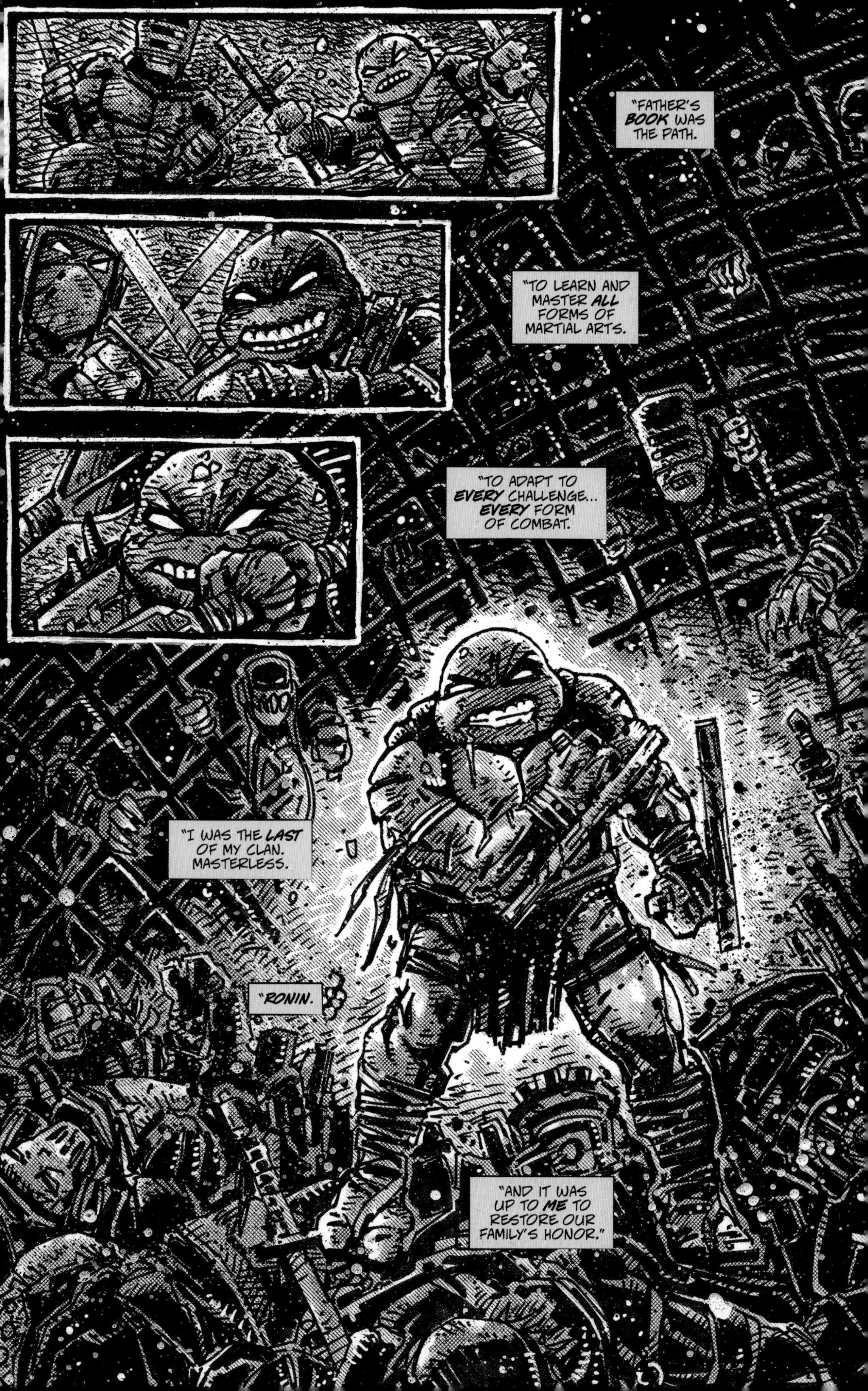
"FATHER'S BOOK WAS THE PATH.
"TO LEARN AND MASTER ALL FORMS OF MARTIAL ARTS.
"TO ADAPT TO EVERY CHALLENGE... EVERY FORM OF COMBAT.
"I WAS THE LAST OF MY CLAN. MASTERLESS.
"RONIN.
"AND IT WAS UP TO ME TO RESTORE OUR FAMILY'S HONOR."

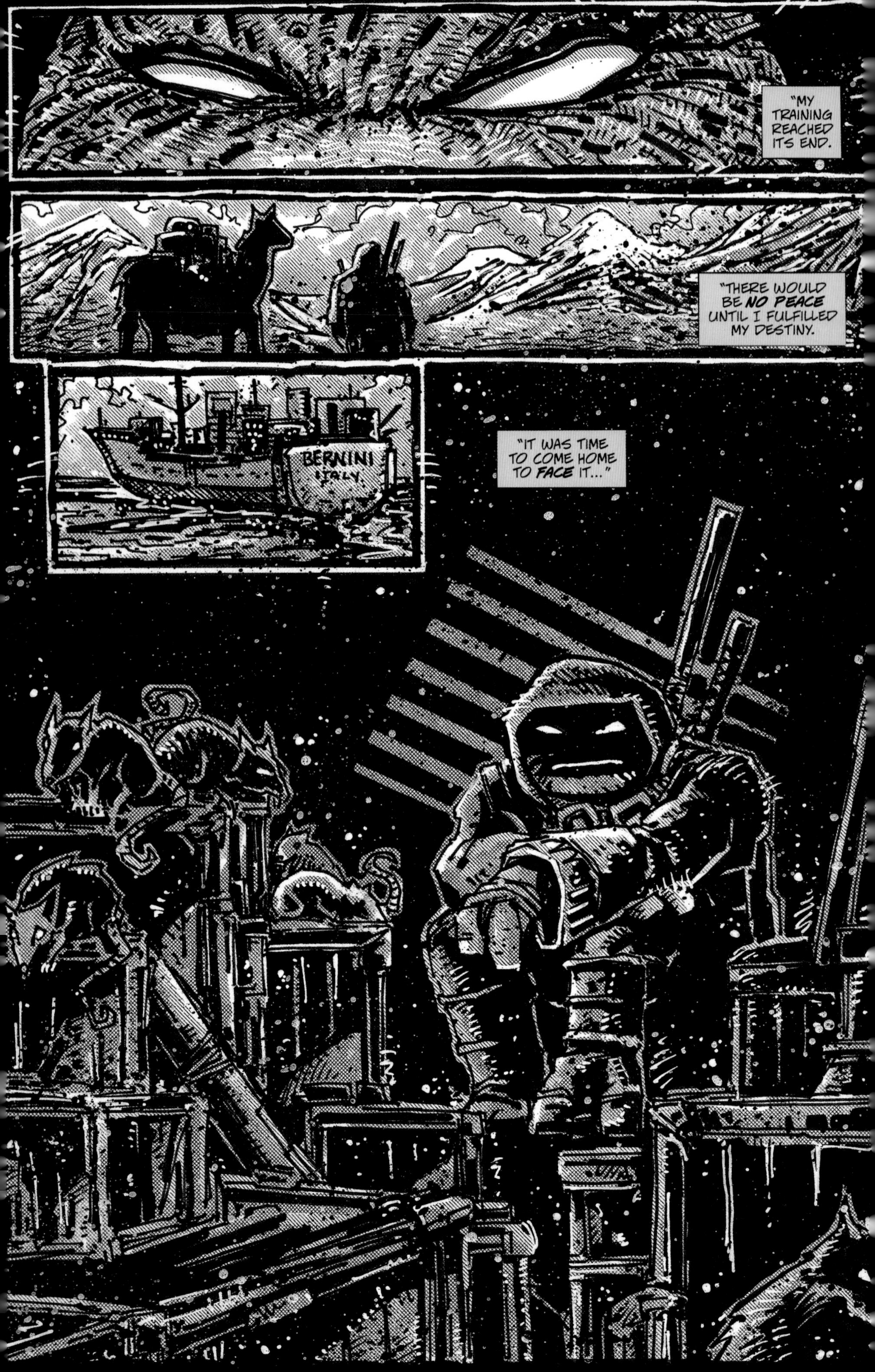
"MY TRAINING REACHED ITS END.
"THERE WOULD BE NO PEACE UNTIL I FULFILLED MY DESTINY.
BERNINI ITALY
"IT WAS TIME TO COME HOME TO FACE IT..."

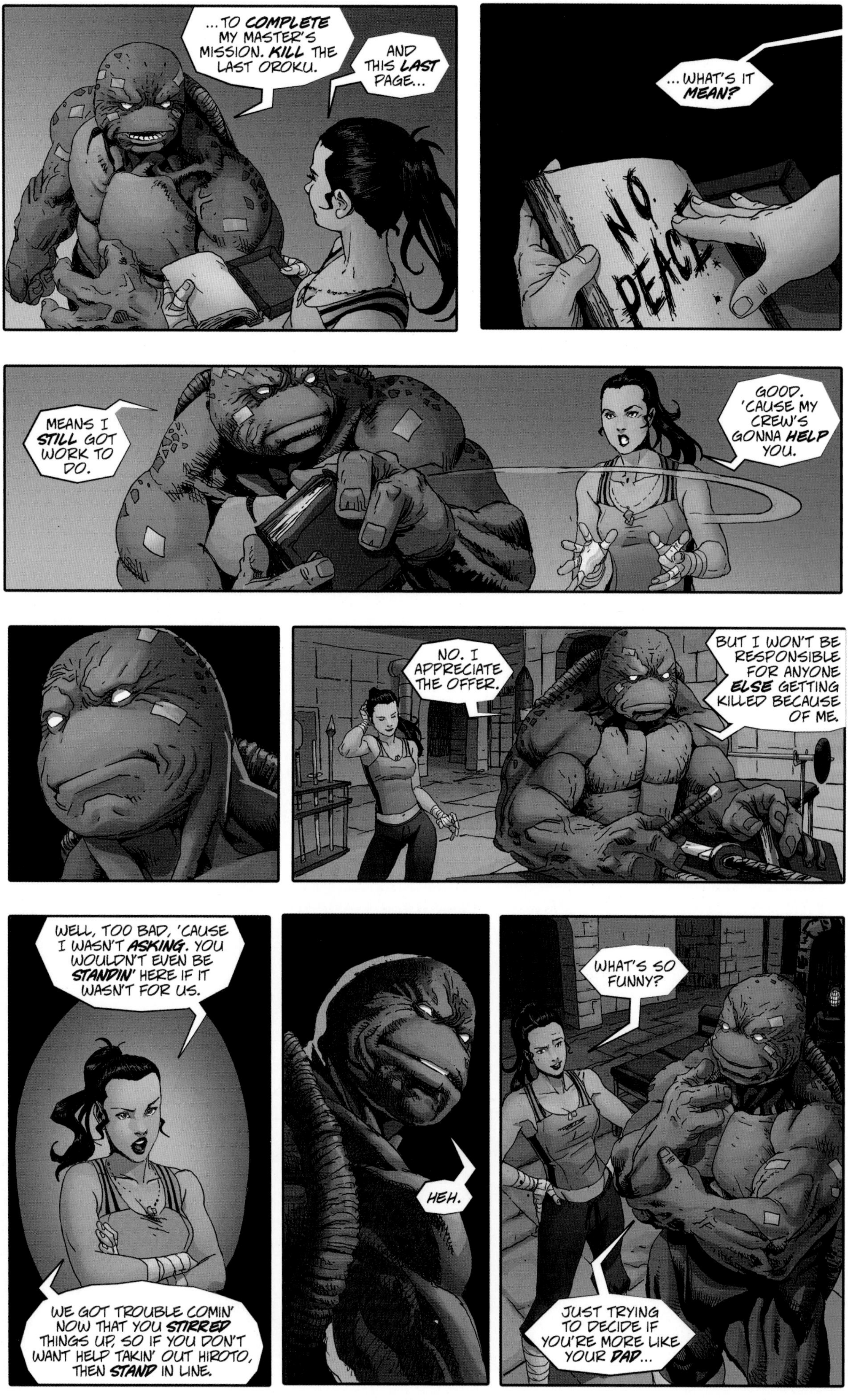
...TO COMPLETE MY MASTER'S MISSION. KILL THE LAST OROKU.
AND THIS LAST PAGE...
...WHAT'S IT MEAN?
NO PEACE
MEANS I STILL GOT WORK TO DO.
GOOD. 'CAUSE MY CREW'S GONNA HELP YOU.
NO. I APPRECIATE THE OFFER.
BUT I WON'T BE RESPONSIBLE FOR ANYONE ELSE GETTING KILLED BECAUSE OF ME.
WELL, TOO BAD, 'CAUSE I WASN'T ASKING. YOU WOULDN'T EVEN BE STANDIN' HERE IF IT WASN'T FOR US.
WE GOT TROUBLE COMIN' NOW THAT YOU STIRRED THINGS UP, SO IF YOU DON'T WANT HELP TAKIN' OUT HIROTO, THEN STAND IN LINE.
HEH.
WHAT'S SO FUNNY?
JUST TRYING TO DECIDE IF YOU'RE MORE LIKE YOUR DAD...

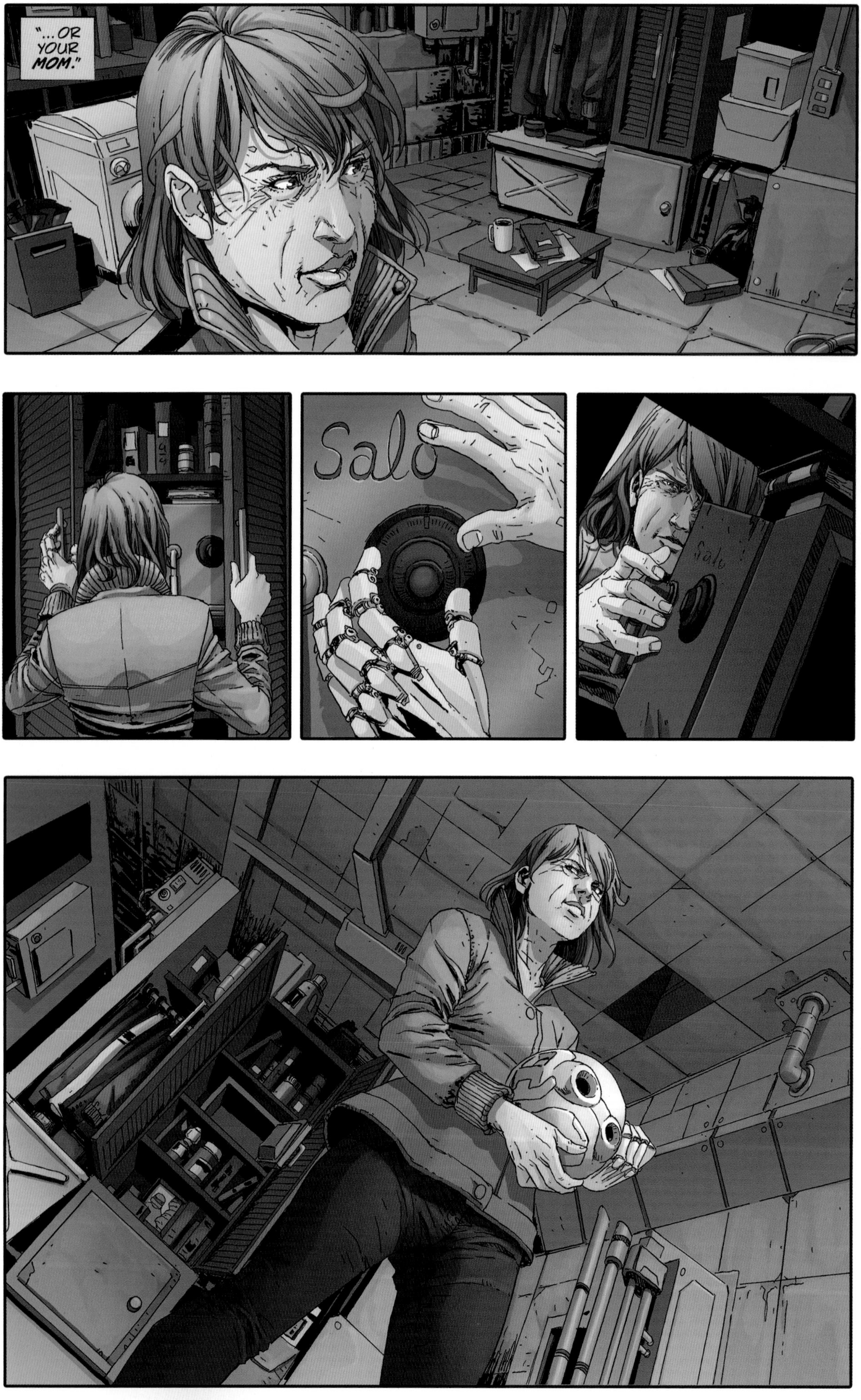
"...OR YOUR MOM."
Salo
Salo

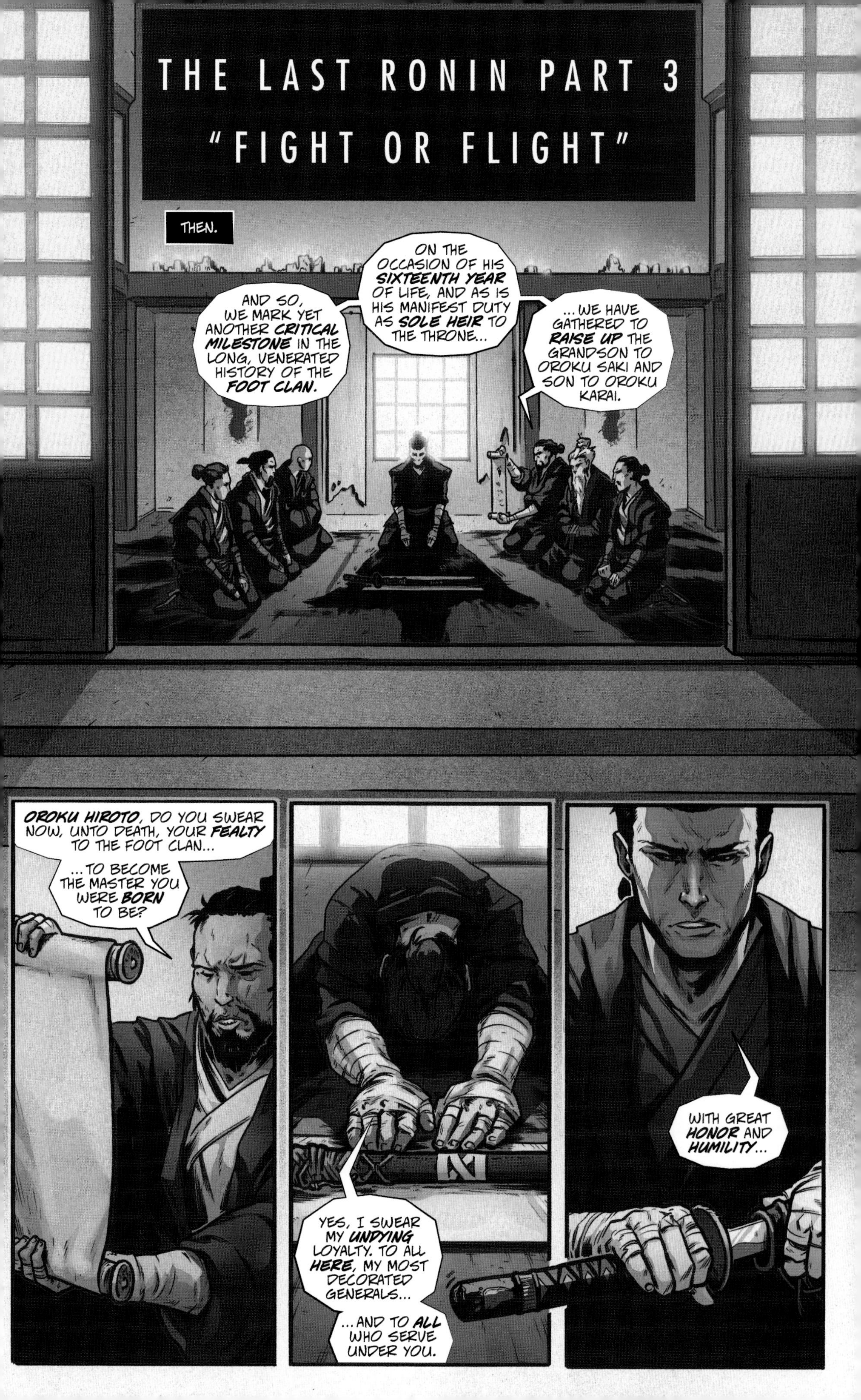
THE LAST RONIN PART 3
"FIGHT OR FLIGHT"
THEN.
AND SO, WE MARK YET ANOTHER CRITICAL MILESTONE IN THE LONG, VENERATED HISTORY OF THE FOOT CLAN.
ON THE OCCASION OF HIS SIXTEENTH YEAR OF LIFE, AND AS IS HIS MANIFEST DUTY AS SOLE HEIR TO THE THRONE...
...WE HAVE GATHERED TO RAISE UP THE GRANDSON TO OROKU SAKI AND SON TO OROKU KARAI.
OROKU HIROTO, DO YOU SWEAR NOW, UNTO DEATH, YOUR FEALTY TO THE FOOT CLAN...
...TO BECOME THE MASTER YOU WERE BORN TO BE?
YES, I SWEAR MY UNDYING LOYALTY. TO ALL HERE, MY MOST DECORATED GENERALS...
...AND TO ALL WHO SERVE UNDER YOU.
WITH GREAT HONOR AND HUMILITY...

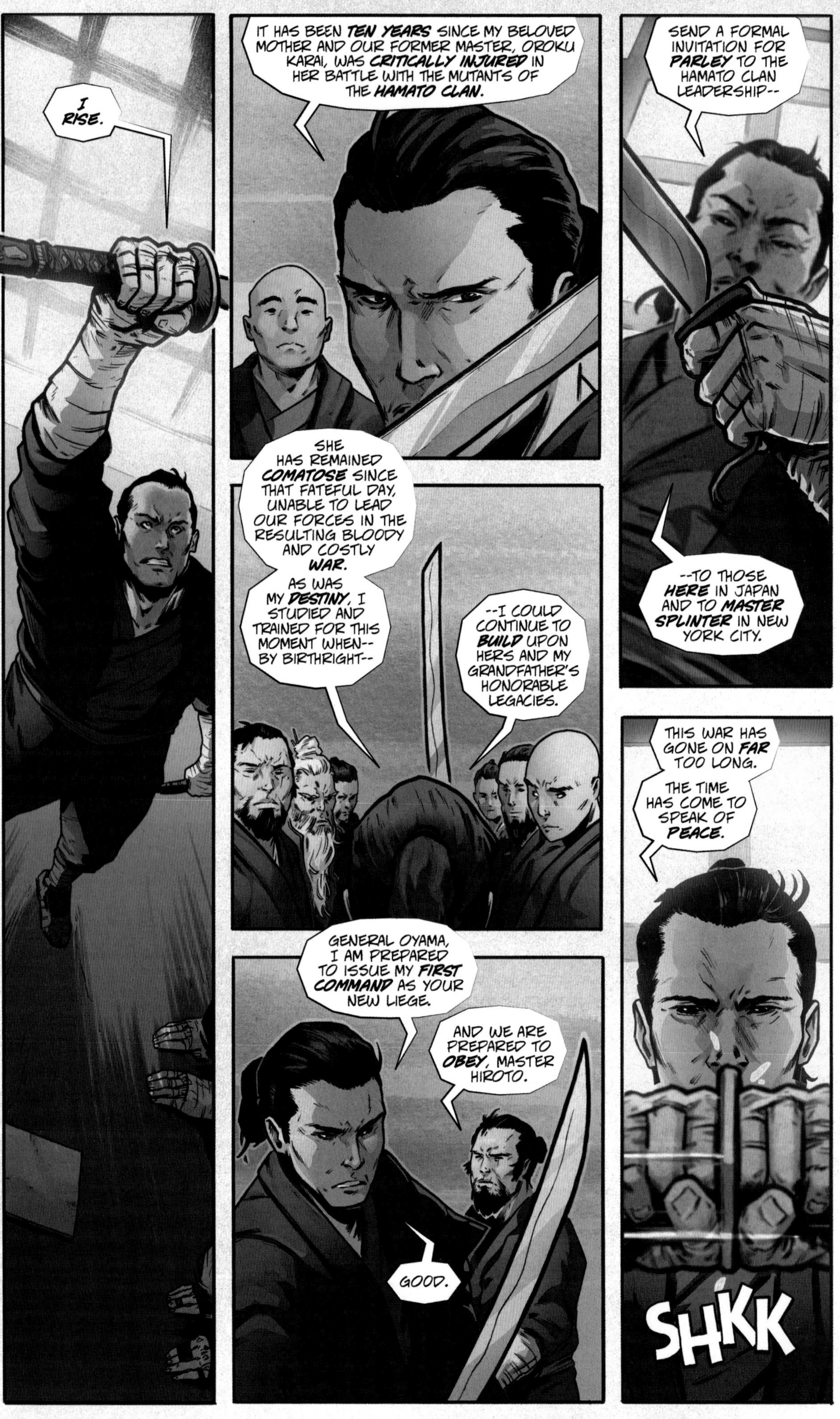
I RISE.
IT HAS BEEN TEN YEARS SINCE MY BELOVED MOTHER AND OUR FORMER MASTER, OROKU KARAI, WAS CRITICALLY INJURED IN HER BATTLE WITH THE MUTANTS OF THE HAMATO CLAN.
SHE HAS REMAINED COMATOSE SINCE THAT FATEFUL DAY, UNABLE TO LEAD OUR FORCES IN THE RESULTING BLOODY AND COSTLY WAR.
AS WAS MY DESTINY, I STUDIED AND TRAINED FOR THIS MOMENT WHEN--BY BIRTHRIGHT--
--I COULD CONTINUE TO BUILD UPON HERS AND MY GRANDFATHER'S HONORABLE LEGACIES.
GENERAL OYAMA, I AM PREPARED TO ISSUE MY FIRST COMMAND AS YOUR NEW LIEGE.
AND WE ARE PREPARED TO OBEY, MASTER HIROTO.
GOOD.
SEND A FORMAL INVITATION FOR PARLEY TO THE HAMATO CLAN LEADERSHIP--
--TO THOSE HERE IN JAPAN AND TO MASTER SPLINTER IN NEW YORK CITY.
THIS WAR HAS GONE ON FAR TOO LONG.
THE TIME HAS COME TO SPEAK OF PEACE.
SHKK

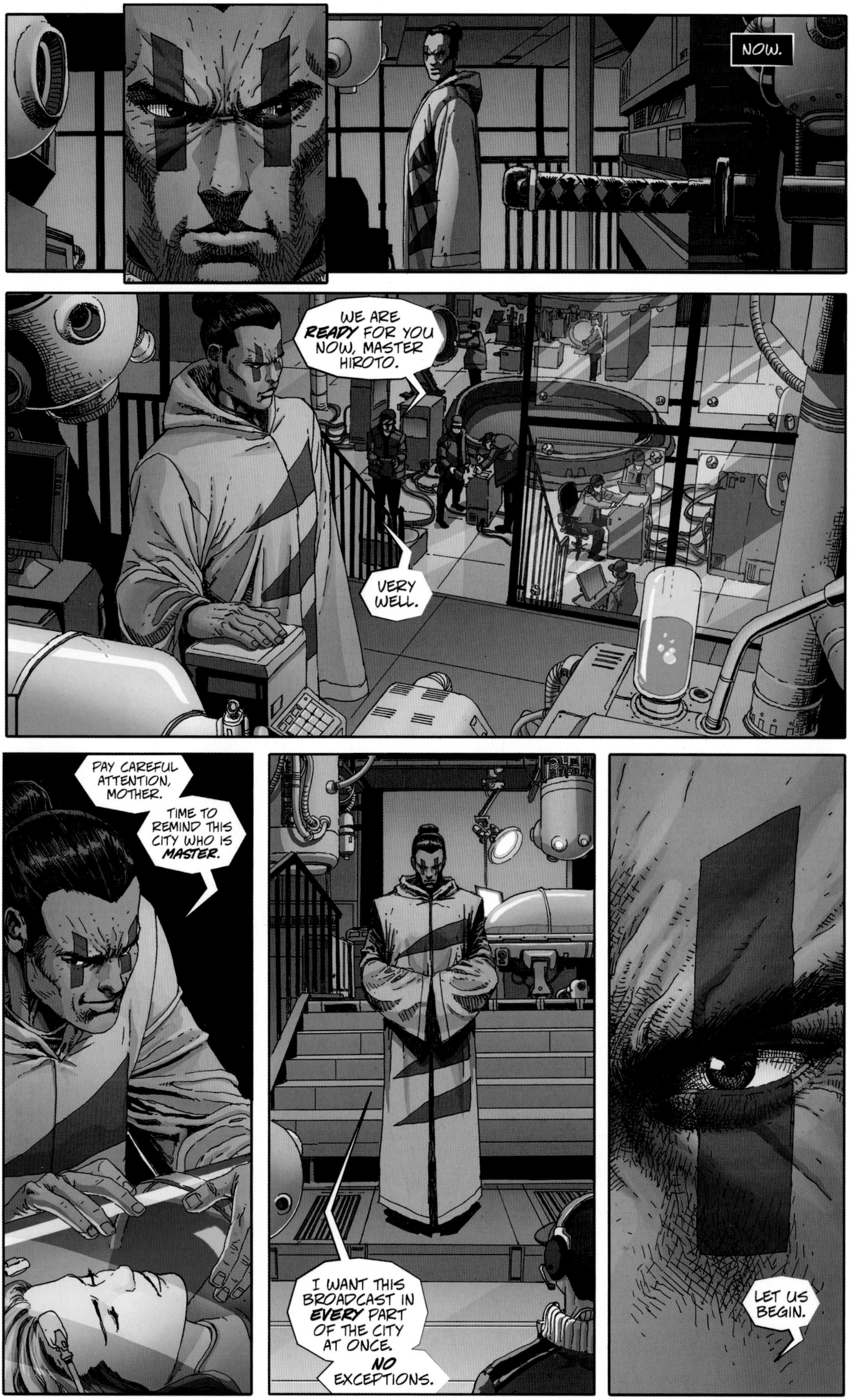
NOW.
WE ARE READY FOR YOU NOW, MASTER HIROTO.
VERY WELL.
PAY CAREFUL ATTENTION, MOTHER.
TIME TO REMIND THIS CITY WHO IS MASTER.
I WANT THIS BROADCAST IN EVERY PART OF THE CITY AT ONCE.
NO EXCEPTIONS.
LET US BEGIN.

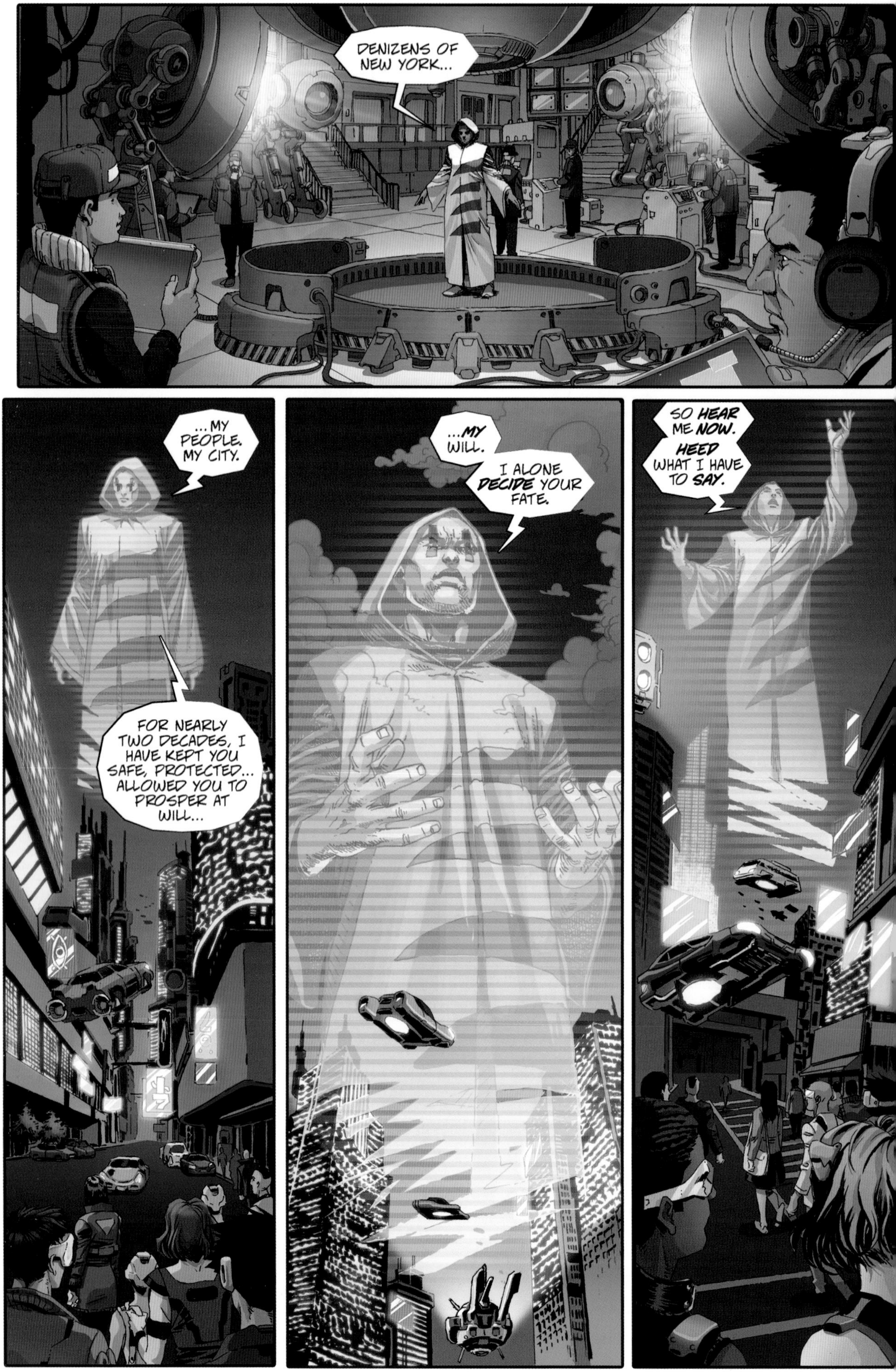
DENIZENS OF NEW YORK...
...MY PEOPLE. MY CITY.
FOR NEARLY TWO DECADES, I HAVE KEPT YOU SAFE, PROTECTED... ALLOWED YOU TO PROSPER AT WILL...
...MY WILL.
I ALONE DECIDE YOUR FATE.
SO HEAR ME NOW.
HEED WHAT I HAVE TO SAY.

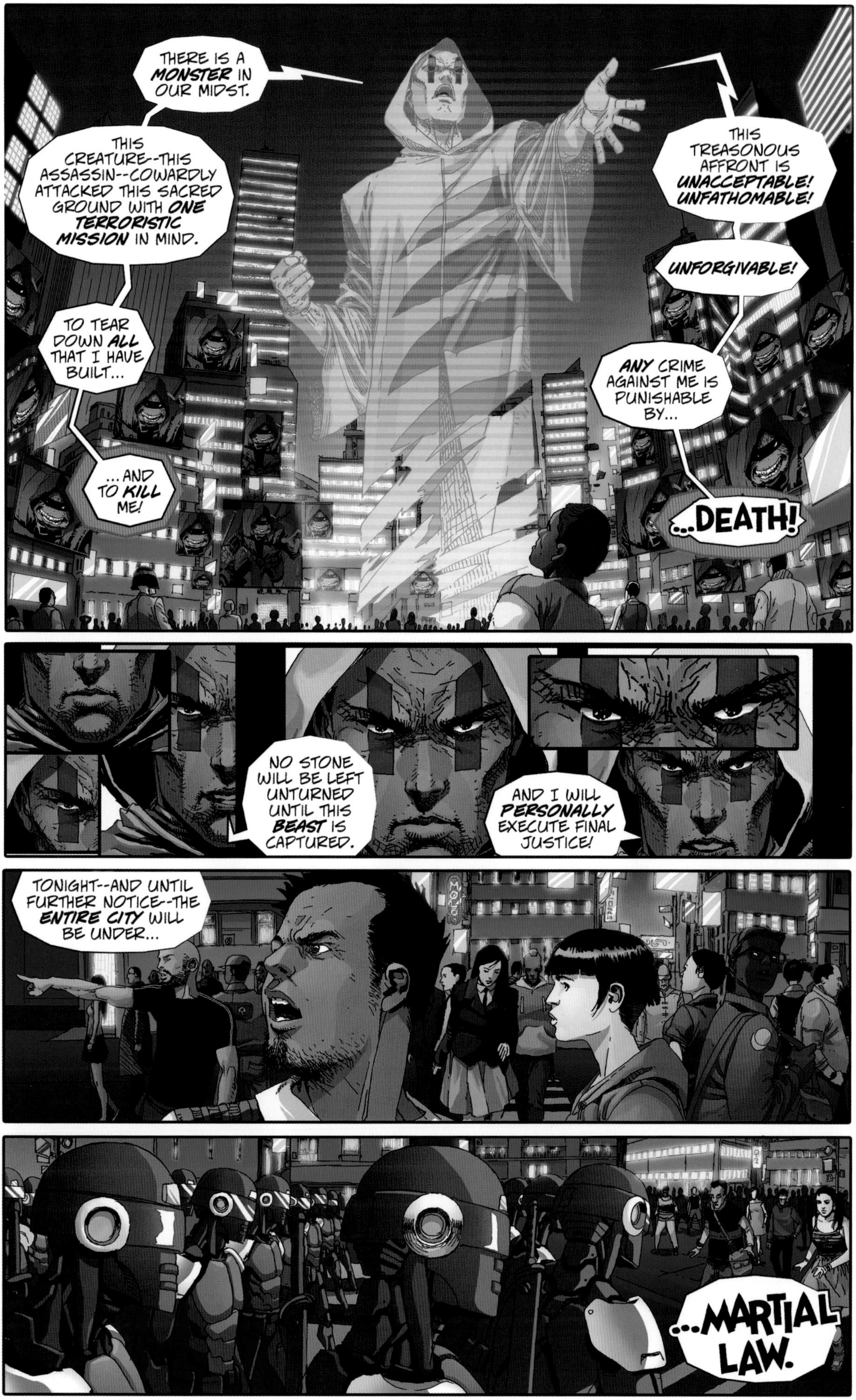
THERE IS A MONSTER IN OUR MIDST.
THIS CREATURE--THIS ASSASSIN--COWARDLY ATTACKED THIS SACRED GROUND WITH ONE TERRORISTIC MISSION IN MIND.
TO TEAR DOWN ALL THAT I HAVE BUILT...
...AND TO KILL ME!
THIS TREASONOUS AFFRONT IS UNACCEPTABLE! UNFATHOMABLE!
UNFORGIVABLE!
ANY CRIME AGAINST ME IS PUNISHABLE BY...
...DEATH!
NO STONE WILL BE LEFT UNTURNED UNTIL THIS BEAST IS CAPTURED.
AND I WILL PERSONALLY EXECUTE FINAL JUSTICE!
TONIGHT--AND UNTIL FURTHER NOTICE--THE ENTIRE CITY WILL BE UNDER...
...MARTIAL LAW.

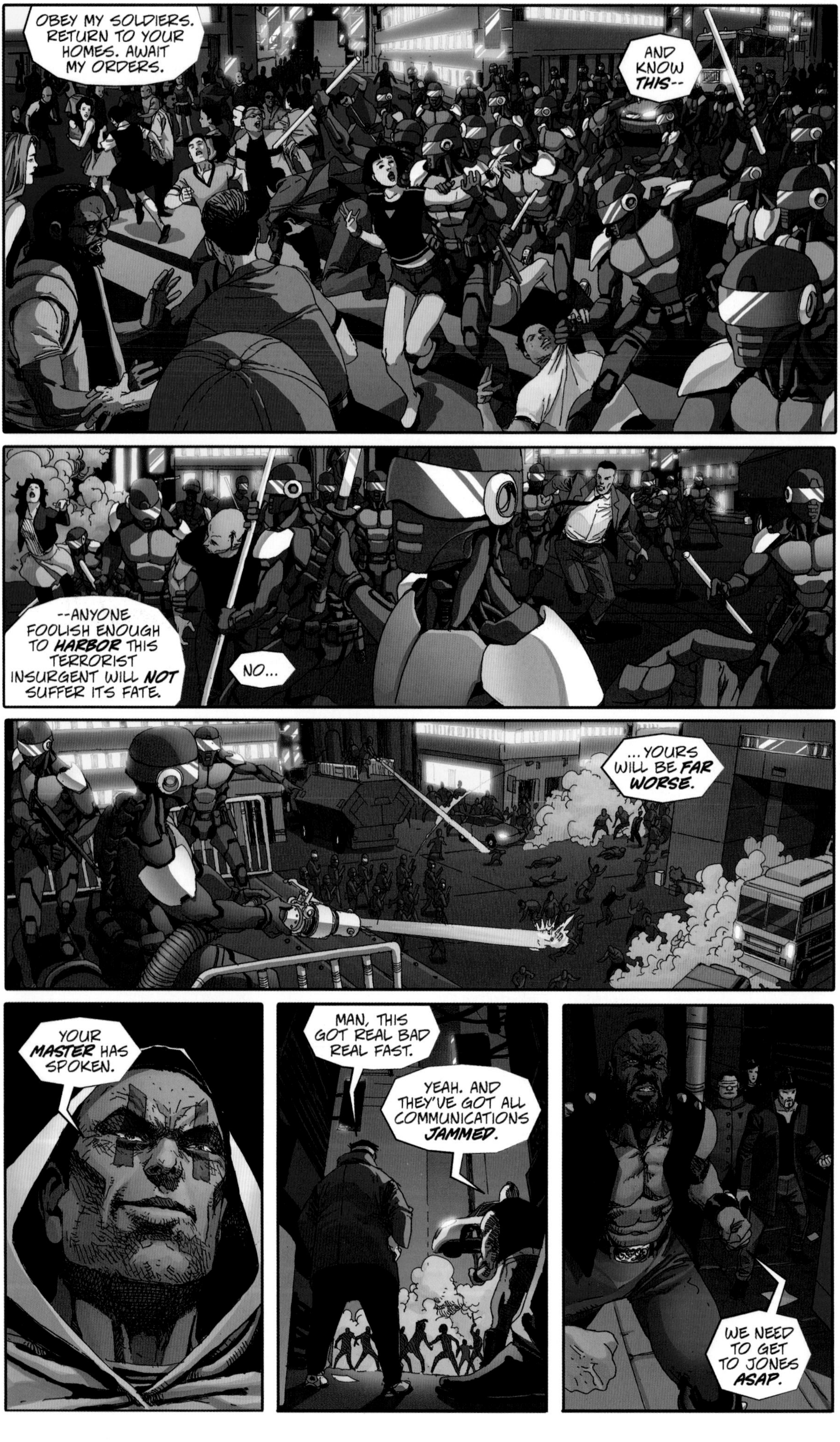
OBEY MY SOLDIERS. RETURN TO YOUR HOMES. AWAIT MY ORDERS.
AND KNOW *THIS*--
--ANYONE FOOLISH ENOUGH TO ***HARBOR*** THIS TERRORIST INSURGENT WILL ***NOT*** SUFFER ITS FATE.
NO...
...YOURS WILL BE ***FAR WORSE***.
YOUR ***MASTER*** HAS SPOKEN.
MAN, THIS GOT REAL BAD REAL FAST.
YEAH. AND THEY'VE GOT ALL COMMUNICATIONS ***JAMMED***.
WE NEED TO GET TO JONES ***ASAP***.

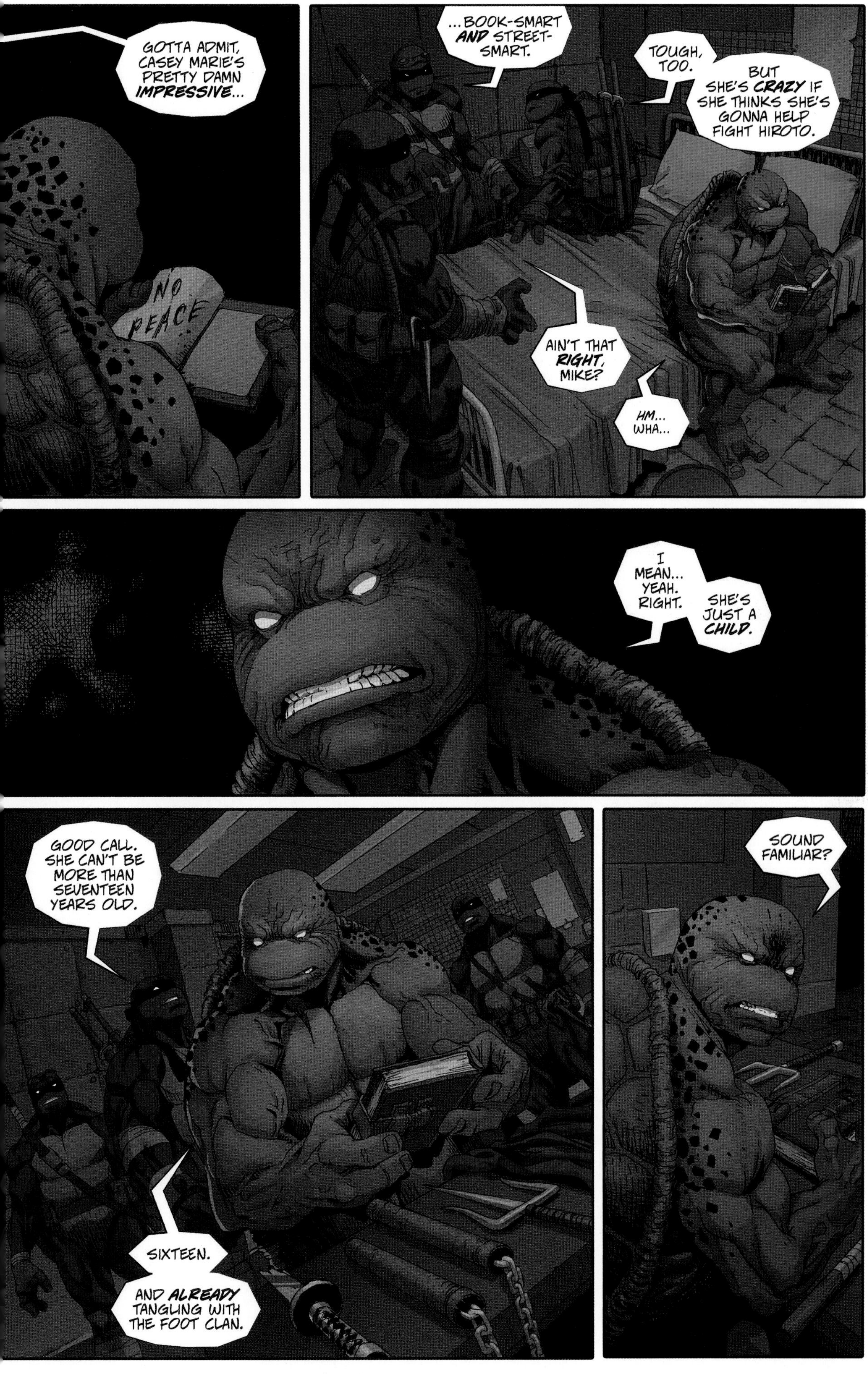
GOTTA ADMIT, CASEY MARIE'S PRETTY DAMN **IMPRESSIVE**...
NO PEACE
...BOOK-SMART **AND** STREET-SMART.
TOUGH, TOO.
BUT SHE'S **CRAZY** IF SHE THINKS SHE'S GONNA HELP FIGHT HIROTO.
AIN'T THAT **RIGHT**, MIKE?
HM... WHA...
I MEAN... YEAH. RIGHT.
SHE'S JUST A **CHILD**.
GOOD CALL. SHE CAN'T BE MORE THAN SEVENTEEN YEARS OLD.
SIXTEEN.
AND **ALREADY** TANGLING WITH THE FOOT CLAN.
SOUND FAMILIAR?

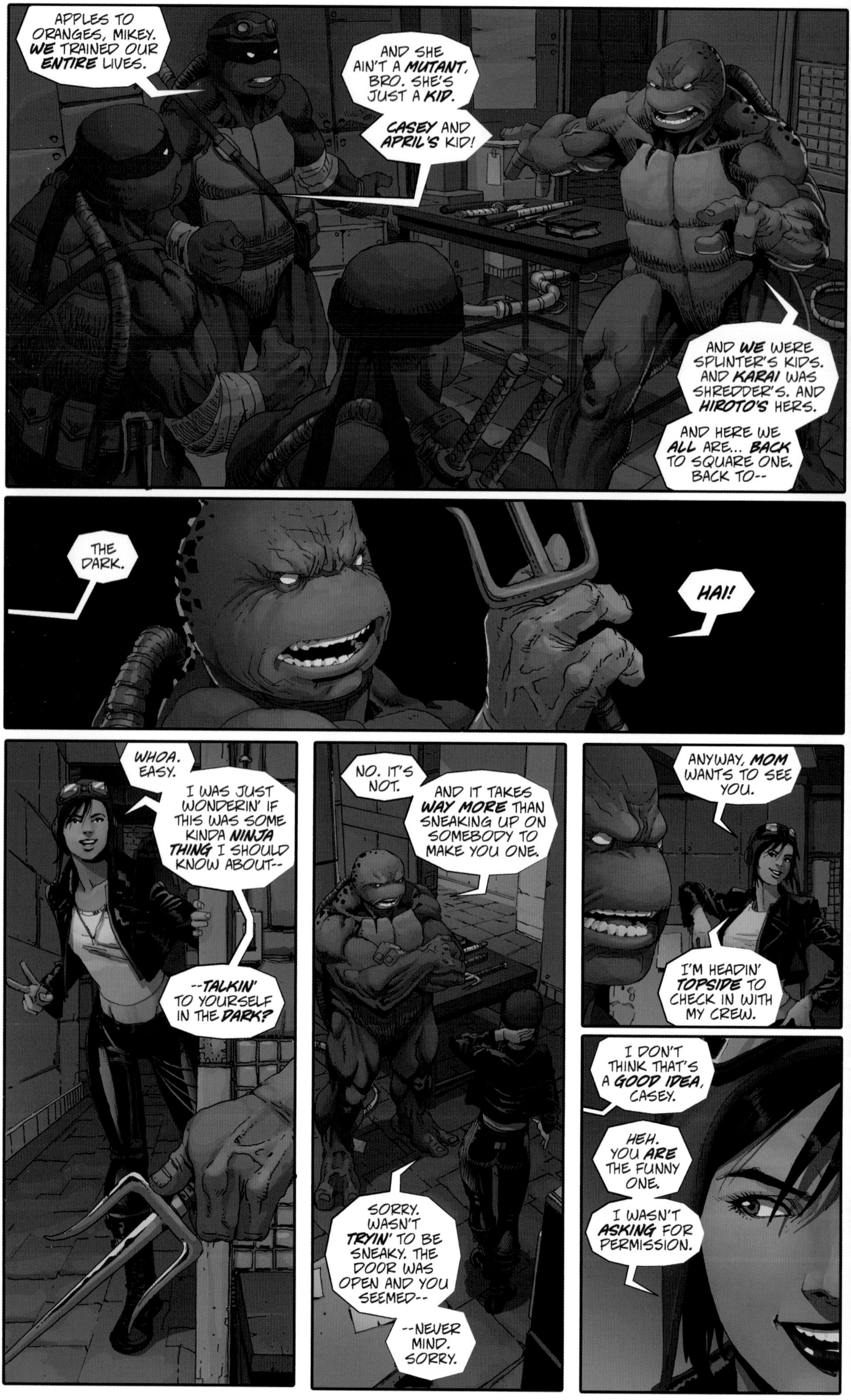
APPLES TO ORANGES, MIKEY. WE TRAINED OUR ENTIRE LIVES.
AND SHE AIN'T A MUTANT, BRO. SHE'S JUST A KID.
CASEY AND APRIL'S KID!
AND WE WERE SPLINTER'S KIDS. AND KARAI WAS SHREDDER'S. AND HIROTO'S HERS.
AND HERE WE ALL ARE... BACK TO SQUARE ONE. BACK TO--
THE DARK.
HAI!
WHOA. EASY.
I WAS JUST WONDERIN' IF THIS WAS SOME KINDA NINJA THING I SHOULD KNOW ABOUT--
--TALKIN' TO YOURSELF IN THE DARK?
NO. IT'S NOT.
AND IT TAKES WAY MORE THAN SNEAKING UP ON SOMEBODY TO MAKE YOU ONE.
SORRY. WASN'T TRYIN' TO BE SNEAKY. THE DOOR WAS OPEN AND YOU SEEMED--
--NEVER MIND. SORRY.
ANYWAY, MOM WANTS TO SEE YOU.
I'M HEADIN' TOPSIDE TO CHECK IN WITH MY CREW.
I DON'T THINK THAT'S A GOOD IDEA, CASEY.
HEH. YOU ARE THE FUNNY ONE.
I WASN'T ASKING FOR PERMISSION.

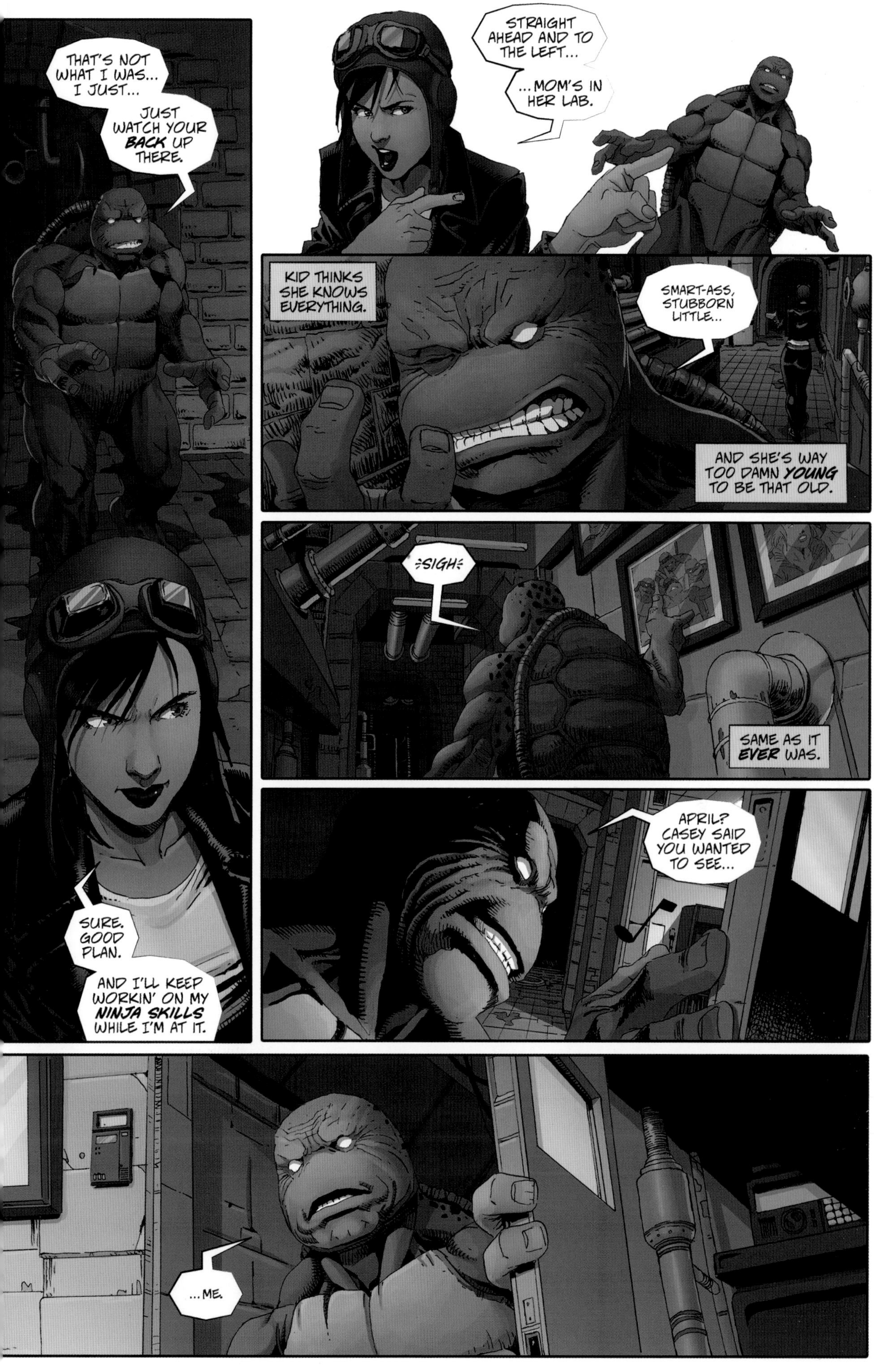
THAT'S NOT WHAT I WAS... I JUST...
JUST WATCH YOUR BACK UP THERE.
STRAIGHT AHEAD AND TO THE LEFT...
...MOM'S IN HER LAB.
SURE. GOOD PLAN.
AND I'LL KEEP WORKIN' ON MY NINJA SKILLS WHILE I'M AT IT.
KID THINKS SHE KNOWS EVERYTHING.
SMART-ASS, STUBBORN LITTLE...
AND SHE'S WAY TOO DAMN YOUNG TO BE THAT OLD.
SIGH
SAME AS IT EVER WAS.
APRIL? CASEY SAID YOU WANTED TO SEE...
...ME.

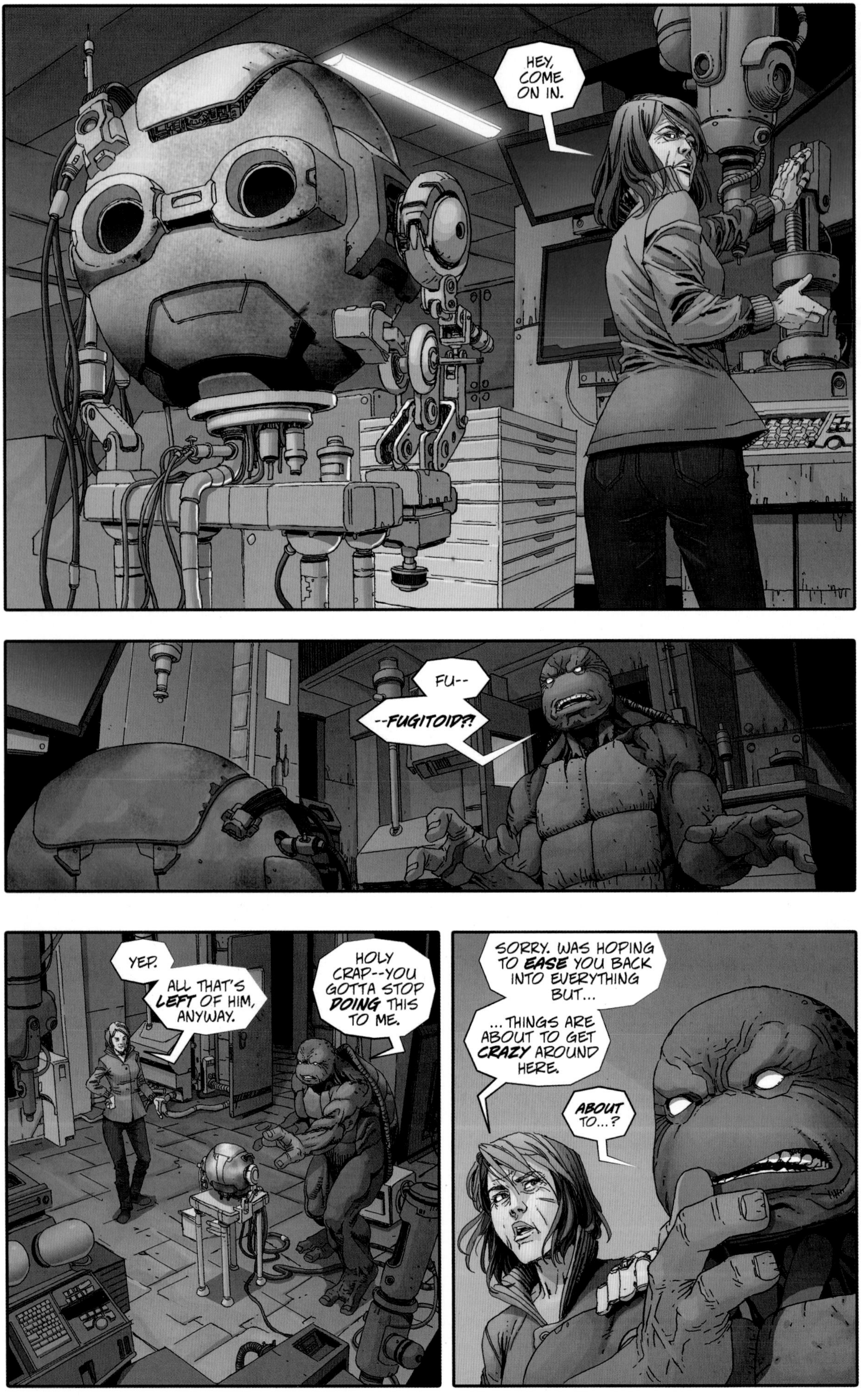
HEY, COME ON IN.
FU--
--FUGITOID?!
YEP.
ALL THAT'S LEFT OF HIM, ANYWAY.
HOLY CRAP--YOU GOTTA STOP DOING THIS TO ME.
SORRY. WAS HOPING TO EASE YOU BACK INTO EVERYTHING BUT...
...THINGS ARE ABOUT TO GET CRAZY AROUND HERE.
ABOUT TO...?

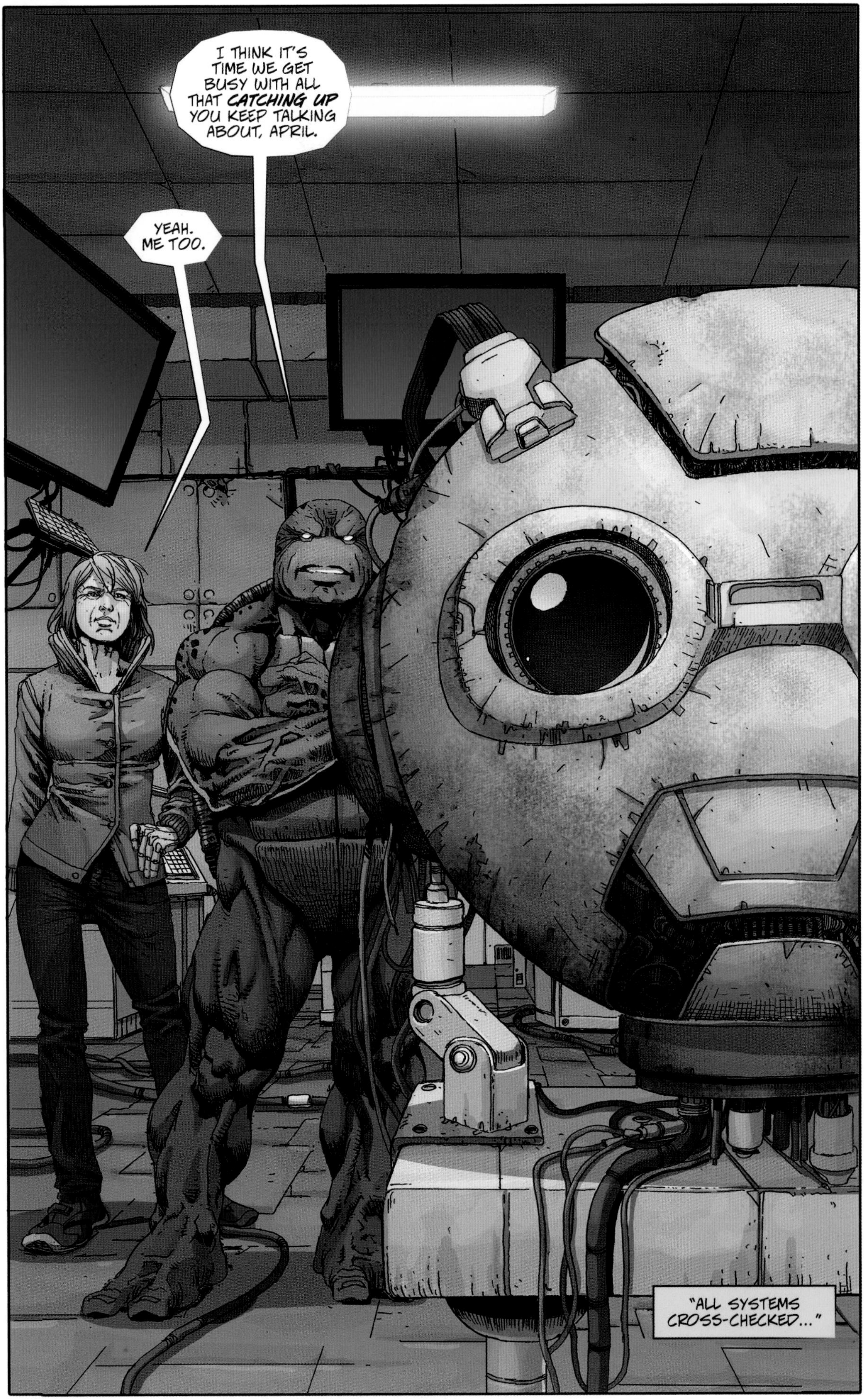
I THINK IT'S TIME WE GET BUSY WITH ALL THAT **CATCHING UP** YOU KEEP TALKING ABOUT, APRIL.
YEAH. ME TOO.
"ALL SYSTEMS CROSS-CHECKED..."

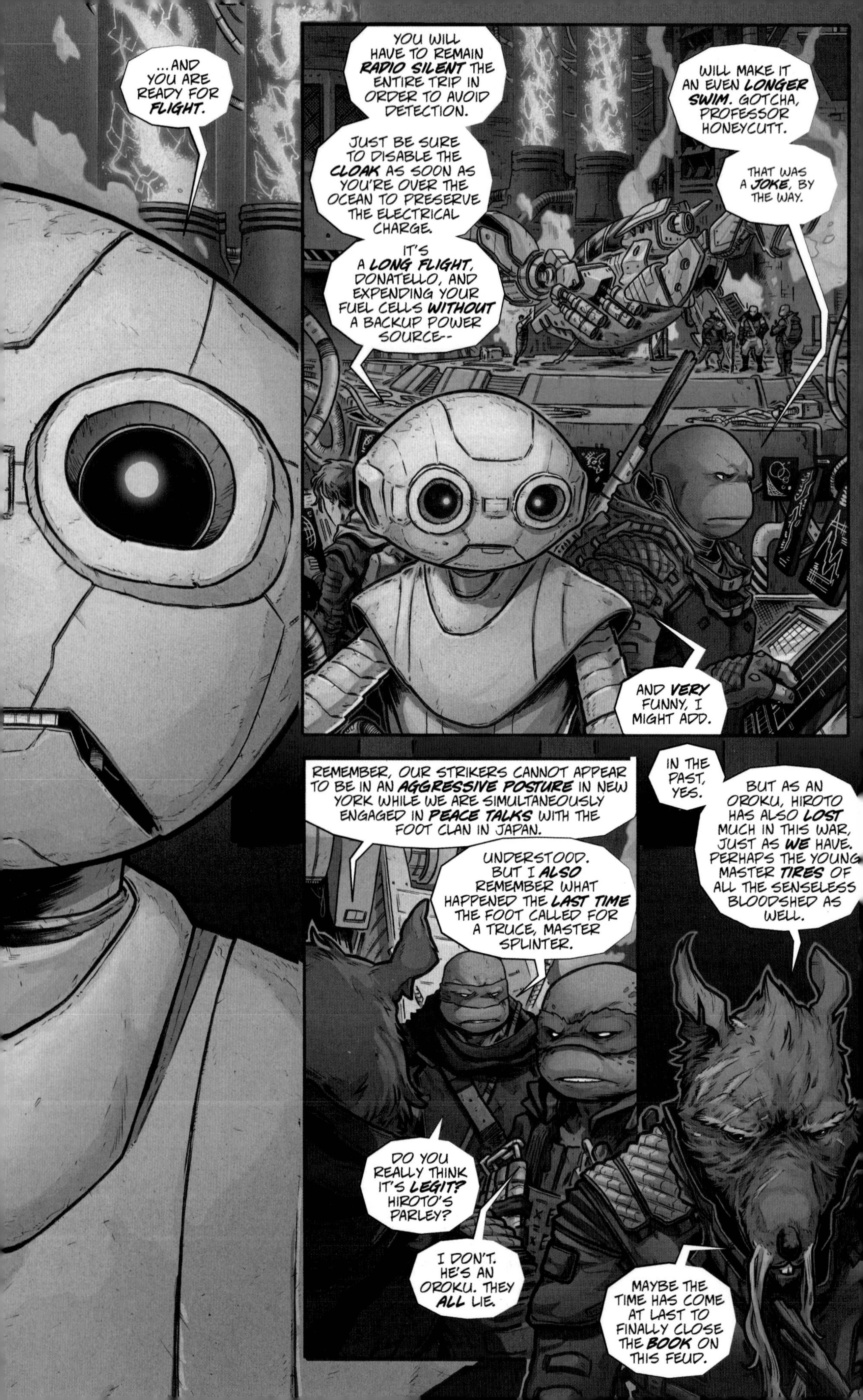
...AND YOU ARE READY FOR FLIGHT.
YOU WILL HAVE TO REMAIN RADIO SILENT THE ENTIRE TRIP IN ORDER TO AVOID DETECTION.
JUST BE SURE TO DISABLE THE CLOAK AS SOON AS YOU'RE OVER THE OCEAN TO PRESERVE THE ELECTRICAL CHARGE.
IT'S A LONG FLIGHT, DONATELLO, AND EXPENDING YOUR FUEL CELLS WITHOUT A BACKUP POWER SOURCE--
WILL MAKE IT AN EVEN LONGER SWIM. GOTCHA, PROFESSOR HONEYCUTT.
THAT WAS A JOKE, BY THE WAY.
AND VERY FUNNY, I MIGHT ADD.
REMEMBER, OUR STRIKERS CANNOT APPEAR TO BE IN AN AGGRESSIVE POSTURE IN NEW YORK WHILE WE ARE SIMULTANEOUSLY ENGAGED IN PEACE TALKS WITH THE FOOT CLAN IN JAPAN.
UNDERSTOOD. BUT I ALSO REMEMBER WHAT HAPPENED THE LAST TIME THE FOOT CALLED FOR A TRUCE, MASTER SPLINTER.
IN THE PAST, YES.
BUT AS AN OROKU, HIROTO HAS ALSO LOST MUCH IN THIS WAR, JUST AS WE HAVE. PERHAPS THE YOUNG MASTER TIRES OF ALL THE SENSELESS BLOODSHED AS WELL.
DO YOU REALLY THINK IT'S LEGIT? HIROTO'S PARLEY?
I DON'T. HE'S AN OROKU. THEY ALL LIE.
MAYBE THE TIME HAS COME AT LAST TO FINALLY CLOSE THE BOOK ON THIS FEUD.

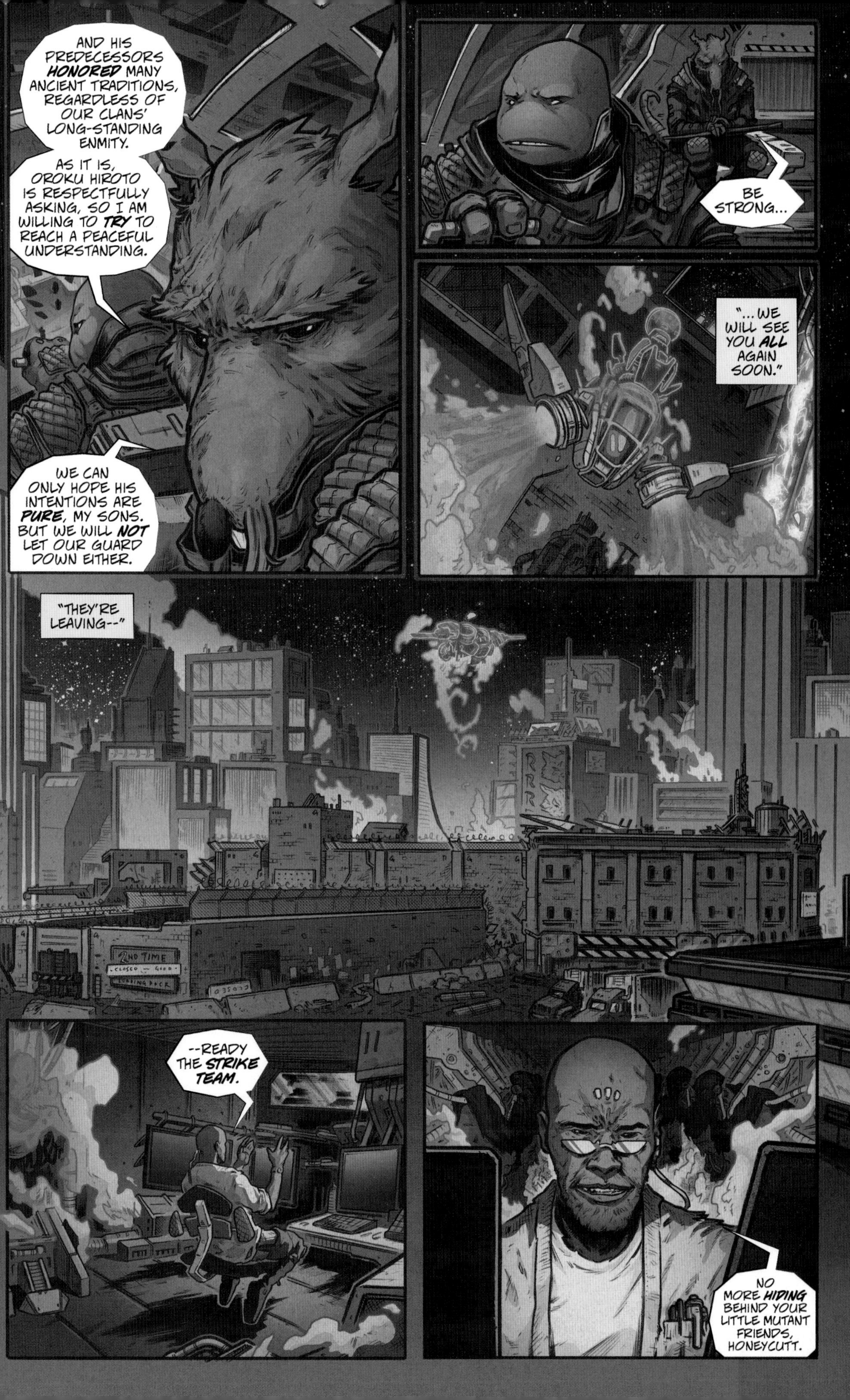
AND HIS PREDECESSORS HONORED MANY ANCIENT TRADITIONS, REGARDLESS OF OUR CLANS' LONG-STANDING ENMITY.
AS IT IS, OROKU HIROTO IS RESPECTFULLY ASKING, SO I AM WILLING TO TRY TO REACH A PEACEFUL UNDERSTANDING.
WE CAN ONLY HOPE HIS INTENTIONS ARE PURE, MY SONS. BUT WE WILL NOT LET OUR GUARD DOWN EITHER.
BE STRONG...
"...WE WILL SEE YOU ALL AGAIN SOON."
"THEY'RE LEAVING--"
2ND TIME
CLOSED — GOOD
LOADING DOCK
--READY THE STRIKE TEAM.
NO MORE HIDING BEHIND YOUR LITTLE MUTANT FRIENDS, HONEYCUTT.

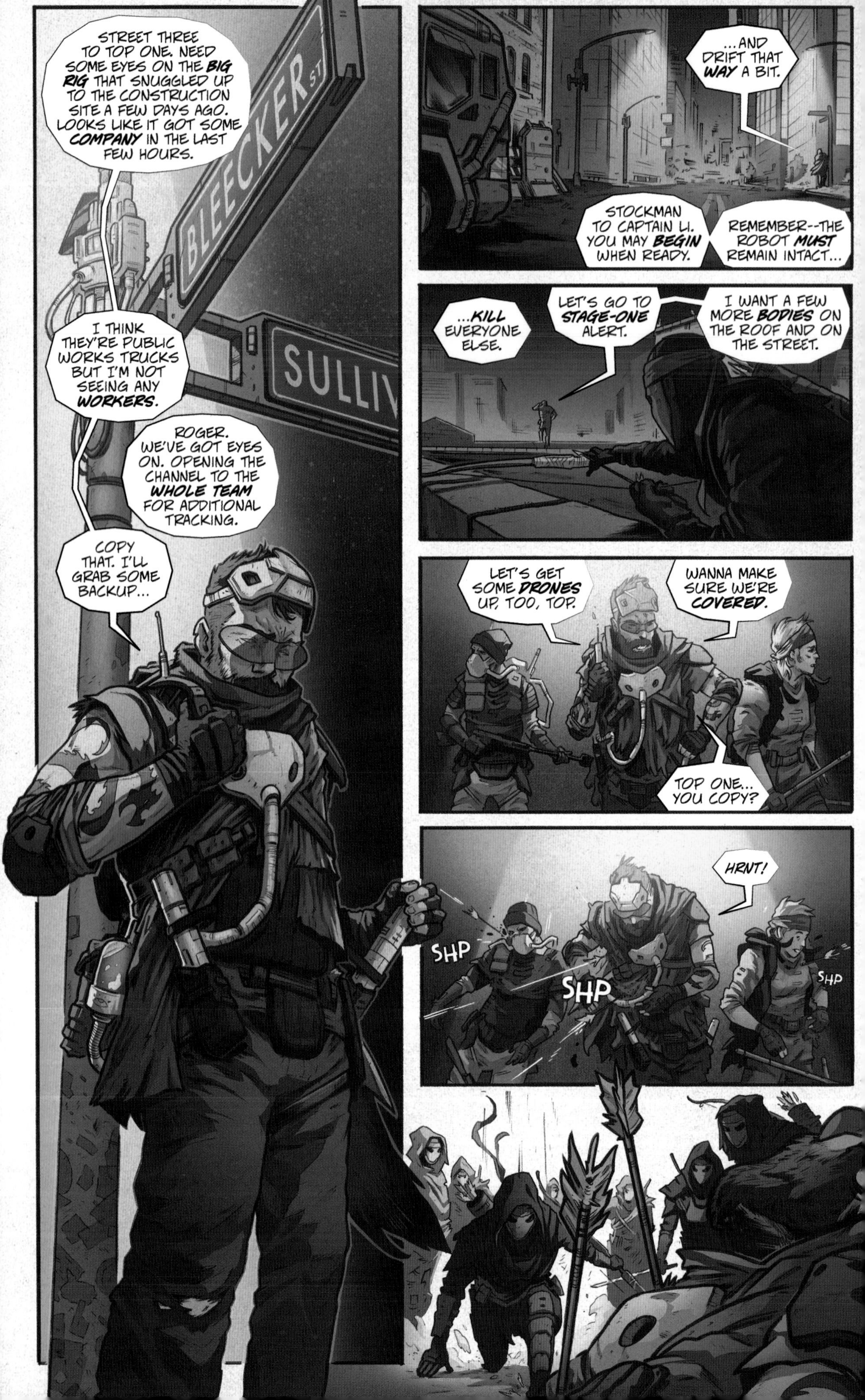

STREET THREE TO TOP ONE. NEED SOME EYES ON THE **BIG RIG** THAT SNUGGLED UP TO THE CONSTRUCTION SITE A FEW DAYS AGO. LOOKS LIKE IT GOT SOME **COMPANY** IN THE LAST FEW HOURS.
BLEECKER ST
SULLIV
I THINK THEY'RE PUBLIC WORKS TRUCKS BUT I'M NOT SEEING ANY **WORKERS**.
ROGER. WE'VE GOT EYES ON. OPENING THE CHANNEL TO THE **WHOLE TEAM** FOR ADDITIONAL TRACKING.
COPY THAT. I'LL GRAB SOME BACKUP...
...AND DRIFT THAT **WAY** A BIT.
STOCKMAN TO CAPTAIN LI. YOU MAY **BEGIN** WHEN READY.
REMEMBER--THE ROBOT **MUST** REMAIN INTACT...
...**KILL** EVERYONE ELSE.
LET'S GO TO **STAGE-ONE** ALERT.
I WANT A FEW MORE **BODIES** ON THE ROOF AND ON THE STREET.
LET'S GET SOME **DRONES** UP, TOO, TOP.
WANNA MAKE SURE WE'RE **COVERED**.
TOP ONE... YOU COPY?
HRNT!
SHP
SHP
SHP

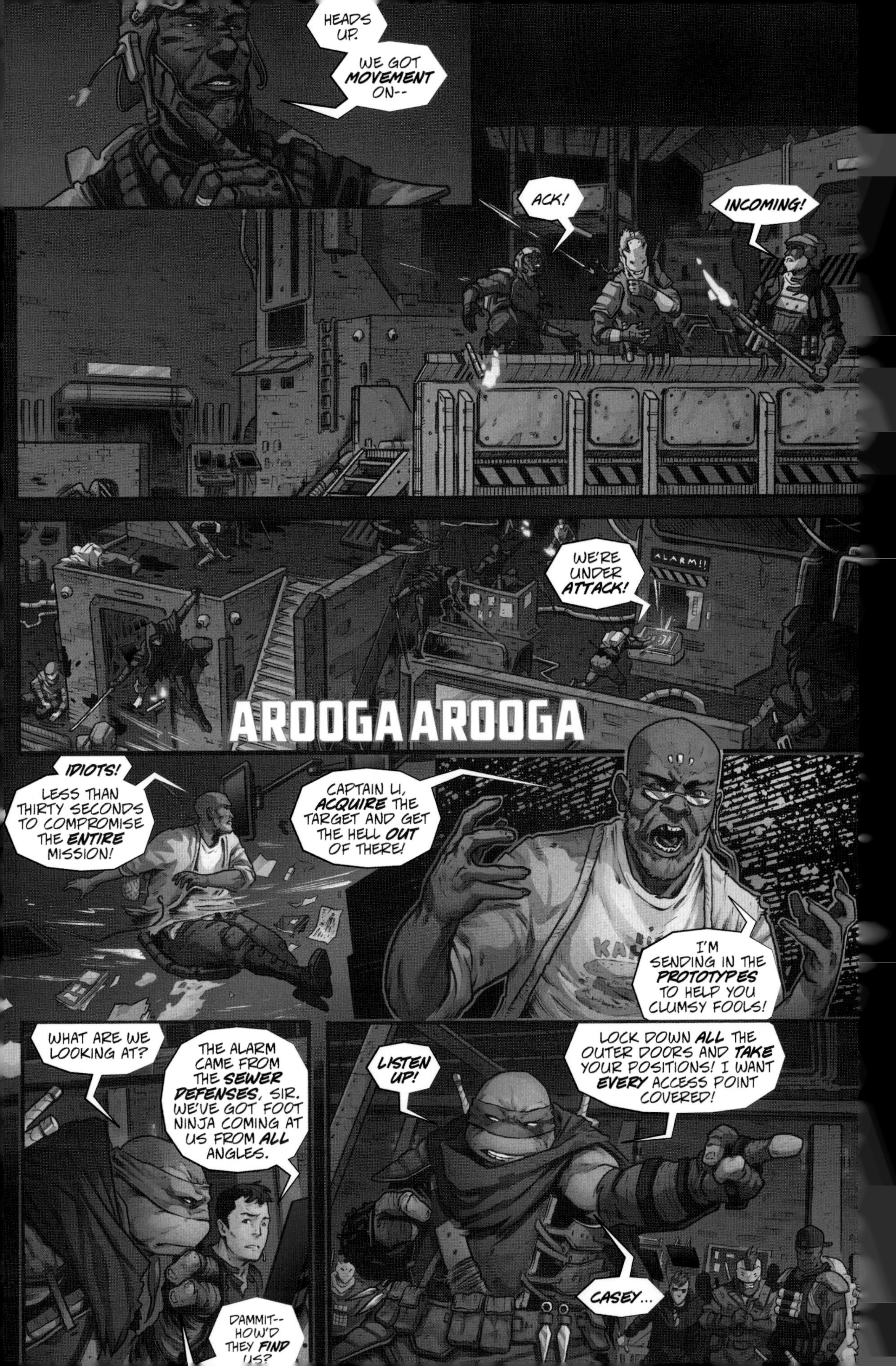
HEADS UP.
WE GOT MOVEMENT ON--
ACK!
INCOMING!
WE'RE UNDER ATTACK!
ALARM!!
AROOGA AROOGA
IDIOTS! LESS THAN THIRTY SECONDS TO COMPROMISE THE ENTIRE MISSION!
CAPTAIN LI, ACQUIRE THE TARGET AND GET THE HELL OUT OF THERE!
I'M SENDING IN THE PROTOTYPES TO HELP YOU CLUMSY FOOLS!
WHAT ARE WE LOOKING AT?
THE ALARM CAME FROM THE SEWER DEFENSES, SIR. WE'VE GOT FOOT NINJA COMING AT US FROM ALL ANGLES.
DAMMIT-- HOW'D THEY FIND US?
LISTEN UP!
LOCK DOWN ALL THE OUTER DOORS AND TAKE YOUR POSITIONS! I WANT EVERY ACCESS POINT COVERED!
CASEY...

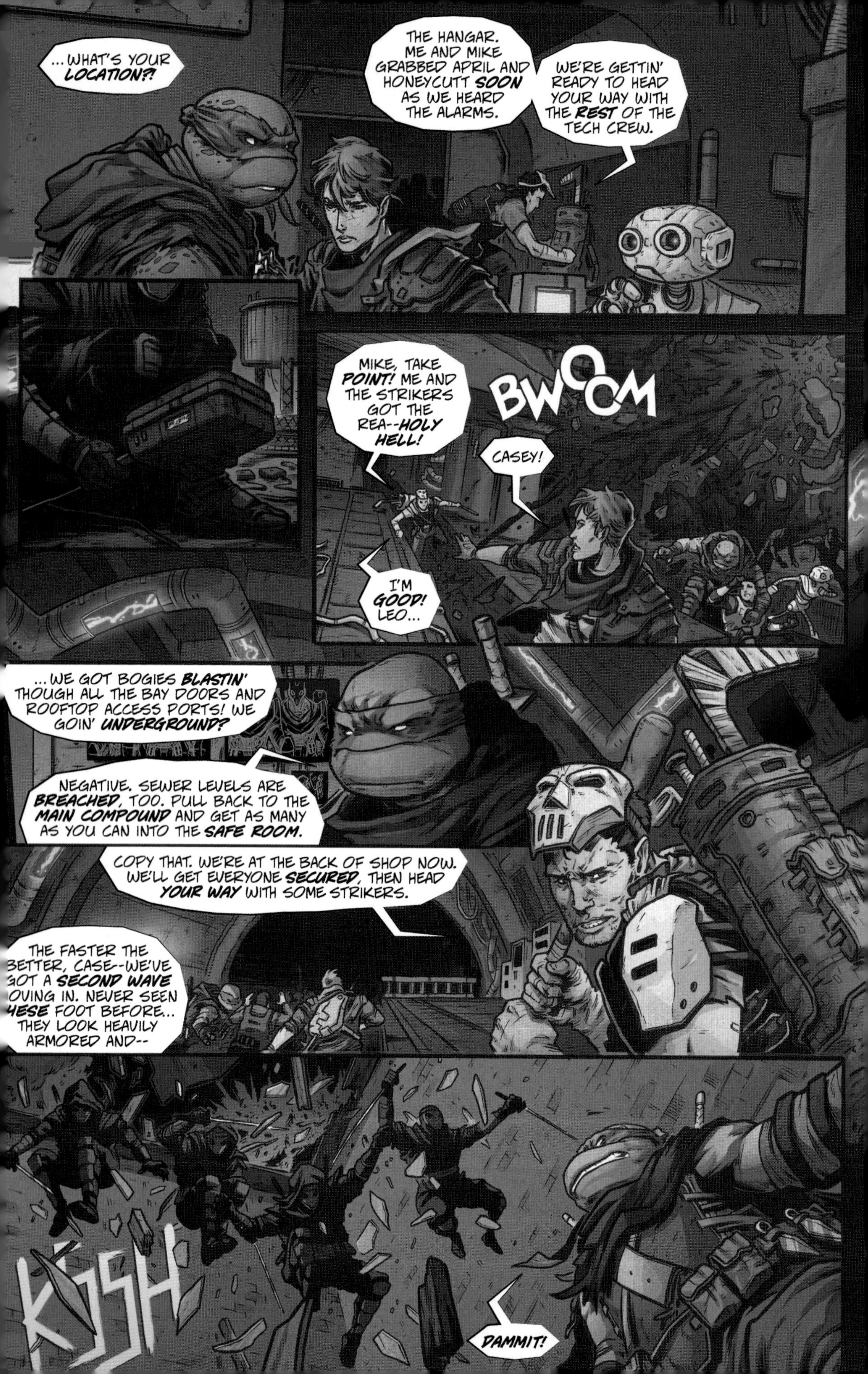
...WHAT'S YOUR LOCATION?!
THE HANGAR. ME AND MIKE GRABBED APRIL AND HONEYCUTT SOON AS WE HEARD THE ALARMS.
WE'RE GETTIN' READY TO HEAD YOUR WAY WITH THE REST OF THE TECH CREW.
MIKE, TAKE POINT! ME AND THE STRIKERS GOT THE REA--HOLY HELL!
BWOOOM
CASEY!
I'M GOOD! LEO...
...WE GOT BOGIES BLASTIN' THOUGH ALL THE BAY DOORS AND ROOFTOP ACCESS PORTS! WE GOIN' UNDERGROUND?
NEGATIVE. SEWER LEVELS ARE BREACHED, TOO. PULL BACK TO THE MAIN COMPOUND AND GET AS MANY AS YOU CAN INTO THE SAFE ROOM.
COPY THAT. WE'RE AT THE BACK OF SHOP NOW. WE'LL GET EVERYONE SECURED, THEN HEAD YOUR WAY WITH SOME STRIKERS.
THE FASTER THE BETTER, CASE--WE'VE GOT A SECOND WAVE OVING IN. NEVER SEEN HESE FOOT BEFORE... THEY LOOK HEAVILY ARMORED AND--
KSSH
DAMMIT!

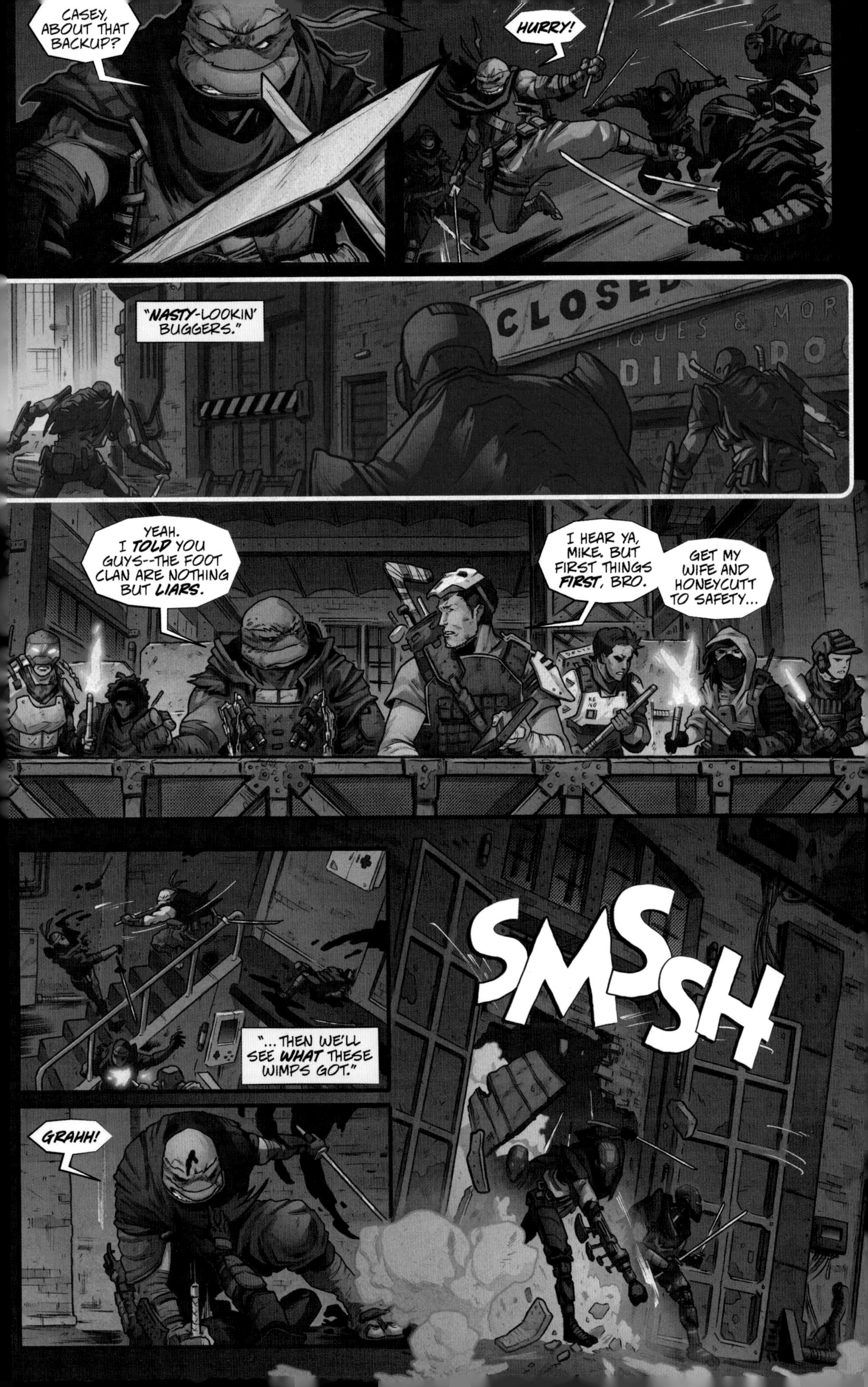

CASEY, ABOUT THAT BACKUP?
HURRY!
"NASTY-LOOKIN' BUGGERS."
CLOSED
YEAH. I TOLD YOU GUYS--THE FOOT CLAN ARE NOTHING BUT LIARS.
I HEAR YA, MIKE. BUT FIRST THINGS FIRST, BRO.
GET MY WIFE AND HONEYCUTT TO SAFETY...
SMSSH
"...THEN WE'LL SEE WHAT THESE WIMPS GOT."
GRAHH!

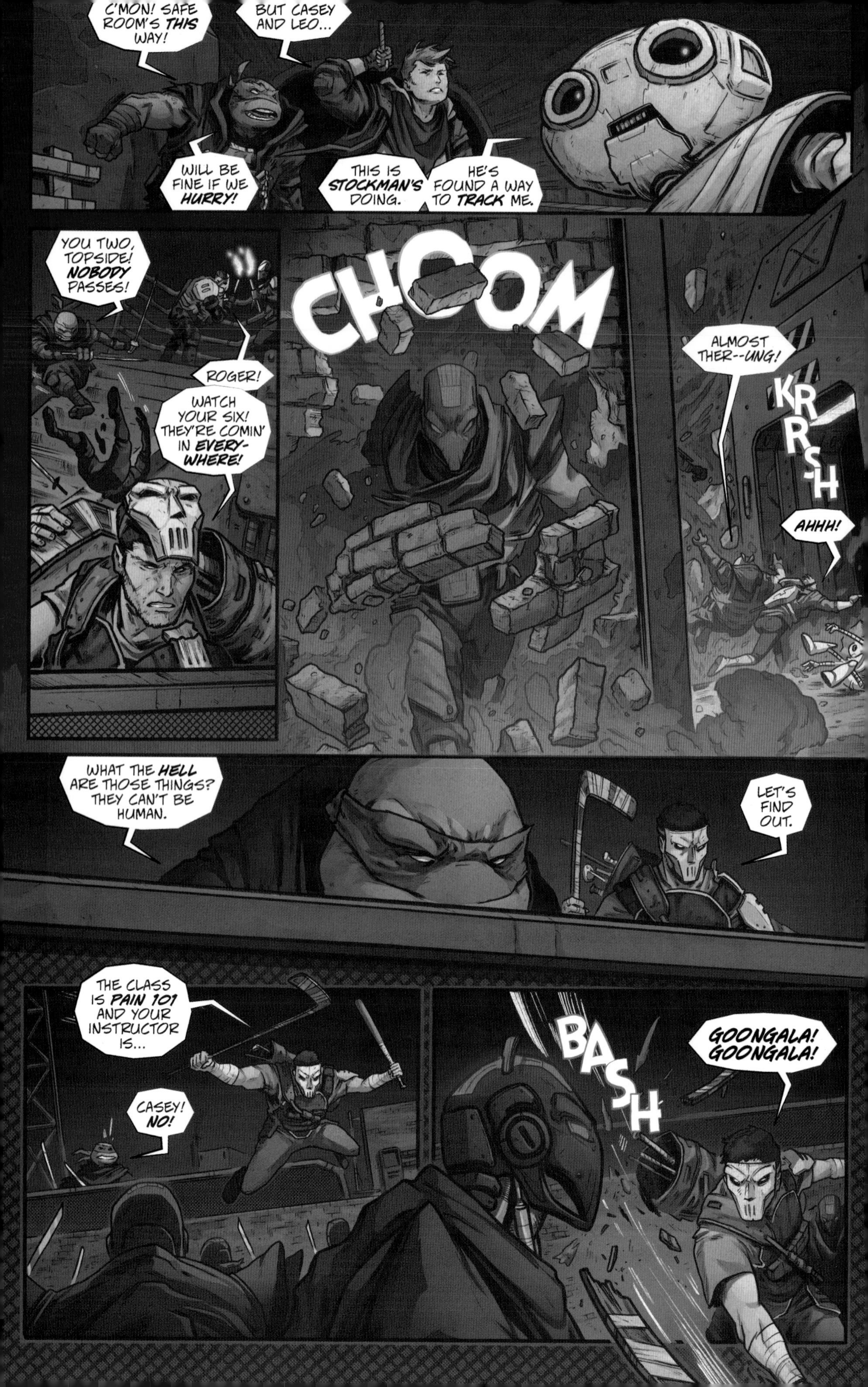

C'MON! SAFE ROOM'S **THIS** WAY!
BUT CASEY AND LEO...
WILL BE FINE IF WE **HURRY!**
THIS IS **STOCKMAN'S** DOING.
HE'S FOUND A WAY TO **TRACK** ME.
YOU TWO, TOPSIDE! **NOBODY** PASSES!
ROGER!
WATCH YOUR SIX! THEY'RE COMIN' IN **EVERY-WHERE!**
CHOOM
ALMOST THER--*UNG!*
KRRSH
AHHH!
WHAT THE **HELL** ARE THOSE THINGS? THEY CAN'T BE HUMAN.
LET'S FIND OUT.
THE CLASS IS **PAIN 101** AND YOUR INSTRUCTOR IS...
CASEY! **NO!**
BASH
GOONGALA! GOONGALA!

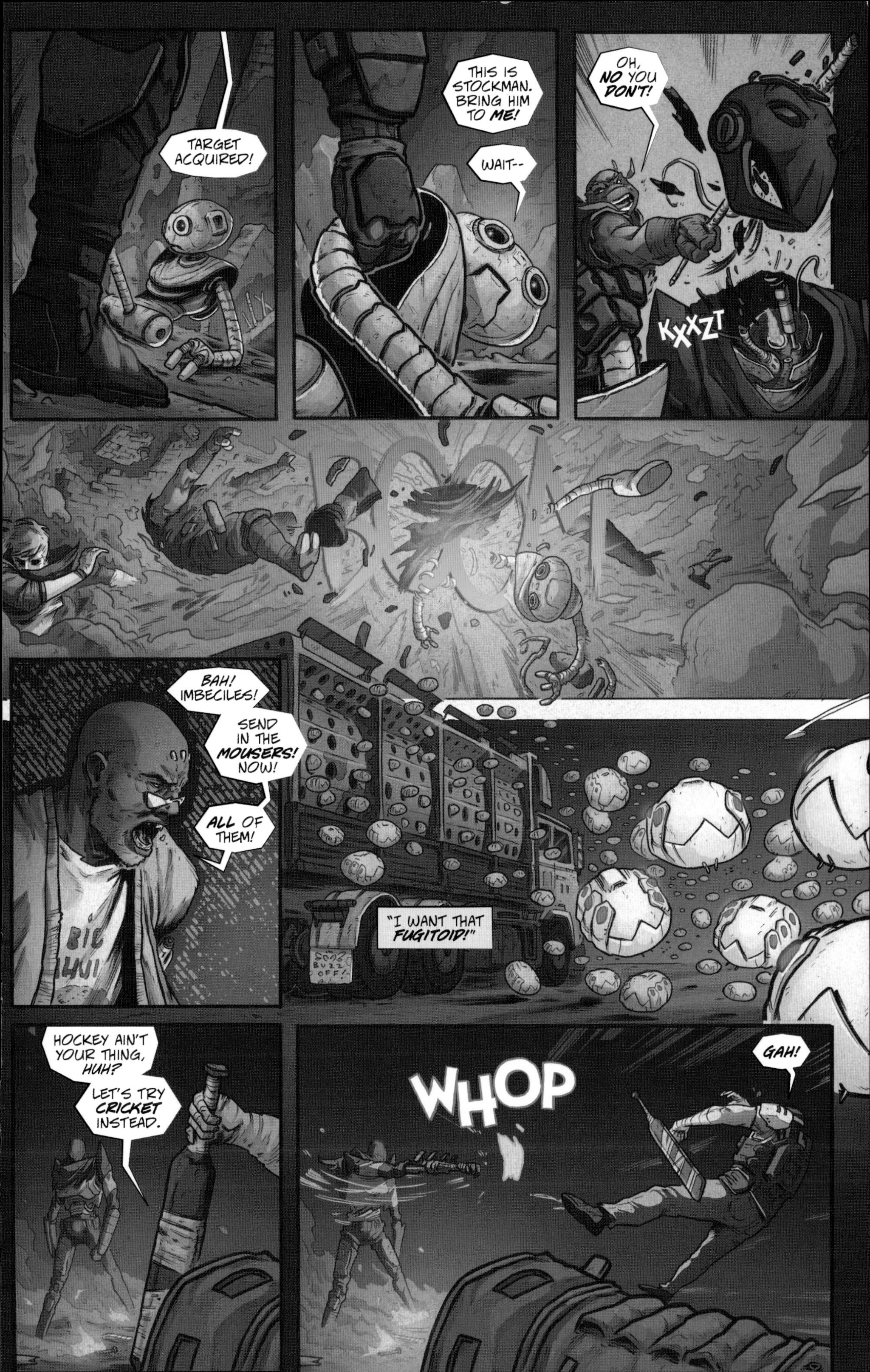
TARGET ACQUIRED!
THIS IS STOCKMAN. BRING HIM TO ME!
WAIT--
OH, NO YOU DON'T!
KXXZT
BAH! IMBECILES!
SEND IN THE MOUSERS! NOW!
ALL OF THEM!
"I WANT THAT FUGITOID!"
BUZZ OFF!
HOCKEY AIN'T YOUR THING, HUH?
LET'S TRY CRICKET INSTEAD.
WHOP
GAH!

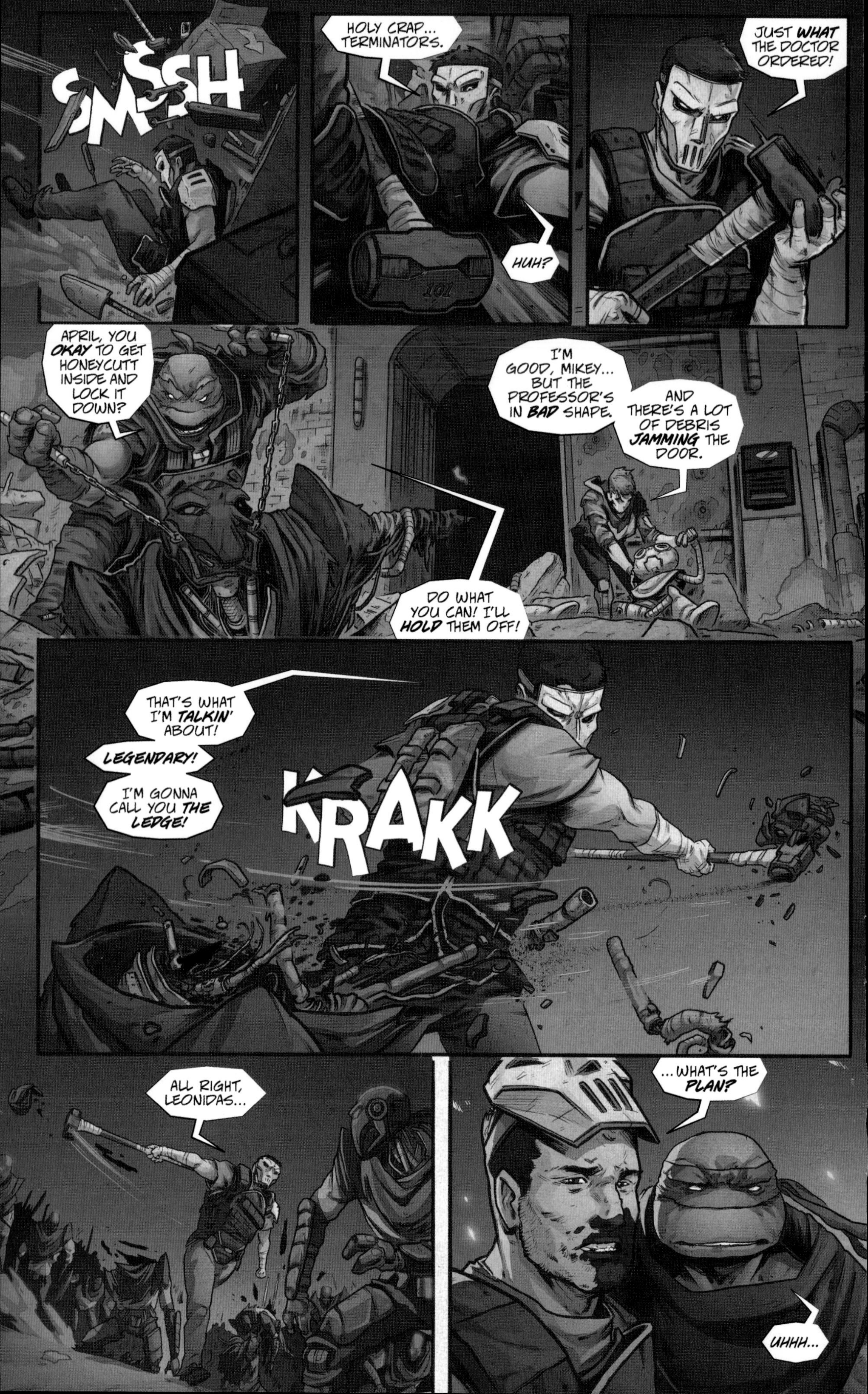
SMSSH
HOLY CRAP... TERMINATORS.
HUH?
JUST WHAT THE DOCTOR ORDERED!
APRIL, YOU OKAY TO GET HONEYCUTT INSIDE AND LOCK IT DOWN?
I'M GOOD, MIKEY... BUT THE PROFESSOR'S IN BAD SHAPE.
AND THERE'S A LOT OF DEBRIS JAMMING THE DOOR.
DO WHAT YOU CAN! I'LL HOLD THEM OFF!
THAT'S WHAT I'M TALKIN' ABOUT!
LEGENDARY!
I'M GONNA CALL YOU THE LEDGE!
KRAKK
ALL RIGHT, LEONIDAS...
...WHAT'S THE PLAN?
UHHH...

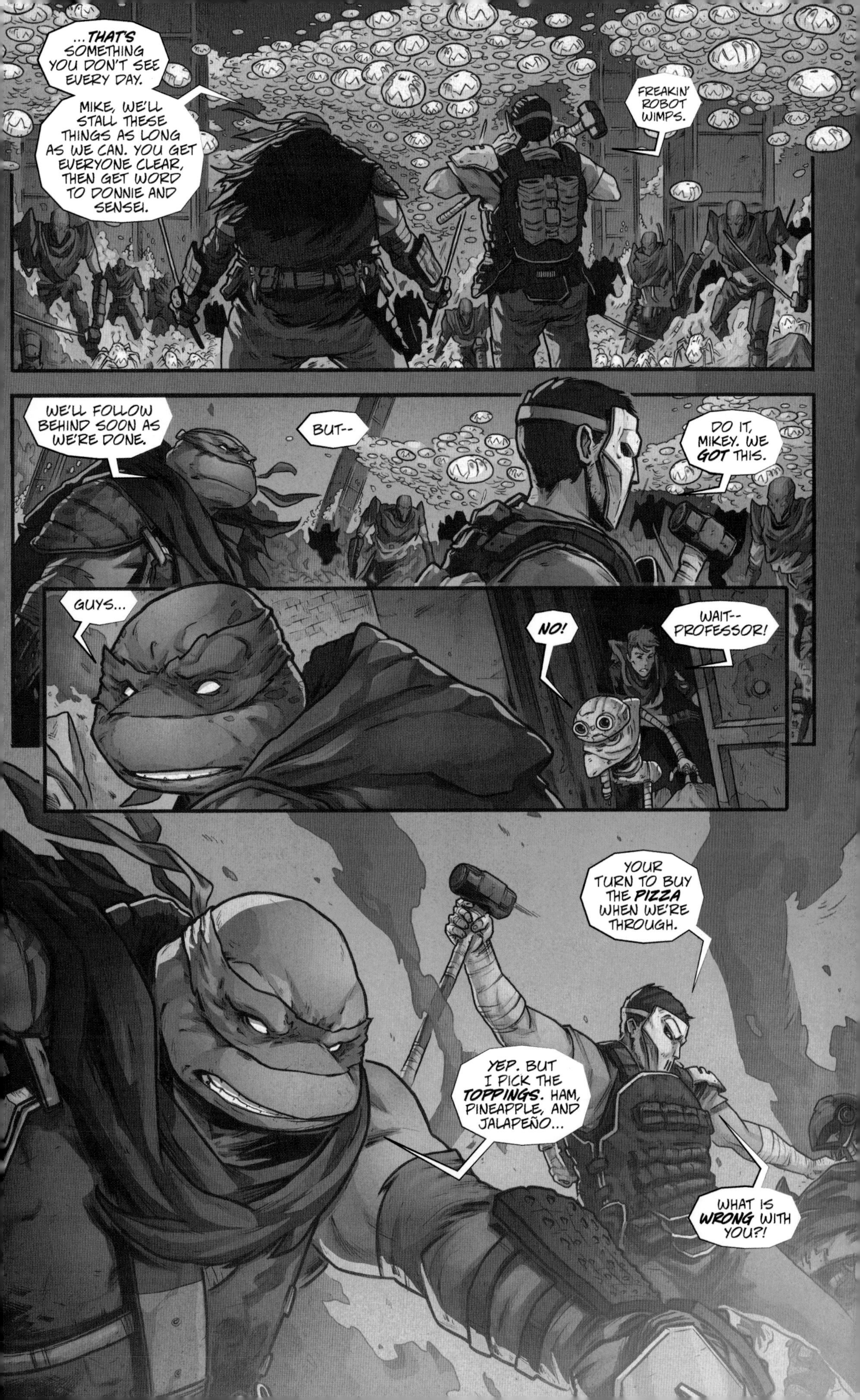
...THAT'S SOMETHING YOU DON'T SEE EVERY DAY.
MIKE, WE'LL STALL THESE THINGS AS LONG AS WE CAN. YOU GET EVERYONE CLEAR, THEN GET WORD TO DONNIE AND SENSEI.
FREAKIN' ROBOT WIMPS.
WE'LL FOLLOW BEHIND SOON AS WE'RE DONE.
BUT--
DO IT, MIKEY. WE GOT THIS.
GUYS...
NO!
WAIT-- PROFESSOR!
YOUR TURN TO BUY THE PIZZA WHEN WE'RE THROUGH.
YEP. BUT I PICK THE TOPPINGS. HAM, PINEAPPLE, AND JALAPEÑO...
WHAT IS WRONG WITH YOU?!

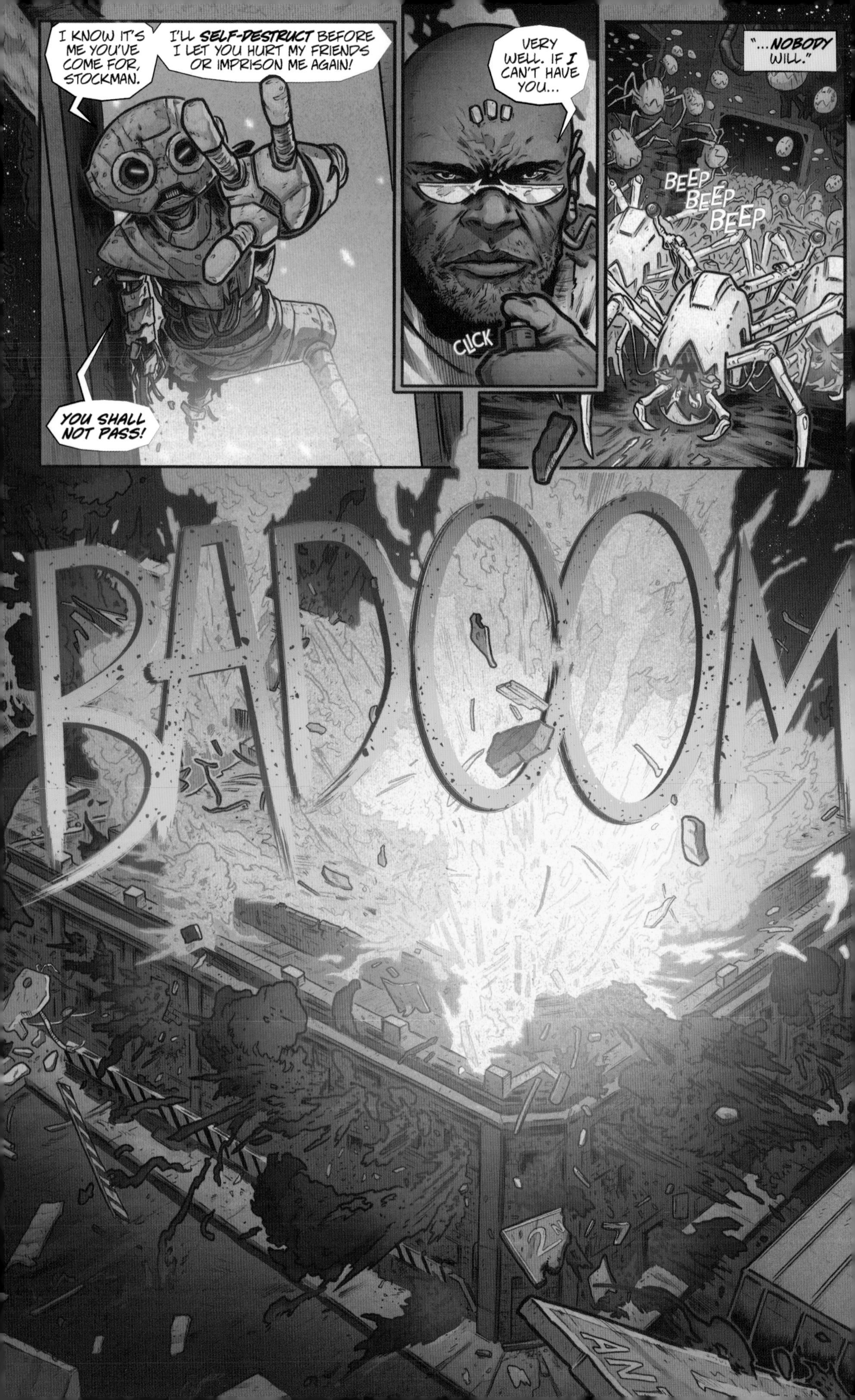
I KNOW IT'S ME YOU'VE COME FOR, STOCKMAN.
I'LL SELF-DESTRUCT BEFORE I LET YOU HURT MY FRIENDS OR IMPRISON ME AGAIN!
YOU SHALL NOT PASS!
VERY WELL. IF I CAN'T HAVE YOU...
CLICK
"...NOBODY WILL."
BEEP BEEP BEEP
BADOOM

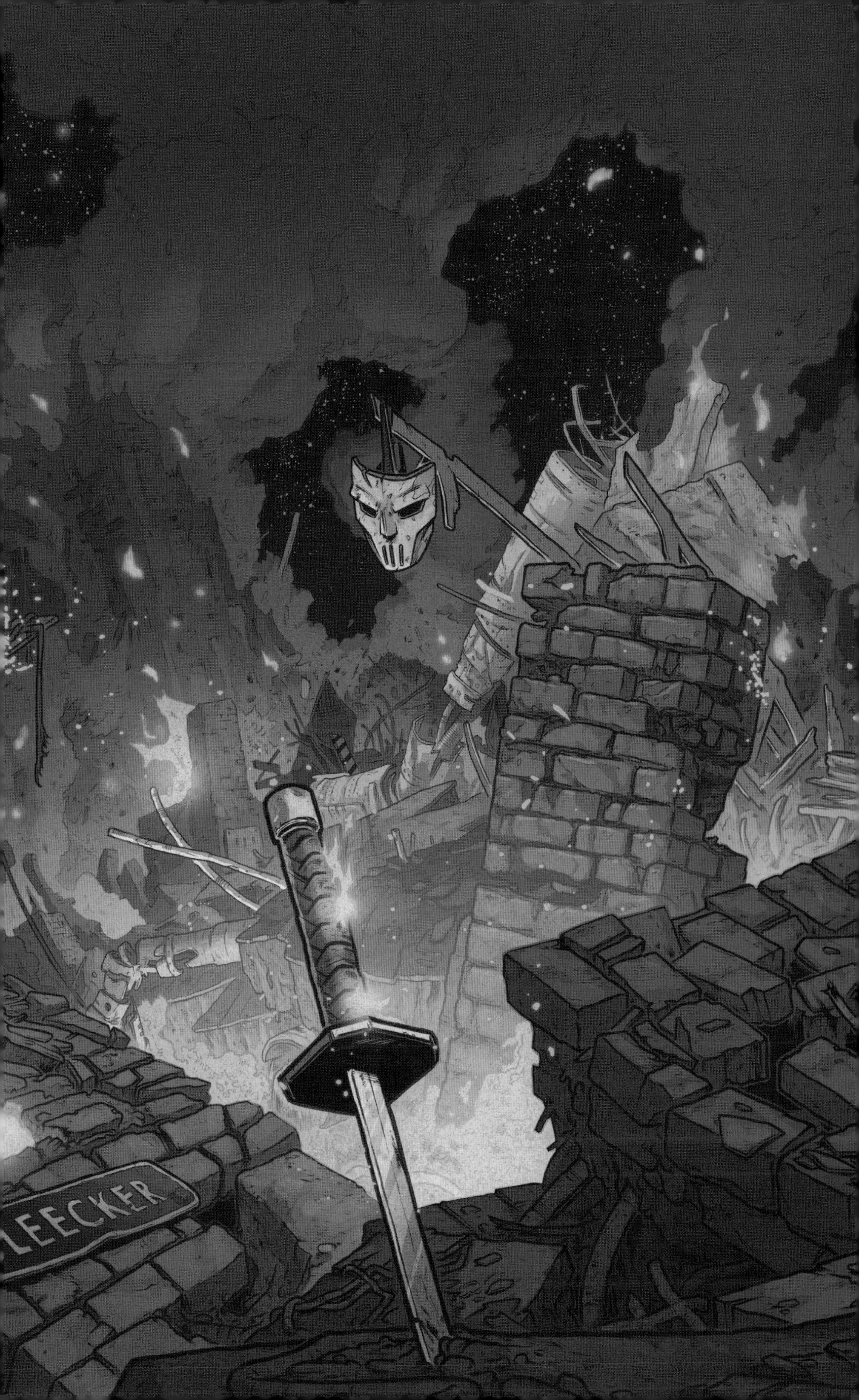
LEECKER

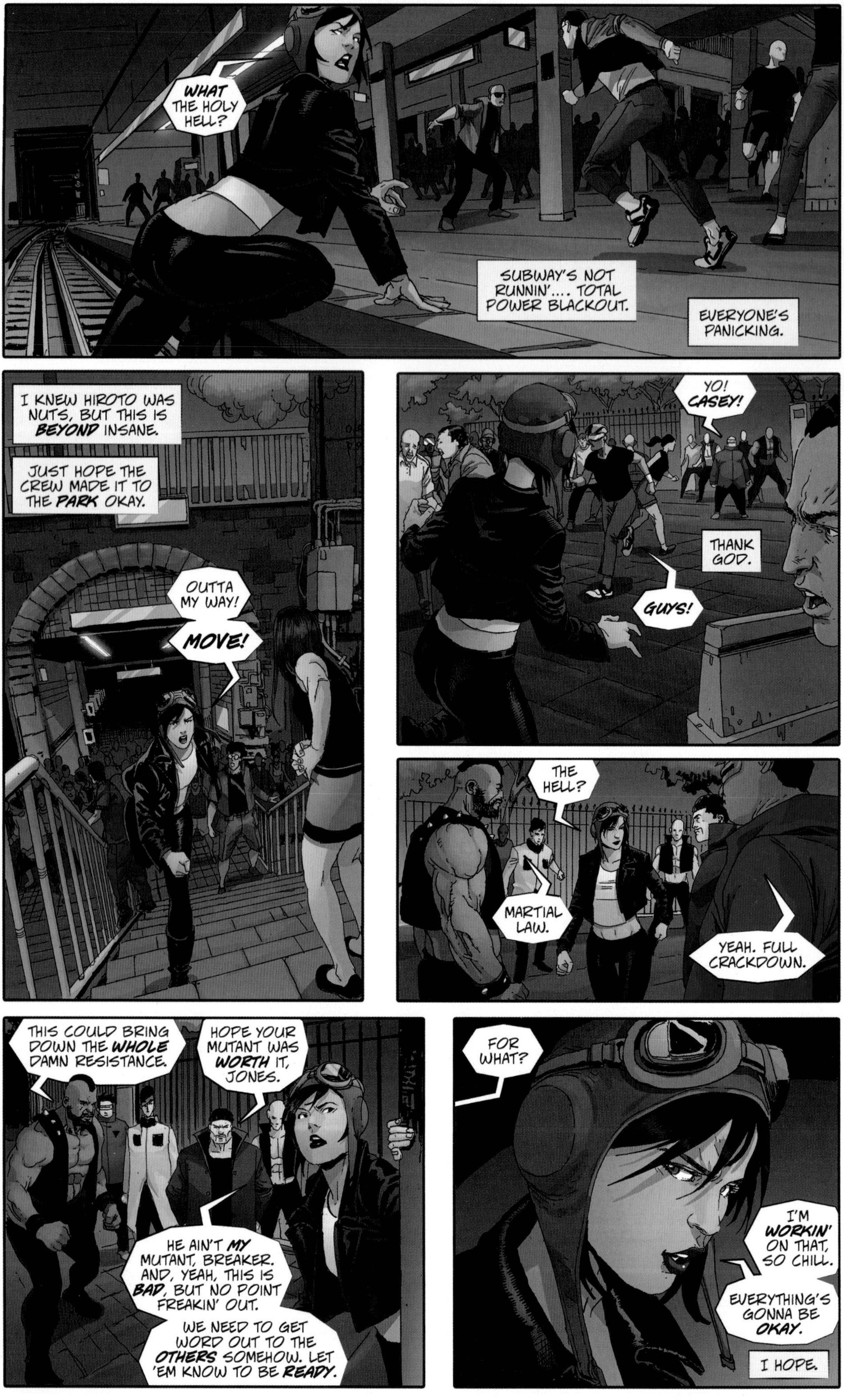
WHAT THE HOLY HELL?
SUBWAY'S NOT RUNNIN'.... TOTAL POWER BLACKOUT.
EVERYONE'S PANICKING.
I KNEW HIROTO WAS NUTS, BUT THIS IS BEYOND INSANE.
JUST HOPE THE CREW MADE IT TO THE PARK OKAY.
OUTTA MY WAY!
MOVE!
YO! CASEY!
THANK GOD.
GUYS!
THE HELL?
MARTIAL LAW.
YEAH. FULL CRACKDOWN.
THIS COULD BRING DOWN THE WHOLE DAMN RESISTANCE.
HOPE YOUR MUTANT WAS WORTH IT, JONES.
HE AIN'T MY MUTANT, BREAKER. AND, YEAH, THIS IS BAD, BUT NO POINT FREAKIN' OUT.
WE NEED TO GET WORD OUT TO THE OTHERS SOMEHOW. LET 'EM KNOW TO BE READY.
FOR WHAT?
I'M WORKIN' ON THAT, SO CHILL.
EVERYTHING'S GONNA BE OKAY.
I HOPE.

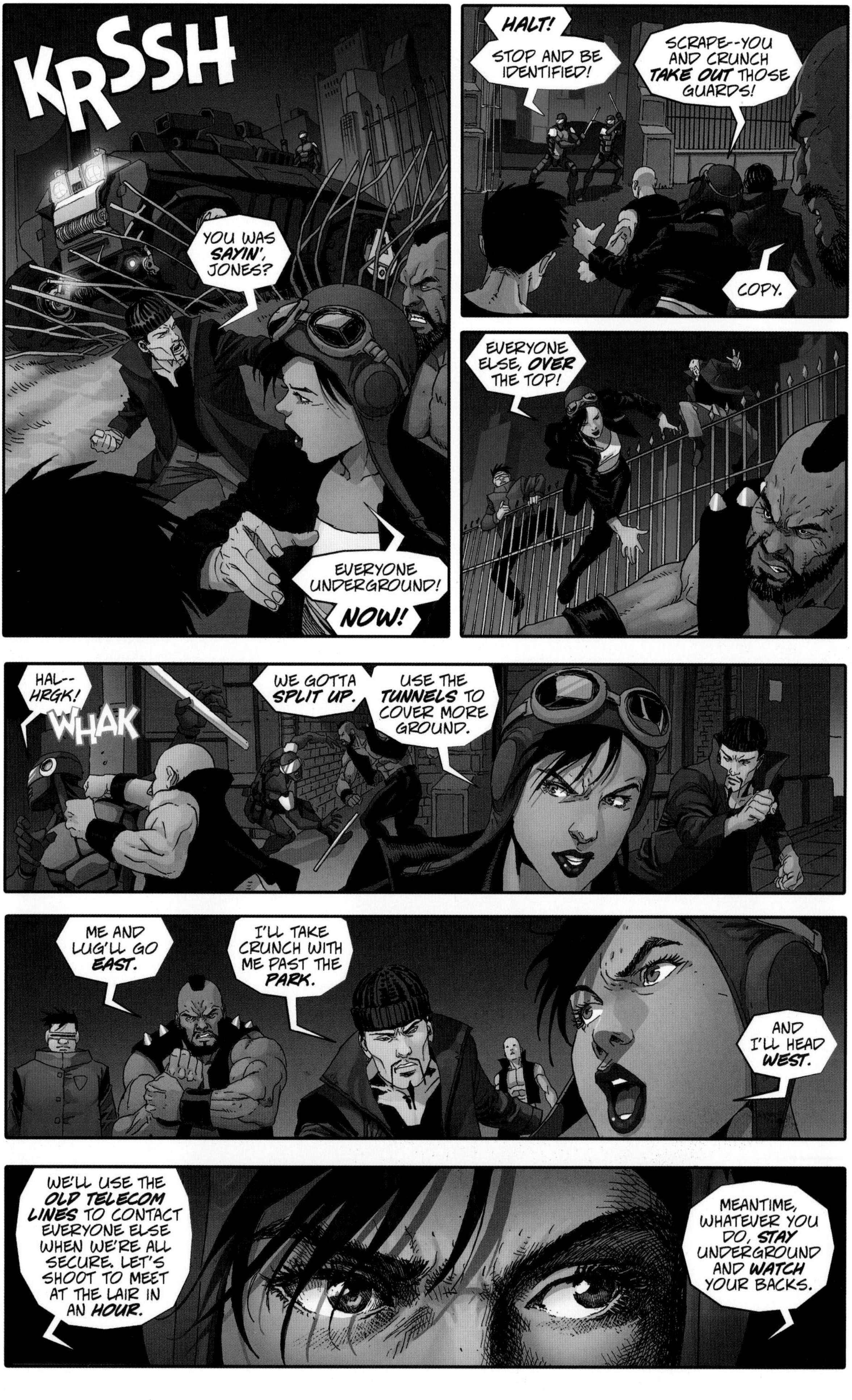
KRSSH
YOU WAS SAYIN', JONES?
EVERYONE UNDERGROUND! NOW!
HALT!
STOP AND BE IDENTIFIED!
SCRAPE--YOU AND CRUNCH TAKE OUT THOSE GUARDS!
COPY.
EVERYONE ELSE, OVER THE TOP!
HAL-- HRGK!
WHAK
WE GOTTA SPLIT UP.
USE THE TUNNELS TO COVER MORE GROUND.
ME AND LUG'LL GO EAST.
I'LL TAKE CRUNCH WITH ME PAST THE PARK.
AND I'LL HEAD WEST.
WE'LL USE THE OLD TELECOM LINES TO CONTACT EVERYONE ELSE WHEN WE'RE ALL SECURE. LET'S SHOOT TO MEET AT THE LAIR IN AN HOUR.
MEANTIME, WHATEVER YOU DO, STAY UNDERGROUND AND WATCH YOUR BACKS.

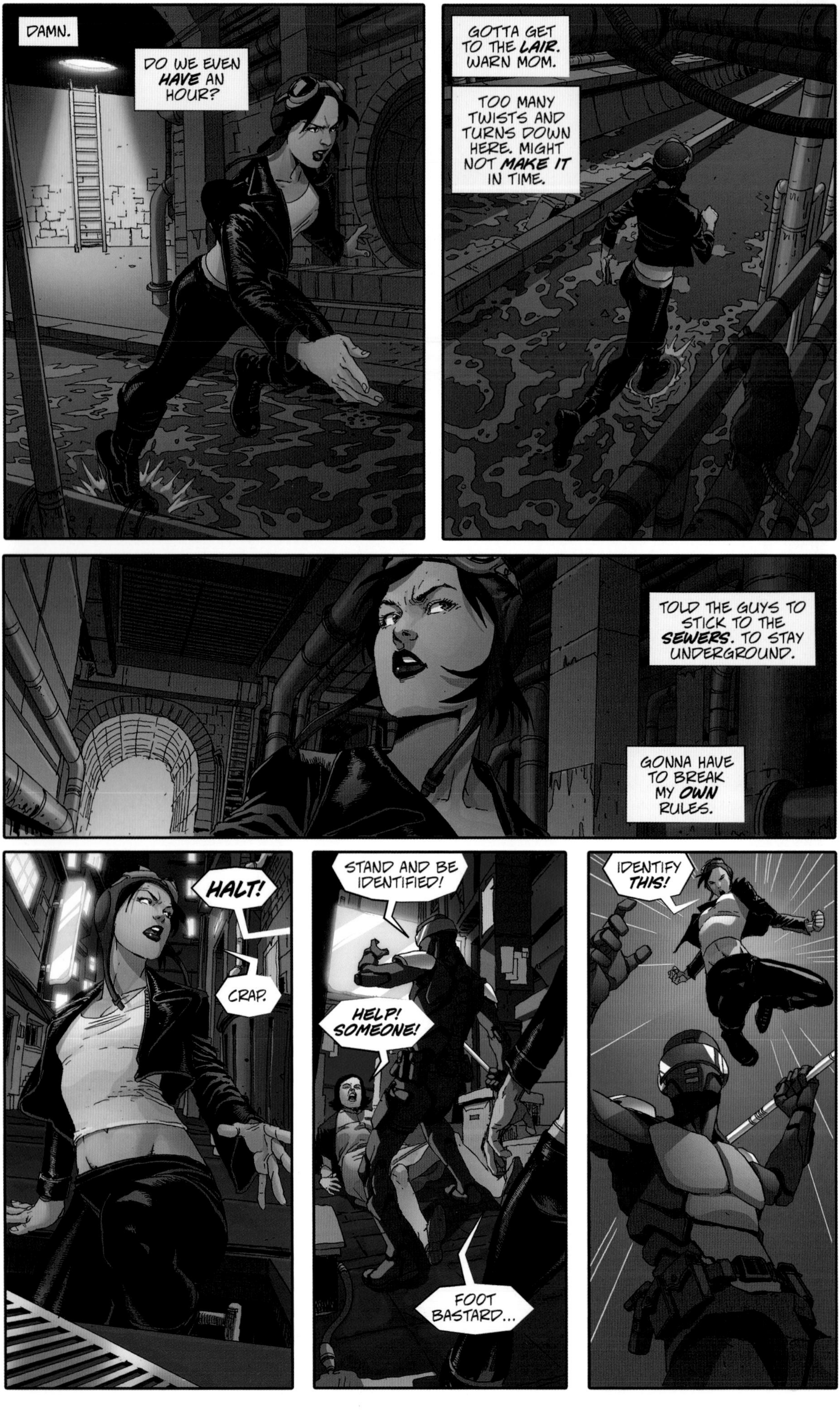
DAMN.
DO WE EVEN HAVE AN HOUR?
GOTTA GET TO THE LAIR. WARN MOM.
TOO MANY TWISTS AND TURNS DOWN HERE. MIGHT NOT MAKE IT IN TIME.
TOLD THE GUYS TO STICK TO THE SEWERS. TO STAY UNDERGROUND.
GONNA HAVE TO BREAK MY OWN RULES.
HALT!
CRAP.
STAND AND BE IDENTIFIED!
HELP! SOMEONE!
FOOT BASTARD...
IDENTIFY THIS!

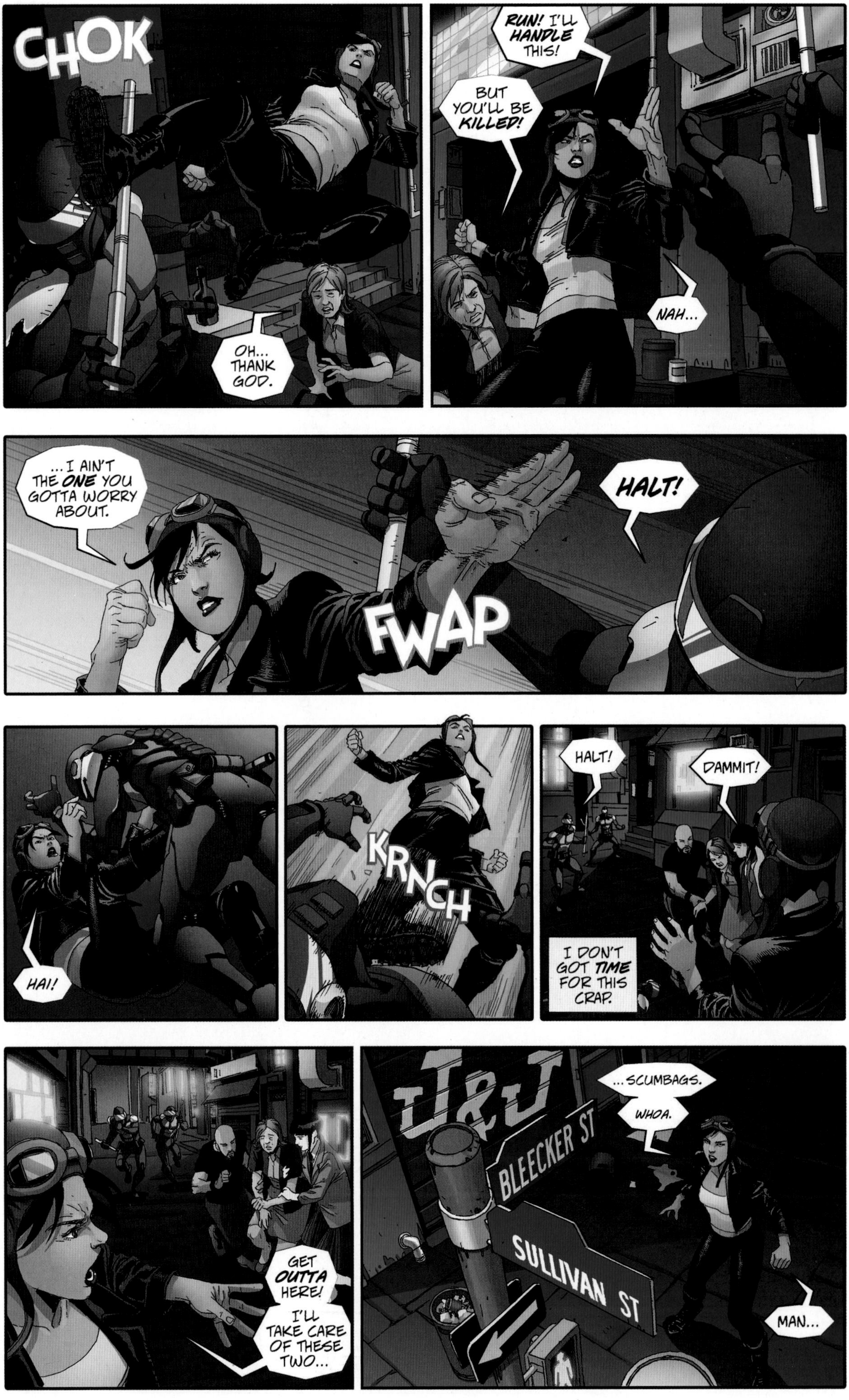
CHOK
OH... THANK GOD.
RUN! I'LL HANDLE THIS!
BUT YOU'LL BE KILLED!
NAH...
...I AIN'T THE ONE YOU GOTTA WORRY ABOUT.
HALT!
FWAP
HAI!
KRNCH
HALT!
DAMMIT!
I DON'T GOT TIME FOR THIS CRAP.
GET OUTTA HERE!
I'LL TAKE CARE OF THESE TWO...
...SCUMBAGS.
WHOA.
BLEECKER ST
SULLIVAN ST
MAN...

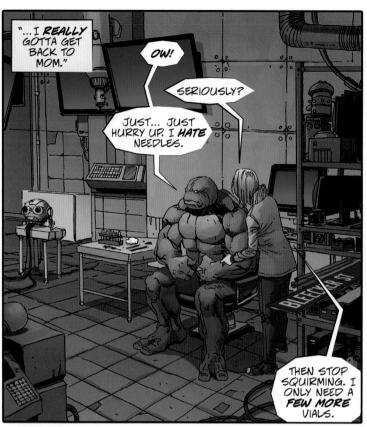

"...I *REALLY* GOTTA GET BACK TO MOM."

OW!

SERIOUSLY?

JUST... JUST HURRY UP. I *HATE* NEEDLES.

THEN STOP SQUIRMING. I ONLY NEED A *FEW MORE* VIALS.

I GET THAT YOU SCIENTISTS CAN'T HELP POKING AND PRODDING EVERYTHING, BUT AM I GONNA HAVE *ANY* BLOOD LEFT AFTER THIS?

WHAT ARE YOU, FIVE YEARS OLD? IT'S BARELY ANY BLOOD.

I NEED TO SEE WHAT YOUR *ADVANCED MUTATION* IS DOING TO YOUR BODY.

BUT I CAN GET YOU A *LOLLIPOP* WHEN I'M DONE IF THAT HELPS.

WHATEVER. JUST HURRY UP.

SO... HOW BADLY DAMAGED *IS* HE?

IS HONEYCUTT STILL *IN* THERE?

I... DON'T KNOW. I THINK SO.

I *HOPE* SO.

IT'S JUST... I'M PRETTY SURE STOCKMAN FOUND US *LAST TIME* BY HACKING THE SECURITY FIREWALLS FUGITOID HAD DEVELOPED TO KEEP US *HIDDEN* DURING THE WAR.

REACTIVATING HIM NOW WOULD BE LIKE BLASTING *ANOTHER* "COME KILL US" SIGNAL TO THE BAD GUYS.

WELL, COME *KILL* THE *REST* OF US, AT LEAST.

APRIL, AFTER THE EXPLOSION... HOW...

HOW'D I END UP *HERE?*

DIDN'T HAPPEN *OVERNIGHT*, THAT'S FOR SURE.

AFTER THE SMOKE CLEARED, A RESCUE TEAM PULLED ME OUT OF THE RUBBLE AND GOT ME TO THE HOSPITAL...

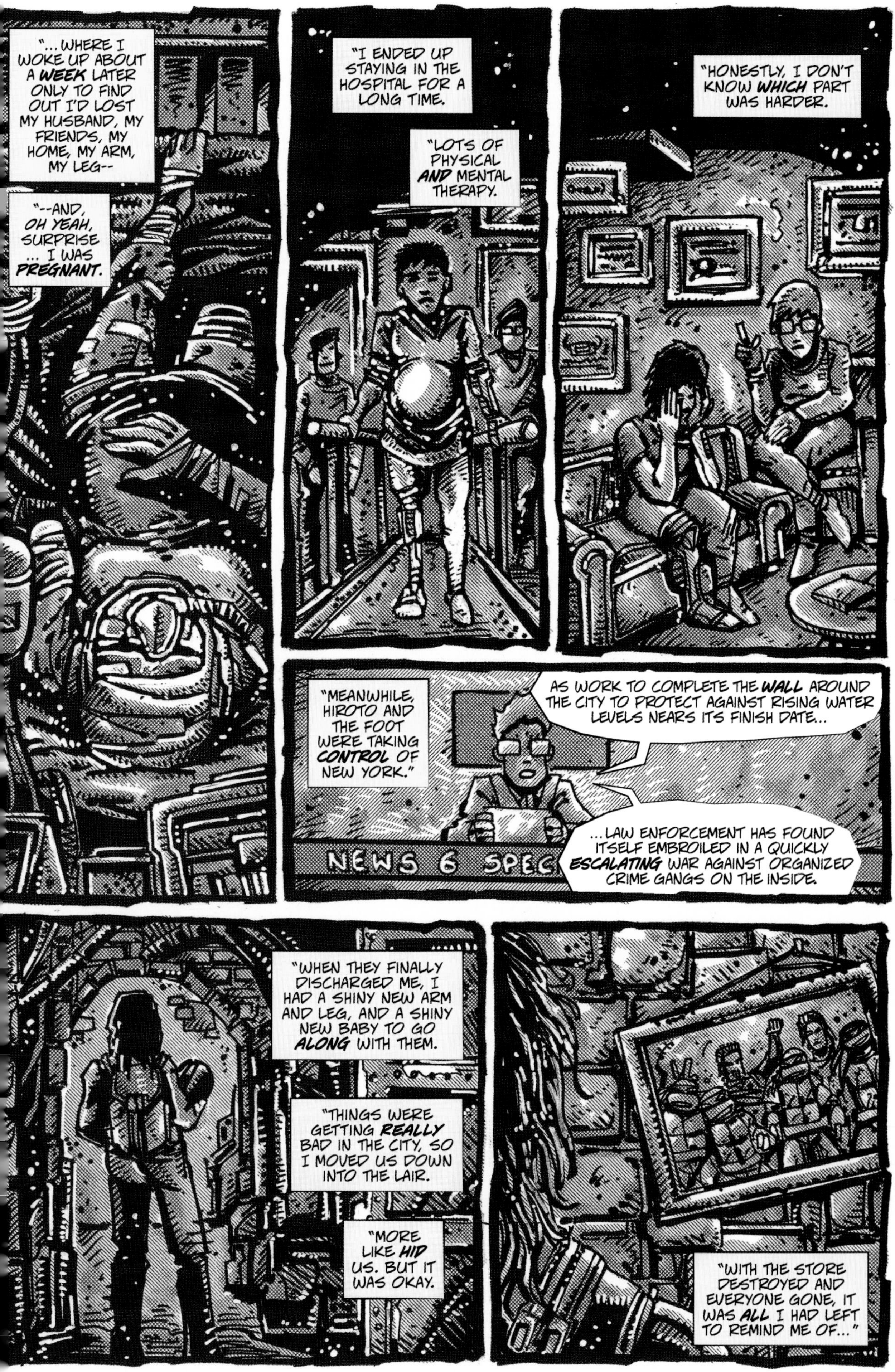
"...WHERE I WOKE UP ABOUT A WEEK LATER ONLY TO FIND OUT I'D LOST MY HUSBAND, MY FRIENDS, MY HOME, MY ARM, MY LEG--
"--AND, OH YEAH, SURPRISE ... I WAS PREGNANT.
"I ENDED UP STAYING IN THE HOSPITAL FOR A LONG TIME.
"LOTS OF PHYSICAL AND MENTAL THERAPY.
"HONESTLY, I DON'T KNOW WHICH PART WAS HARDER.
"MEANWHILE, HIROTO AND THE FOOT WERE TAKING CONTROL OF NEW YORK."
AS WORK TO COMPLETE THE WALL AROUND THE CITY TO PROTECT AGAINST RISING WATER LEVELS NEARS ITS FINISH DATE...
...LAW ENFORCEMENT HAS FOUND ITSELF EMBROILED IN A QUICKLY ESCALATING WAR AGAINST ORGANIZED CRIME GANGS ON THE INSIDE.
NEWS 6 SPEC
"WHEN THEY FINALLY DISCHARGED ME, I HAD A SHINY NEW ARM AND LEG, AND A SHINY NEW BABY TO GO ALONG WITH THEM.
"THINGS WERE GETTING REALLY BAD IN THE CITY, SO I MOVED US DOWN INTO THE LAIR.
"MORE LIKE HID US. BUT IT WAS OKAY.
"WITH THE STORE DESTROYED AND EVERYONE GONE, IT WAS ALL I HAD LEFT TO REMIND ME OF..."

...WELL. YOU KNOW.

OKAY. ALL DONE.

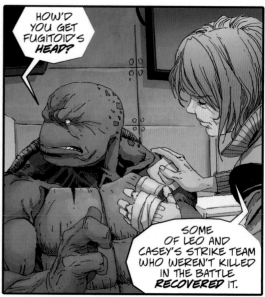

HOW'D YOU GET FUGITOID'S *HEAD?*

SOME OF LEO AND CASEY'S STRIKE TEAM WHO WEREN'T KILLED IN THE BATTLE *RECOVERED* IT.

YEAH?

WHERE ARE *THOSE GUYS* NOW?

MOST OF THEM *DIED* FIGHTING HIROTO'S FORCES WHEN HE TOOK OVER.

THE FEW THAT ARE LEFT ARE COMMANDING UNDERGROUND RESISTANCE UNITS IN *OTHER* PARTS OF THE CITY.

YOU KNOW, CASEY MARIE TOLD ME ABOUT THE TRAINING *YOU* DID IN ASIA AND EUROPE...

...BUT SHE DIDN'T SAY HOW THE HELL YOU *GOT* ALL THE WAY OVER THERE.

IN A *FOG,* MOSTLY.

LAST THING I REMEMBER CLEARLY WAS TRYING TO GET YOU AND THE FUGITOID TO *SAFETY...*

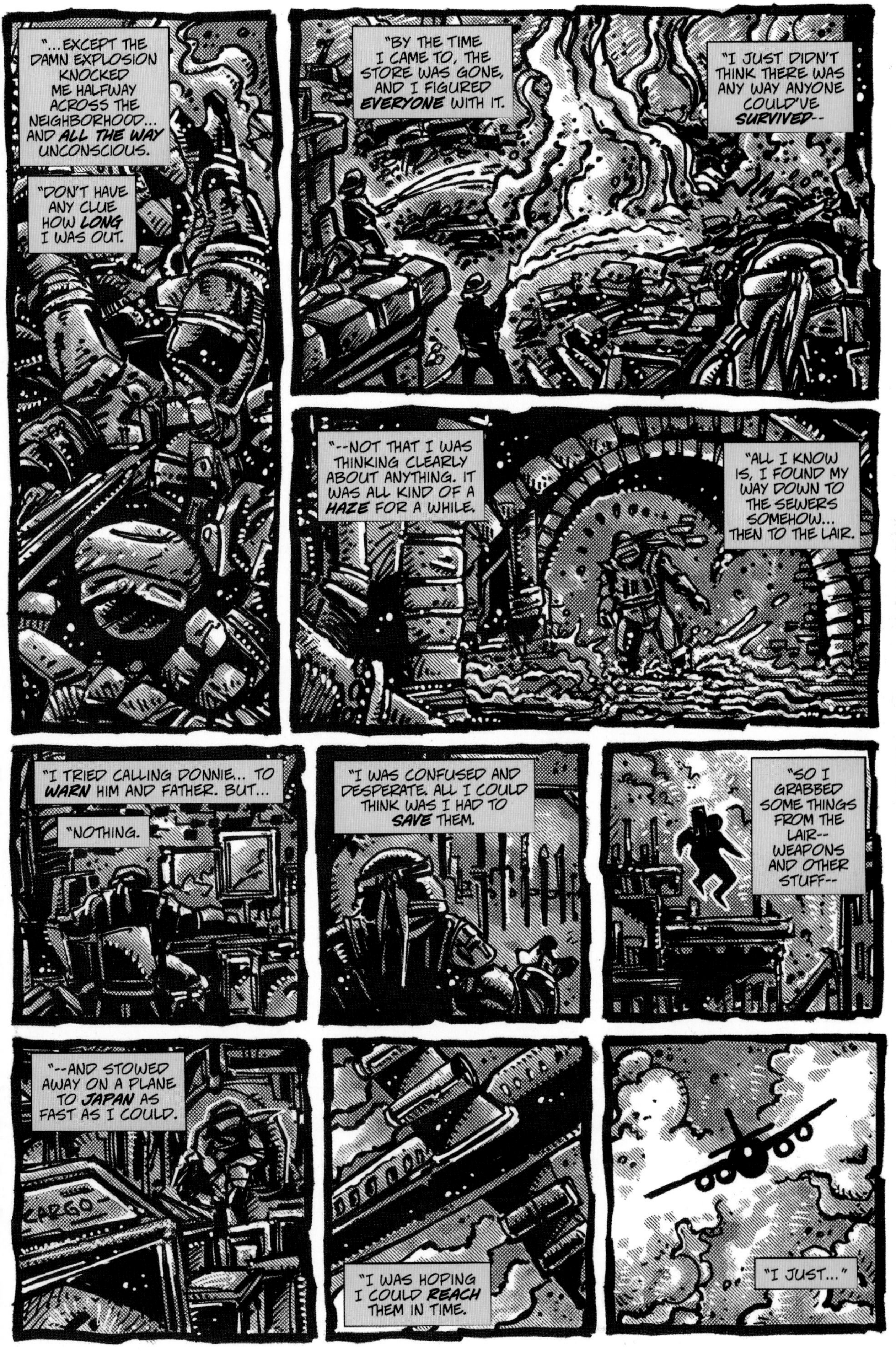
"...EXCEPT THE DAMN EXPLOSION KNOCKED ME HALFWAY ACROSS THE NEIGHBORHOOD... AND ALL THE WAY UNCONSCIOUS.
"DON'T HAVE ANY CLUE HOW LONG I WAS OUT.
"BY THE TIME I CAME TO, THE STORE WAS GONE, AND I FIGURED EVERYONE WITH IT.
"I JUST DIDN'T THINK THERE WAS ANY WAY ANYONE COULD'VE SURVIVED--
"--NOT THAT I WAS THINKING CLEARLY ABOUT ANYTHING. IT WAS ALL KIND OF A HAZE FOR A WHILE.
"ALL I KNOW IS, I FOUND MY WAY DOWN TO THE SEWERS SOMEHOW... THEN TO THE LAIR.
"I TRIED CALLING DONNIE... TO WARN HIM AND FATHER. BUT...
"NOTHING.
"I WAS CONFUSED AND DESPERATE. ALL I COULD THINK WAS I HAD TO SAVE THEM.
"SO I GRABBED SOME THINGS FROM THE LAIR-- WEAPONS AND OTHER STUFF--
"--AND STOWED AWAY ON A PLANE TO JAPAN AS FAST AS I COULD.
CARGO
"I WAS HOPING I COULD REACH THEM IN TIME.
"I JUST..."

...DIDN'T KNOW WHAT *ELSE* TO DO.

I KNOW WHAT YOU'RE THINKING, BUT IT'S NOT *YOUR* FAULT, MIKEY. *NONE* OF IT.

THE COUNSELORS I WORKED WITH CALLED IT *SURVIVOR'S GUILT,* AND I HAD *PLENTY* OF IT AFTER THE EXPLOSION.

IT TOOK A WHILE--LOTS OF THERAPY, LOTS OF TEARS--BUT I FINALLY REALIZED THERE WAS *NOTHING* I COULD'VE DONE TO CHANGE THE THINGS THAT HAPPENED.

BUT THAT DOESN'T MEAN I HAVE TO ACCEPT WHAT'S HAPPENING *NOW.*

NONE OF *US* DO.

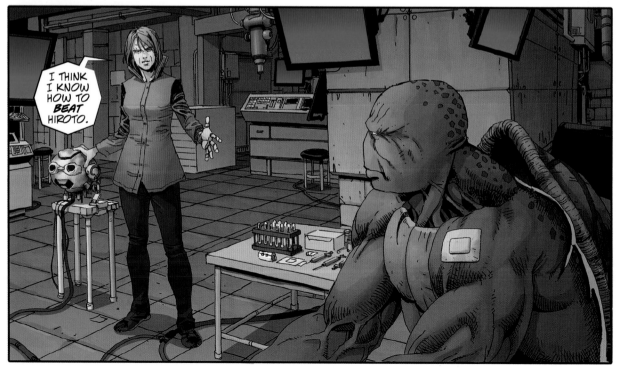

I THINK I KNOW HOW TO *BEAT* HIROTO.

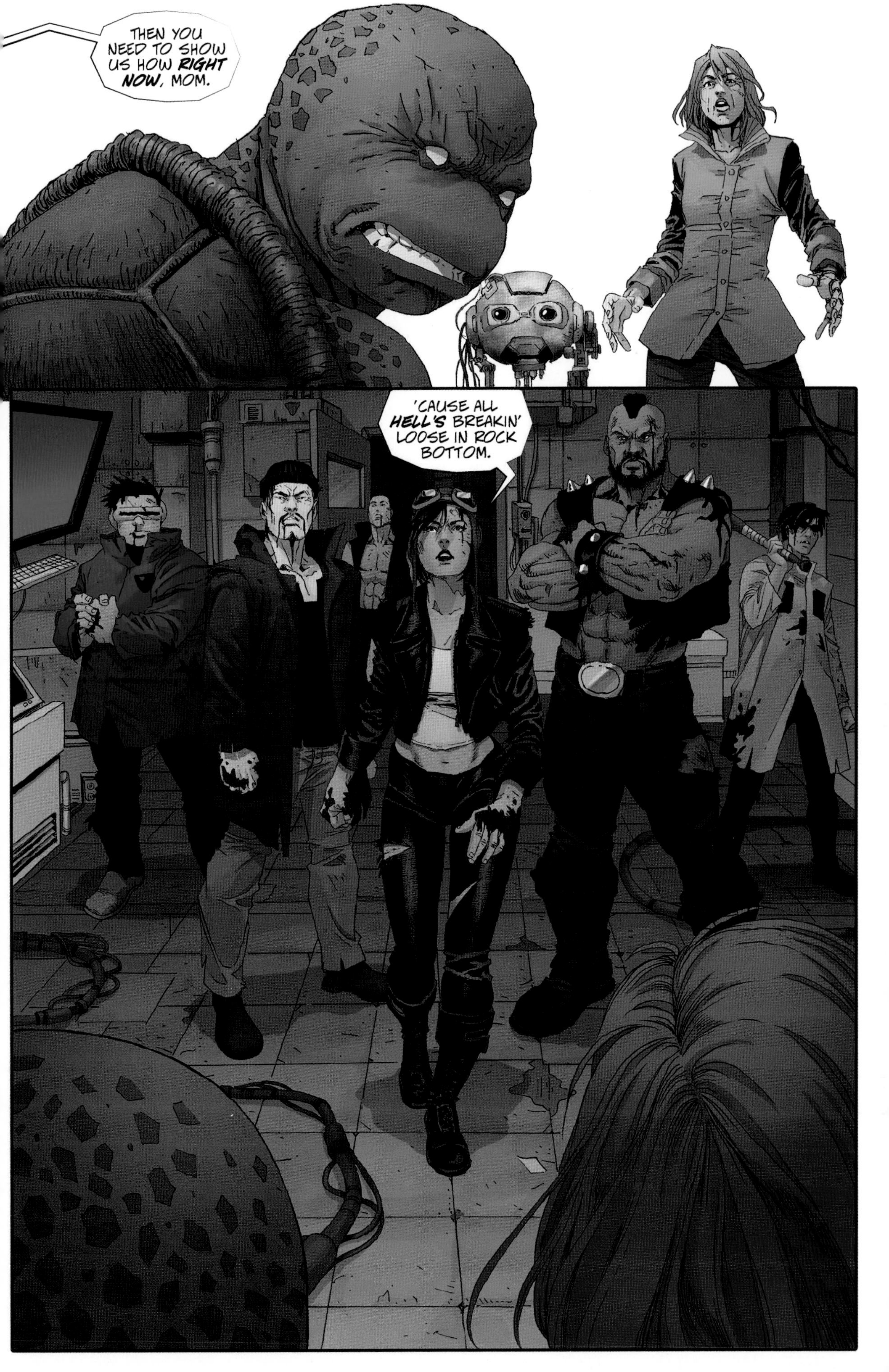
THEN YOU NEED TO SHOW US HOW RIGHT NOW, MOM.
'CAUSE ALL HELL'S BREAKIN' LOOSE IN ROCK BOTTOM.

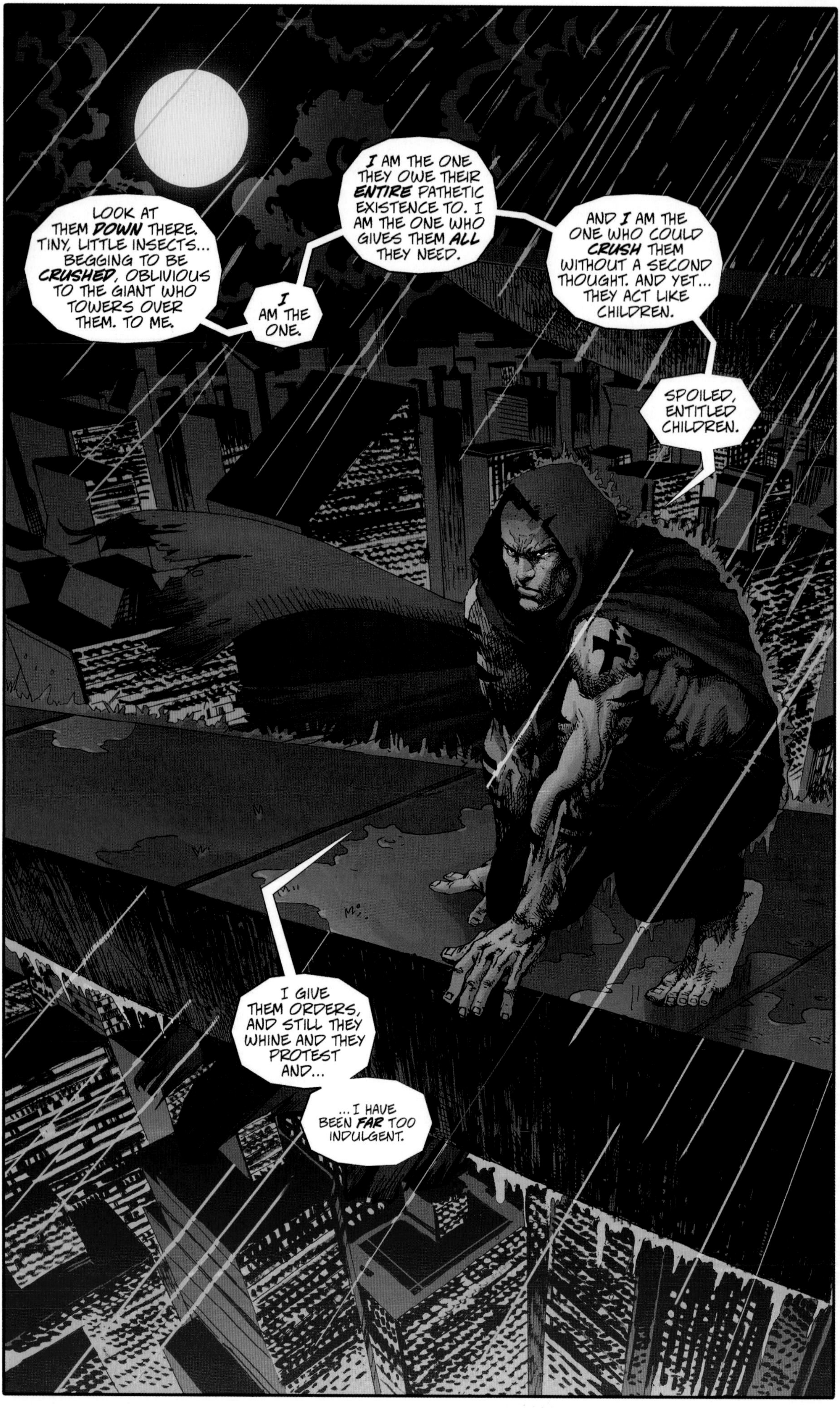
LOOK AT THEM DOWN THERE. TINY, LITTLE INSECTS... BEGGING TO BE CRUSHED, OBLIVIOUS TO THE GIANT WHO TOWERS OVER THEM. TO ME.
I AM THE ONE.
I AM THE ONE THEY OWE THEIR ENTIRE PATHETIC EXISTENCE TO. I AM THE ONE WHO GIVES THEM ALL THEY NEED.
AND I AM THE ONE WHO COULD CRUSH THEM WITHOUT A SECOND THOUGHT. AND YET... THEY ACT LIKE CHILDREN.
SPOILED, ENTITLED CHILDREN.
I GIVE THEM ORDERS, AND STILL THEY WHINE AND THEY PROTEST AND...
...I HAVE BEEN FAR TOO INDULGENT.

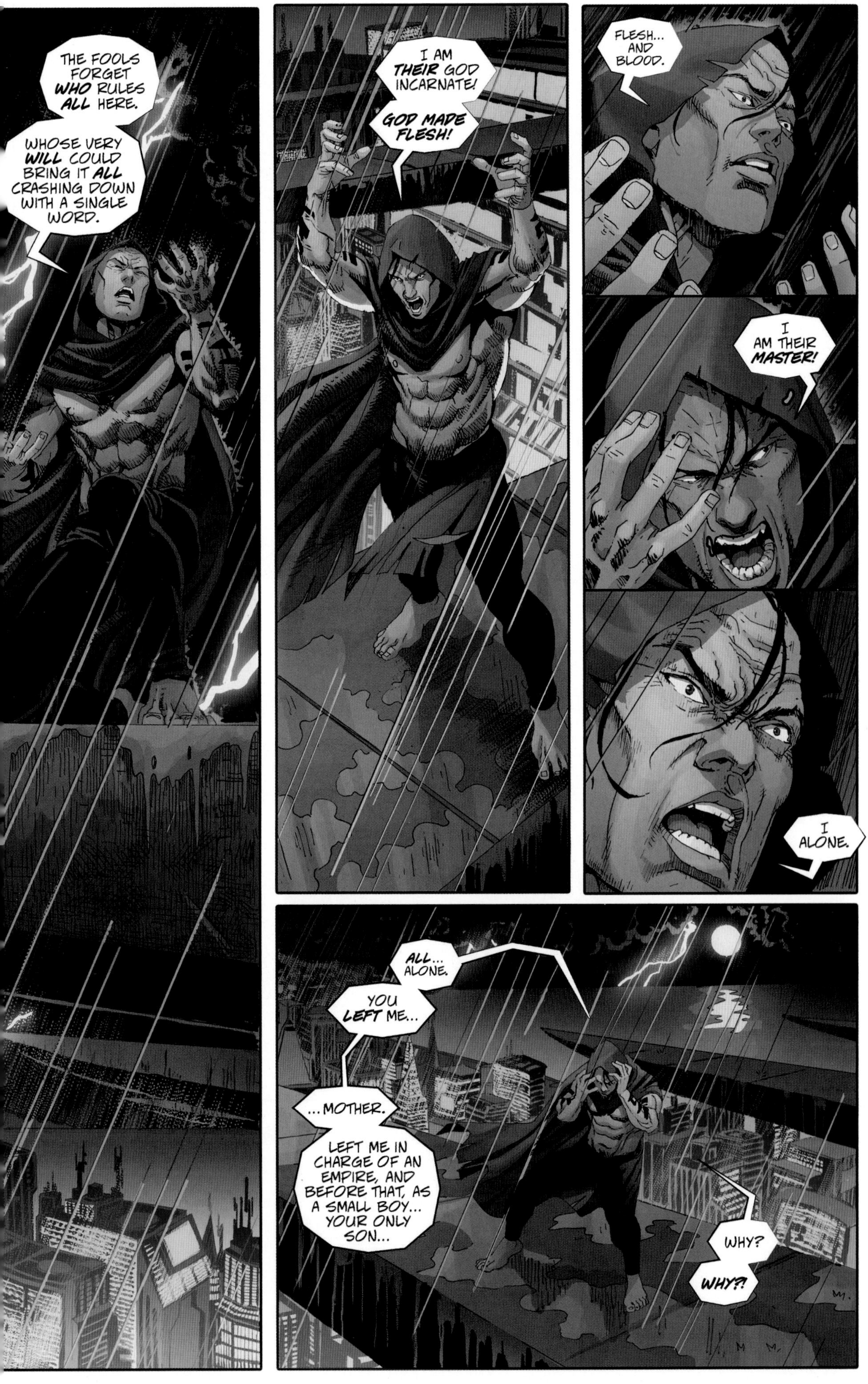
THE FOOLS FORGET **WHO** RULES **ALL** HERE.
WHOSE VERY **WILL** COULD BRING IT **ALL** CRASHING DOWN WITH A SINGLE WORD.
I AM **THEIR** GOD INCARNATE!
GOD MADE FLESH!
FLESH... AND BLOOD.
I AM THEIR **MASTER!**
I ALONE.
ALL... ALONE.
YOU **LEFT** ME...
...MOTHER.
LEFT ME IN CHARGE OF AN EMPIRE, AND BEFORE THAT, AS A SMALL BOY... YOUR ONLY SON...
WHY?
WHY?!

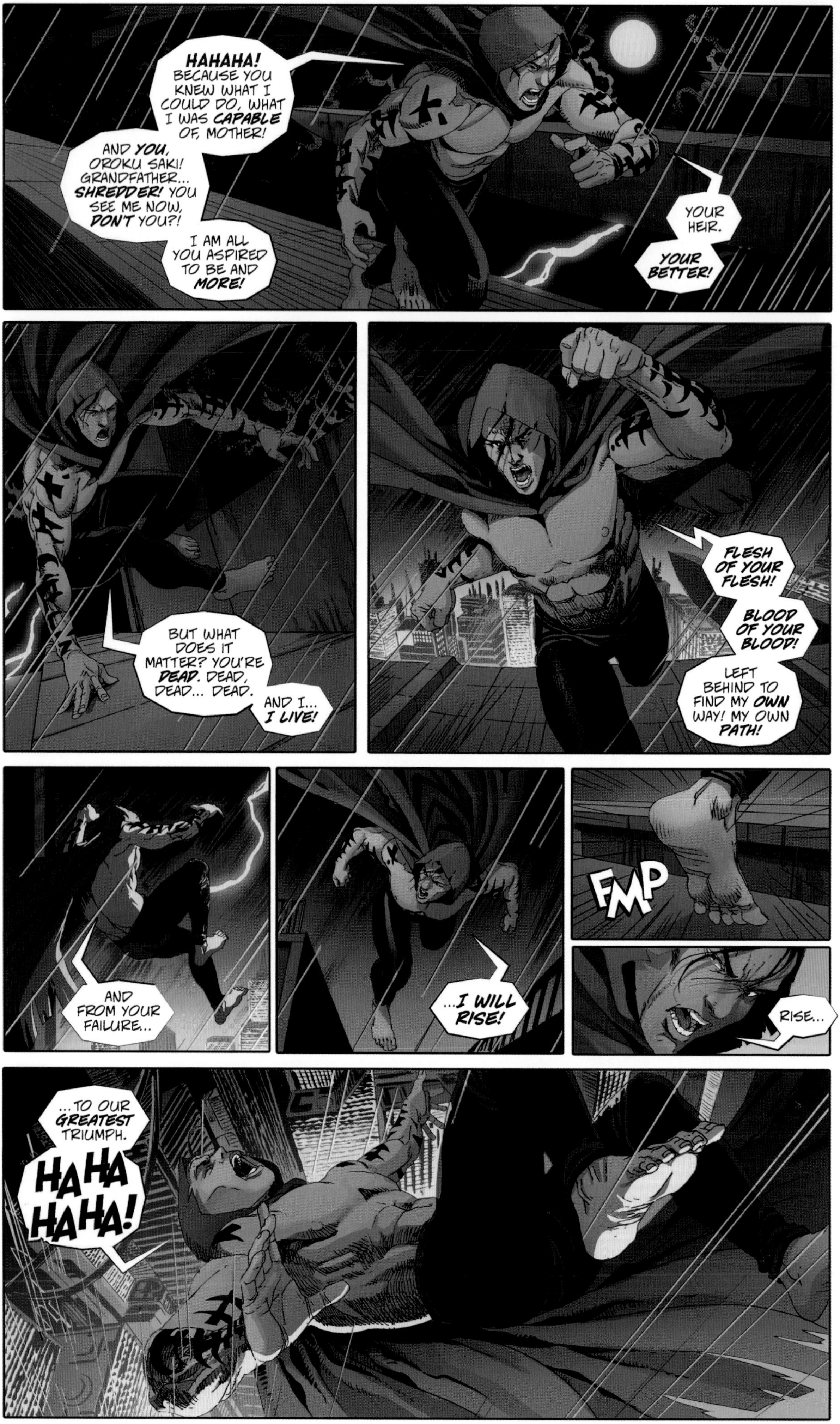
HAHAHA! BECAUSE YOU KNEW WHAT I COULD DO, WHAT I WAS CAPABLE OF, MOTHER!
AND YOU, OROKU SAKI! GRANDFATHER... SHREDDER! YOU SEE ME NOW, DON'T YOU?!
I AM ALL YOU ASPIRED TO BE AND MORE!
YOUR HEIR.
YOUR BETTER!
BUT WHAT DOES IT MATTER? YOU'RE DEAD. DEAD, DEAD... DEAD.
AND I... I LIVE!
FLESH OF YOUR FLESH!
BLOOD OF YOUR BLOOD!
LEFT BEHIND TO FIND MY OWN WAY! MY OWN PATH!
AND FROM YOUR FAILURE...
...I WILL RISE!
FMP
RISE...
...TO OUR GREATEST TRIUMPH.
HAHA HAHA!

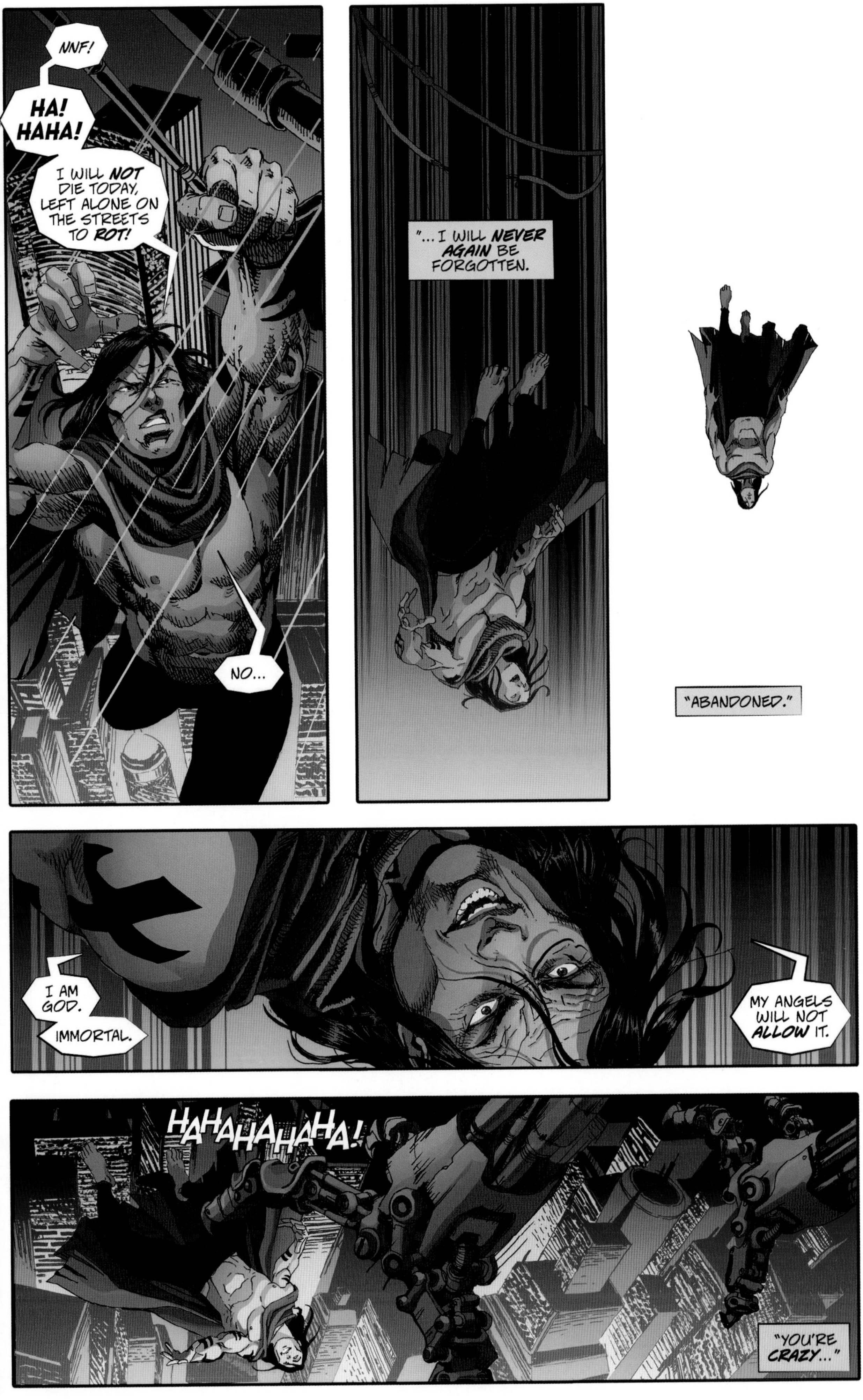
NNF!
HA! HAHA!
I WILL NOT DIE TODAY, LEFT ALONE ON THE STREETS TO ROT!
NO...
"...I WILL NEVER AGAIN BE FORGOTTEN.
"ABANDONED."
I AM GOD.
IMMORTAL.
MY ANGELS WILL NOT ALLOW IT.
HAHAHAHAHAHA!
"YOU'RE CRAZY..."

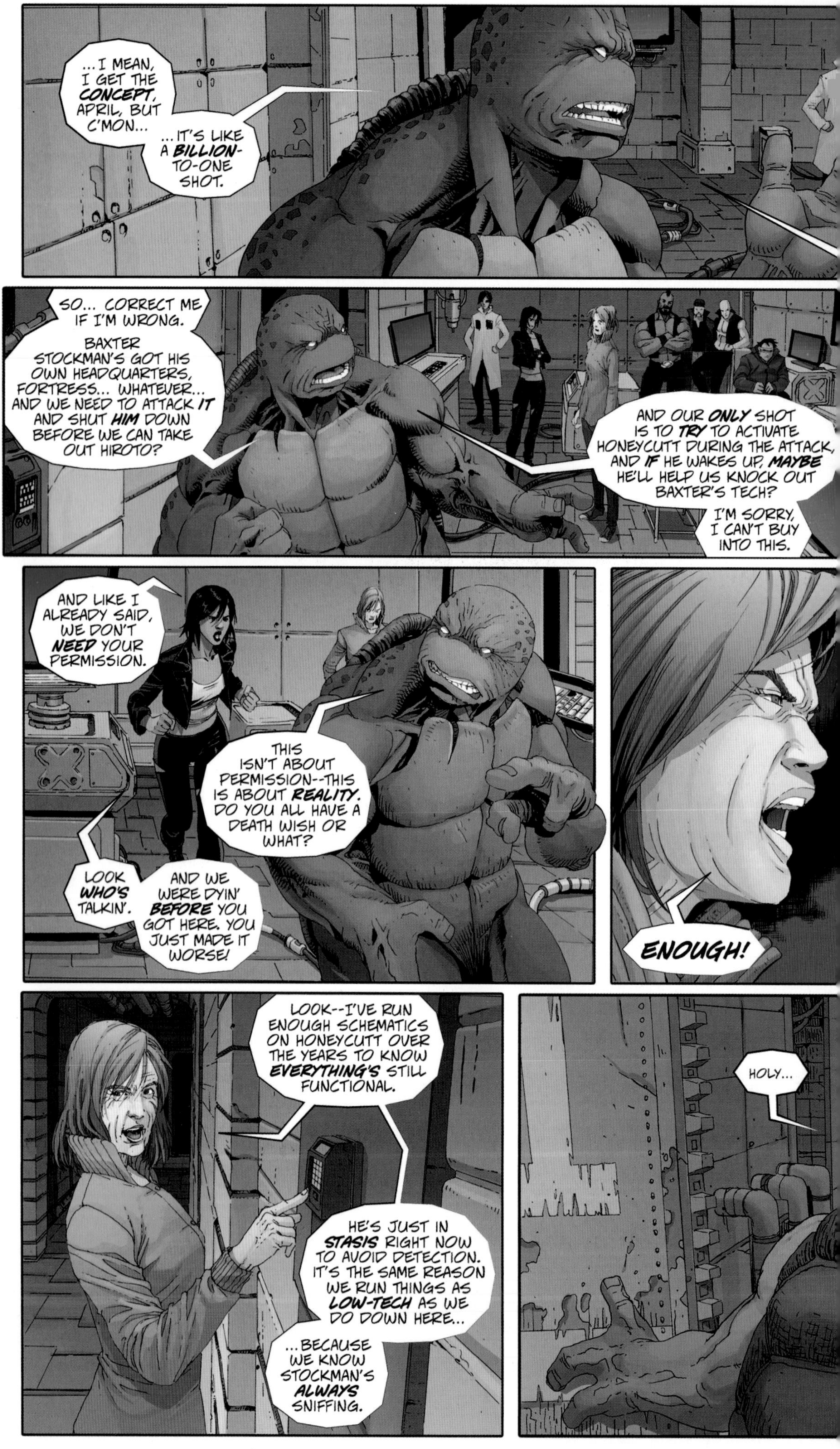
...I MEAN, I GET THE CONCEPT, APRIL, BUT C'MON...
...IT'S LIKE A BILLION-TO-ONE SHOT.
SO... CORRECT ME IF I'M WRONG.
BAXTER STOCKMAN'S GOT HIS OWN HEADQUARTERS, FORTRESS... WHATEVER... AND WE NEED TO ATTACK IT AND SHUT HIM DOWN BEFORE WE CAN TAKE OUT HIROTO?
AND OUR ONLY SHOT IS TO TRY TO ACTIVATE HONEYCUTT DURING THE ATTACK, AND IF HE WAKES UP, MAYBE HE'LL HELP US KNOCK OUT BAXTER'S TECH?
I'M SORRY, I CAN'T BUY INTO THIS.
AND LIKE I ALREADY SAID, WE DON'T NEED YOUR PERMISSION.
THIS ISN'T ABOUT PERMISSION--THIS IS ABOUT REALITY. DO YOU ALL HAVE A DEATH WISH OR WHAT?
LOOK WHO'S TALKIN'.
AND WE WERE DYIN' BEFORE YOU GOT HERE. YOU JUST MADE IT WORSE!
ENOUGH!
LOOK--I'VE RUN ENOUGH SCHEMATICS ON HONEYCUTT OVER THE YEARS TO KNOW EVERYTHING'S STILL FUNCTIONAL.
HE'S JUST IN STASIS RIGHT NOW TO AVOID DETECTION. IT'S THE SAME REASON WE RUN THINGS AS LOW-TECH AS WE DO DOWN HERE...
...BECAUSE WE KNOW STOCKMAN'S ALWAYS SNIFFING.
HOLY...

MORE LIKE OUR **ONLY** SHOT, MIKEY.

WITH **WAY** TOO MANY VARIABLES, TOO MANY MOVING PARTS... TOO MANY LIVES LOST.

EVERY PLAN, NO MATTER THE ODDS, HAS RISKS. YOU **KNOW** THAT.

AT LEAST THESE ARE BETTER ODDS THAN A 100-YEAR-OLD MUTANT ATTACKIN' HIROTO **DIRECTLY.**

COME WITH ME, MIKEY. THERE'S SOMETHING **ELSE** YOU NEED TO SEE.

APRIL, THEY'RE JUST KIDS. YOU NEED TO LET ME DO MY **OWN** THING.

JUST HUMOR ME, OKAY?

FINE.

BUT I **WON'T** CHANGE MY MIND.

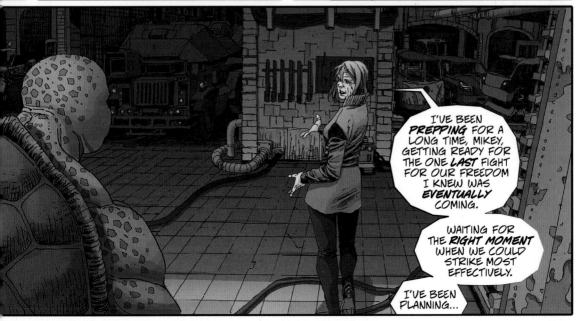

I'VE BEEN **PREPPING** FOR A LONG TIME, MIKEY, GETTING READY FOR THE ONE **LAST** FIGHT FOR OUR FREEDOM I KNEW WAS **EVENTUALLY** COMING.

WAITING FOR THE **RIGHT MOMENT** WHEN WE COULD STRIKE MOST EFFECTIVELY.

I'VE BEEN PLANNING...

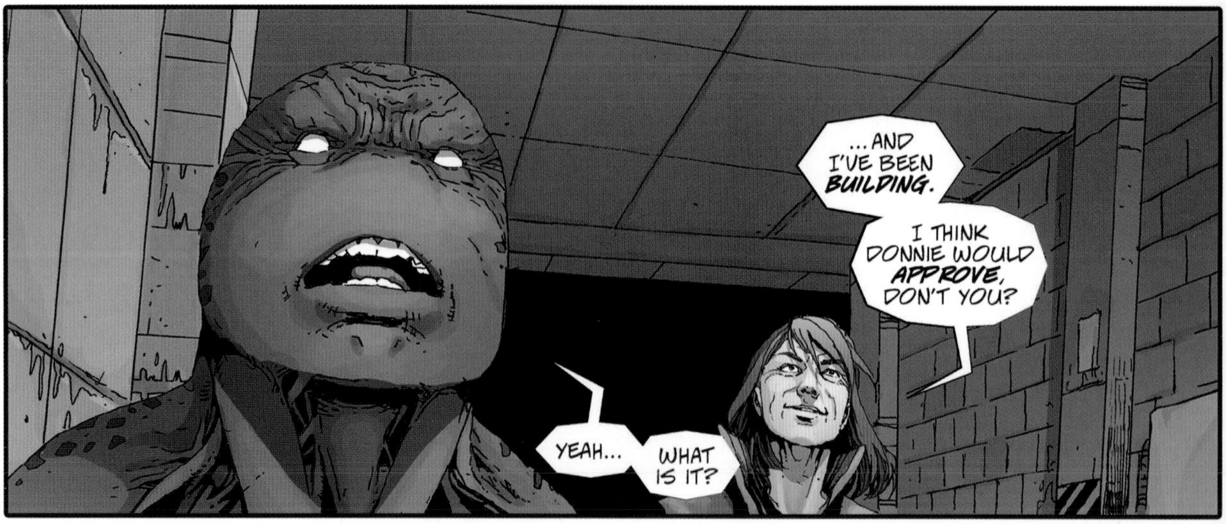
...AND I'VE BEEN **BUILDING**.
I THINK DONNIE WOULD **APPROVE**, DON'T YOU?
YEAH...
WHAT IS IT?

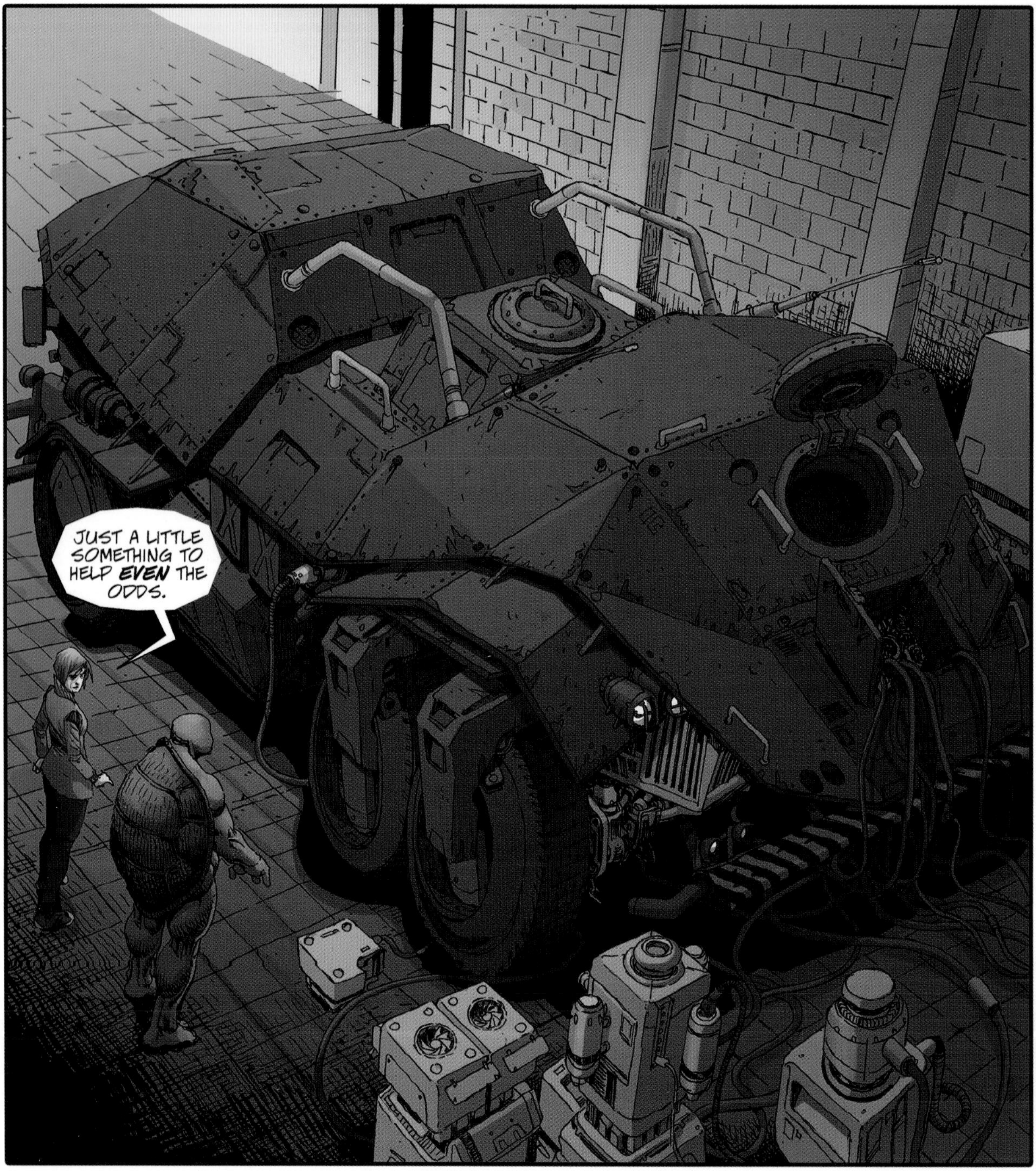
JUST A LITTLE SOMETHING TO HELP **EVEN** THE ODDS.

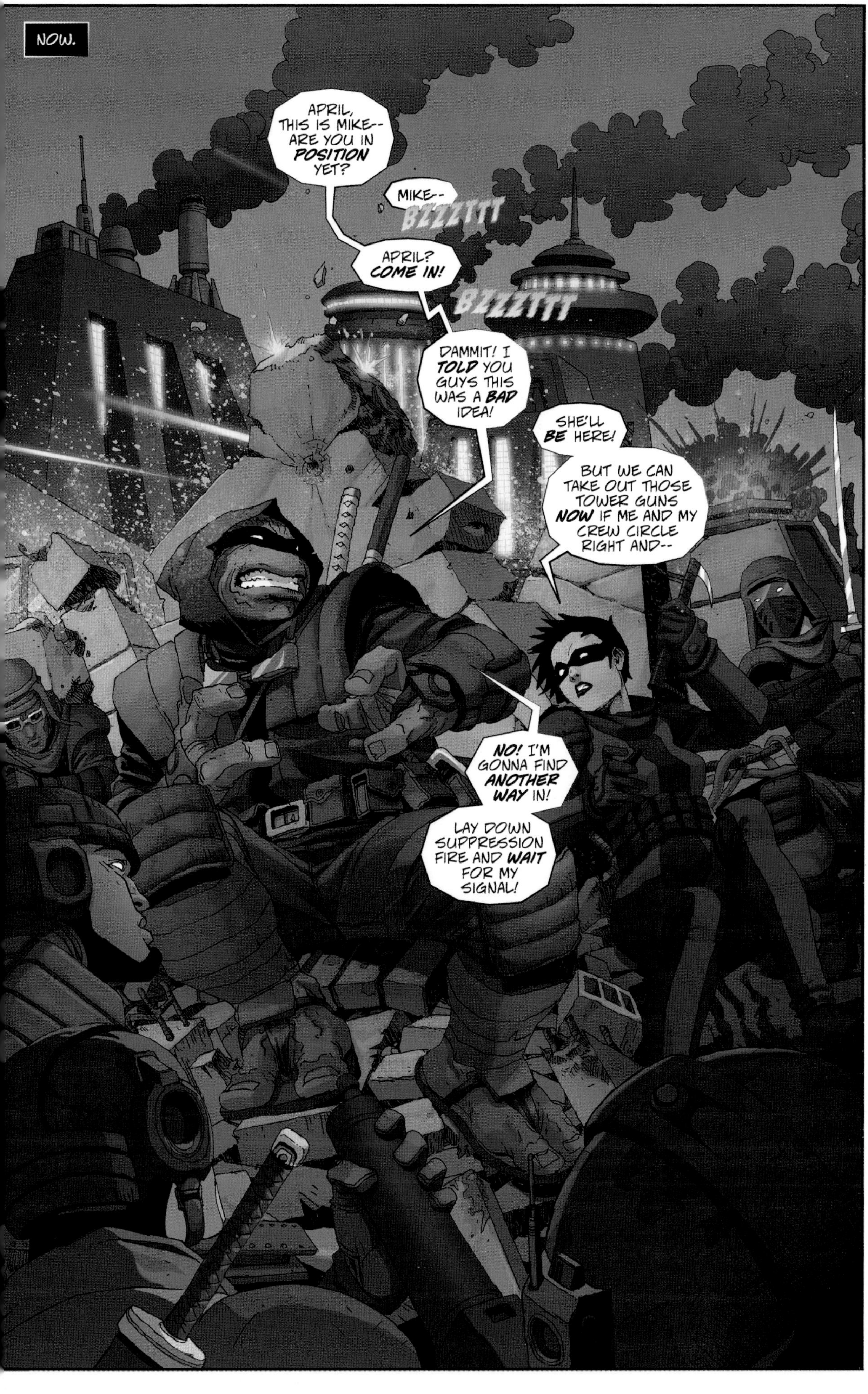
NOW.
APRIL, THIS IS MIKE--ARE YOU IN POSITION YET?
MIKE--
BZZZTTT
APRIL? COME IN!
BZZZTTT
DAMMIT! I TOLD YOU GUYS THIS WAS A BAD IDEA!
SHE'LL BE HERE!
BUT WE CAN TAKE OUT THOSE TOWER GUNS NOW IF ME AND MY CREW CIRCLE RIGHT AND--
NO! I'M GONNA FIND ANOTHER WAY IN!
LAY DOWN SUPPRESSION FIRE AND WAIT FOR MY SIGNAL!

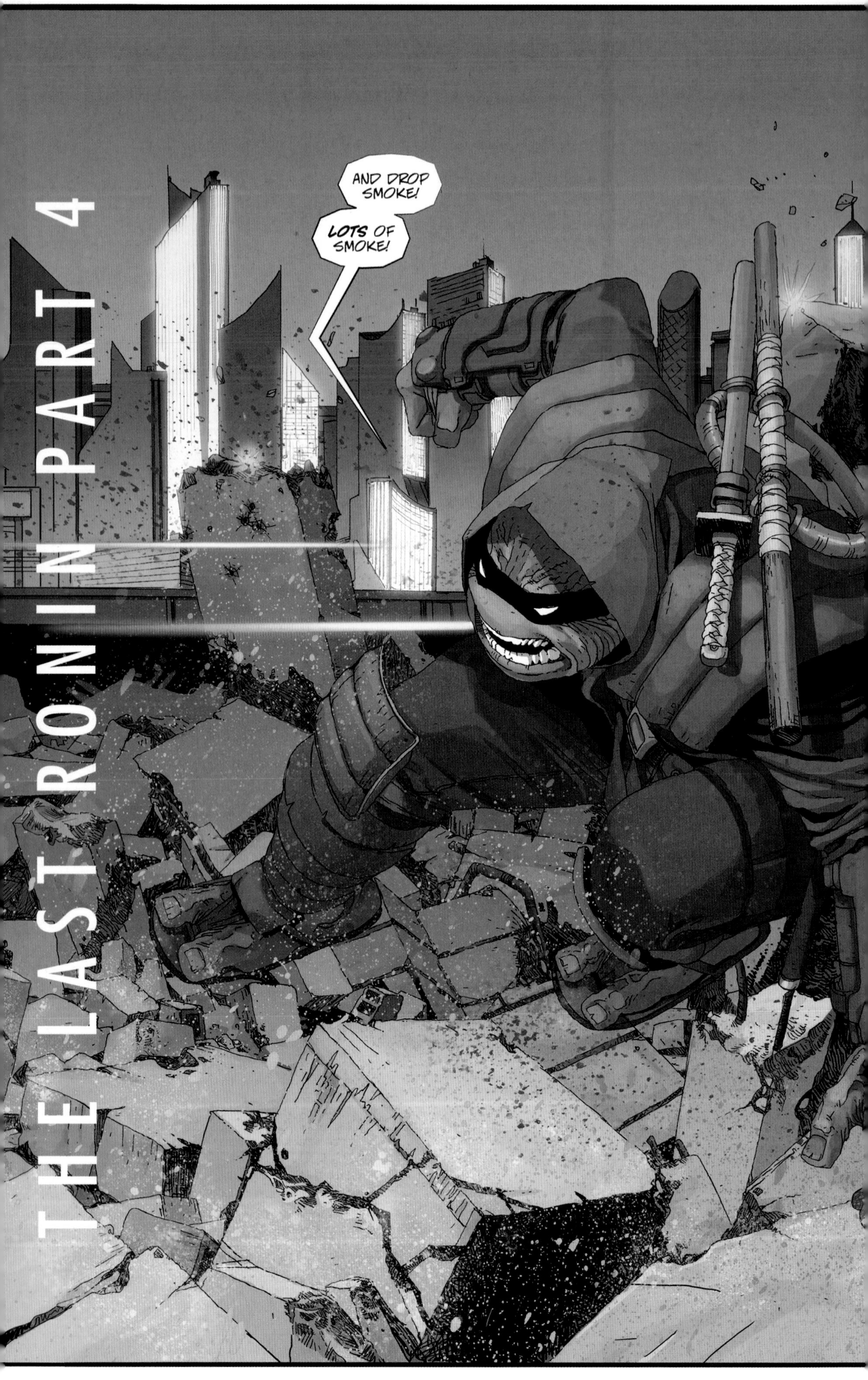
THE LAST RONIN PART 4
AND DROP SMOKE!
LOTS OF SMOKE!

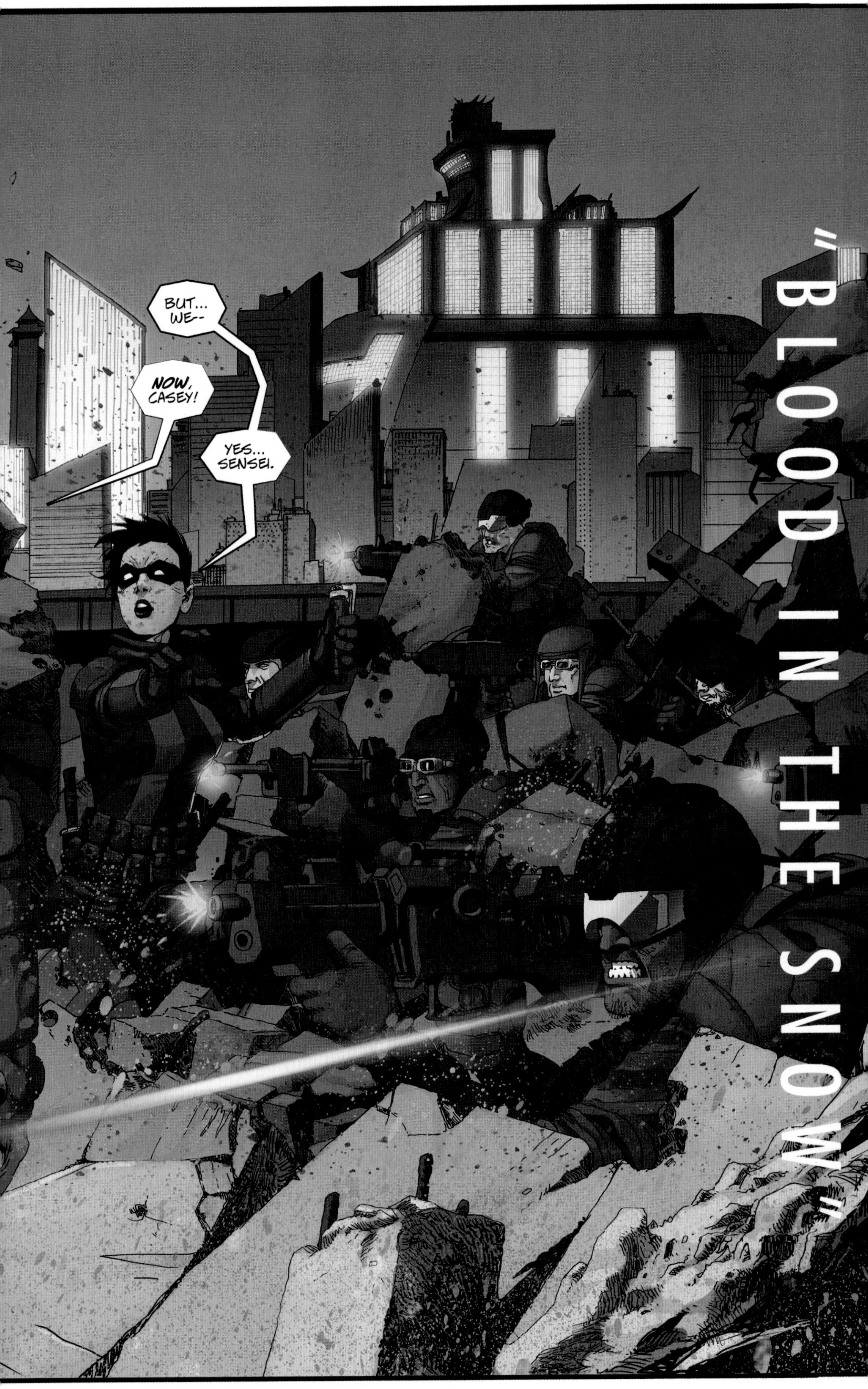
"BLOOD IN THE SNOW"
BUT... WE--
NOW, CASEY!
YES... SENSEI.

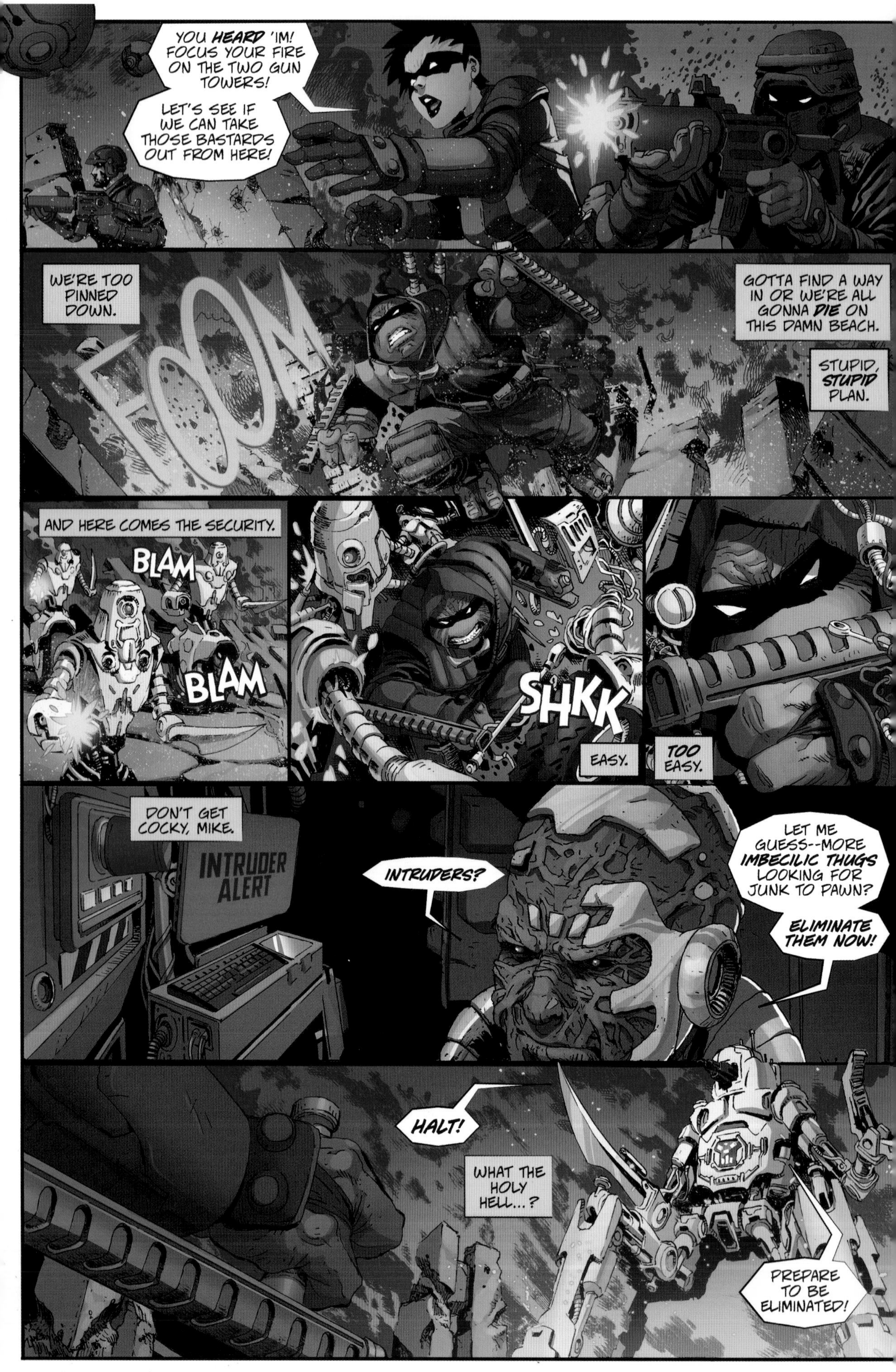
YOU HEARD 'IM! FOCUS YOUR FIRE ON THE TWO GUN TOWERS!
LET'S SEE IF WE CAN TAKE THOSE BASTARDS OUT FROM HERE!
WE'RE TOO PINNED DOWN.
FOOM
GOTTA FIND A WAY IN OR WE'RE ALL GONNA DIE ON THIS DAMN BEACH.
STUPID, STUPID PLAN.
AND HERE COMES THE SECURITY.
BLAM
BLAM
SHKK
EASY.
TOO EASY.
DON'T GET COCKY, MIKE.
INTRUDER ALERT
INTRUDERS?
LET ME GUESS--MORE IMBECILIC THUGS LOOKING FOR JUNK TO PAWN?
ELIMINATE THEM NOW!
HALT!
WHAT THE HOLY HELL...?
PREPARE TO BE ELIMINATED!

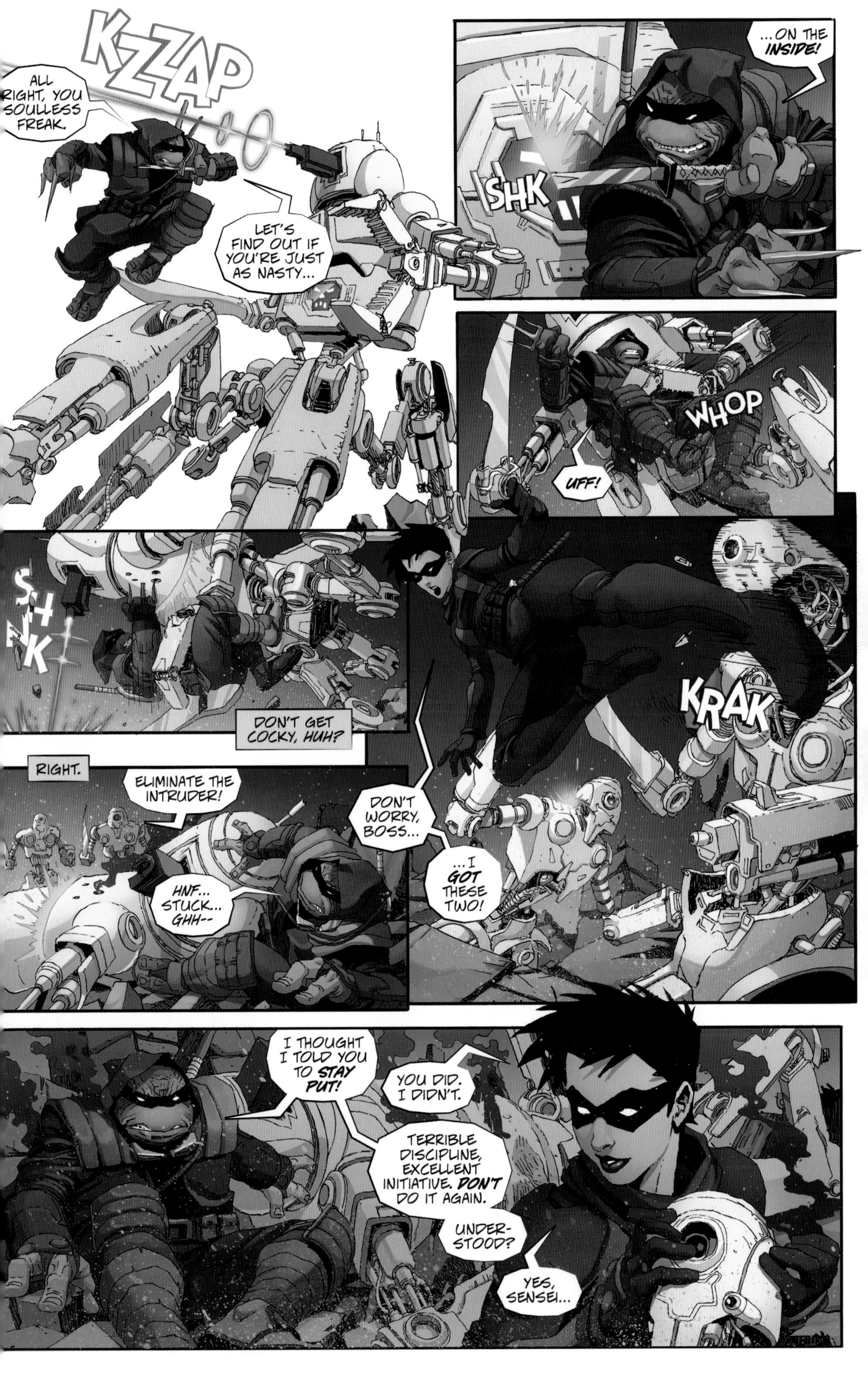
K-ZZAP
ALL RIGHT, YOU SOULLESS FREAK.
LET'S FIND OUT IF YOU'RE JUST AS NASTY...
...ON THE INSIDE!
SHK
WHOP
UFF!
SHNK
DON'T GET COCKY, HUH?
KRAK
RIGHT.
ELIMINATE THE INTRUDER!
HNF... STUCK... GHH--
DON'T WORRY, BOSS...
...I GOT THESE TWO!
I THOUGHT I TOLD YOU TO STAY PUT!
YOU DID. I DIDN'T.
TERRIBLE DISCIPLINE, EXCELLENT INITIATIVE. DON'T DO IT AGAIN.
UNDER-STOOD?
YES, SENSEI...

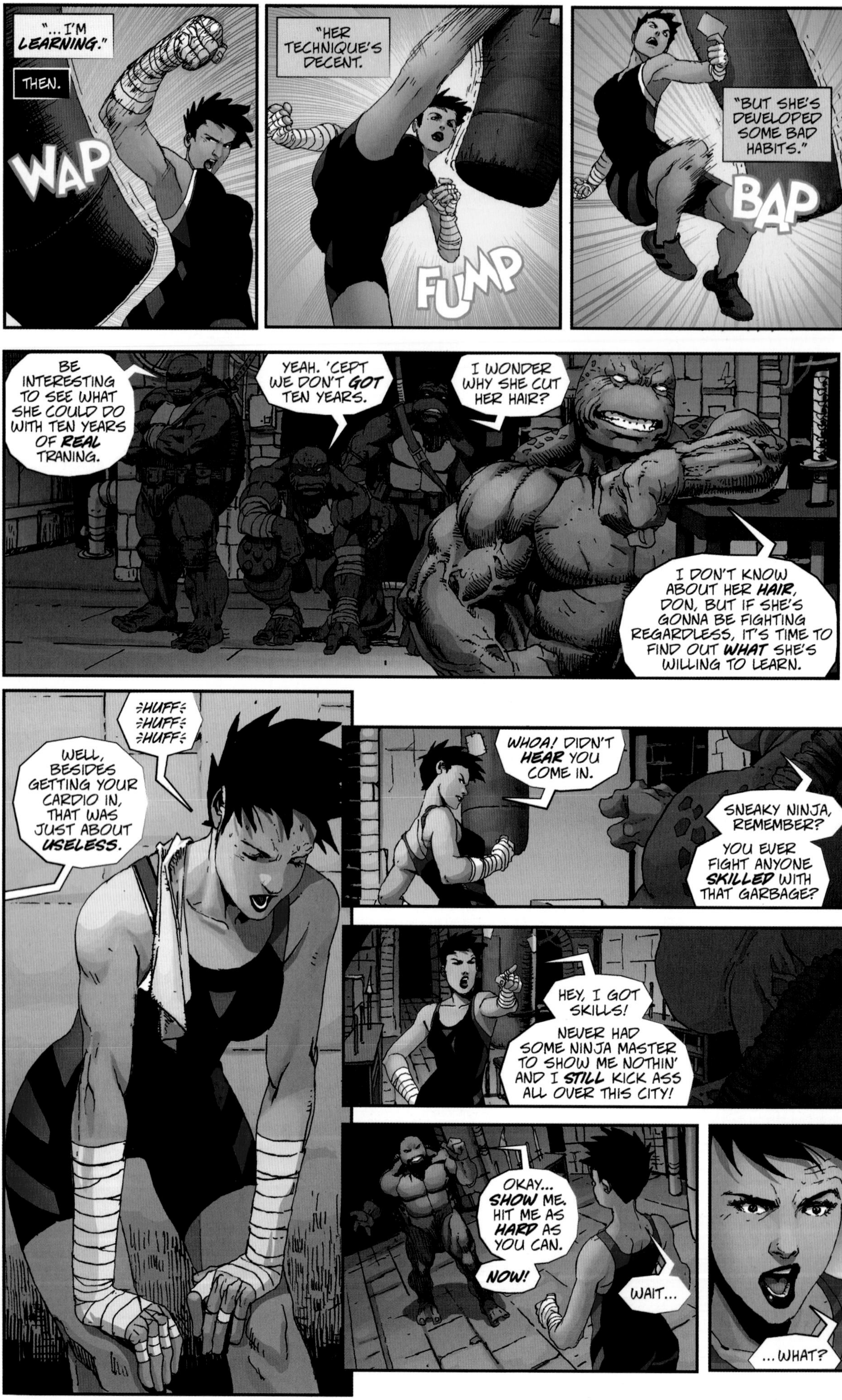
"... I'M LEARNING."
THEN.
WAP
"HER TECHNIQUE'S DECENT.
FUMP
"BUT SHE'S DEVELOPED SOME BAD HABITS."
BAP
BE INTERESTING TO SEE WHAT SHE COULD DO WITH TEN YEARS OF REAL TRANING.
YEAH. 'CEPT WE DON'T GOT TEN YEARS.
I WONDER WHY SHE CUT HER HAIR?
I DON'T KNOW ABOUT HER HAIR, DON, BUT IF SHE'S GONNA BE FIGHTING REGARDLESS, IT'S TIME TO FIND OUT WHAT SHE'S WILLING TO LEARN.
HUFF HUFF HUFF
WELL, BESIDES GETTING YOUR CARDIO IN, THAT WAS JUST ABOUT USELESS.
WHOA! DIDN'T HEAR YOU COME IN.
SNEAKY NINJA, REMEMBER?
YOU EVER FIGHT ANYONE SKILLED WITH THAT GARBAGE?
HEY, I GOT SKILLS!
NEVER HAD SOME NINJA MASTER TO SHOW ME NOTHIN' AND I STILL KICK ASS ALL OVER THIS CITY!
OKAY... SHOW ME. HIT ME AS HARD AS YOU CAN.
NOW!
WAIT...
... WHAT?

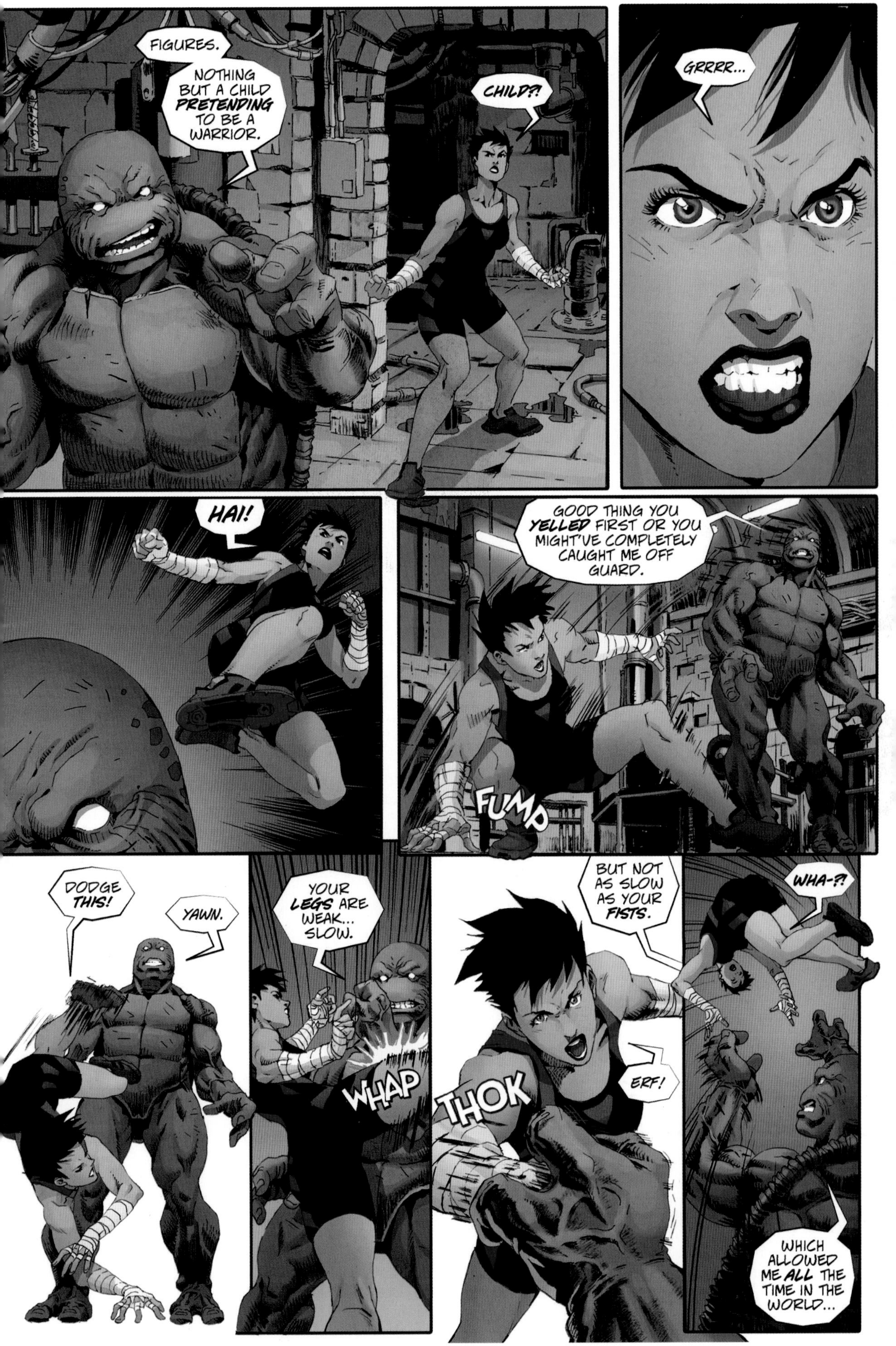
FIGURES.
NOTHING BUT A CHILD PRETENDING TO BE A WARRIOR.
CHILD?!
GRRRR...
HAI!
GOOD THING YOU YELLED FIRST OR YOU MIGHT'VE COMPLETELY CAUGHT ME OFF GUARD.
FUMP
DODGE THIS!
YAWN.
YOUR LEGS ARE WEAK... SLOW.
WHAP
BUT NOT AS SLOW AS YOUR FISTS.
THOK
ERF!
WHA-?!
WHICH ALLOWED ME ALL THE TIME IN THE WORLD...

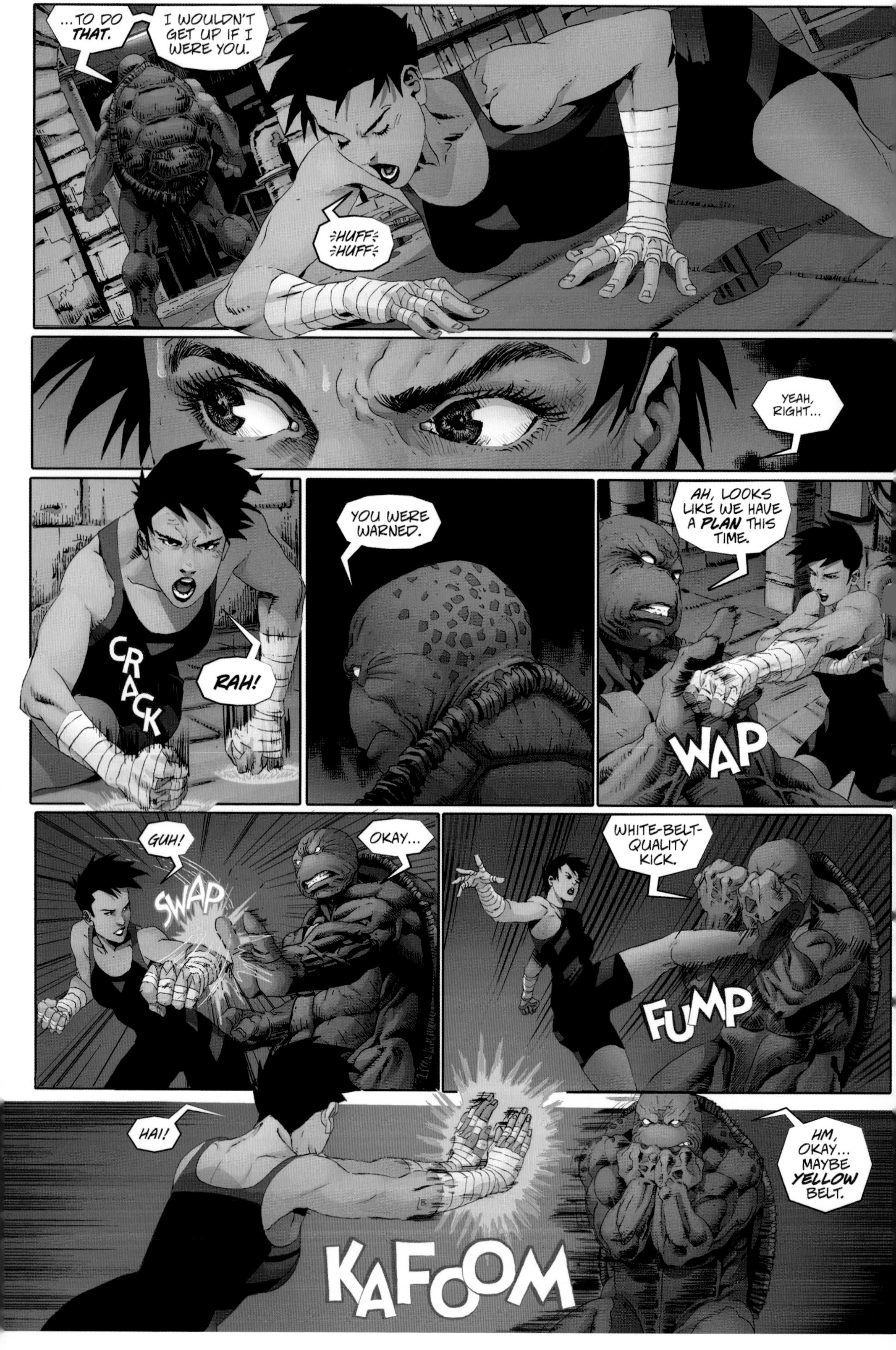
...TO DO THAT.
I WOULDN'T GET UP IF I WERE YOU.
HUFF HUFF
YEAH, RIGHT...
CRACK
RAH!
YOU WERE WARNED.
AH, LOOKS LIKE WE HAVE A PLAN THIS TIME.
WAP
GUH!
SWAP
OKAY...
WHITE-BELT-QUALITY KICK.
FUMP
HAI!
HM, OKAY... MAYBE YELLOW BELT.
KAFOOM

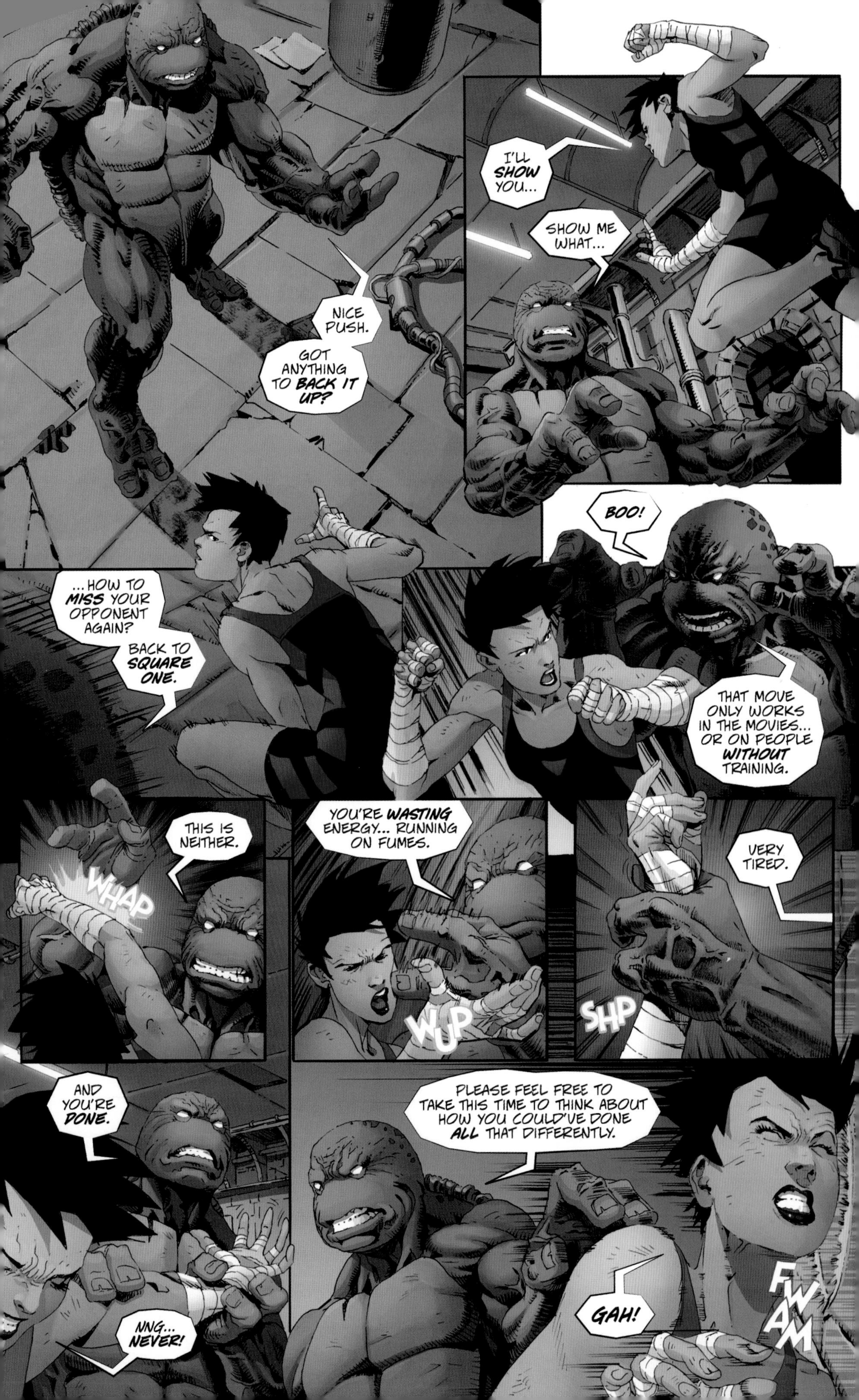
NICE PUSH.
GOT ANYTHING TO BACK IT UP?
I'LL SHOW YOU...
SHOW ME WHAT...
...HOW TO MISS YOUR OPPONENT AGAIN?
BACK TO SQUARE ONE.
BOO!
THAT MOVE ONLY WORKS IN THE MOVIES... OR ON PEOPLE WITHOUT TRAINING.
THIS IS NEITHER.
WHAP
YOU'RE WASTING ENERGY... RUNNING ON FUMES.
WUP
VERY TIRED.
SHP
AND YOU'RE DONE.
NNG... NEVER!
PLEASE FEEL FREE TO TAKE THIS TIME TO THINK ABOUT HOW YOU COULD'VE DONE ALL THAT DIFFERENTLY.
GAH!
FWAM

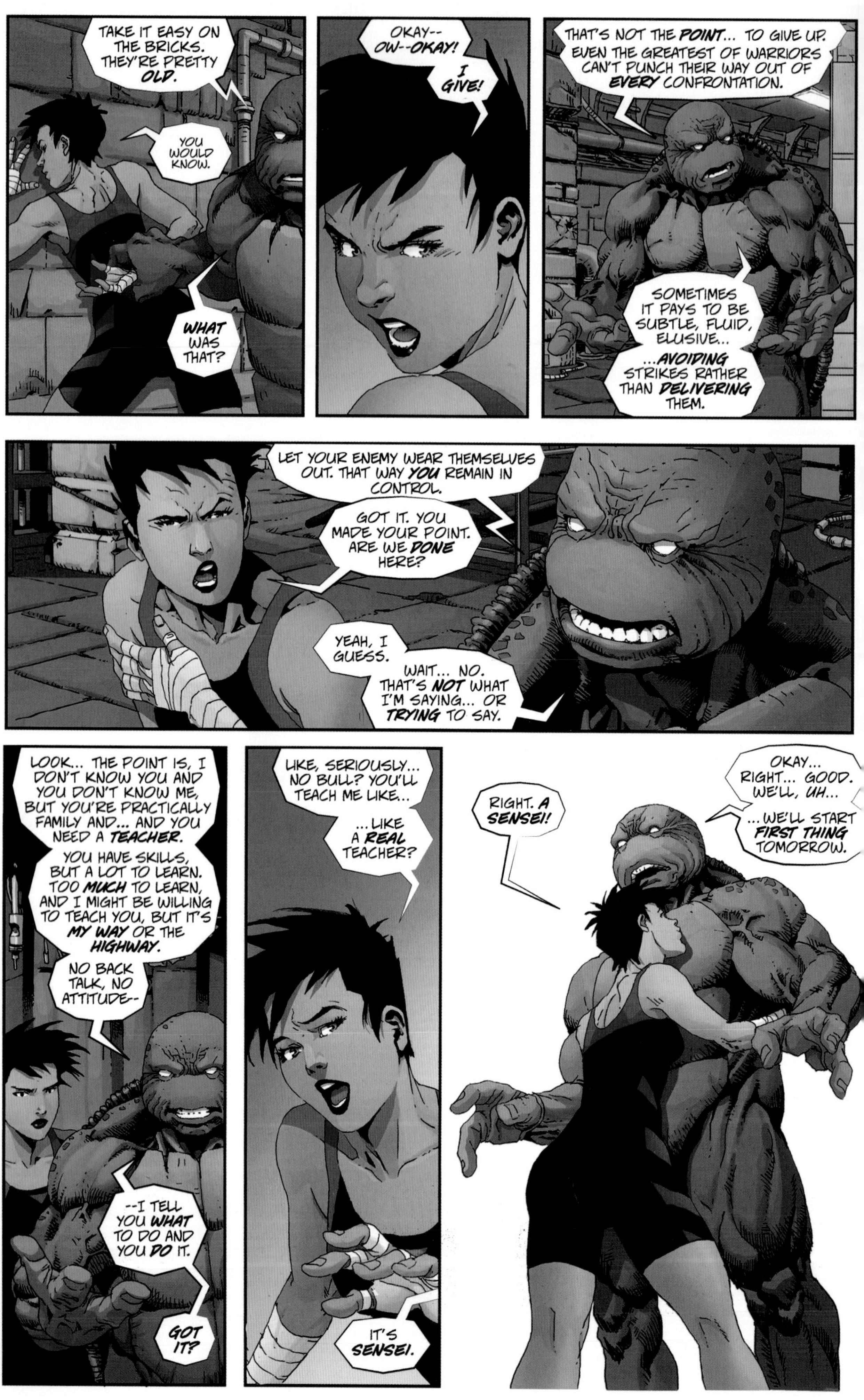
TAKE IT EASY ON THE BRICKS. THEY'RE PRETTY OLD.
YOU WOULD KNOW.
WHAT WAS THAT?
OKAY-- OW--OKAY!
I GIVE!
THAT'S NOT THE POINT... TO GIVE UP. EVEN THE GREATEST OF WARRIORS CAN'T PUNCH THEIR WAY OUT OF EVERY CONFRONTATION.
SOMETIMES IT PAYS TO BE SUBTLE, FLUID, ELUSIVE...
...AVOIDING STRIKES RATHER THAN DELIVERING THEM.
LET YOUR ENEMY WEAR THEMSELVES OUT. THAT WAY YOU REMAIN IN CONTROL.
GOT IT. YOU MADE YOUR POINT. ARE WE DONE HERE?
YEAH, I GUESS.
WAIT... NO. THAT'S NOT WHAT I'M SAYING... OR TRYING TO SAY.
LOOK... THE POINT IS, I DON'T KNOW YOU AND YOU DON'T KNOW ME, BUT YOU'RE PRACTICALLY FAMILY AND... AND YOU NEED A TEACHER.
YOU HAVE SKILLS, BUT A LOT TO LEARN. TOO MUCH TO LEARN, AND I MIGHT BE WILLING TO TEACH YOU, BUT IT'S MY WAY OR THE HIGHWAY.
NO BACK TALK, NO ATTITUDE--
--I TELL YOU WHAT TO DO AND YOU DO IT.
GOT IT?
LIKE, SERIOUSLY... NO BULL? YOU'LL TEACH ME LIKE...
...LIKE A REAL TEACHER?
IT'S SENSEI.
RIGHT. A SENSEI!
OKAY... RIGHT... GOOD. WE'LL, UH...
...WE'LL START FIRST THING TOMORROW.

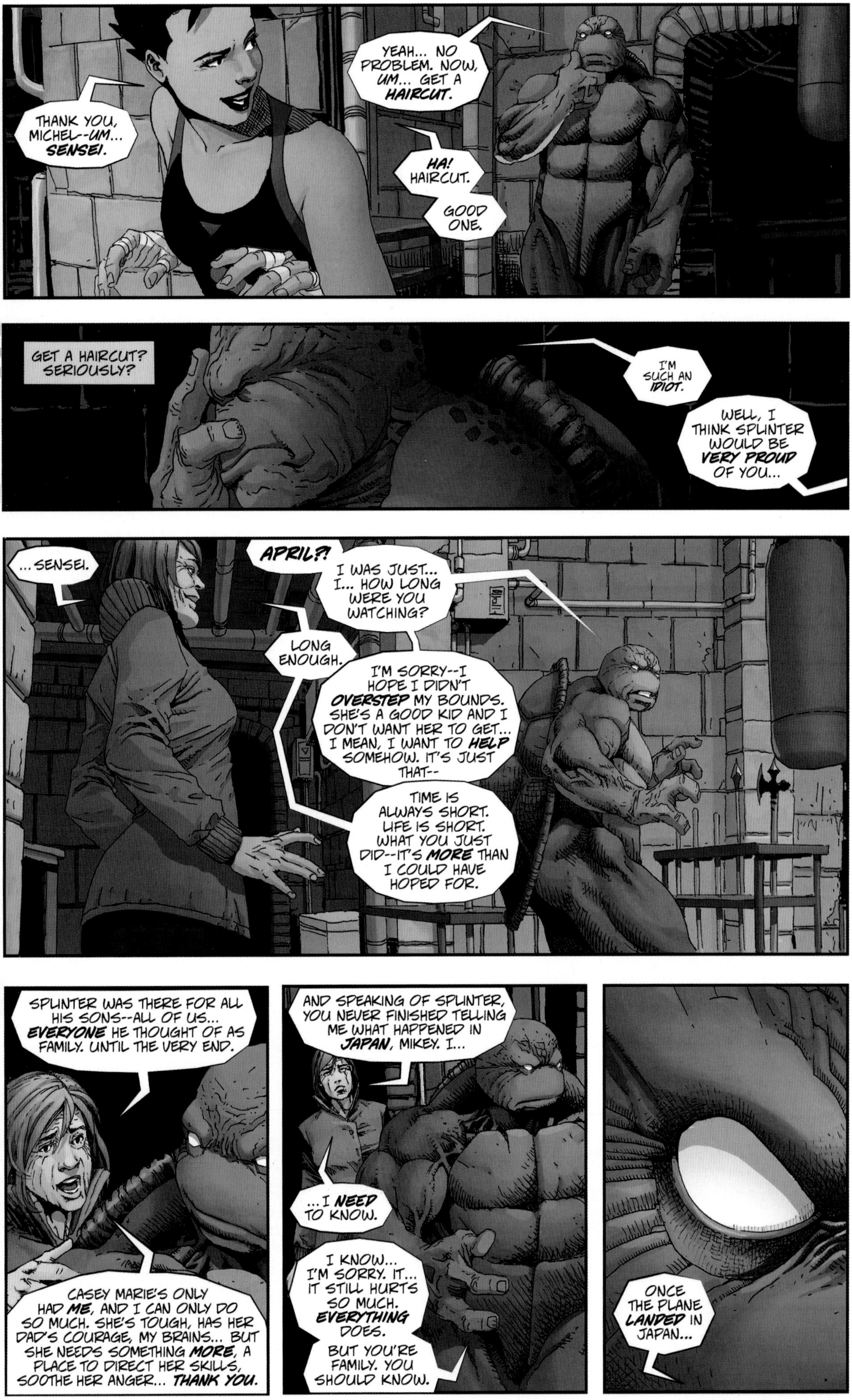
THANK YOU, MICHEL--UM... SENSEI.
YEAH... NO PROBLEM. NOW, UM... GET A HAIRCUT.
HA! HAIRCUT.
GOOD ONE.
GET A HAIRCUT? SERIOUSLY?
I'M SUCH AN IDIOT.
WELL, I THINK SPLINTER WOULD BE VERY PROUD OF YOU...
...SENSEI.
APRIL?!
I WAS JUST... I... HOW LONG WERE YOU WATCHING?
LONG ENOUGH.
I'M SORRY--I HOPE I DIDN'T OVERSTEP MY BOUNDS. SHE'S A GOOD KID AND I DON'T WANT HER TO GET... I MEAN, I WANT TO HELP SOMEHOW. IT'S JUST THAT--
TIME IS ALWAYS SHORT. LIFE IS SHORT. WHAT YOU JUST DID--IT'S MORE THAN I COULD HAVE HOPED FOR.
SPLINTER WAS THERE FOR ALL HIS SONS--ALL OF US... EVERYONE HE THOUGHT OF AS FAMILY. UNTIL THE VERY END.
CASEY MARIE'S ONLY HAD ME, AND I CAN ONLY DO SO MUCH. SHE'S TOUGH, HAS HER DAD'S COURAGE, MY BRAINS... BUT SHE NEEDS SOMETHING MORE, A PLACE TO DIRECT HER SKILLS, SOOTHE HER ANGER... THANK YOU.
AND SPEAKING OF SPLINTER, YOU NEVER FINISHED TELLING ME WHAT HAPPENED IN JAPAN, MIKEY. I...
...I NEED TO KNOW.
I KNOW... I'M SORRY. IT... IT STILL HURTS SO MUCH. EVERYTHING DOES.
BUT YOU'RE FAMILY. YOU SHOULD KNOW.
ONCE THE PLANE LANDED IN JAPAN...

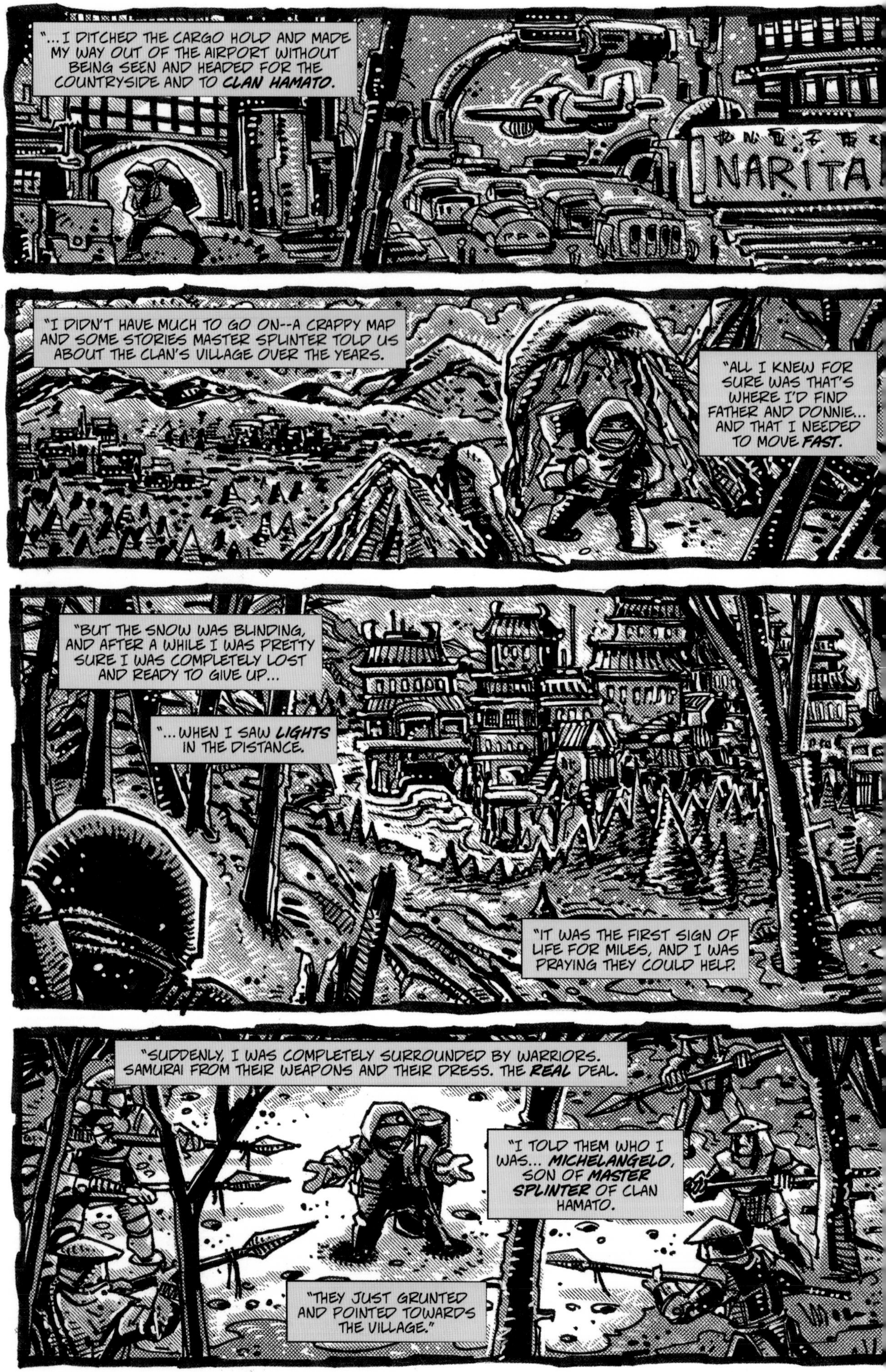
"...I DITCHED THE CARGO HOLD AND MADE MY WAY OUT OF THE AIRPORT WITHOUT BEING SEEN AND HEADED FOR THE COUNTRYSIDE AND TO CLAN HAMATO.
NARITA
"I DIDN'T HAVE MUCH TO GO ON--A CRAPPY MAP AND SOME STORIES MASTER SPLINTER TOLD US ABOUT THE CLAN'S VILLAGE OVER THE YEARS.
"ALL I KNEW FOR SURE WAS THAT'S WHERE I'D FIND FATHER AND DONNIE... AND THAT I NEEDED TO MOVE FAST.
"BUT THE SNOW WAS BLINDING, AND AFTER A WHILE I WAS PRETTY SURE I WAS COMPLETELY LOST AND READY TO GIVE UP...
"...WHEN I SAW LIGHTS IN THE DISTANCE.
"IT WAS THE FIRST SIGN OF LIFE FOR MILES, AND I WAS PRAYING THEY COULD HELP.
"SUDDENLY, I WAS COMPLETELY SURROUNDED BY WARRIORS. SAMURAI FROM THEIR WEAPONS AND THEIR DRESS. THE REAL DEAL.
"I TOLD THEM WHO I WAS... MICHELANGELO, SON OF MASTER SPLINTER OF CLAN HAMATO.
"THEY JUST GRUNTED AND POINTED TOWARDS THE VILLAGE."

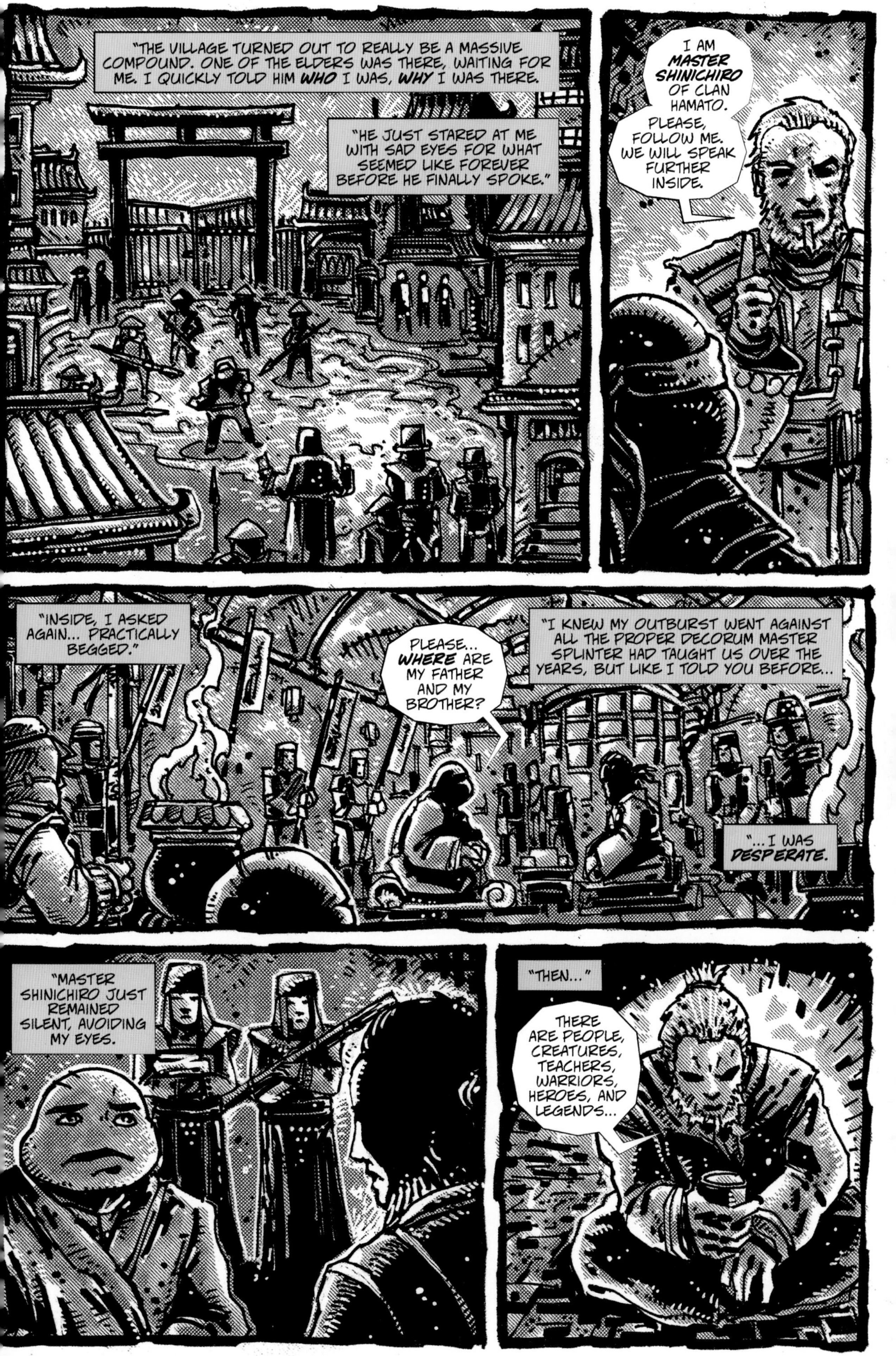
"THE VILLAGE TURNED OUT TO REALLY BE A MASSIVE COMPOUND. ONE OF THE ELDERS WAS THERE, WAITING FOR ME. I QUICKLY TOLD HIM WHO I WAS, WHY I WAS THERE.
"HE JUST STARED AT ME WITH SAD EYES FOR WHAT SEEMED LIKE FOREVER BEFORE HE FINALLY SPOKE."
I AM MASTER SHINICHIRO OF CLAN HAMATO.
PLEASE, FOLLOW ME. WE WILL SPEAK FURTHER INSIDE.
"INSIDE, I ASKED AGAIN... PRACTICALLY BEGGED."
PLEASE... WHERE ARE MY FATHER AND MY BROTHER?
"I KNEW MY OUTBURST WENT AGAINST ALL THE PROPER DECORUM MASTER SPLINTER HAD TAUGHT US OVER THE YEARS, BUT LIKE I TOLD YOU BEFORE...
"...I WAS DESPERATE.
"MASTER SHINICHIRO JUST REMAINED SILENT, AVOIDING MY EYES.
"THEN..."
THERE ARE PEOPLE, CREATURES, TEACHERS, WARRIORS, HEROES, AND LEGENDS...

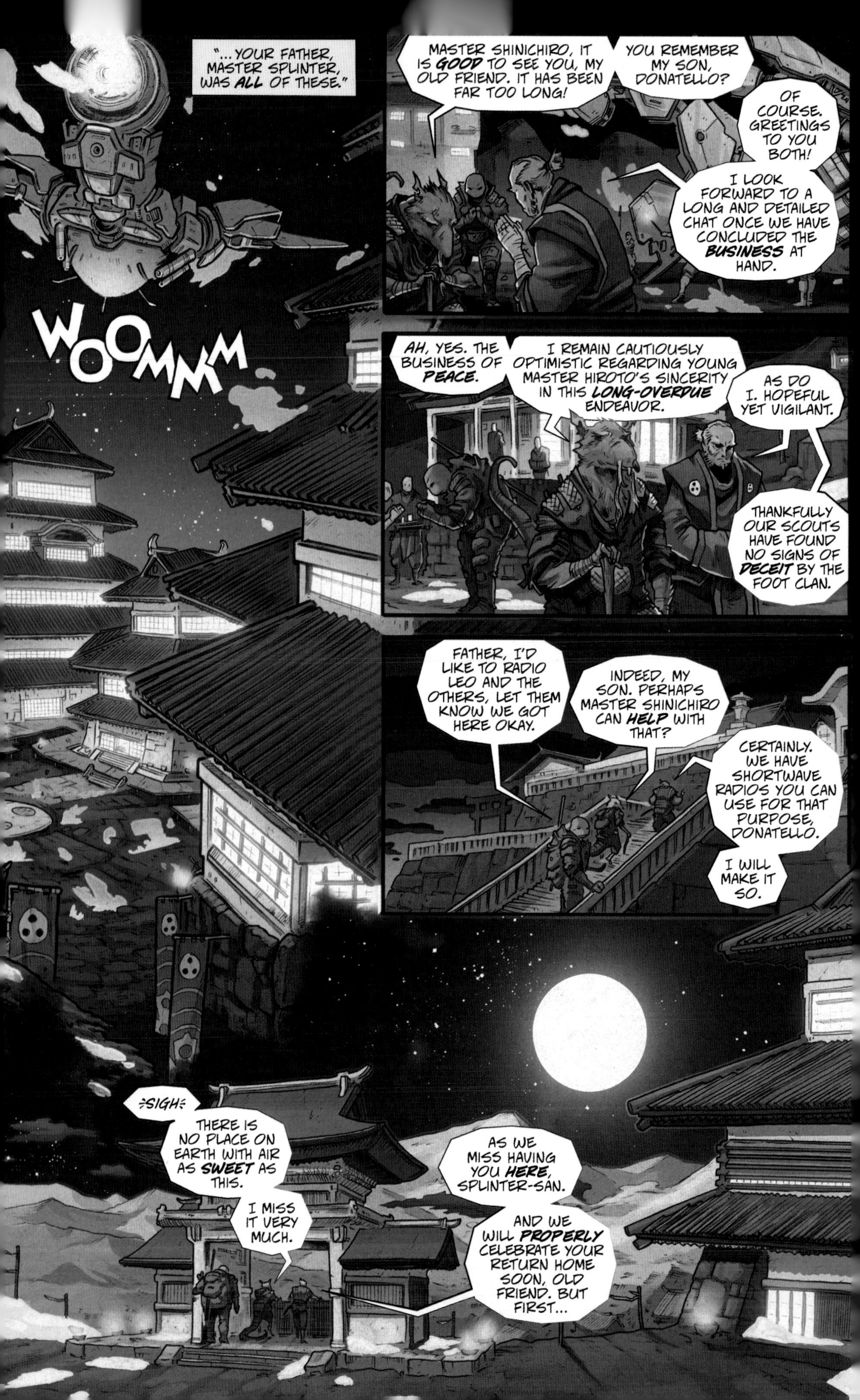
"...YOUR FATHER, MASTER SPLINTER, WAS ALL OF THESE."
MASTER SHINICHIRO, IT IS GOOD TO SEE YOU, MY OLD FRIEND. IT HAS BEEN FAR TOO LONG!
YOU REMEMBER MY SON, DONATELLO?
OF COURSE. GREETINGS TO YOU BOTH!
I LOOK FORWARD TO A LONG AND DETAILED CHAT ONCE WE HAVE CONCLUDED THE BUSINESS AT HAND.
WOOMNKM
AH, YES. THE BUSINESS OF PEACE.
I REMAIN CAUTIOUSLY OPTIMISTIC REGARDING YOUNG MASTER HIROTO'S SINCERITY IN THIS LONG-OVERDUE ENDEAVOR.
AS DO I. HOPEFUL YET VIGILANT.
THANKFULLY OUR SCOUTS HAVE FOUND NO SIGNS OF DECEIT BY THE FOOT CLAN.
FATHER, I'D LIKE TO RADIO LEO AND THE OTHERS, LET THEM KNOW WE GOT HERE OKAY.
INDEED, MY SON. PERHAPS MASTER SHINICHIRO CAN HELP WITH THAT?
CERTAINLY. WE HAVE SHORTWAVE RADIOS YOU CAN USE FOR THAT PURPOSE, DONATELLO.
I WILL MAKE IT SO.
SIGH
THERE IS NO PLACE ON EARTH WITH AIR AS SWEET AS THIS.
I MISS IT VERY MUCH.
AS WE MISS HAVING YOU HERE, SPLINTER-SAN.
AND WE WILL PROPERLY CELEBRATE YOUR RETURN HOME SOON, OLD FRIEND. BUT FIRST...

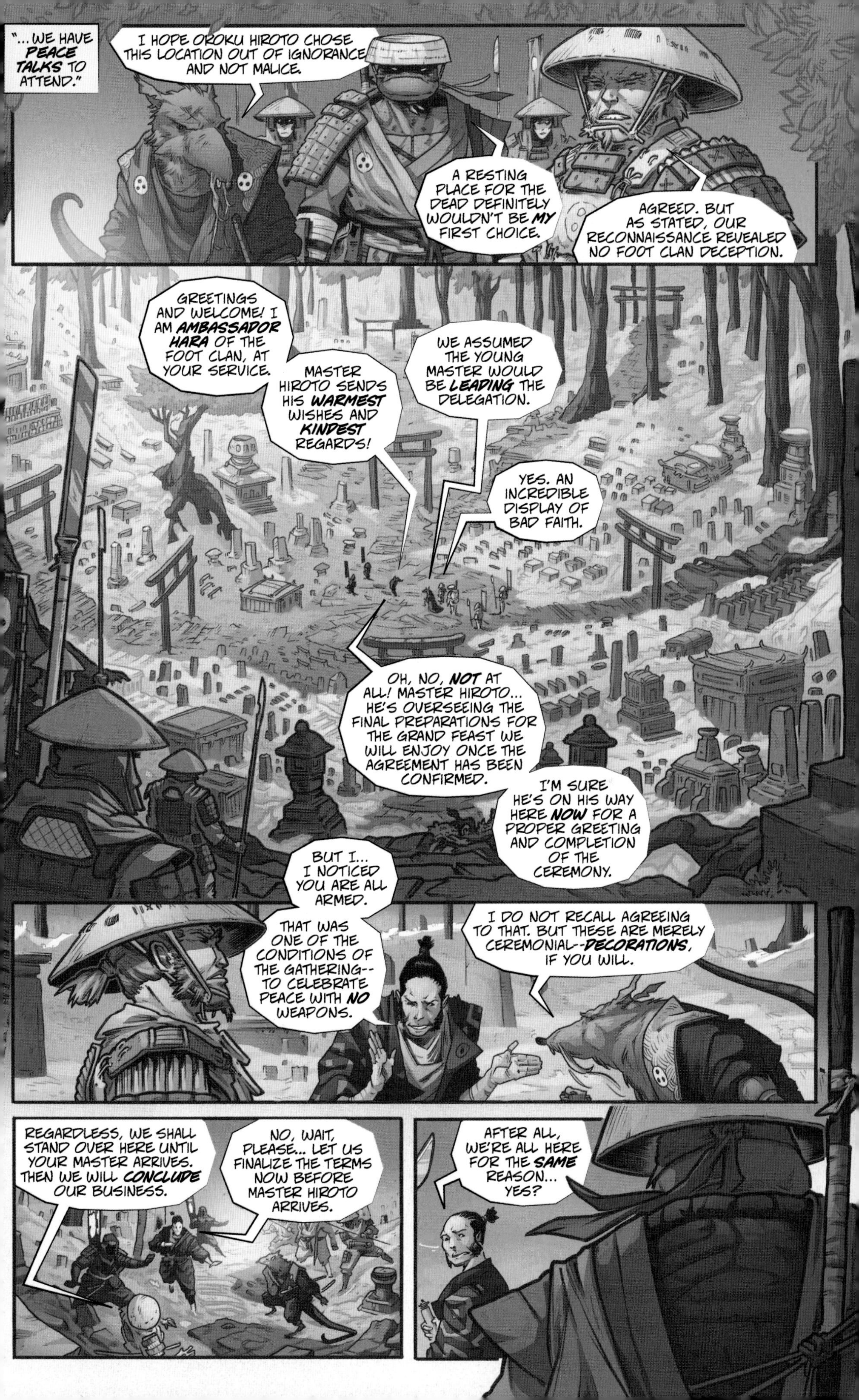

"...WE HAVE PEACE TALKS TO ATTEND."
I HOPE OROKU HIROTO CHOSE THIS LOCATION OUT OF IGNORANCE AND NOT MALICE.
A RESTING PLACE FOR THE DEAD DEFINITELY WOULDN'T BE MY FIRST CHOICE.
AGREED. BUT AS STATED, OUR RECONNAISSANCE REVEALED NO FOOT CLAN DECEPTION.
GREETINGS AND WELCOME! I AM AMBASSADOR HARA OF THE FOOT CLAN, AT YOUR SERVICE.
MASTER HIROTO SENDS HIS WARMEST WISHES AND KINDEST REGARDS!
WE ASSUMED THE YOUNG MASTER WOULD BE LEADING THE DELEGATION.
YES. AN INCREDIBLE DISPLAY OF BAD FAITH.
OH, NO, NOT AT ALL! MASTER HIROTO... HE'S OVERSEEING THE FINAL PREPARATIONS FOR THE GRAND FEAST WE WILL ENJOY ONCE THE AGREEMENT HAS BEEN CONFIRMED.
I'M SURE HE'S ON HIS WAY HERE NOW FOR A PROPER GREETING AND COMPLETION OF THE CEREMONY.
BUT I... I NOTICED YOU ARE ALL ARMED.
THAT WAS ONE OF THE CONDITIONS OF THE GATHERING--TO CELEBRATE PEACE WITH NO WEAPONS.
I DO NOT RECALL AGREEING TO THAT. BUT THESE ARE MERELY CEREMONIAL--DECORATIONS, IF YOU WILL.
REGARDLESS, WE SHALL STAND OVER HERE UNTIL YOUR MASTER ARRIVES. THEN WE WILL CONCLUDE OUR BUSINESS.
NO, WAIT, PLEASE... LET US FINALIZE THE TERMS NOW BEFORE MASTER HIROTO ARRIVES.
AFTER ALL, WE'RE ALL HERE FOR THE SAME REASON... YES?

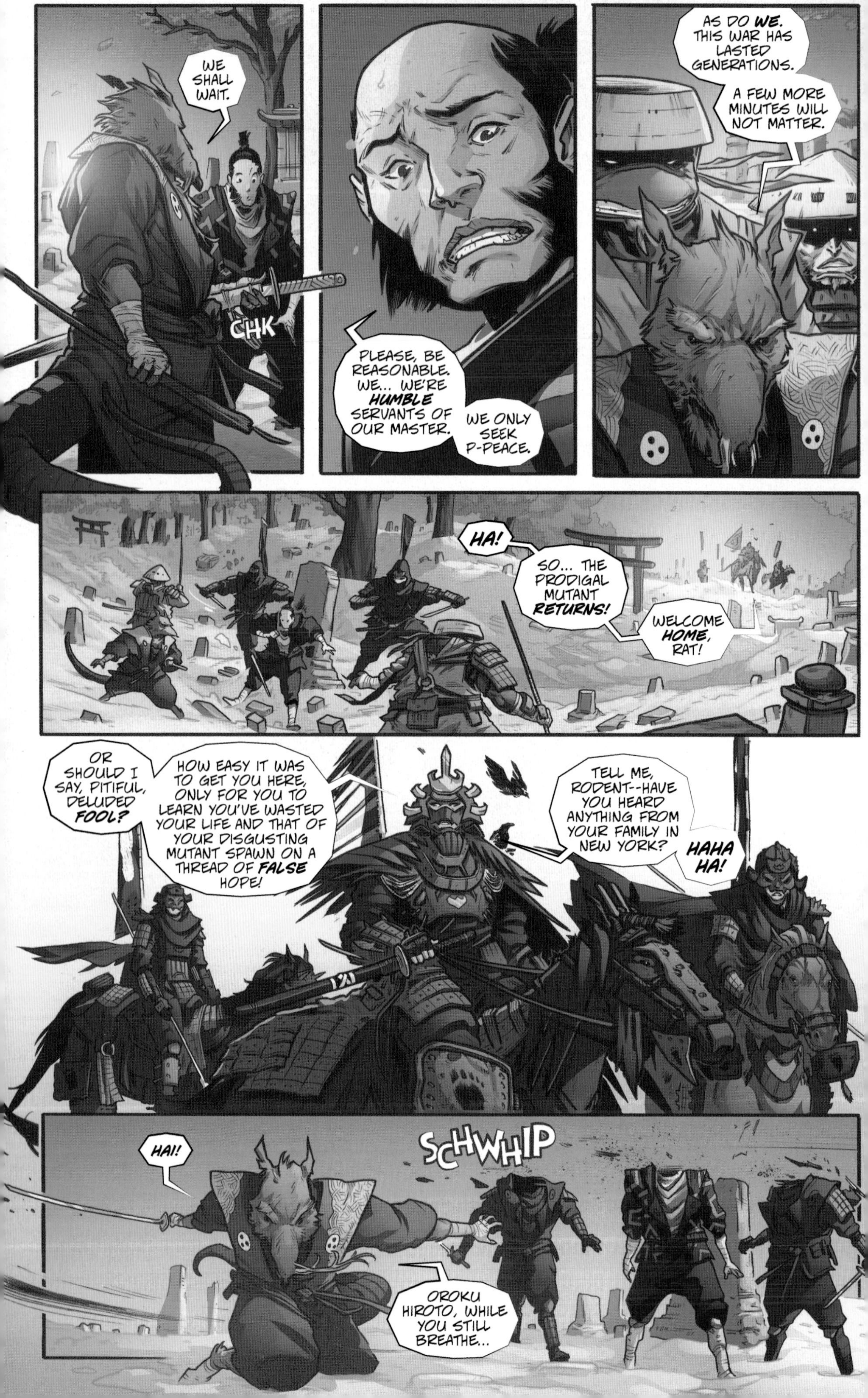

WE SHALL WAIT.
CHK
PLEASE, BE REASONABLE. WE... WE'RE HUMBLE SERVANTS OF OUR MASTER.
WE ONLY SEEK P-PEACE.
AS DO WE. THIS WAR HAS LASTED GENERATIONS.
A FEW MORE MINUTES WILL NOT MATTER.
HA!
SO... THE PRODIGAL MUTANT RETURNS!
WELCOME HOME, RAT!
OR SHOULD I SAY, PITIFUL, DELUDED FOOL?
HOW EASY IT WAS TO GET YOU HERE, ONLY FOR YOU TO LEARN YOU'VE WASTED YOUR LIFE AND THAT OF YOUR DISGUSTING MUTANT SPAWN ON A THREAD OF FALSE HOPE!
TELL ME, RODENT--HAVE YOU HEARD ANYTHING FROM YOUR FAMILY IN NEW YORK?
HAHA HA!
HAI!
SCHWHIP
OROKU HIROTO, WHILE YOU STILL BREATHE...

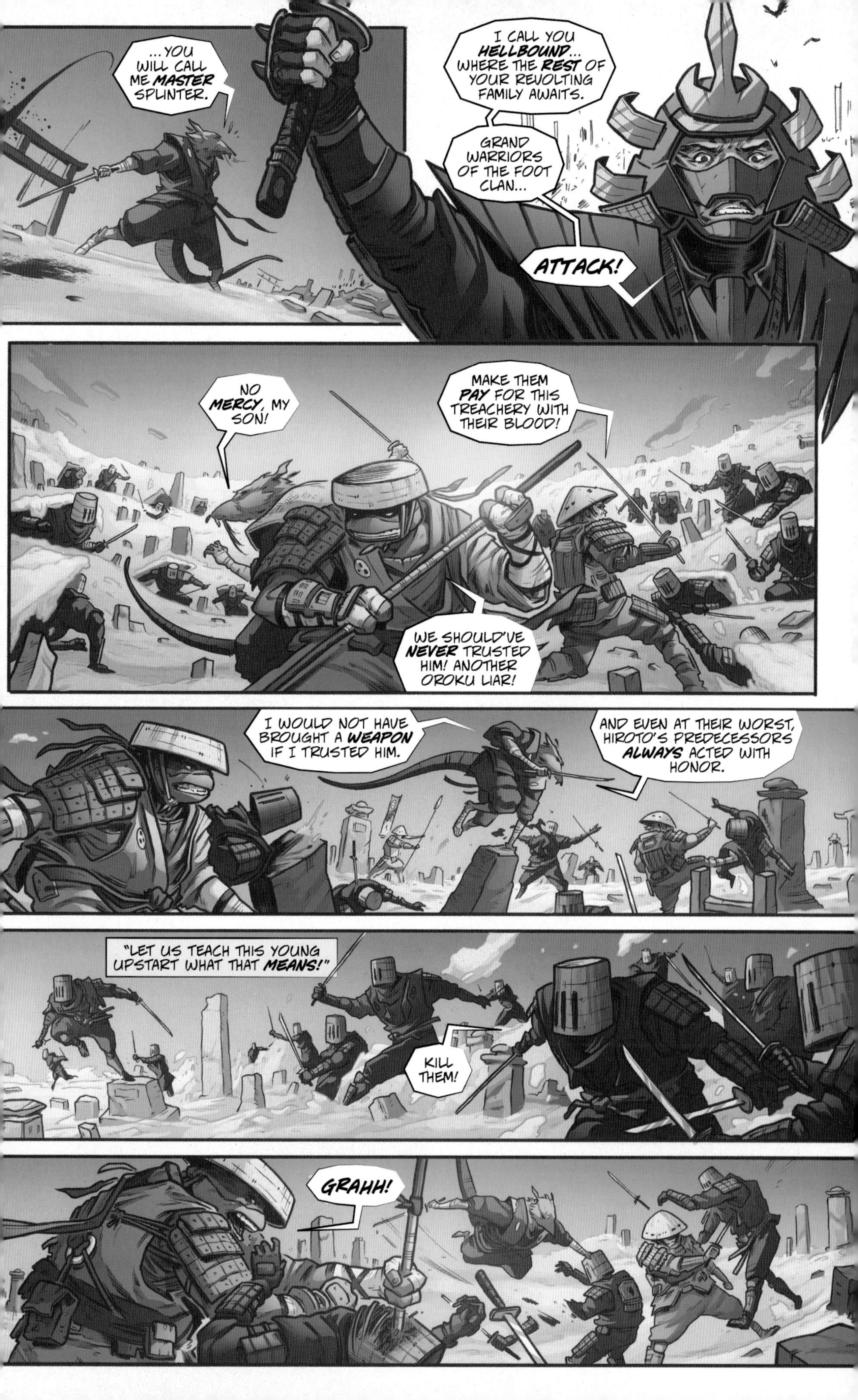
...YOU WILL CALL ME **MASTER** SPLINTER.
I CALL YOU **HELLBOUND**... WHERE THE **REST** OF YOUR REVOLTING FAMILY AWAITS.
GRAND WARRIORS OF THE FOOT CLAN...
ATTACK!
NO **MERCY**, MY SON!
MAKE THEM **PAY** FOR THIS TREACHERY WITH THEIR BLOOD!
WE SHOULD'VE **NEVER** TRUSTED HIM! ANOTHER OROKU LIAR!
I WOULD NOT HAVE BROUGHT A **WEAPON** IF I TRUSTED HIM.
AND EVEN AT THEIR WORST, HIROTO'S PREDECESSORS **ALWAYS** ACTED WITH HONOR.
"LET US TEACH THIS YOUNG UPSTART WHAT THAT **MEANS!**"
KILL THEM!
GRAHH!

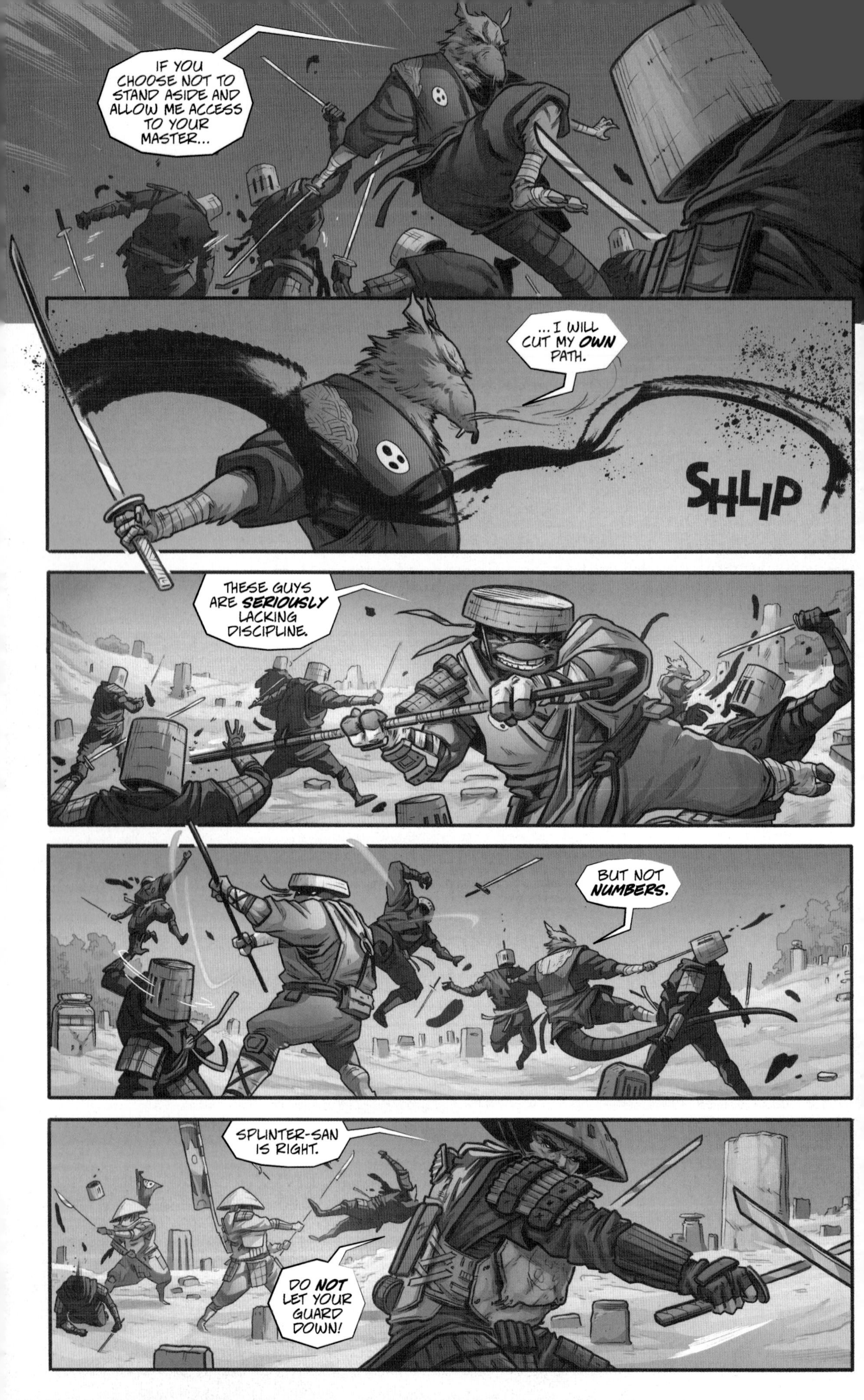
IF YOU CHOOSE NOT TO STAND ASIDE AND ALLOW ME ACCESS TO YOUR MASTER...
...I WILL CUT MY OWN PATH.
SHLIP
THESE GUYS ARE SERIOUSLY LACKING DISCIPLINE.
BUT NOT NUMBERS.
SPLINTER-SAN IS RIGHT.
DO NOT LET YOUR GUARD DOWN!

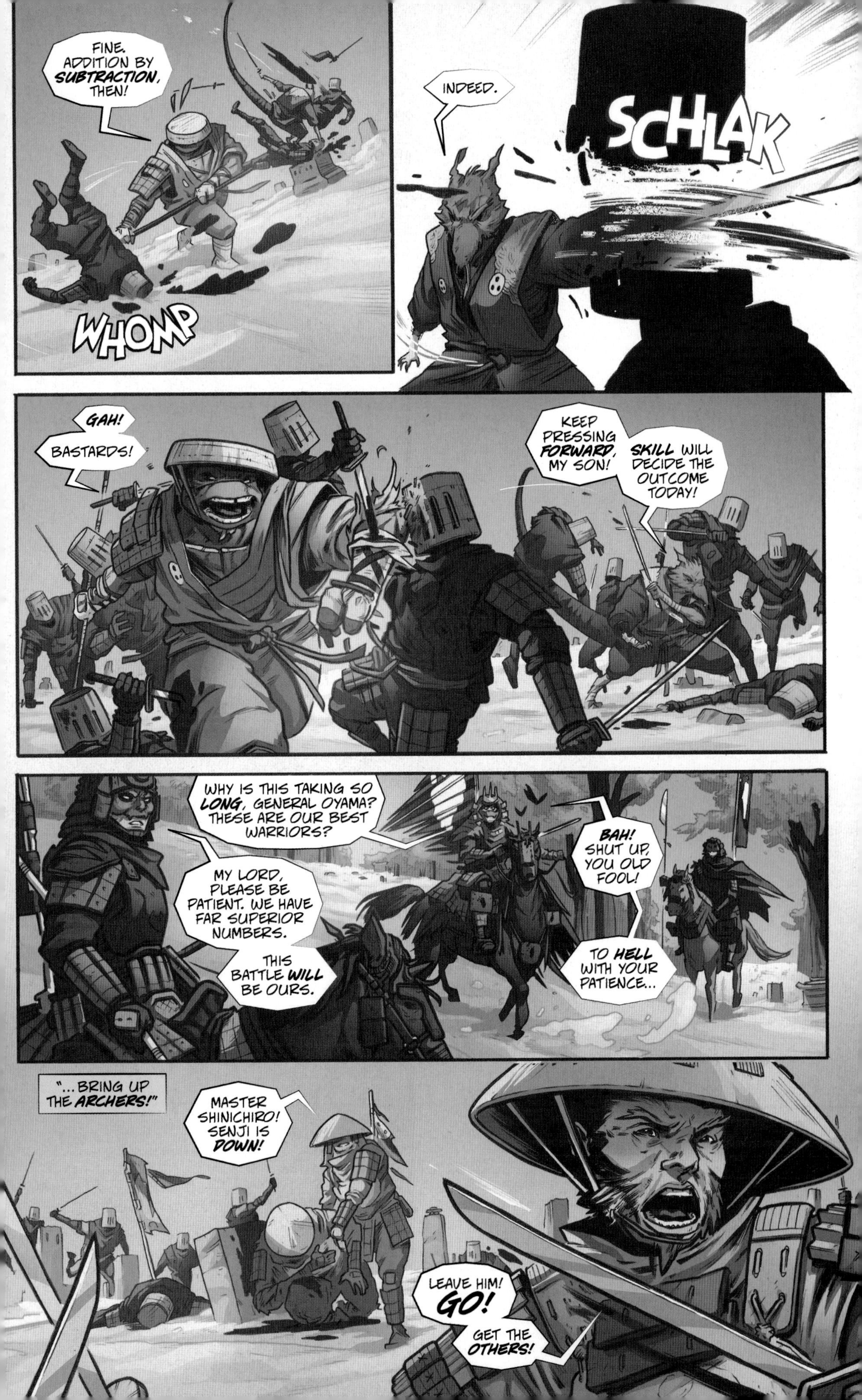
FINE. ADDITION BY SUBTRACTION, THEN!
WHOMP
INDEED.
SCHLAK
GAH!
BASTARDS!
KEEP PRESSING FORWARD, MY SON!
SKILL WILL DECIDE THE OUTCOME TODAY!
WHY IS THIS TAKING SO LONG, GENERAL OYAMA? THESE ARE OUR BEST WARRIORS?
MY LORD, PLEASE BE PATIENT. WE HAVE FAR SUPERIOR NUMBERS.
THIS BATTLE WILL BE OURS.
BAH! SHUT UP, YOU OLD FOOL!
TO HELL WITH YOUR PATIENCE...
"...BRING UP THE ARCHERS!"
MASTER SHINICHIRO! SENJI IS DOWN!
LEAVE HIM! GO!
GET THE OTHERS!

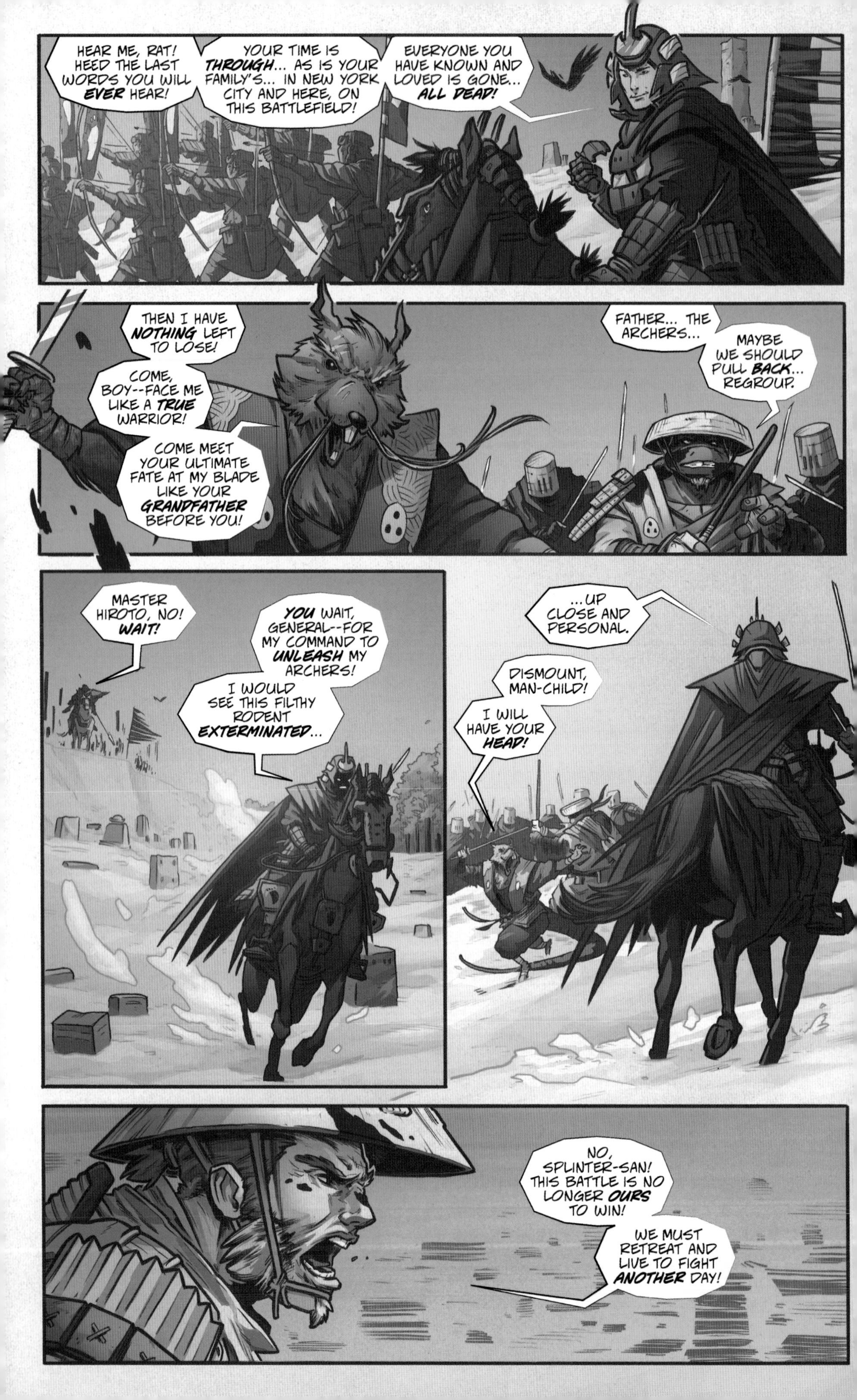
HEAR ME, RAT! HEED THE LAST WORDS YOU WILL EVER HEAR!
YOUR TIME IS THROUGH... AS IS YOUR FAMILY'S... IN NEW YORK CITY AND HERE, ON THIS BATTLEFIELD!
EVERYONE YOU HAVE KNOWN AND LOVED IS GONE... ALL DEAD!
THEN I HAVE NOTHING LEFT TO LOSE!
COME, BOY--FACE ME LIKE A TRUE WARRIOR!
COME MEET YOUR ULTIMATE FATE AT MY BLADE LIKE YOUR GRANDFATHER BEFORE YOU!
FATHER... THE ARCHERS...
MAYBE WE SHOULD PULL BACK... REGROUP.
MASTER HIROTO, NO! WAIT!
YOU WAIT, GENERAL--FOR MY COMMAND TO UNLEASH MY ARCHERS!
I WOULD SEE THIS FILTHY RODENT EXTERMINATED...
...UP CLOSE AND PERSONAL.
DISMOUNT, MAN-CHILD!
I WILL HAVE YOUR HEAD!
NO, SPLINTER-SAN! THIS BATTLE IS NO LONGER OURS TO WIN!
WE MUST RETREAT AND LIVE TO FIGHT ANOTHER DAY!

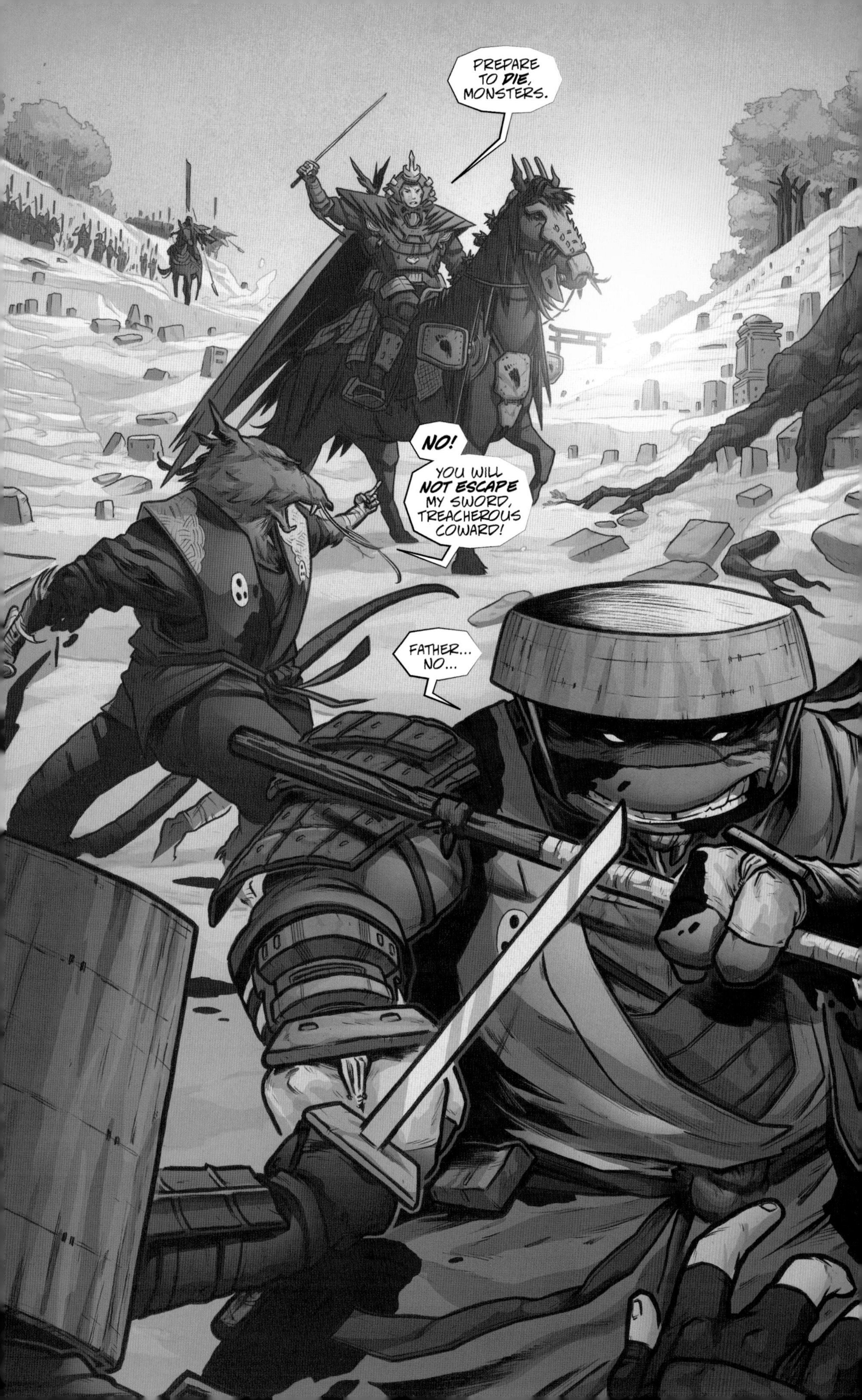
PREPARE TO DIE, MONSTERS.
NO!
YOU WILL NOT ESCAPE MY SWORD, TREACHEROUS COWARD!
FATHER... NO...

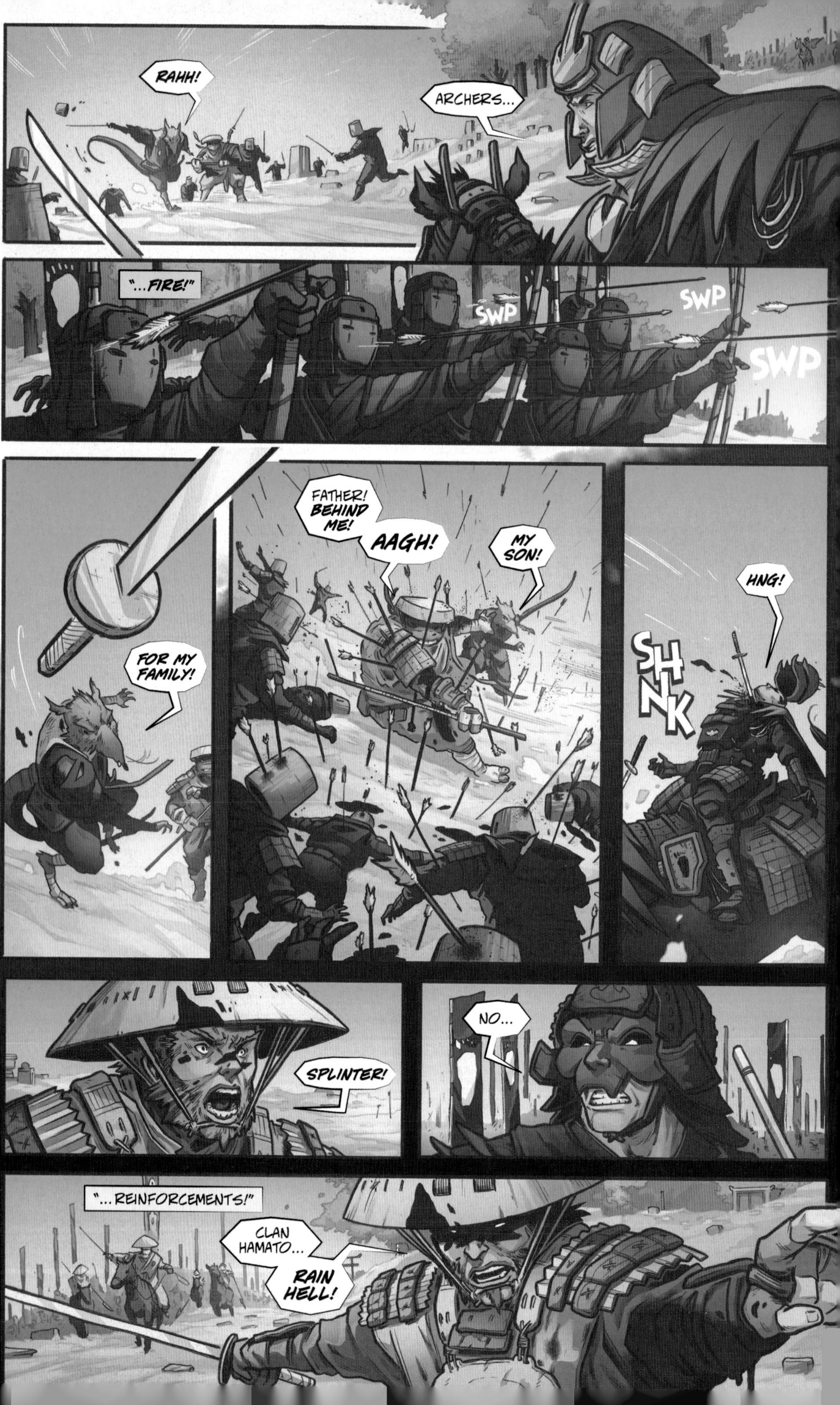
RAHH!
ARCHERS...
"...FIRE!"
SWP
SWP
SWP
FOR MY FAMILY!
FATHER! BEHIND ME!
AAGH!
MY SON!
HNG!
SHNK
SPLINTER!
NO...
"...REINFORCEMENTS!"
CLAN HAMATO...
RAIN HELL!

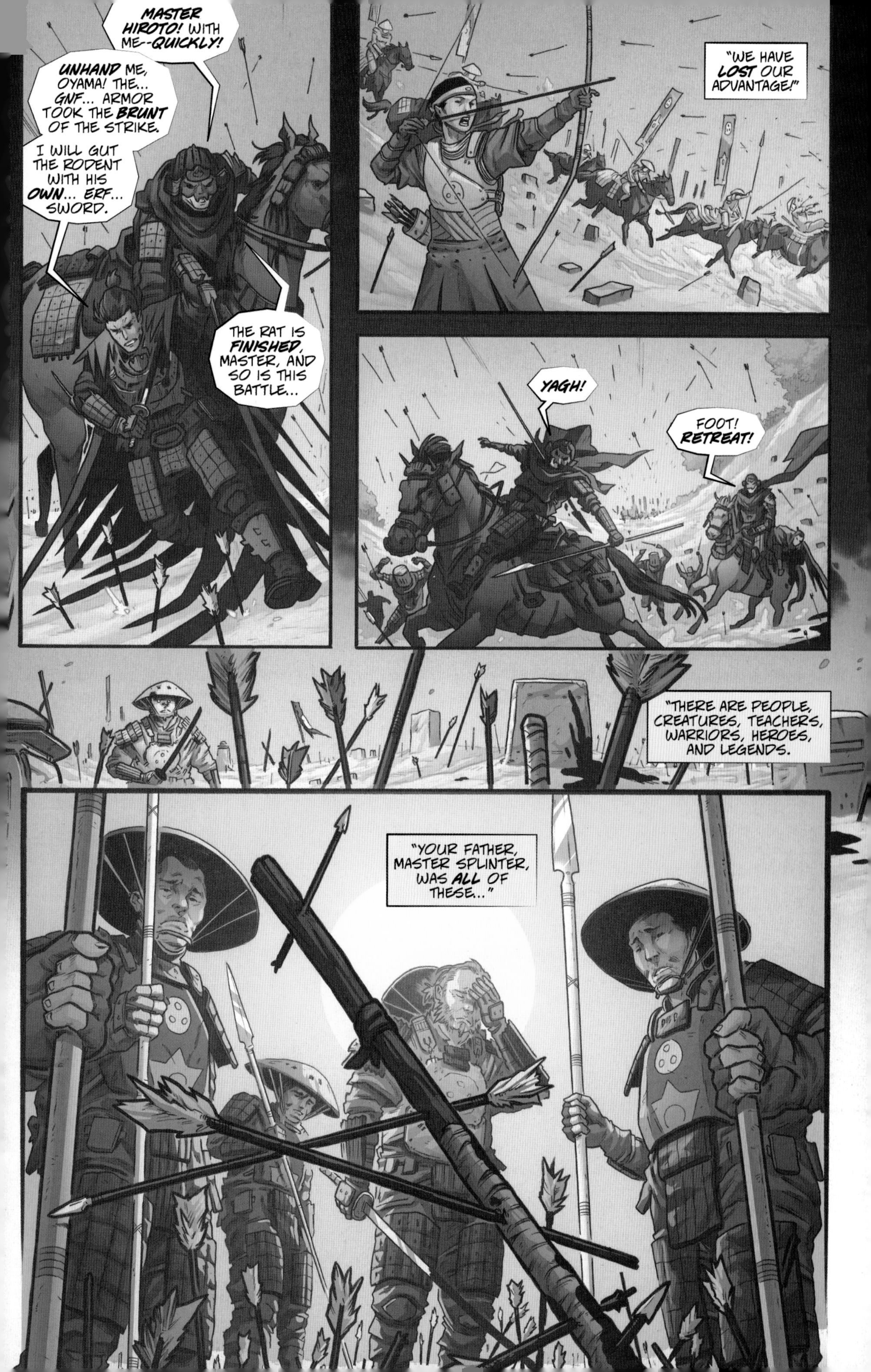
MASTER HIROTO! WITH ME--QUICKLY!
UNHAND ME, OYAMA! THE... GNF... ARMOR TOOK THE BRUNT OF THE STRIKE.
I WILL GUT THE RODENT WITH HIS OWN... ERF... SWORD.
THE RAT IS FINISHED, MASTER, AND SO IS THIS BATTLE...
"WE HAVE LOST OUR ADVANTAGE!"
YAGH!
FOOT! RETREAT!
"THERE ARE PEOPLE, CREATURES, TEACHERS, WARRIORS, HEROES, AND LEGENDS.
"YOUR FATHER, MASTER SPLINTER, WAS ALL OF THESE..."

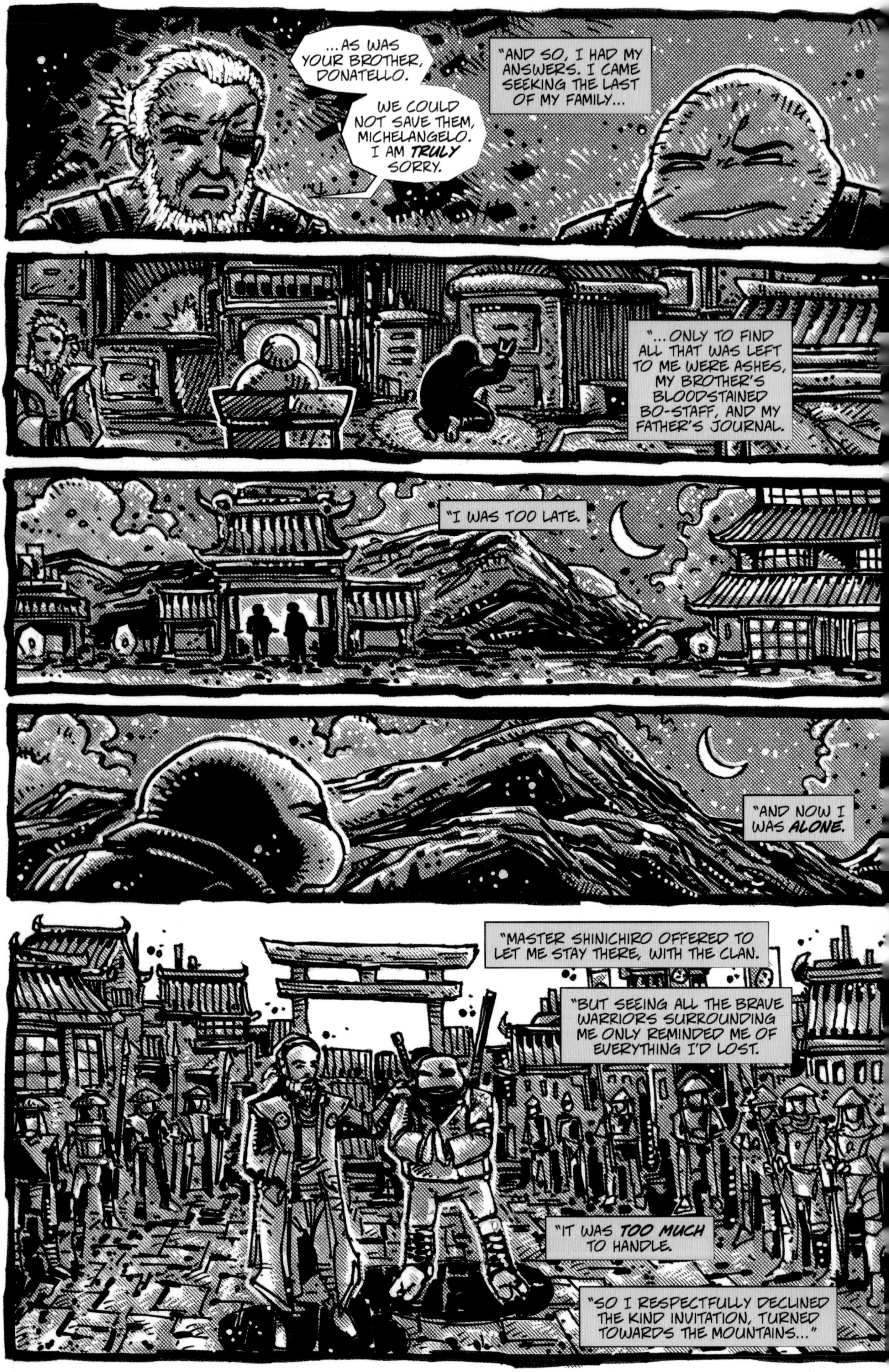

...AS WAS YOUR BROTHER, DONATELLO.
WE COULD NOT SAVE THEM, MICHELANGELO. I AM **TRULY** SORRY.
"AND SO, I HAD MY ANSWERS. I CAME SEEKING THE LAST OF MY FAMILY...
"...ONLY TO FIND ALL THAT WAS LEFT TO ME WERE ASHES, MY BROTHER'S BLOODSTAINED BO-STAFF, AND MY FATHER'S JOURNAL.
"I WAS TOO LATE.
"AND NOW I WAS **ALONE**.
"MASTER SHINICHIRO OFFERED TO LET ME STAY THERE, WITH THE CLAN.
"BUT SEEING ALL THE BRAVE WARRIORS SURROUNDING ME ONLY REMINDED ME OF EVERYTHING I'D LOST.
"IT WAS **TOO MUCH** TO HANDLE.
"SO I RESPECTFULLY DECLINED THE KIND INVITATION, TURNED TOWARDS THE MOUNTAINS..."

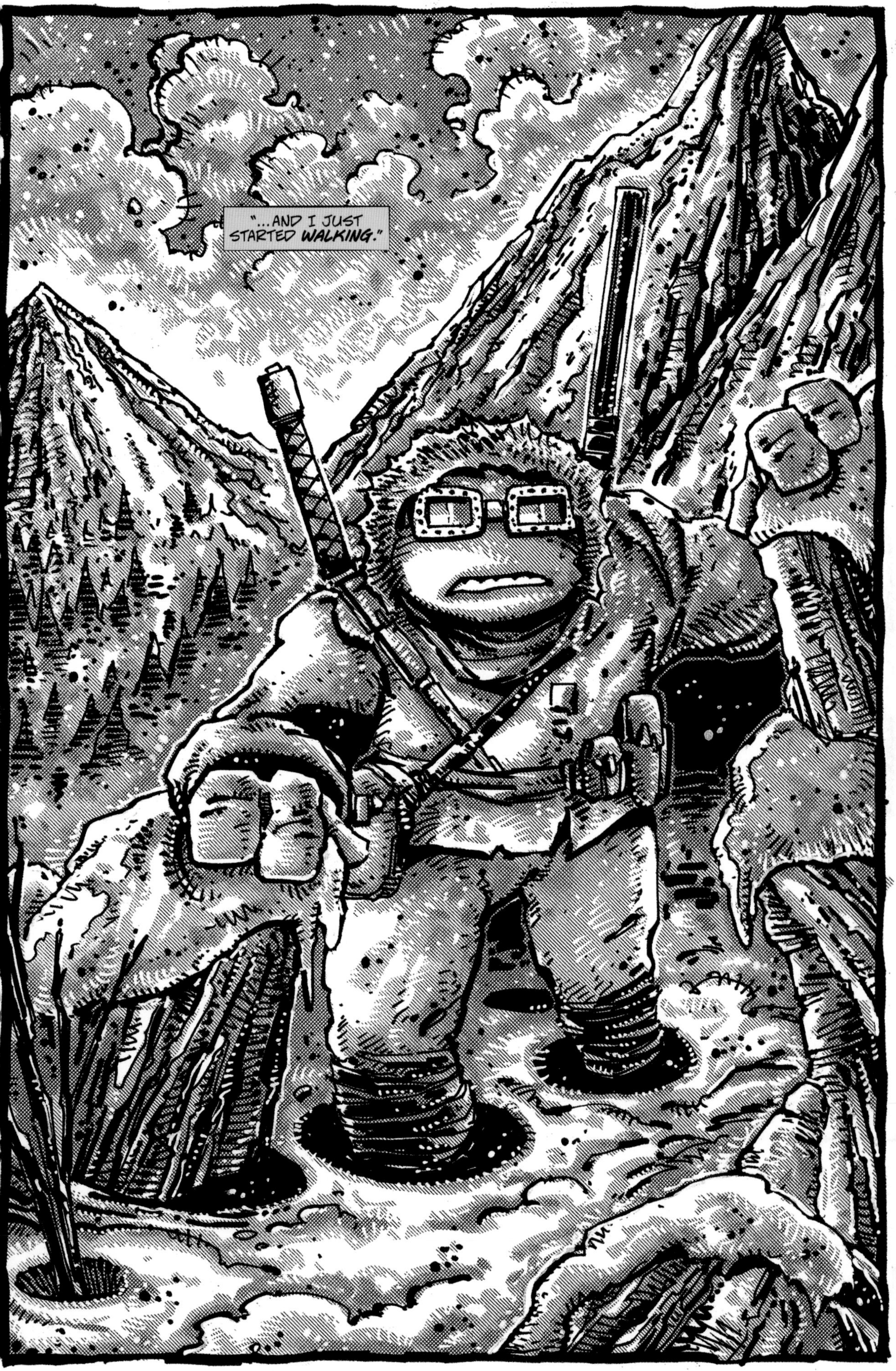
"...AND I JUST STARTED WALKING."

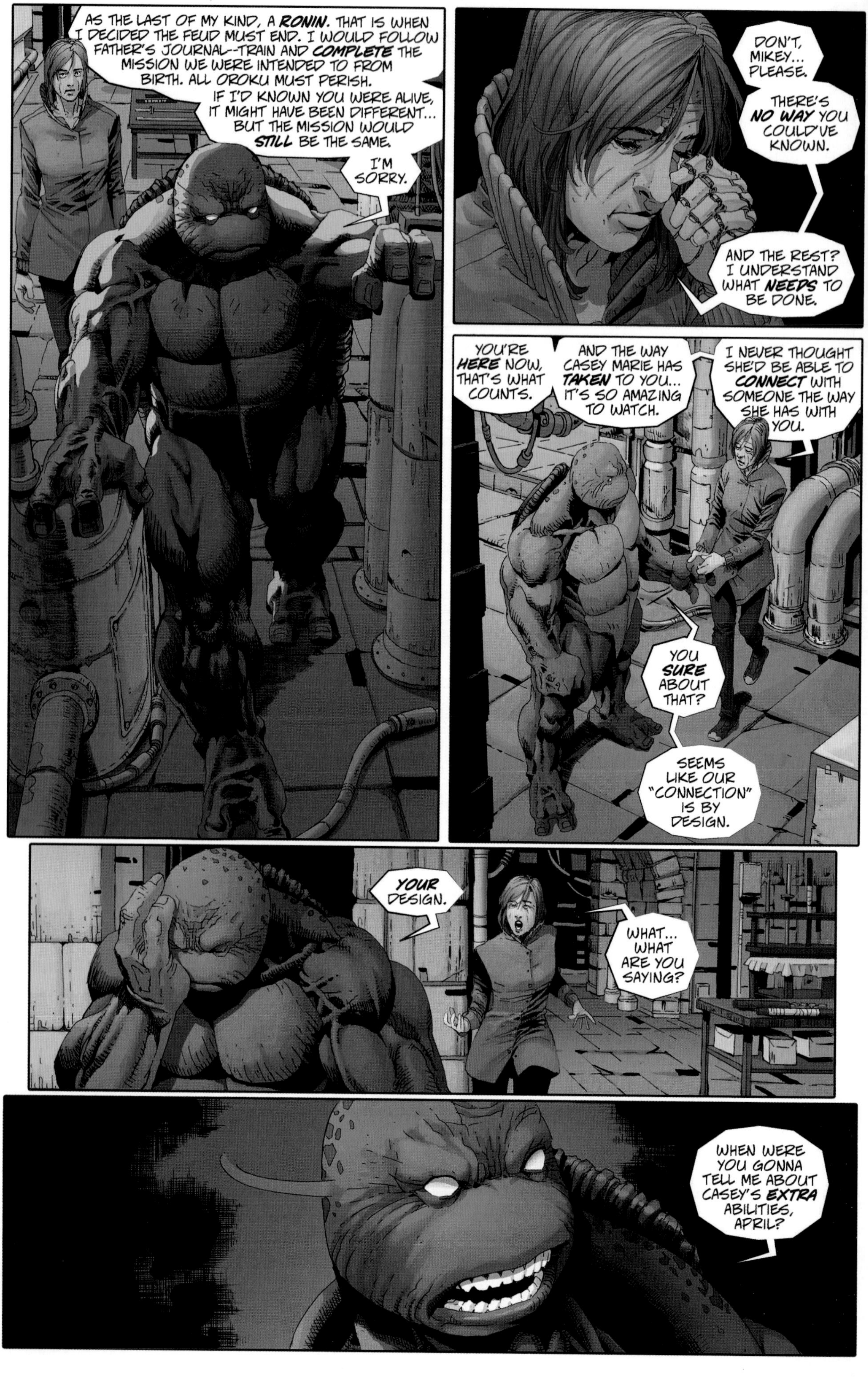

AS THE LAST OF MY KIND, A RONIN. THAT IS WHEN I DECIDED THE FEUD MUST END. I WOULD FOLLOW FATHER'S JOURNAL--TRAIN AND COMPLETE THE MISSION WE WERE INTENDED TO FROM BIRTH. ALL OROKU MUST PERISH.
IF I'D KNOWN YOU WERE ALIVE, IT MIGHT HAVE BEEN DIFFERENT... BUT THE MISSION WOULD STILL BE THE SAME.
I'M SORRY.
DON'T, MIKEY... PLEASE.
THERE'S NO WAY YOU COULD'VE KNOWN.
AND THE REST? I UNDERSTAND WHAT NEEDS TO BE DONE.
YOU'RE HERE NOW, THAT'S WHAT COUNTS.
AND THE WAY CASEY MARIE HAS TAKEN TO YOU... IT'S SO AMAZING TO WATCH.
I NEVER THOUGHT SHE'D BE ABLE TO CONNECT WITH SOMEONE THE WAY SHE HAS WITH YOU.
YOU SURE ABOUT THAT?
SEEMS LIKE OUR "CONNECTION" IS BY DESIGN.
YOUR DESIGN.
WHAT... WHAT ARE YOU SAYING?
WHEN WERE YOU GONNA TELL ME ABOUT CASEY'S EXTRA ABILITIES, APRIL?

WHY WOULD YOU KEEP THAT *AWAY* FROM ME?

I WASN'T KEEPING IT AWAY... NOT EXACTLY.

YOU DIDN'T *INJECT* HER, DID YOU?!

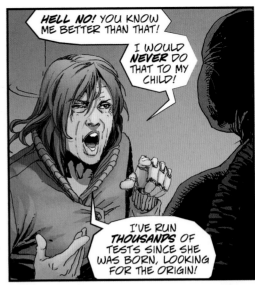

HELL NO! YOU KNOW ME BETTER THAN THAT! I WOULD *NEVER* DO THAT TO MY CHILD!

I'VE RUN *THOUSANDS* OF TESTS SINCE SHE WAS BORN, LOOKING FOR THE ORIGIN!

AS... AS FAR AS I CAN TELL, TRACE AMOUNTS OF THE MUTAGEN DNA WERE *PASSED ON* FROM HER BIRTH PARENTS--

--WHO HAPPENED TO HAVE NEARLY *LIFELONG EXPOSURE* TO IT FROM THE COMPANY THEY KEPT.

WAIT... SERIOUSLY? *US?*

WE CONTAMINATED ALL OF YOU?!

YOU DIDN'T KNOW. WE *ALL* DIDN'T KNOW!

LOOK, SHE'S BASICALLY NORMAL IN *ALL* ASPECTS OTHER THAN STRENGTH AND SPEED... AND HER HEALING ABILITY.

ALL OF WHICH HAVE *INCREASED* WITH AGE, WHICH IS WHY I WANTED SAMPLES OF YOUR BLOOD.

DOES *SHE* KNOW?

SHE'S *AWARE* SHE'S DIFFERENT, BUT I HAVEN'T TOLD HER EVERYTHING.

NOT *YET,* AT LEAST. BUT SOON.

UNTIL THEN, I NEED YOU TO KEEP THIS BETWEEN *US,* OKAY?

YEAH. SURE. OUR SECRET.

THANK YOU.

NOW, I NEED TO GET SOME FOOD IN ME. AND GALLONS OF CAFFEINE.

COME ON, WE'LL TALK MORE IN THE KITCHEN. I HAVE SOME *FRIENDS* COMING OVER I WANT YOU TO MEET.

FRIENDS?

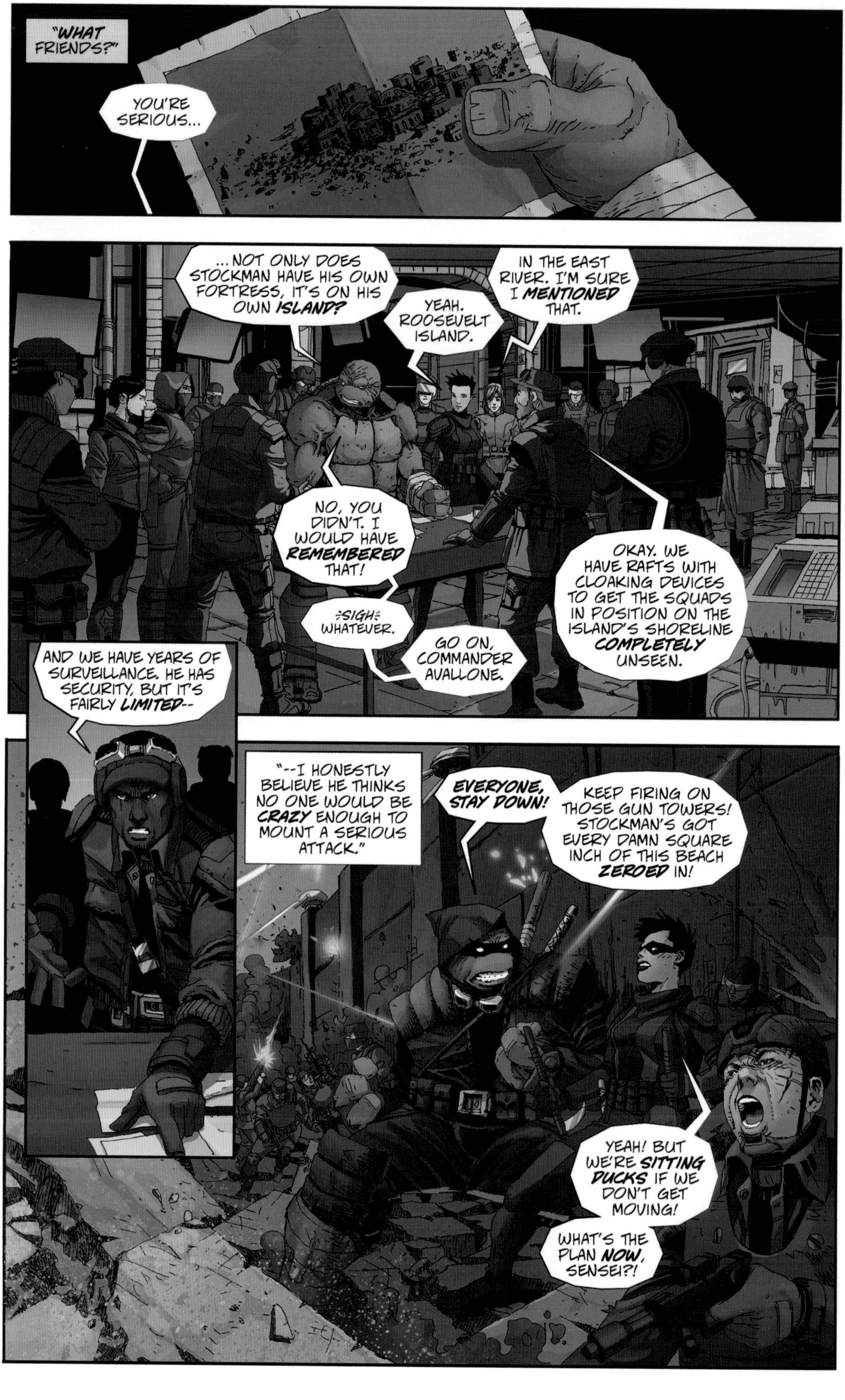
"WHAT FRIENDS?"
YOU'RE SERIOUS...
...NOT ONLY DOES STOCKMAN HAVE HIS OWN FORTRESS, IT'S ON HIS OWN ISLAND?
YEAH. ROOSEVELT ISLAND.
IN THE EAST RIVER. I'M SURE I MENTIONED THAT.
NO, YOU DIDN'T. I WOULD HAVE REMEMBERED THAT!
SIGH WHATEVER.
GO ON, COMMANDER AVALLONE.
OKAY. WE HAVE RAFTS WITH CLOAKING DEVICES TO GET THE SQUADS IN POSITION ON THE ISLAND'S SHORELINE COMPLETELY UNSEEN.
AND WE HAVE YEARS OF SURVEILLANCE. HE HAS SECURITY, BUT IT'S FAIRLY LIMITED--
"--I HONESTLY BELIEVE HE THINKS NO ONE WOULD BE CRAZY ENOUGH TO MOUNT A SERIOUS ATTACK."
EVERYONE, STAY DOWN!
KEEP FIRING ON THOSE GUN TOWERS! STOCKMAN'S GOT EVERY DAMN SQUARE INCH OF THIS BEACH ZEROED IN!
YEAH! BUT WE'RE SITTING DUCKS IF WE DON'T GET MOVING!
WHAT'S THE PLAN NOW, SENSEI?!

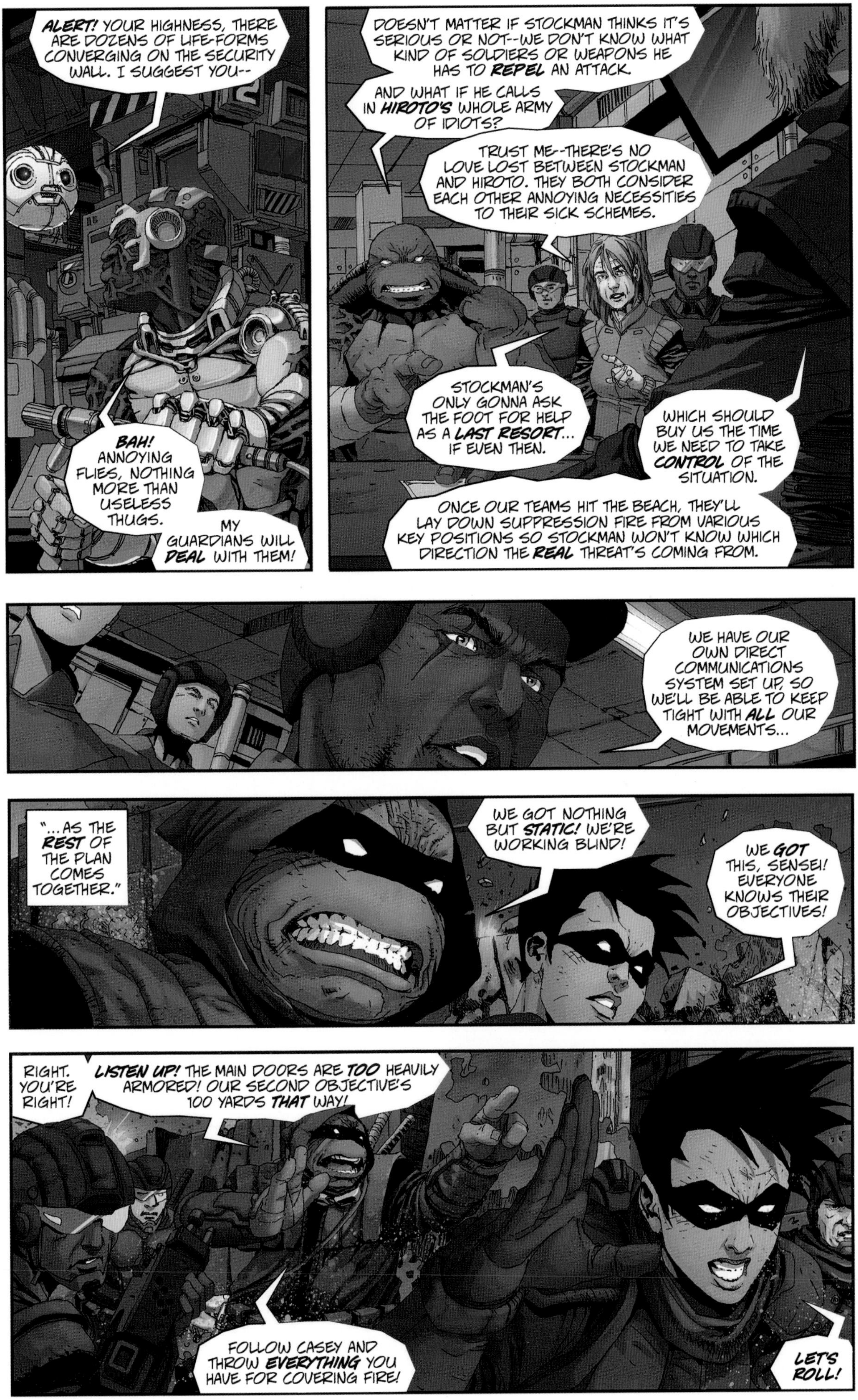
ALERT! YOUR HIGHNESS, THERE ARE DOZENS OF LIFE-FORMS CONVERGING ON THE SECURITY WALL. I SUGGEST YOU--
BAH! ANNOYING FLIES, NOTHING MORE THAN USELESS THUGS.
MY GUARDIANS WILL DEAL WITH THEM!
DOESN'T MATTER IF STOCKMAN THINKS IT'S SERIOUS OR NOT--WE DON'T KNOW WHAT KIND OF SOLDIERS OR WEAPONS HE HAS TO REPEL AN ATTACK.
AND WHAT IF HE CALLS IN HIROTO'S WHOLE ARMY OF IDIOTS?
TRUST ME--THERE'S NO LOVE LOST BETWEEN STOCKMAN AND HIROTO. THEY BOTH CONSIDER EACH OTHER ANNOYING NECESSITIES TO THEIR SICK SCHEMES.
STOCKMAN'S ONLY GONNA ASK THE FOOT FOR HELP AS A LAST RESORT... IF EVEN THEN.
WHICH SHOULD BUY US THE TIME WE NEED TO TAKE CONTROL OF THE SITUATION.
ONCE OUR TEAMS HIT THE BEACH, THEY'LL LAY DOWN SUPPRESSION FIRE FROM VARIOUS KEY POSITIONS SO STOCKMAN WON'T KNOW WHICH DIRECTION THE REAL THREAT'S COMING FROM.
WE HAVE OUR OWN DIRECT COMMUNICATIONS SYSTEM SET UP, SO WE'LL BE ABLE TO KEEP TIGHT WITH ALL OUR MOVEMENTS...
"...AS THE REST OF THE PLAN COMES TOGETHER."
WE GOT NOTHING BUT STATIC! WE'RE WORKING BLIND!
WE GOT THIS, SENSEI! EVERYONE KNOWS THEIR OBJECTIVES!
RIGHT. YOU'RE RIGHT!
LISTEN UP! THE MAIN DOORS ARE TOO HEAVILY ARMORED! OUR SECOND OBJECTIVE'S 100 YARDS THAT WAY!
FOLLOW CASEY AND THROW EVERYTHING YOU HAVE FOR COVERING FIRE!
LET'S ROLL!

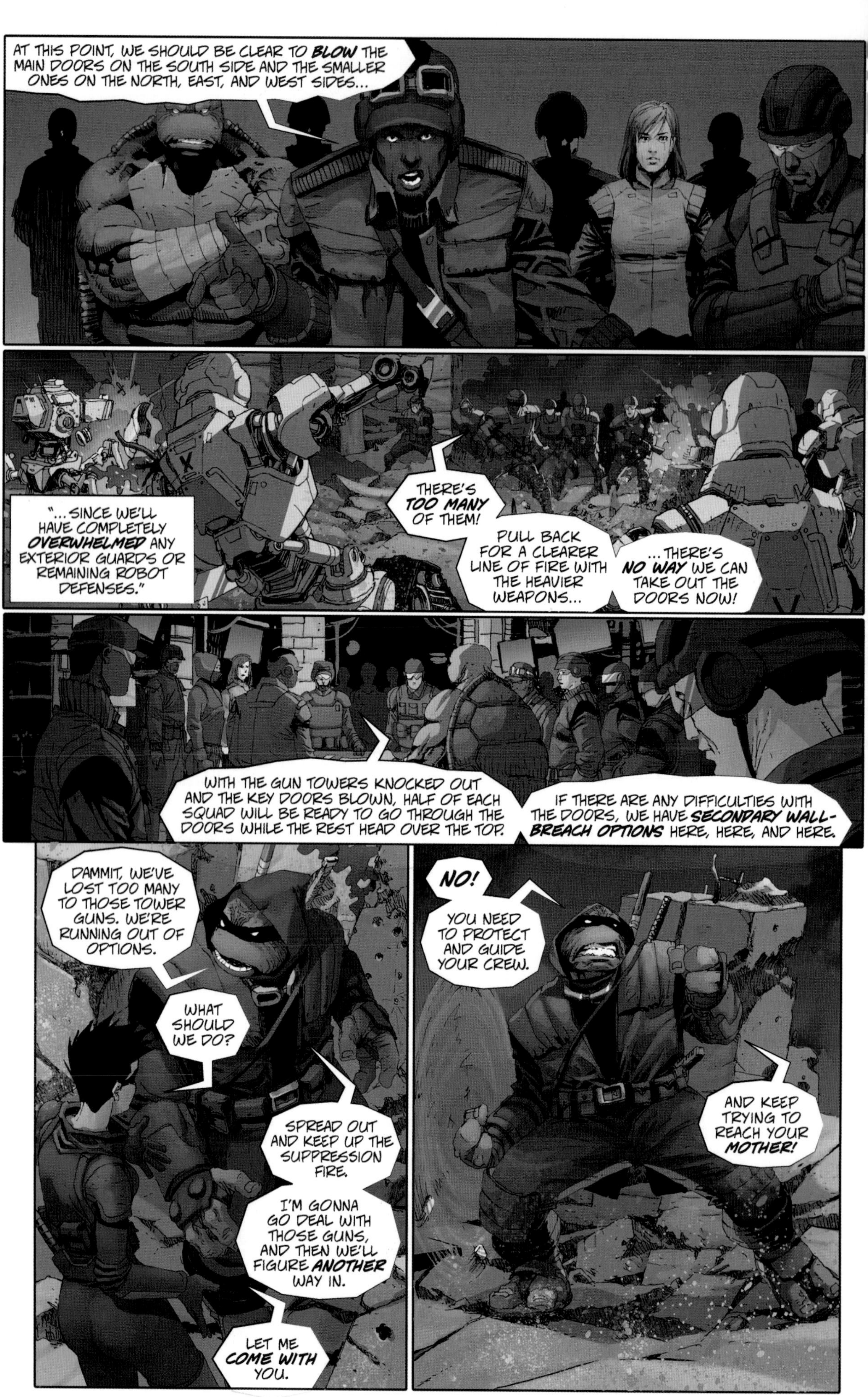
AT THIS POINT, WE SHOULD BE CLEAR TO BLOW THE MAIN DOORS ON THE SOUTH SIDE AND THE SMALLER ONES ON THE NORTH, EAST, AND WEST SIDES...
"...SINCE WE'LL HAVE COMPLETELY OVERWHELMED ANY EXTERIOR GUARDS OR REMAINING ROBOT DEFENSES."
THERE'S TOO MANY OF THEM!
PULL BACK FOR A CLEARER LINE OF FIRE WITH THE HEAVIER WEAPONS...
...THERE'S NO WAY WE CAN TAKE OUT THE DOORS NOW!
WITH THE GUN TOWERS KNOCKED OUT AND THE KEY DOORS BLOWN, HALF OF EACH SQUAD WILL BE READY TO GO THROUGH THE DOORS WHILE THE REST HEAD OVER THE TOP.
IF THERE ARE ANY DIFFICULTIES WITH THE DOORS, WE HAVE SECONDARY WALL-BREACH OPTIONS HERE, HERE, AND HERE.
DAMMIT, WE'VE LOST TOO MANY TO THOSE TOWER GUNS. WE'RE RUNNING OUT OF OPTIONS.
WHAT SHOULD WE DO?
SPREAD OUT AND KEEP UP THE SUPPRESSION FIRE.
I'M GONNA GO DEAL WITH THOSE GUNS, AND THEN WE'LL FIGURE ANOTHER WAY IN.
LET ME COME WITH YOU.
NO!
YOU NEED TO PROTECT AND GUIDE YOUR CREW.
AND KEEP TRYING TO REACH YOUR MOTHER!

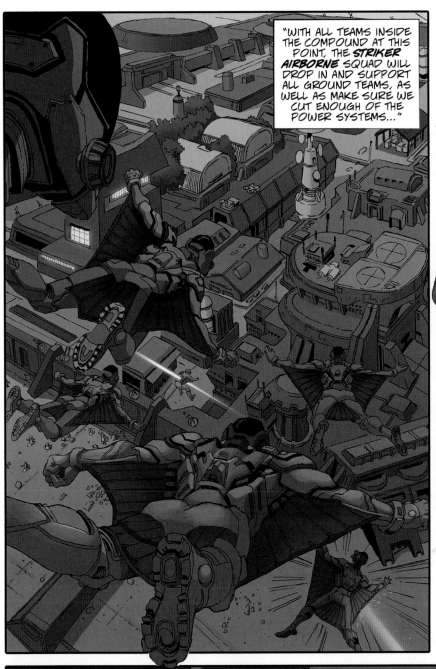

"WITH ALL TEAMS INSIDE THE COMPOUND AT THIS POINT, THE **STRIKER AIRBORNE** SQUAD WILL DROP IN AND SUPPORT ALL GROUND TEAMS, AS WELL AS MAKE SURE WE CUT ENOUGH OF THE POWER SYSTEMS..."

...IN ORDER TO **REPEL** A COUNTERATTACK WHILE WE COMPLETE PHASE TWO.

MRS. JONES WILL PICK UP THE BRIEFING FROM HERE.

DAMMIT! AIRBORNE'S SITTING *DUCKS* FOR THE REMAINING GUN TOWERS!

STUPID ATTACK PLAN!

STUPID!

THIS SHOULD HELP THEM GET ON THE *GROUND.*

SHNKK

NOW TO FIGURE OUT HOW TO KEEP THIS FROM BECOMING A *COMPLETE* MASSACRE.

B O O M

GET *DOWN* IN THE COURTYARD AND TAKE POSITIONS!

WITH EVERYTHING KNOCKED OUT AS COMMANDERS AVALLONE AND ZARAGOZA LAID OUT, I'LL BE ROLLING THROUGH THE MAIN GATES IN THE *AFV*--HEADING STRAIGHT FOR THE LARGEST GENERATOR.

WE'RE GONNA NEED ALL AVAILABLE POWER TO REACTIVATE THE FUGITOID, WHICH SHOULD ENABLE US TO TALK *DIRECTLY* TO PROFESSOR HONEYCUTT, ACCESS STOCKMAN'S NETWORK...

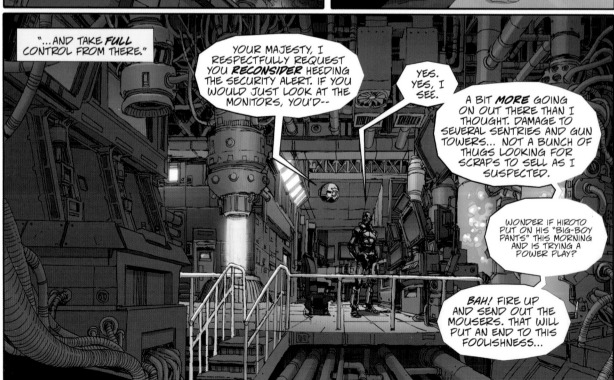

"...AND TAKE *FULL* CONTROL FROM THERE."

YOUR MAJESTY, I RESPECTFULLY REQUEST YOU *RECONSIDER* HEEDING THE SECURITY ALERT. IF YOU WOULD JUST LOOK AT THE MONITORS, YOU'D--

YES. YES, I SEE.

A BIT *MORE* GOING ON OUT THERE THAN I THOUGHT. DAMAGE TO SEVERAL SENTRIES AND GUN TOWERS... NOT A BUNCH OF THUGS LOOKING FOR SCRAPS TO SELL AS I SUSPECTED.

WONDER IF HIROTO PUT ON HIS "BIG-BOY PANTS" THIS MORNING AND IS TRYING A POWER PLAY?

BAH! FIRE UP AND SEND OUT THE MOUSERS. THAT WILL PUT AN END TO THIS FOOLISHNESS...

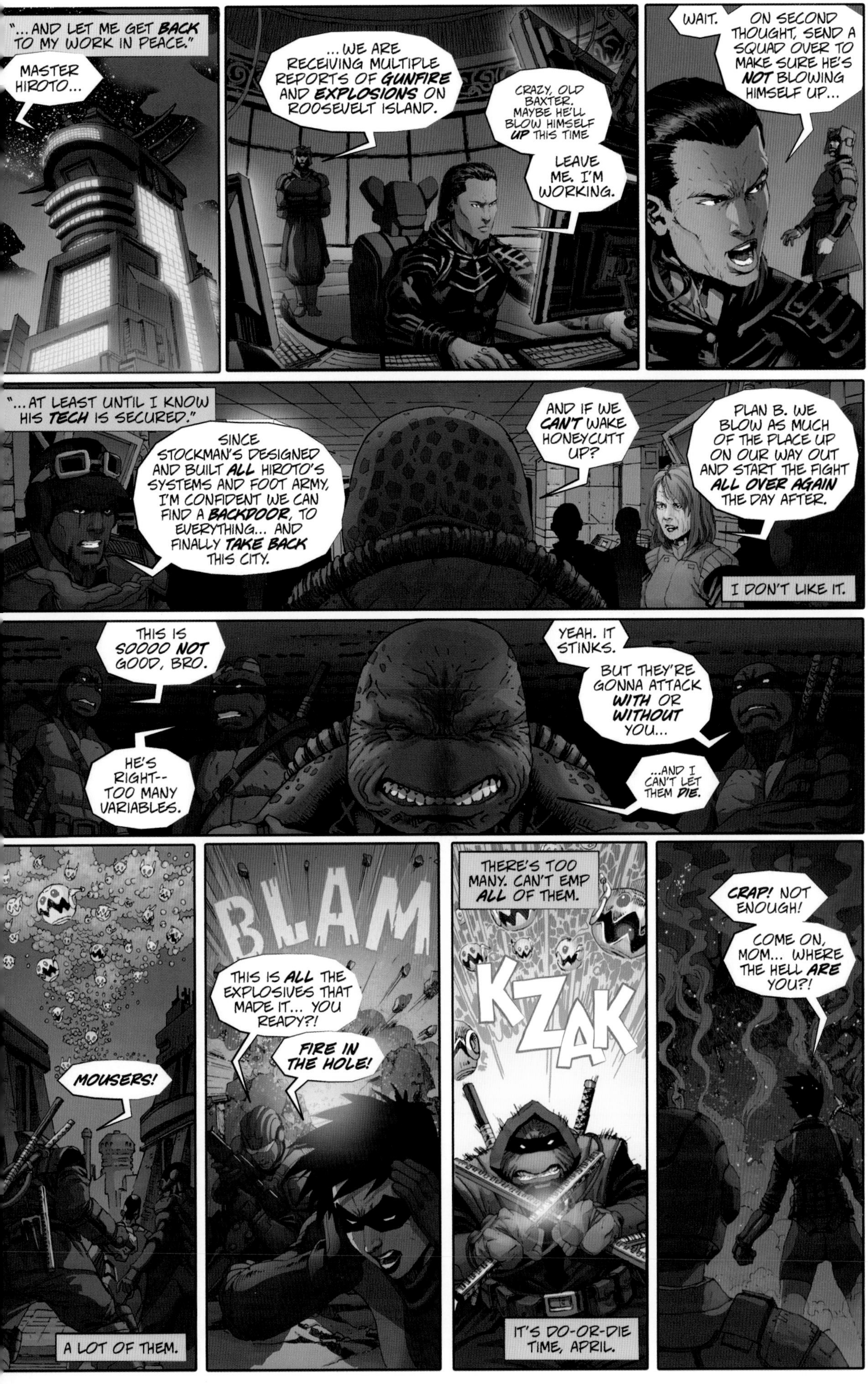
"...AND LET ME GET BACK TO MY WORK IN PEACE."
MASTER HIROTO...
...WE ARE RECEIVING MULTIPLE REPORTS OF GUNFIRE AND EXPLOSIONS ON ROOSEVELT ISLAND.
CRAZY, OLD BAXTER. MAYBE HE'LL BLOW HIMSELF UP THIS TIME
LEAVE ME. I'M WORKING.
WAIT.
ON SECOND THOUGHT, SEND A SQUAD OVER TO MAKE SURE HE'S NOT BLOWING HIMSELF UP...
"...AT LEAST UNTIL I KNOW HIS TECH IS SECURED."
SINCE STOCKMAN'S DESIGNED AND BUILT ALL HIROTO'S SYSTEMS AND FOOT ARMY, I'M CONFIDENT WE CAN FIND A BACKDOOR, TO EVERYTHING... AND FINALLY TAKE BACK THIS CITY.
AND IF WE CAN'T WAKE HONEYCUTT UP?
PLAN B. WE BLOW AS MUCH OF THE PLACE UP ON OUR WAY OUT AND START THE FIGHT ALL OVER AGAIN THE DAY AFTER.
I DON'T LIKE IT.
THIS IS SOOOO NOT GOOD, BRO.
HE'S RIGHT-- TOO MANY VARIABLES.
YEAH. IT STINKS.
BUT THEY'RE GONNA ATTACK WITH OR WITHOUT YOU...
...AND I CAN'T LET THEM DIE.
MOUSERS!
A LOT OF THEM.
BLAM
THIS IS ALL THE EXPLOSIVES THAT MADE IT... YOU READY?!
FIRE IN THE HOLE!
THERE'S TOO MANY. CAN'T EMP ALL OF THEM.
KZAK
IT'S DO-OR-DIE TIME, APRIL.
CRAP! NOT ENOUGH!
COME ON, MOM... WHERE THE HELL ARE YOU?!

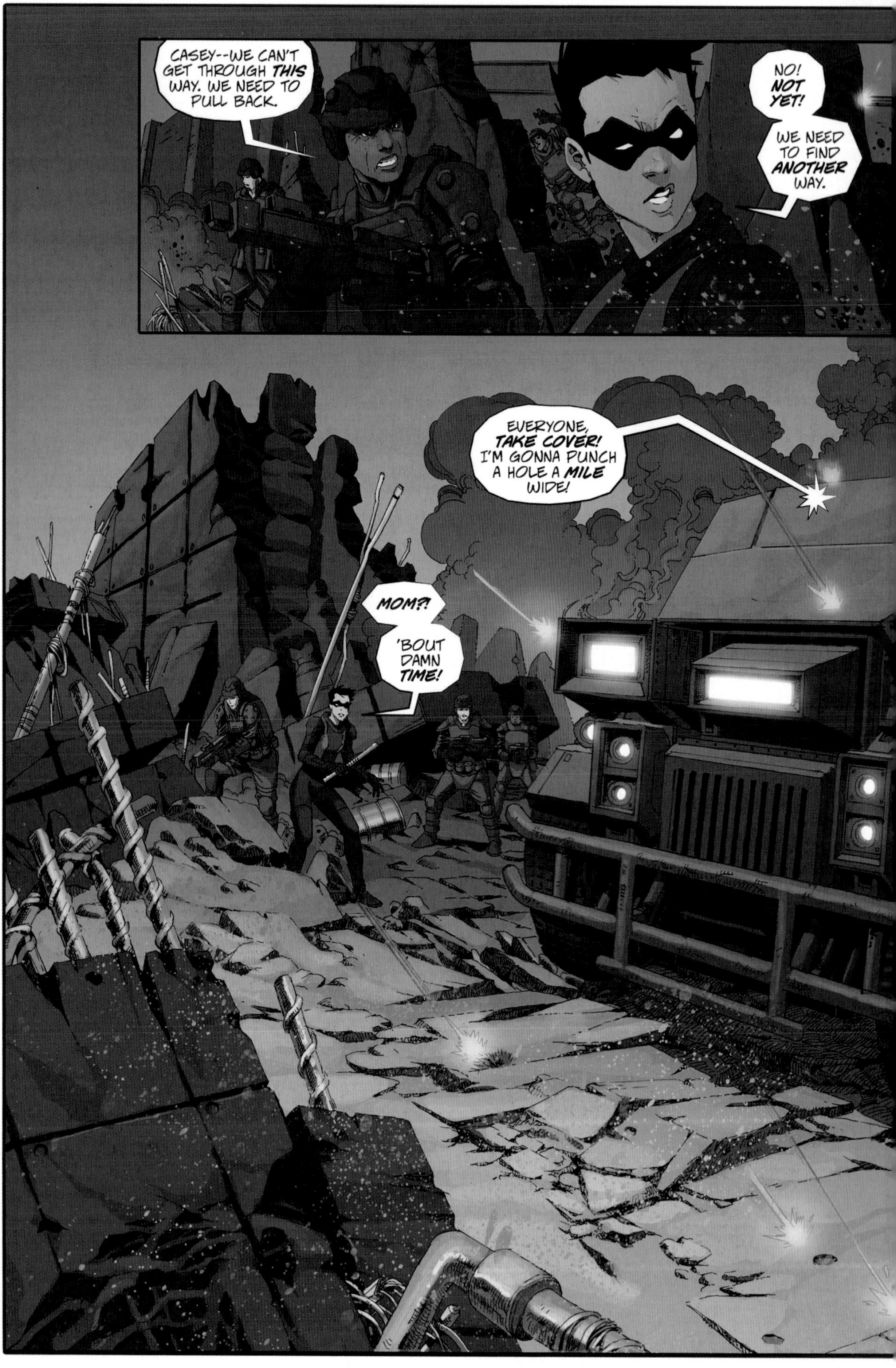
CASEY--WE CAN'T GET THROUGH THIS WAY. WE NEED TO PULL BACK.
NO! NOT YET!
WE NEED TO FIND ANOTHER WAY.
EVERYONE, TAKE COVER! I'M GONNA PUNCH A HOLE A MILE WIDE!
MOM?!
'BOUT DAMN TIME!

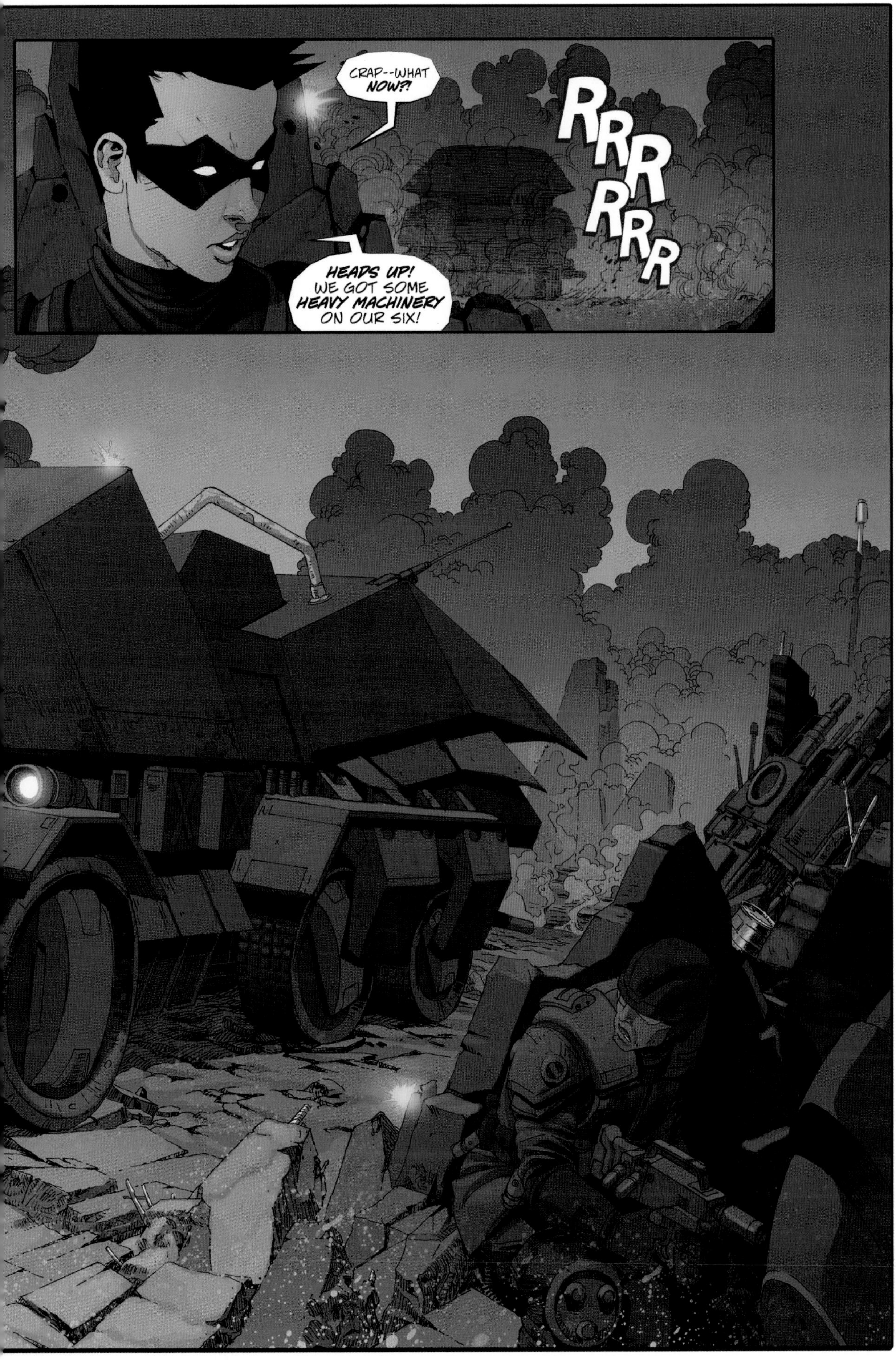
CRAP--WHAT NOW?!
RRRRRRR
HEADS UP! WE GOT SOME HEAVY MACHINERY ON OUR SIX!

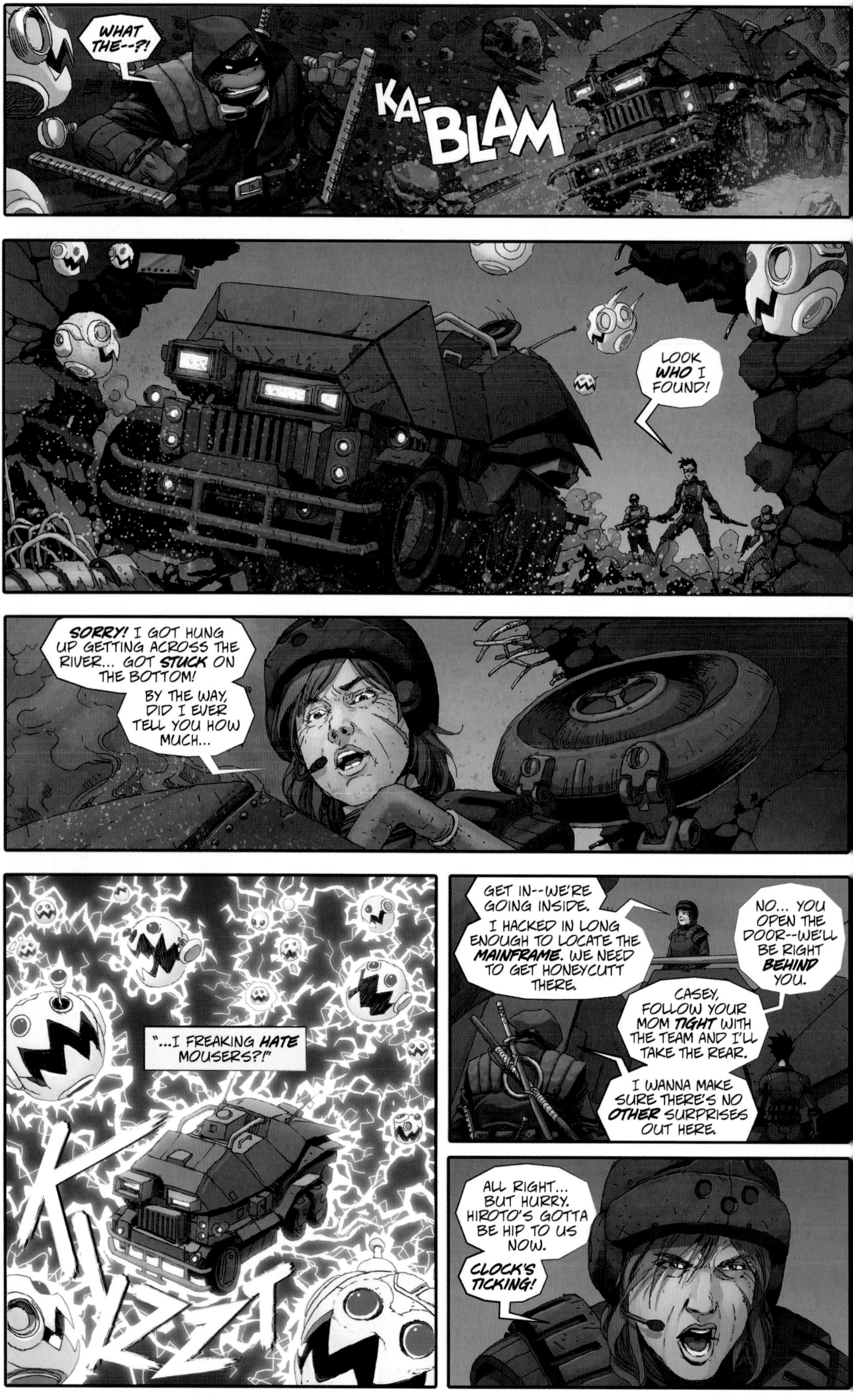
WHAT THE--?!
KA-BLAM
LOOK WHO I FOUND!
SORRY! I GOT HUNG UP GETTING ACROSS THE RIVER... GOT STUCK ON THE BOTTOM!
BY THE WAY, DID I EVER TELL YOU HOW MUCH...
"...I FREAKING HATE MOUSERS?!"
KZZT
GET IN--WE'RE GOING INSIDE.
I HACKED IN LONG ENOUGH TO LOCATE THE MAINFRAME. WE NEED TO GET HONEYCUTT THERE.
NO... YOU OPEN THE DOOR--WE'LL BE RIGHT BEHIND YOU.
CASEY, FOLLOW YOUR MOM TIGHT WITH THE TEAM AND I'LL TAKE THE REAR.
I WANNA MAKE SURE THERE'S NO OTHER SURPRISES OUT HERE.
ALL RIGHT... BUT HURRY. HIROTO'S GOTTA BE HIP TO US NOW.
CLOCK'S TICKING!

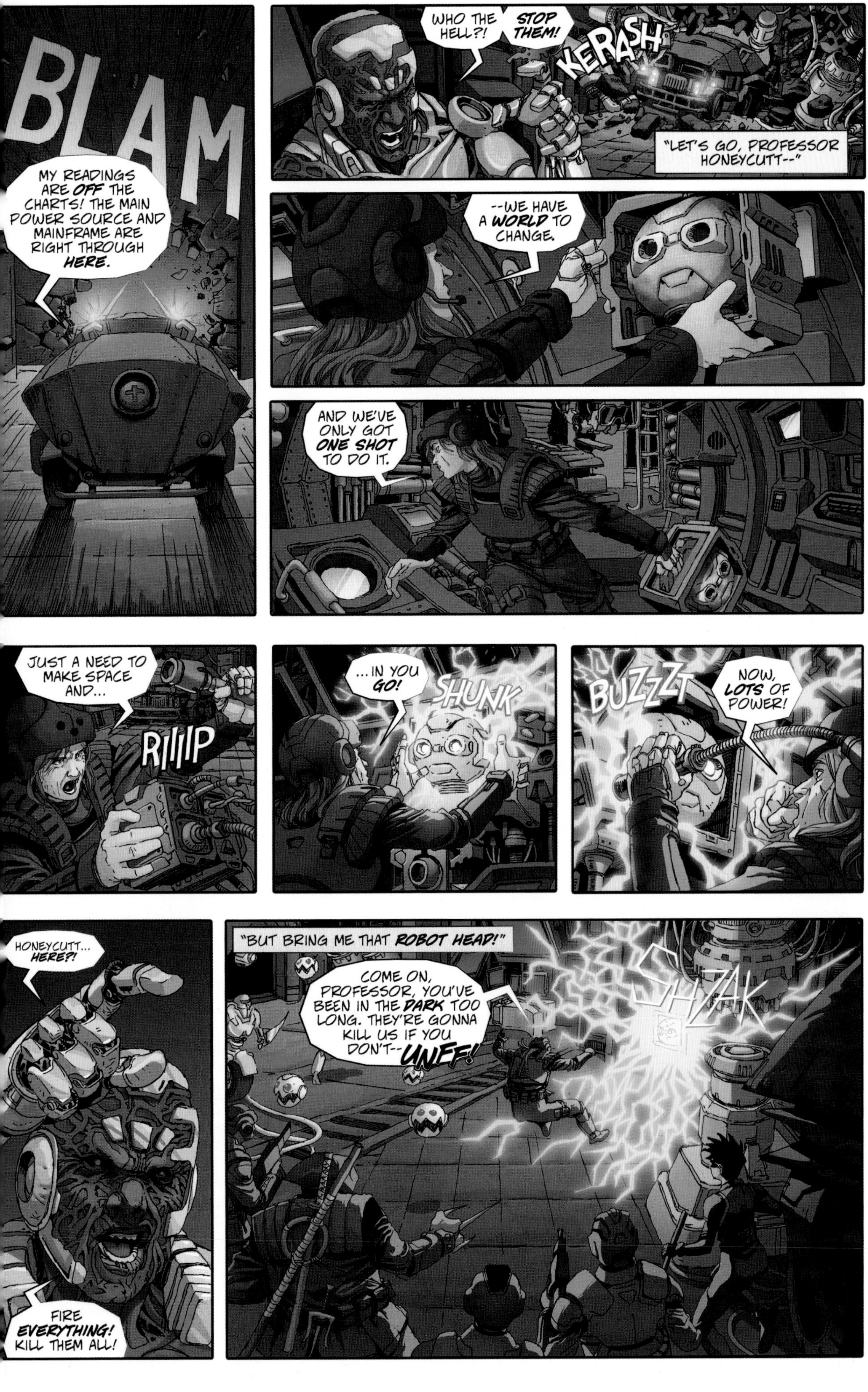
BLAM
MY READINGS ARE OFF THE CHARTS! THE MAIN POWER SOURCE AND MAINFRAME ARE RIGHT THROUGH HERE.
WHO THE HELL?!
STOP THEM!
KERASH
"LET'S GO, PROFESSOR HONEYCUTT--"
--WE HAVE A WORLD TO CHANGE.
AND WE'VE ONLY GOT ONE SHOT TO DO IT.
JUST A NEED TO MAKE SPACE AND...
RIIIIP
...IN YOU GO!
SHUNK
BUZZZT
NOW, LOTS OF POWER!
HONEYCUTT... HERE?!
FIRE EVERYTHING! KILL THEM ALL!
"BUT BRING ME THAT ROBOT HEAD!"
COME ON, PROFESSOR, YOU'VE BEEN IN THE DARK TOO LONG. THEY'RE GONNA KILL US IF YOU DON'T--UNFF!
SHZAK

STOCKMAN'S THROWING **EVERYTHING** HE HAS AT US! WATCH YOUR BACKS!

COME ON, HONEYCUTT...

...IT'S NOW OR NEVER.

WHAT DO YOU THINK YOU'RE DOING?!

SAVING THE WORLD.

BUT FIRST...

KRAK

THIS IS FOR MY **HUSBAND!**

DAMNED WOMAN! I NEARLY **FELT** THAT!

WHAP

NNG!

I'LL FINISH YOU **ALL** MOMENTARILY.

BUT NOT UNTIL I SECURE...

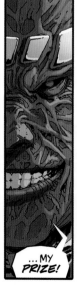

...MY **PRIZE!**

YOU... SHALL... NOT... PASS...

WHAT... DID YOU SAY?

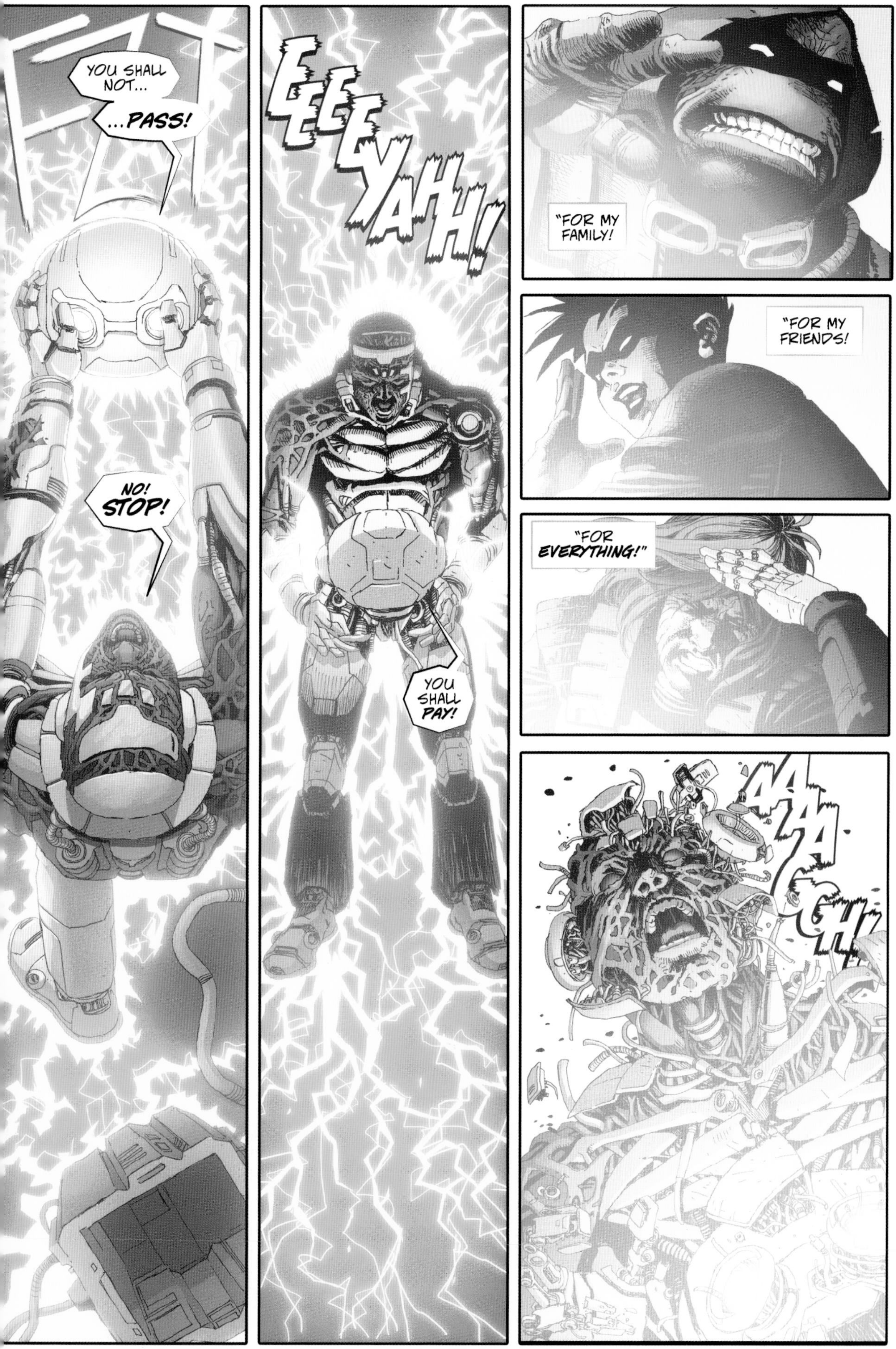
YOU SHALL NOT...
...PASS!
NO! STOP!
EEEEYAHH!
YOU SHALL PAY!
"FOR MY FAMILY!
"FOR MY FRIENDS!
"FOR EVERYTHING!"
AAAAAGH!

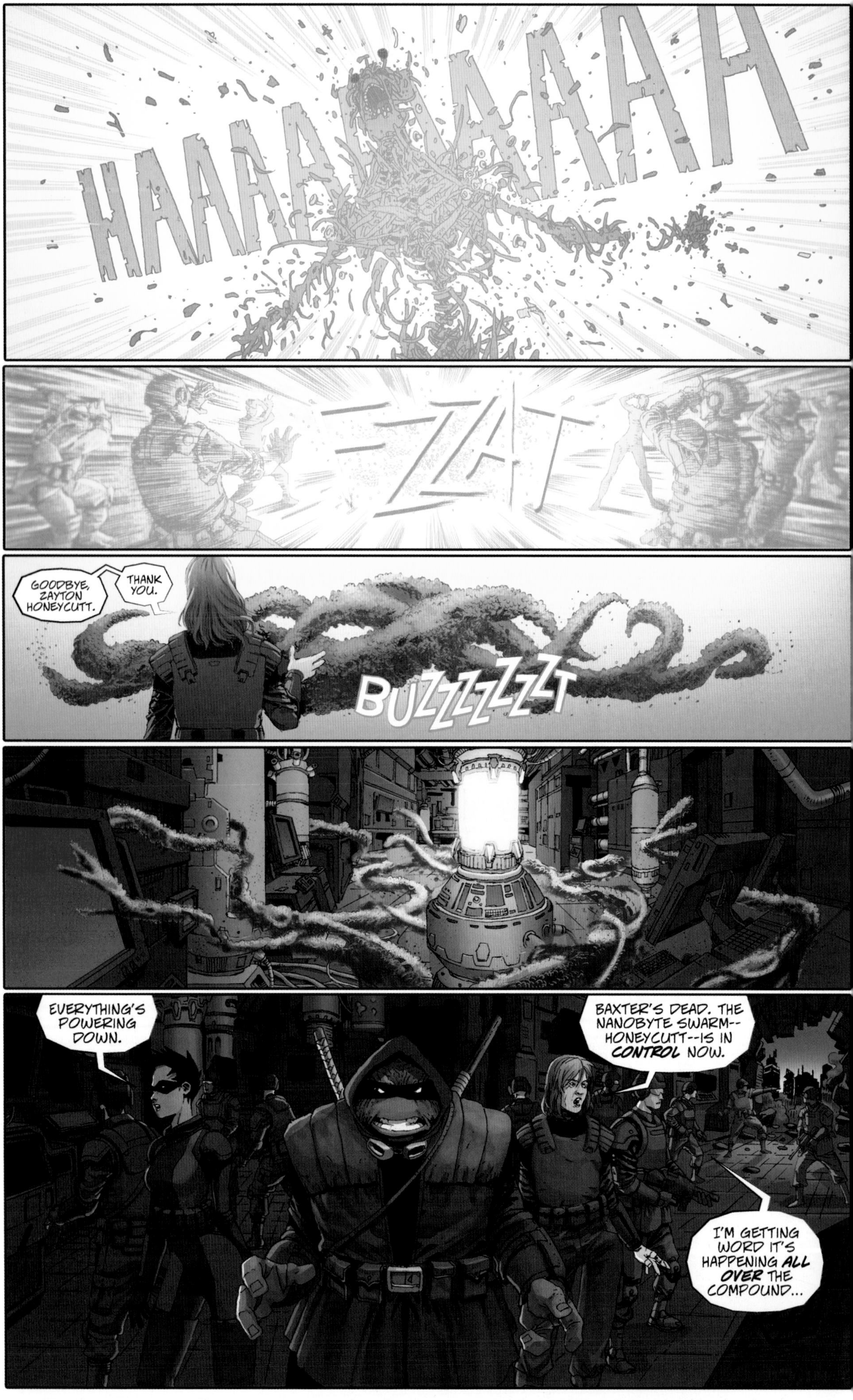
HAAAAAAAAAA
ZZAT
GOODBYE, ZAYTON HONEYCUTT.
THANK YOU.
BUZZZZZZZT
EVERYTHING'S POWERING DOWN.
BAXTER'S DEAD. THE NANOBYTE SWARM--HONEYCUTT--IS IN **CONTROL** NOW.
I'M GETTING WORD IT'S HAPPENING **ALL OVER** THE COMPOUND...

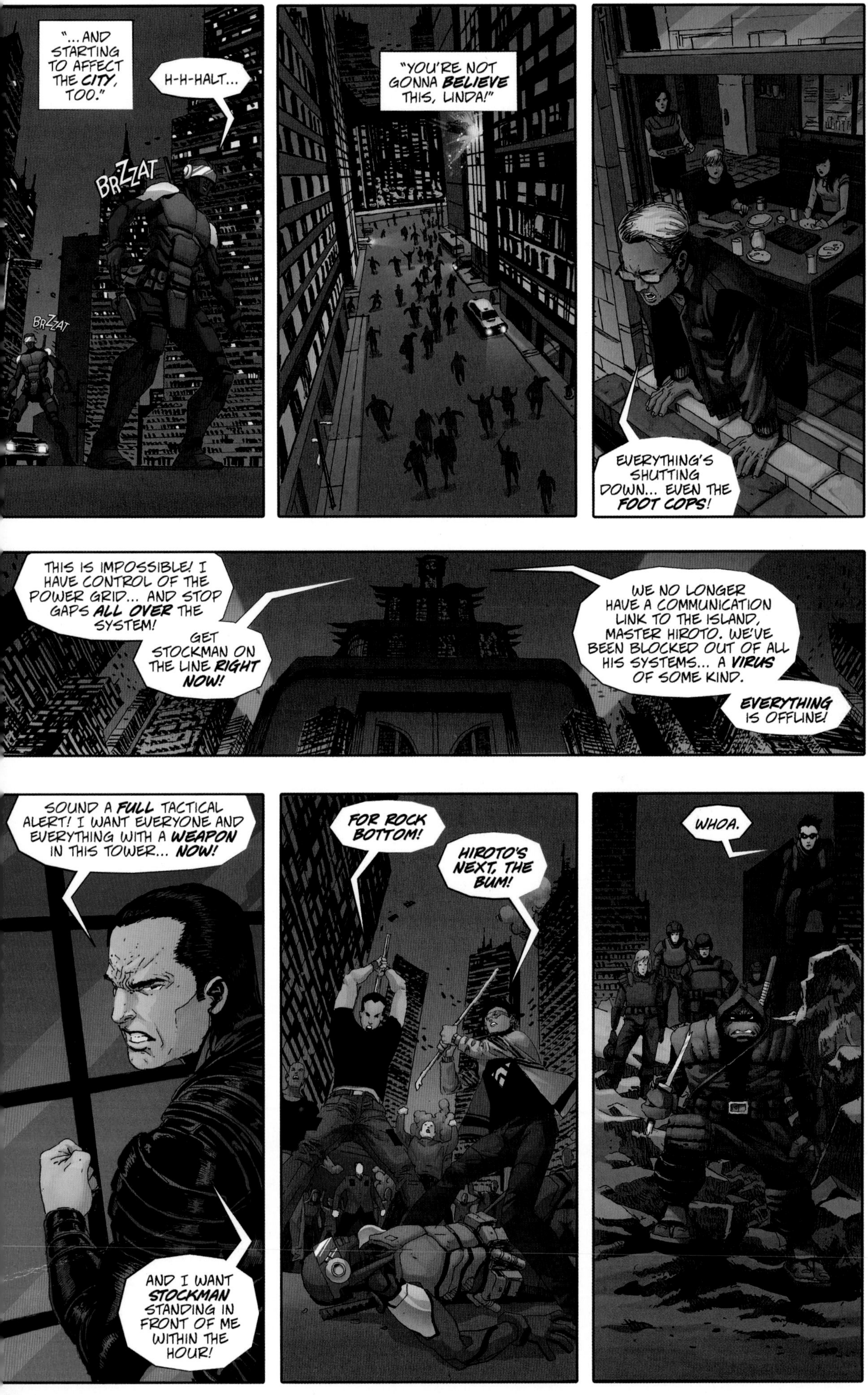
"...AND STARTING TO AFFECT THE CITY, TOO."
H-H-HALT...
BRZZAT
BRZZAT
"YOU'RE NOT GONNA BELIEVE THIS, LINDA!"
EVERYTHING'S SHUTTING DOWN... EVEN THE FOOT COPS!
THIS IS IMPOSSIBLE! I HAVE CONTROL OF THE POWER GRID... AND STOP GAPS ALL OVER THE SYSTEM!
GET STOCKMAN ON THE LINE RIGHT NOW!
WE NO LONGER HAVE A COMMUNICATION LINK TO THE ISLAND, MASTER HIROTO. WE'VE BEEN BLOCKED OUT OF ALL HIS SYSTEMS... A VIRUS OF SOME KIND.
EVERYTHING IS OFFLINE!
SOUND A FULL TACTICAL ALERT! I WANT EVERYONE AND EVERYTHING WITH A WEAPON IN THIS TOWER... NOW!
AND I WANT STOCKMAN STANDING IN FRONT OF ME WITHIN THE HOUR!
FOR ROCK BOTTOM!
HIROTO'S NEXT, THE BUM!
WHOA.

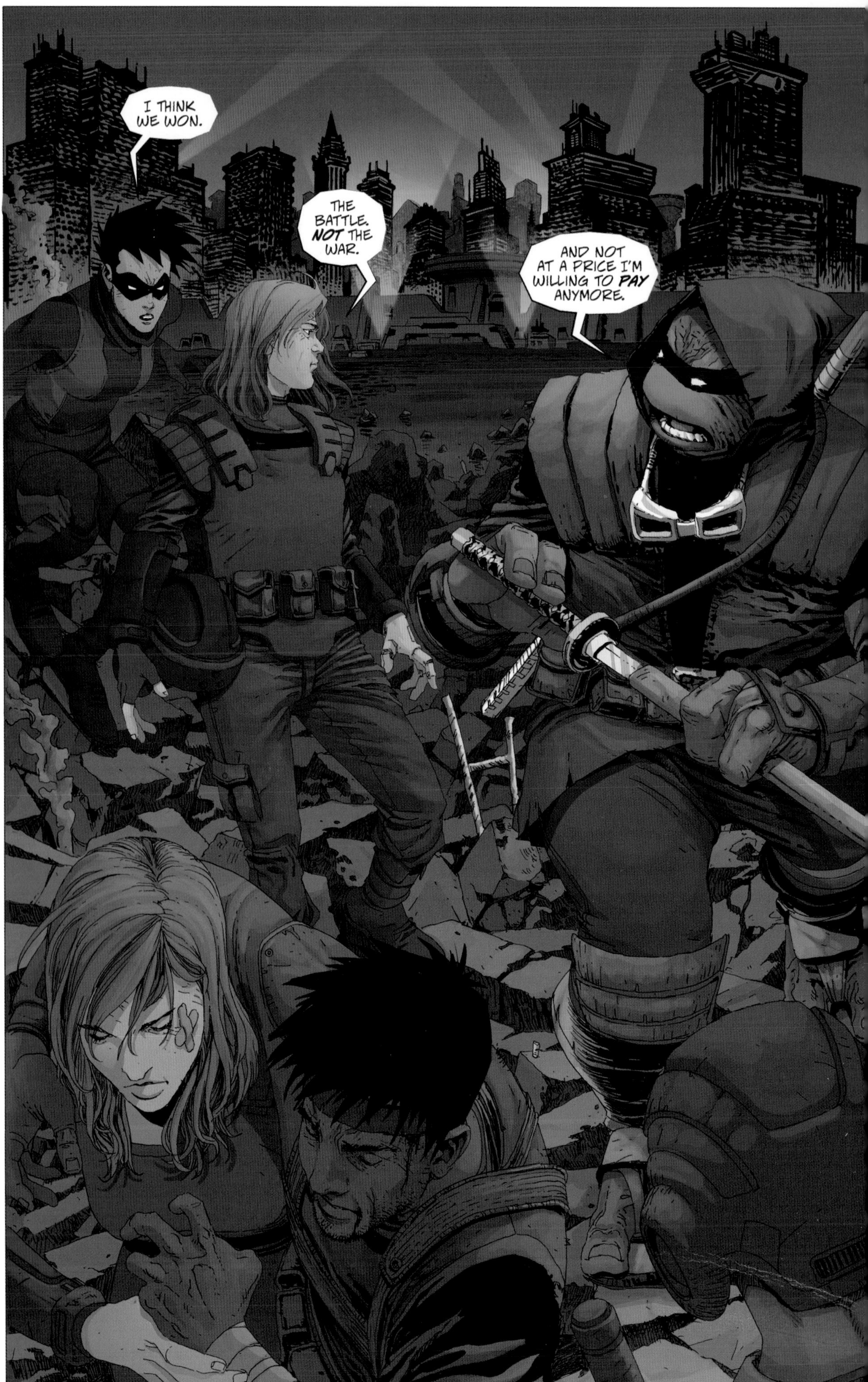
I THINK WE WON.
THE BATTLE. NOT THE WAR.
AND NOT AT A PRICE I'M WILLING TO PAY ANYMORE.

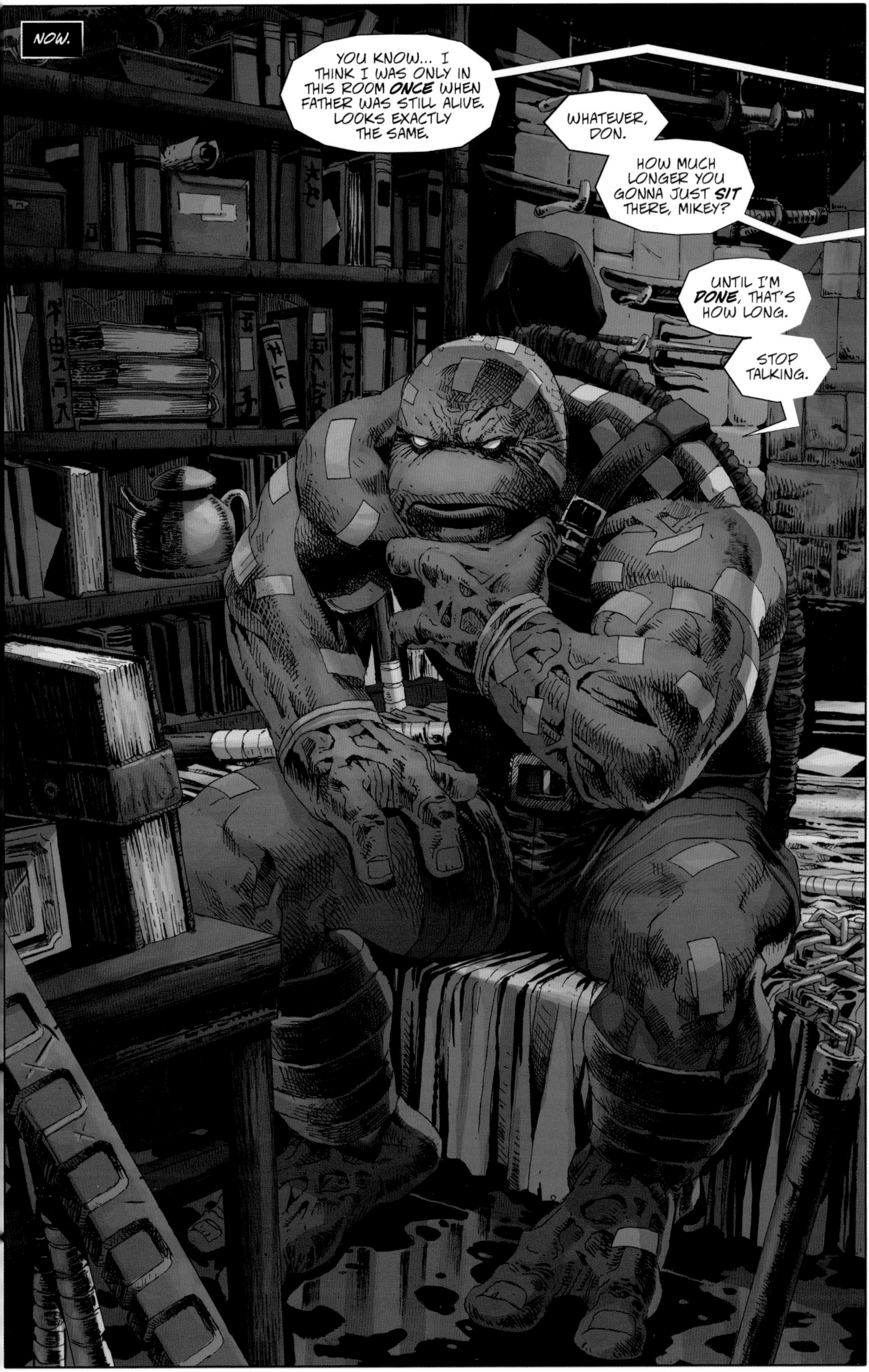
NOW.
YOU KNOW... I THINK I WAS ONLY IN THIS ROOM ONCE WHEN FATHER WAS STILL ALIVE. LOOKS EXACTLY THE SAME.
WHATEVER, DON.
HOW MUCH LONGER YOU GONNA JUST SIT THERE, MIKEY?
UNTIL I'M DONE, THAT'S HOW LONG.
STOP TALKING.

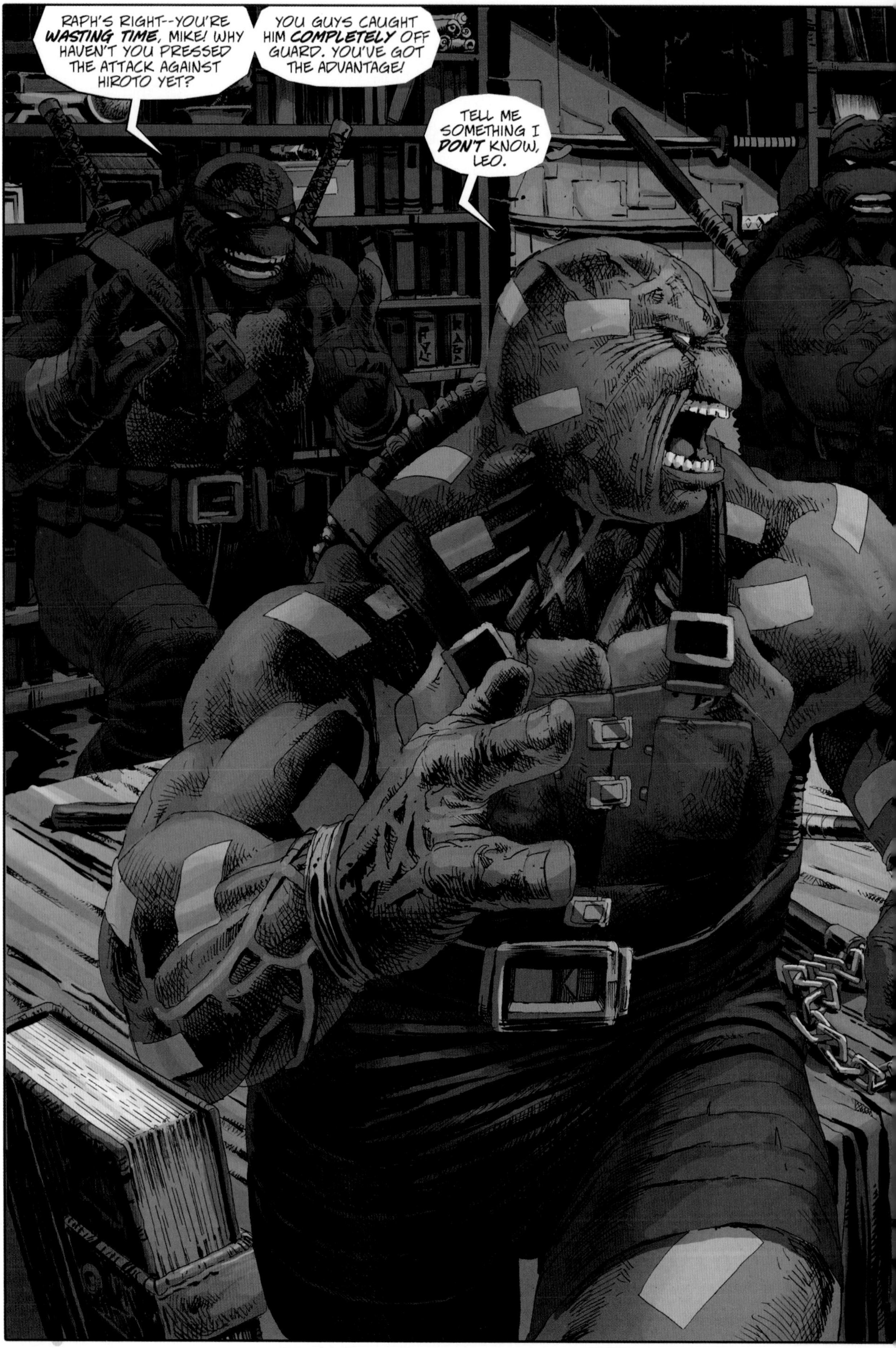
RAPH'S RIGHT--YOU'RE **WASTING TIME**, MIKE! WHY HAVEN'T YOU PRESSED THE ATTACK AGAINST HIROTO YET?
YOU GUYS CAUGHT HIM **COMPLETELY** OFF GUARD. YOU'VE GOT THE ADVANTAGE!
TELL ME SOMETHING I **DON'T** KNOW, LEO.

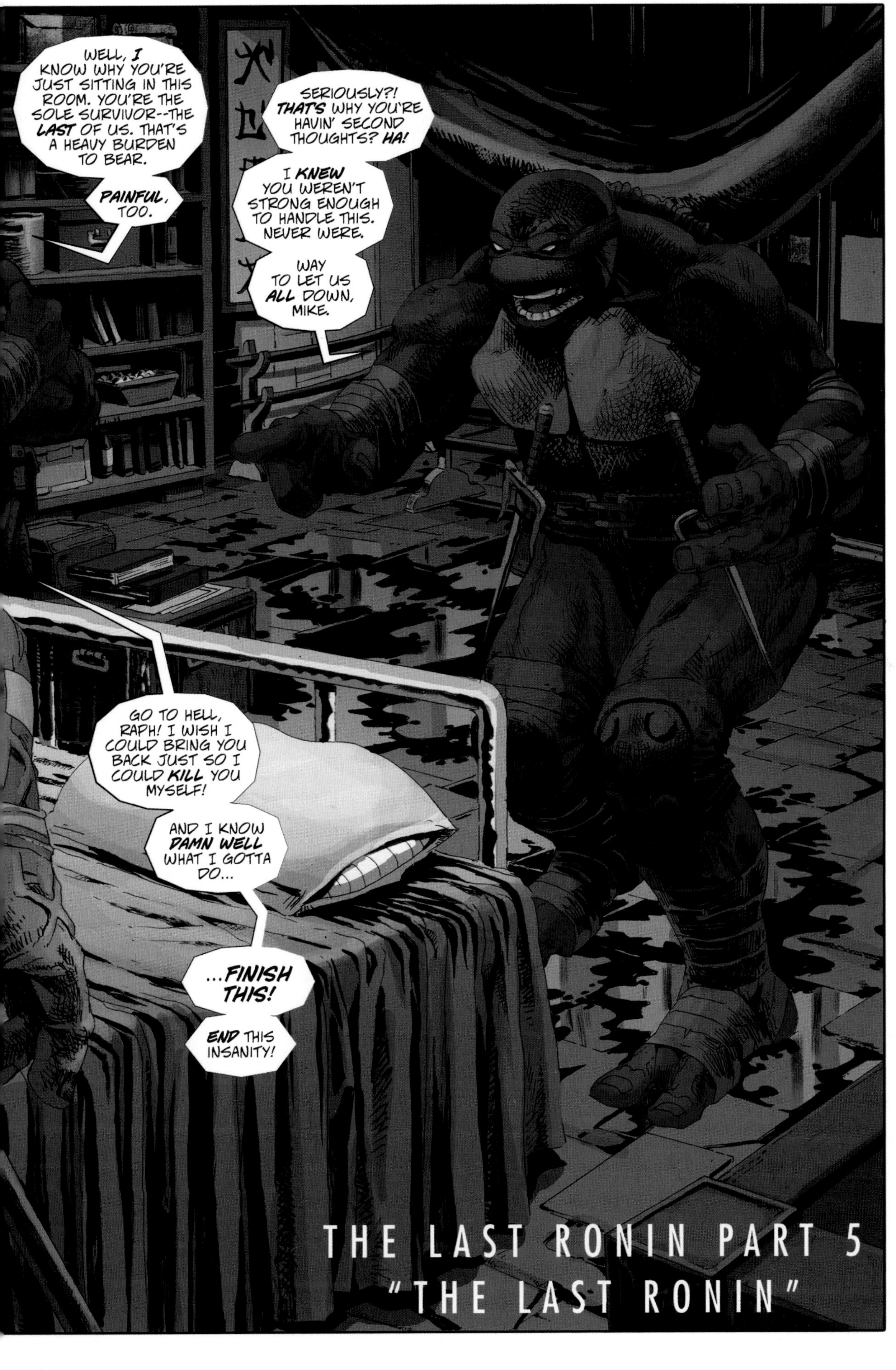
WELL, I KNOW WHY YOU'RE JUST SITTING IN THIS ROOM. YOU'RE THE SOLE SURVIVOR--THE LAST OF US. THAT'S A HEAVY BURDEN TO BEAR.
PAINFUL, TOO.
SERIOUSLY?! THAT'S WHY YOU'RE HAVIN' SECOND THOUGHTS? HA!
I KNEW YOU WEREN'T STRONG ENOUGH TO HANDLE THIS. NEVER WERE.
WAY TO LET US ALL DOWN, MIKE.
GO TO HELL, RAPH! I WISH I COULD BRING YOU BACK JUST SO I COULD KILL YOU MYSELF!
AND I KNOW DAMN WELL WHAT I GOTTA DO...
...FINISH THIS!
END THIS INSANITY!
THE LAST RONIN PART 5
"THE LAST RONIN"

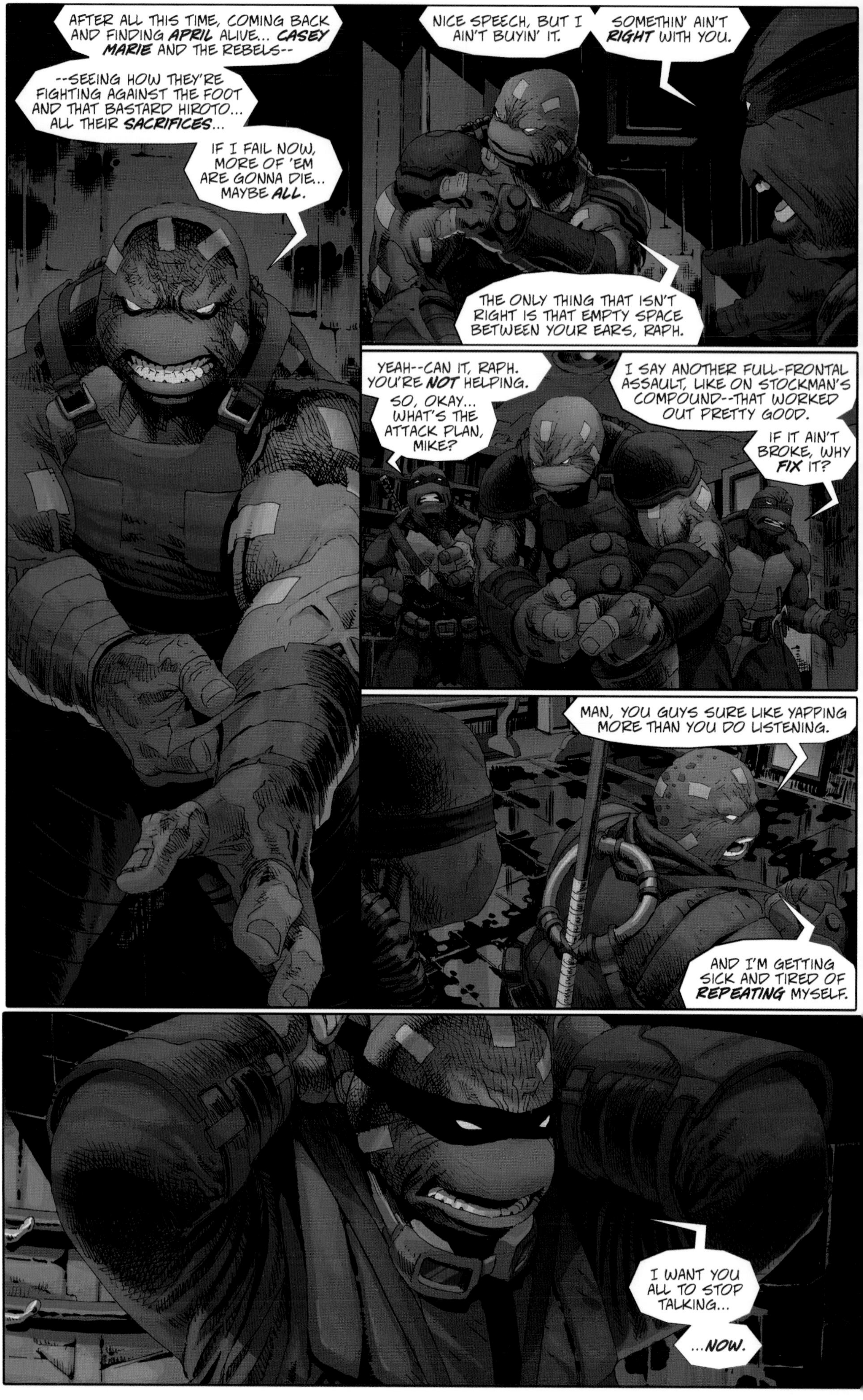
AFTER ALL THIS TIME, COMING BACK AND FINDING APRIL ALIVE... CASEY MARIE AND THE REBELS--
--SEEING HOW THEY'RE FIGHTING AGAINST THE FOOT AND THAT BASTARD HIROTO... ALL THEIR SACRIFICES...
IF I FAIL NOW, MORE OF 'EM ARE GONNA DIE... MAYBE ALL.
NICE SPEECH, BUT I AIN'T BUYIN' IT.
SOMETHIN' AIN'T RIGHT WITH YOU.
THE ONLY THING THAT ISN'T RIGHT IS THAT EMPTY SPACE BETWEEN YOUR EARS, RAPH.
YEAH--CAN IT, RAPH. YOU'RE NOT HELPING.
SO, OKAY... WHAT'S THE ATTACK PLAN, MIKE?
I SAY ANOTHER FULL-FRONTAL ASSAULT, LIKE ON STOCKMAN'S COMPOUND--THAT WORKED OUT PRETTY GOOD.
IF IT AIN'T BROKE, WHY FIX IT?
MAN, YOU GUYS SURE LIKE YAPPING MORE THAN YOU DO LISTENING.
AND I'M GETTING SICK AND TIRED OF REPEATING MYSELF.
I WANT YOU ALL TO STOP TALKING...
...NOW.

RIGHT. YOU'D BE LOST *WITHOUT* US.

NO. NO, I WOULDN'T.

IT'S WORSE *NOW* THAN WHEN YOU WERE ALIVE... CONSTANTLY TELLING ME WHAT TO DO.

AND WHAT DO I HAVE TO SHOW FOR ALL YOUR ORDERS AND KNOWLEDGE?

THIS!

THIS IS *ALL* THAT'S LEFT.

THAT'S LOW, MIKE. WE *ALL* DID OUR PART.

YEAH. AND TO US, IT WAS *EVERYTHING.*

STINKIN' UNGRATEFUL JERK.

I KNOW WHAT YOU DID! I LIVE WITH IT EVERY DAMN DAY, AND I'VE HAD *ENOUGH!*

LEAVE ME!

LEAVE NOW AND *NEVER* COME...

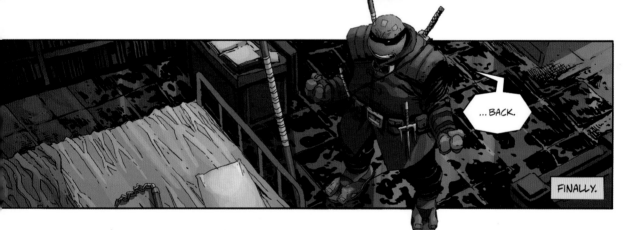

...BACK.

FINALLY.

FWUP

"TOO MANY *INNOCENTS* ARE GETTIN' HURT..."

...WITH THE SYNJAS OFFLINE, THERE'S FREAKIN' LOOTERS EVERYWHERE.

NOT EXACTLY THE REBELLION WE WERE HOPIN' FOR, HUH?

THERE'S JUST NOT ENOUGH OF US.

WE'RE TRYING TO ESTABLISH A ROUGH NETWORK WITH THE RESISTANCE COMMUNITY LEADERS ON THE OLD LANDLINES. IF WE CAN GET THEM TO TAKE CONTROL OF THEIR SECTIONS, WE'LL HAVE A SERIES OF SAFE ZONES TO FIGHT BACK FROM...

"...HOPEFULLY BEFORE IT'S TOO LATE."

YO! FORGET THE STUPID REBELLION!

LET'S BURN THIS MOTHER TO THE GROUND!

DAMMIT!

MOB MENTALITY'S LIKE A STINKIN' VIRUS!

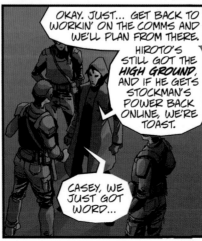

OKAY. JUST... GET BACK TO WORKIN' ON THE COMMS AND WE'LL PLAN FROM THERE.

HIROTO'S STILL GOT THE HIGH GROUND, AND IF HE GETS STOCKMAN'S POWER BACK ONLINE, WE'RE TOAST.

CASEY, WE JUST GOT WORD...

...THE POWER OUTAGE IS CAUSING FLOODING IN THE SEWERS.

OH NO... THE LAIR.

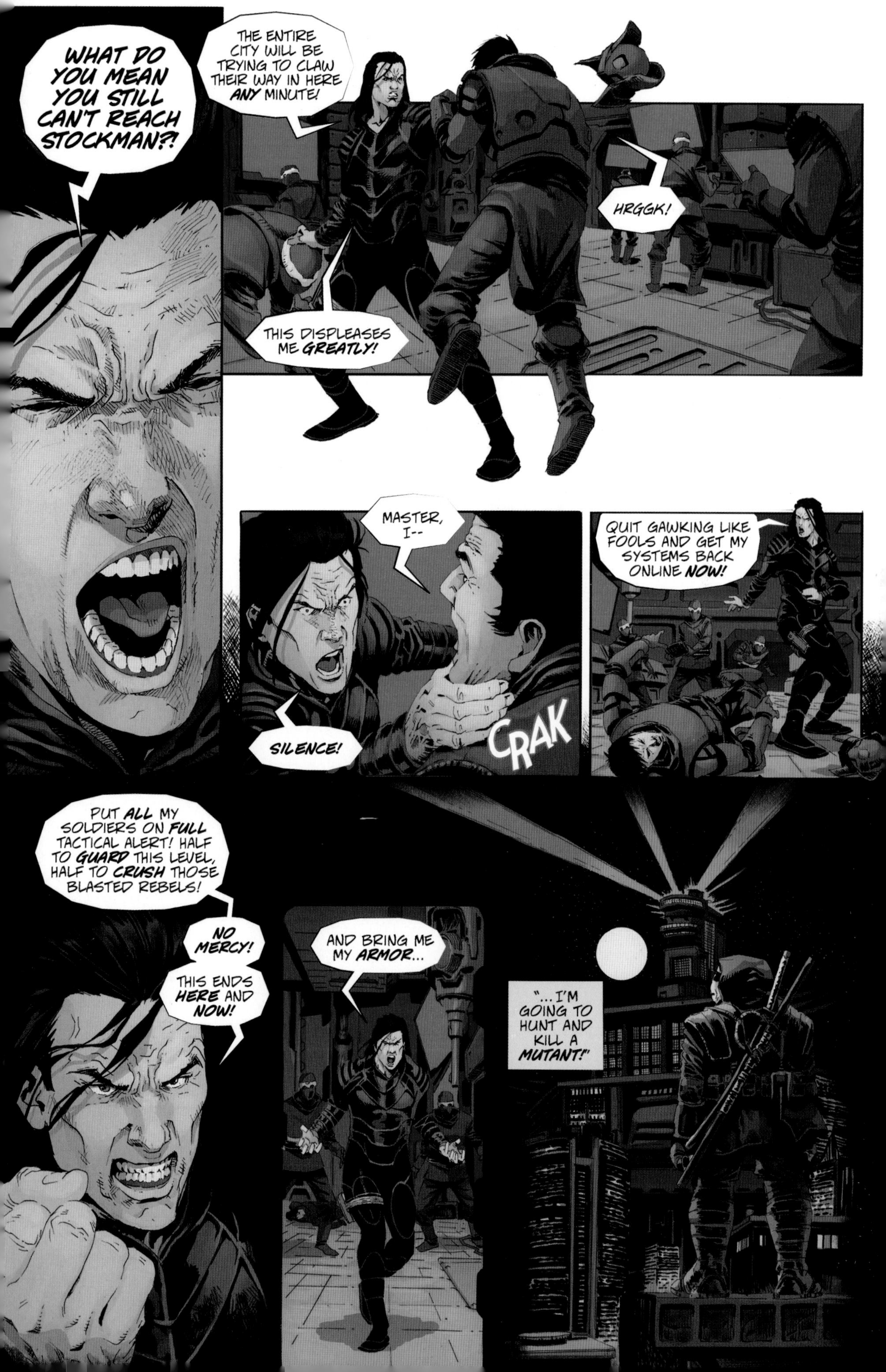
WHAT DO YOU MEAN YOU STILL CAN'T REACH STOCKMAN?!
THE ENTIRE CITY WILL BE TRYING TO CLAW THEIR WAY IN HERE ANY MINUTE!
HRGGK!
THIS DISPLEASES ME GREATLY!
MASTER, I--
SILENCE!
CRAK
QUIT GAWKING LIKE FOOLS AND GET MY SYSTEMS BACK ONLINE NOW!
PUT ALL MY SOLDIERS ON FULL TACTICAL ALERT! HALF TO GUARD THIS LEVEL, HALF TO CRUSH THOSE BLASTED REBELS!
NO MERCY!
THIS ENDS HERE AND NOW!
AND BRING ME MY ARMOR...
"...I'M GOING TO HUNT AND KILL A MUTANT!"

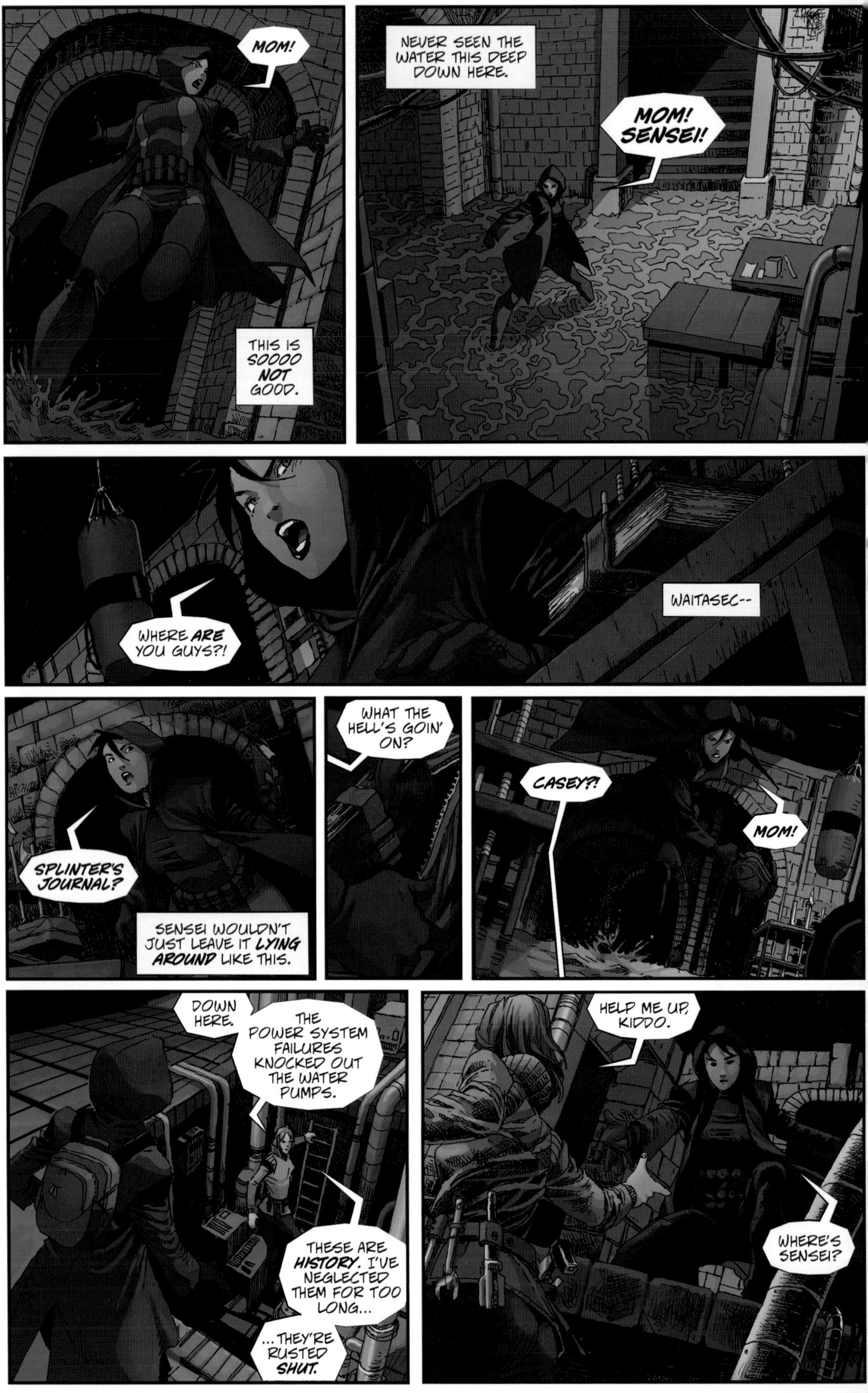
MOM!
THIS IS SOOOO NOT GOOD.
NEVER SEEN THE WATER THIS DEEP DOWN HERE.
MOM! SENSEI!
WHERE ARE YOU GUYS?!
WAITASEC--
SPLINTER'S JOURNAL?
SENSEI WOULDN'T JUST LEAVE IT LYING AROUND LIKE THIS.
WHAT THE HELL'S GOIN' ON?
CASEY?!
MOM!
DOWN HERE.
THE POWER SYSTEM FAILURES KNOCKED OUT THE WATER PUMPS.
THESE ARE HISTORY. I'VE NEGLECTED THEM FOR TOO LONG...
...THEY'RE RUSTED SHUT.
HELP ME UP, KIDDO.
WHERE'S SENSEI?

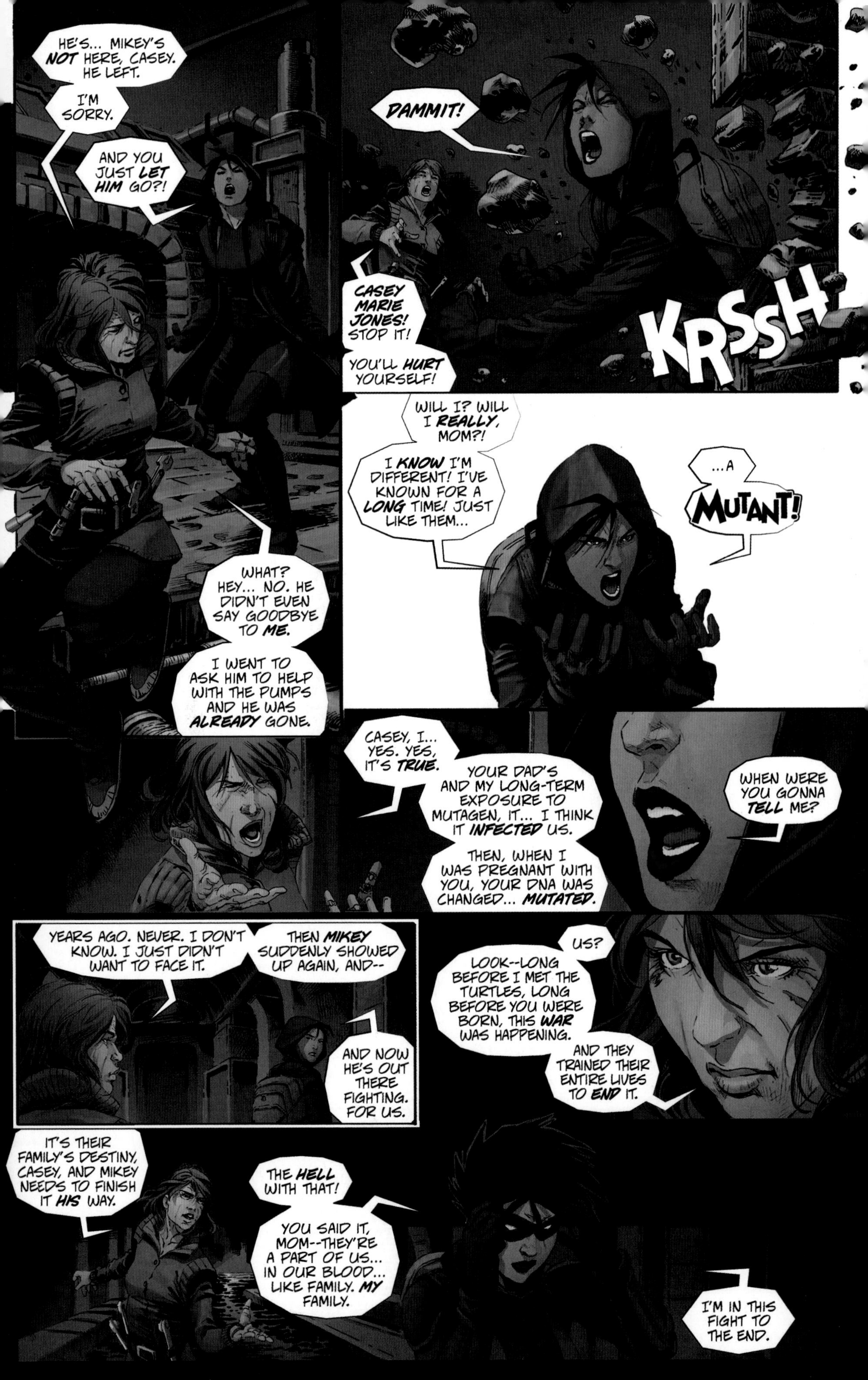
HE'S... MIKEY'S NOT HERE, CASEY. HE LEFT.
I'M SORRY.
AND YOU JUST LET HIM GO?!
WHAT? HEY... NO. HE DIDN'T EVEN SAY GOODBYE TO ME.
I WENT TO ASK HIM TO HELP WITH THE PUMPS AND HE WAS ALREADY GONE.
DAMMIT!
CASEY MARIE JONES! STOP IT!
YOU'LL HURT YOURSELF!
KRSSH
WILL I? WILL I REALLY, MOM?!
I KNOW I'M DIFFERENT! I'VE KNOWN FOR A LONG TIME! JUST LIKE THEM...
...A MUTANT!
CASEY, I... YES. YES, IT'S TRUE.
YOUR DAD'S AND MY LONG-TERM EXPOSURE TO MUTAGEN, IT... I THINK IT INFECTED US.
THEN, WHEN I WAS PREGNANT WITH YOU, YOUR DNA WAS CHANGED... MUTATED.
WHEN WERE YOU GONNA TELL ME?
YEARS AGO. NEVER. I DON'T KNOW. I JUST DIDN'T WANT TO FACE IT.
THEN MIKEY SUDDENLY SHOWED UP AGAIN, AND--
AND NOW HE'S OUT THERE FIGHTING. FOR US.
US?
LOOK--LONG BEFORE I MET THE TURTLES, LONG BEFORE YOU WERE BORN, THIS WAR WAS HAPPENING.
AND THEY TRAINED THEIR ENTIRE LIVES TO END IT.
IT'S THEIR FAMILY'S DESTINY, CASEY, AND MIKEY NEEDS TO FINISH IT HIS WAY.
THE HELL WITH THAT!
YOU SAID IT, MOM--THEY'RE A PART OF US... IN OUR BLOOD... LIKE FAMILY. MY FAMILY.
I'M IN THIS FIGHT TO THE END.

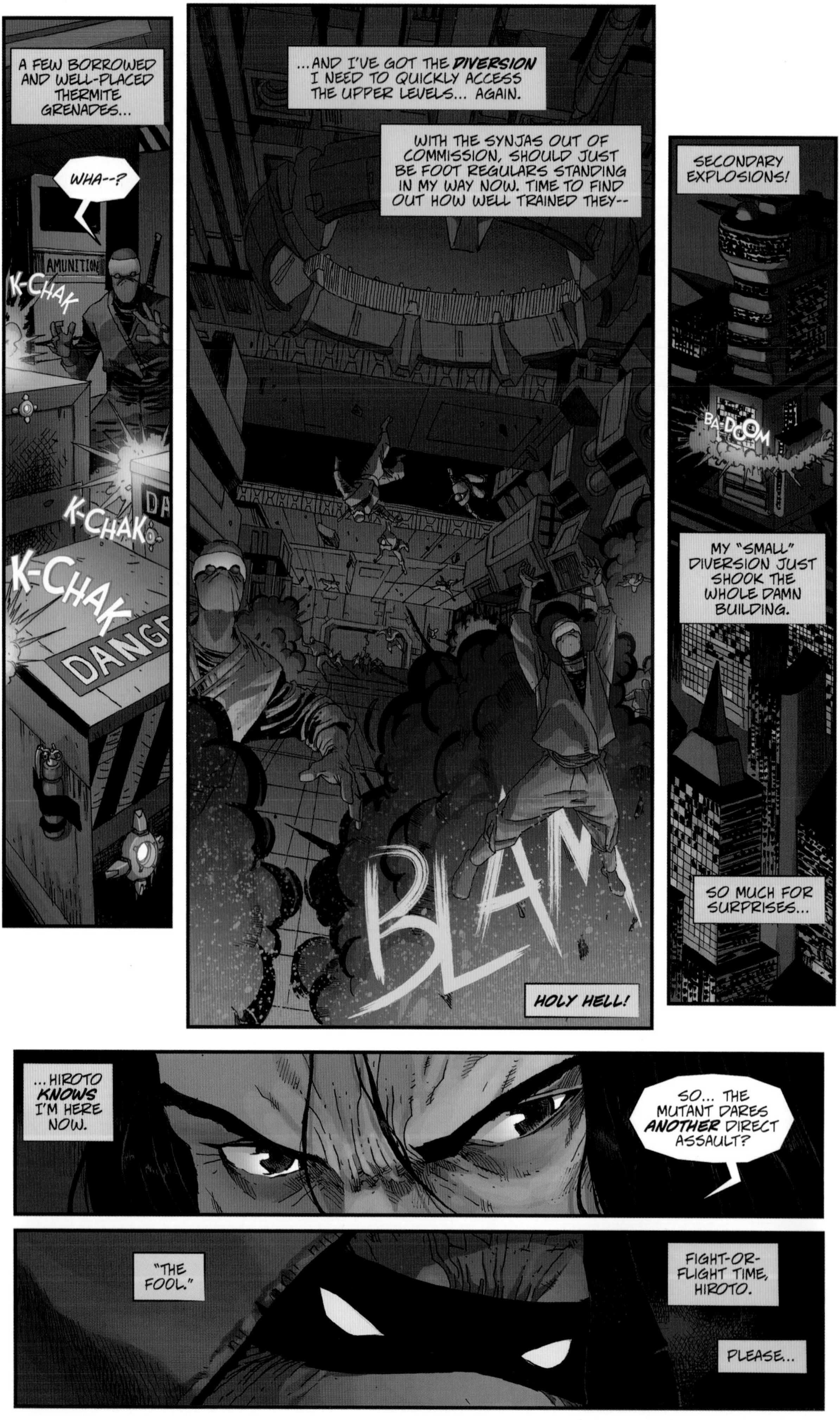
A FEW BORROWED AND WELL-PLACED THERMITE GRENADES...
WHA--?
AMUNITION
K-CHAK
K-CHAK
K-CHAK
DANG
...AND I'VE GOT THE **DIVERSION** I NEED TO QUICKLY ACCESS THE UPPER LEVELS... AGAIN.
WITH THE SYNJAS OUT OF COMMISSION, SHOULD JUST BE FOOT REGULARS STANDING IN MY WAY NOW. TIME TO FIND OUT HOW WELL TRAINED THEY--
BLAM
HOLY HELL!
SECONDARY EXPLOSIONS!
BA-DOOM
MY "SMALL" DIVERSION JUST SHOOK THE WHOLE DAMN BUILDING.
SO MUCH FOR SURPRISES...
...HIROTO **KNOWS** I'M HERE NOW.
SO... THE MUTANT DARES **ANOTHER** DIRECT ASSAULT?
"THE FOOL."
FIGHT-OR-FLIGHT TIME, HIROTO.
PLEASE...

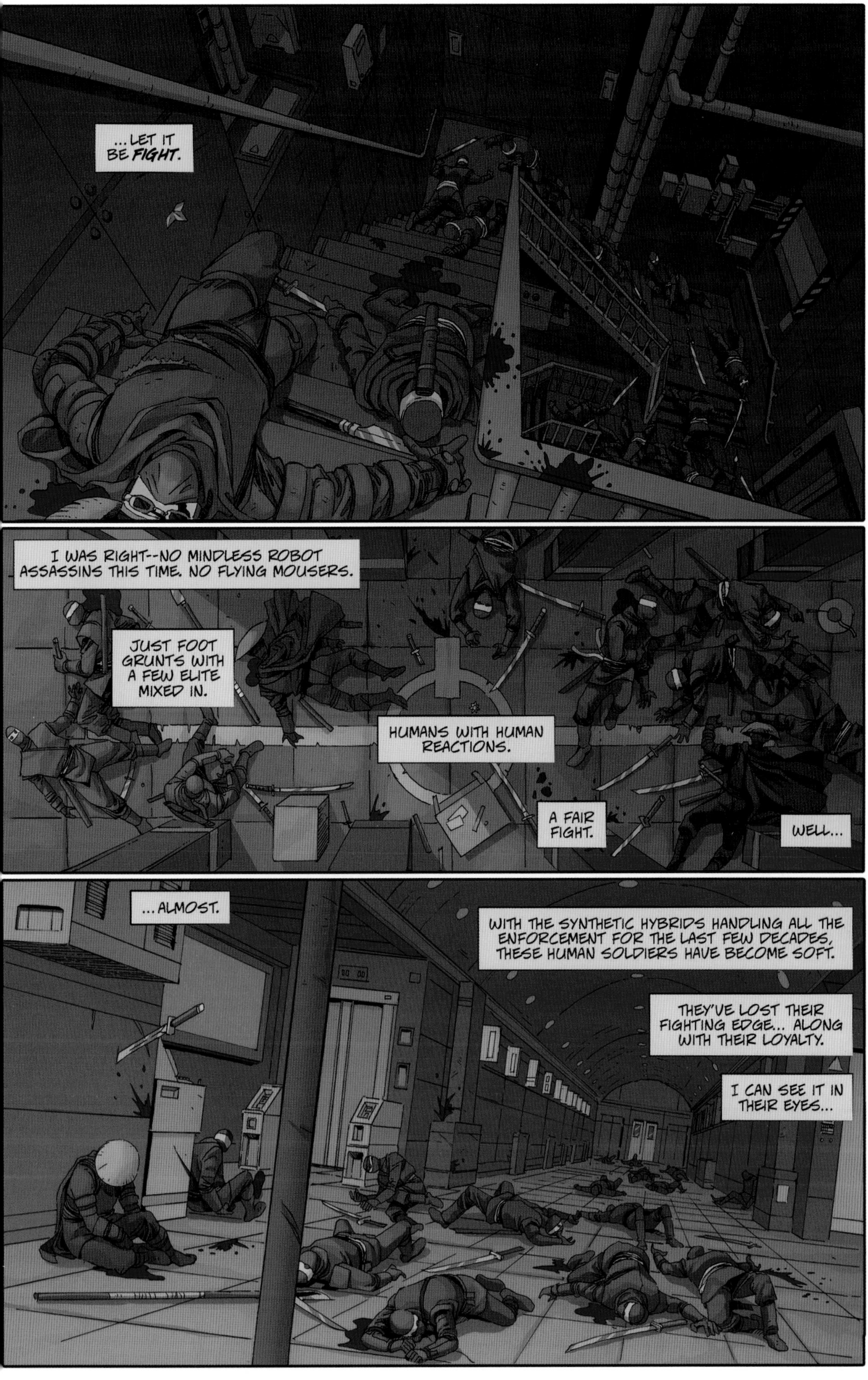
...LET IT BE FIGHT.
I WAS RIGHT--NO MINDLESS ROBOT ASSASSINS THIS TIME. NO FLYING MOUSERS.
JUST FOOT GRUNTS WITH A FEW ELITE MIXED IN.
HUMANS WITH HUMAN REACTIONS.
A FAIR FIGHT.
WELL...
...ALMOST.
WITH THE SYNTHETIC HYBRIDS HANDLING ALL THE ENFORCEMENT FOR THE LAST FEW DECADES, THESE HUMAN SOLDIERS HAVE BECOME SOFT.
THEY'VE LOST THEIR FIGHTING EDGE... ALONG WITH THEIR LOYALTY.
I CAN SEE IT IN THEIR EYES...

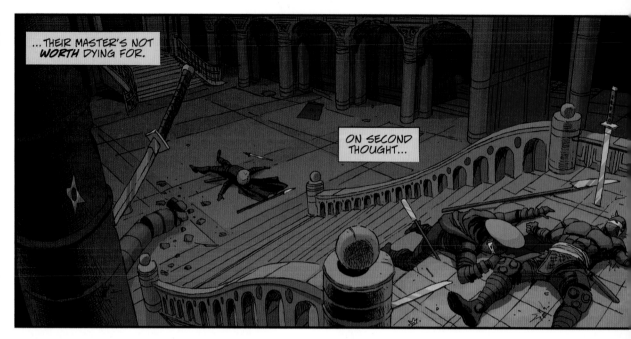

...THEIR MASTER'S NOT *WORTH* DYING FOR.

ON SECOND THOUGHT...

...*THIS* ONE LOOKS PRETTY LOYAL. BIG AS HELL, TOO.

AND HE'S THE ONLY THING BLOCKING MY WAY TO THE TOP FLOOR.

LET'S SEE WHAT HE'S GOT.

FLASH-BANGS.

BOOM

BOOM

HARD TO STRIKE BACK WHEN YOU'RE DEAF AND BLIND.

CONCUSSION BLAST TO OPEN THE DOOR.

WHUMP

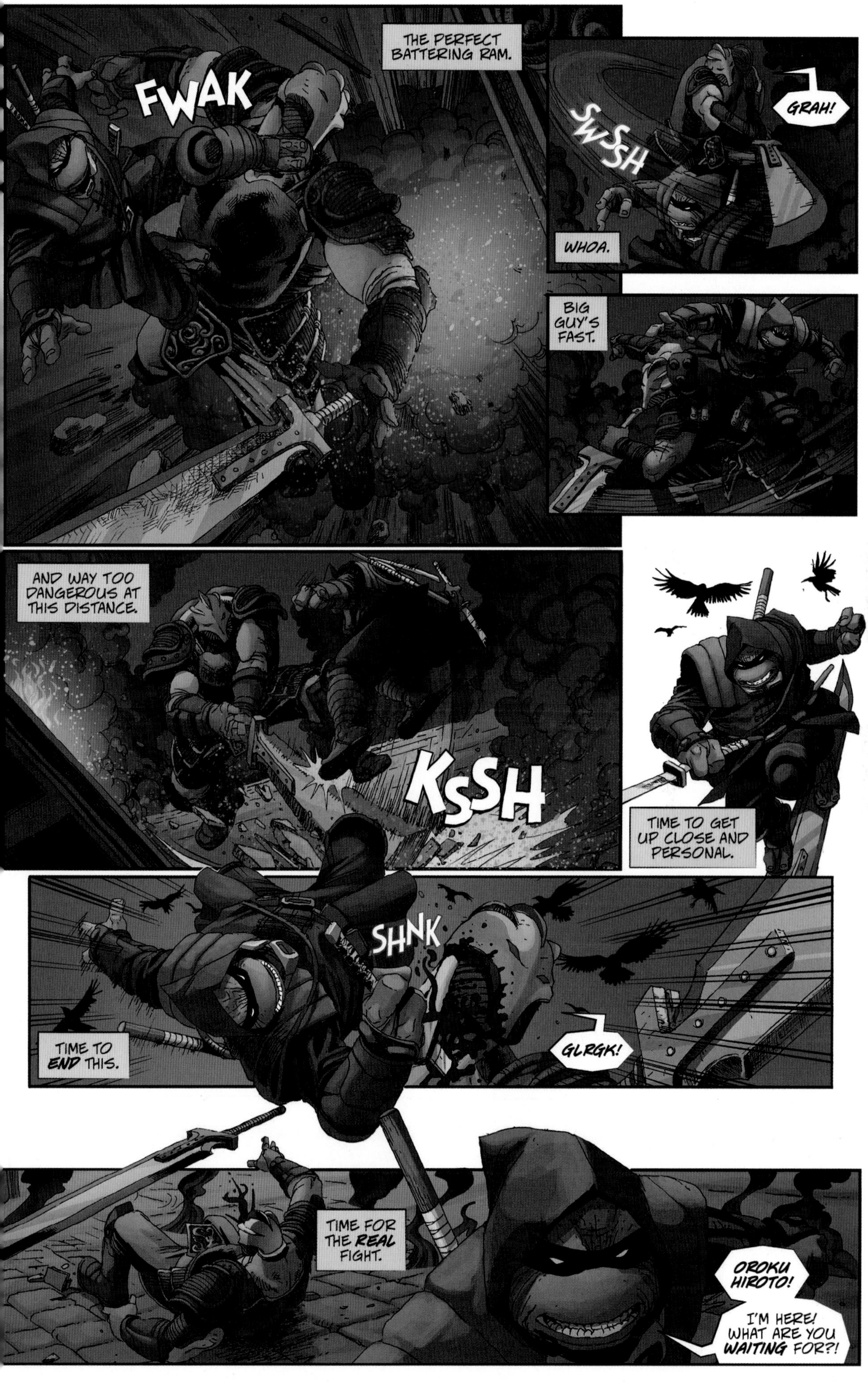
THE PERFECT BATTERING RAM.
FWAK
SWSSH
GRAH!
WHOA.
BIG GUY'S FAST.
AND WAY TOO DANGEROUS AT THIS DISTANCE.
KSSH
TIME TO GET UP CLOSE AND PERSONAL.
SHNK
TIME TO END THIS.
GLRGK!
TIME FOR THE REAL FIGHT.
OROKU HIROTO!
I'M HERE! WHAT ARE YOU WAITING FOR?!

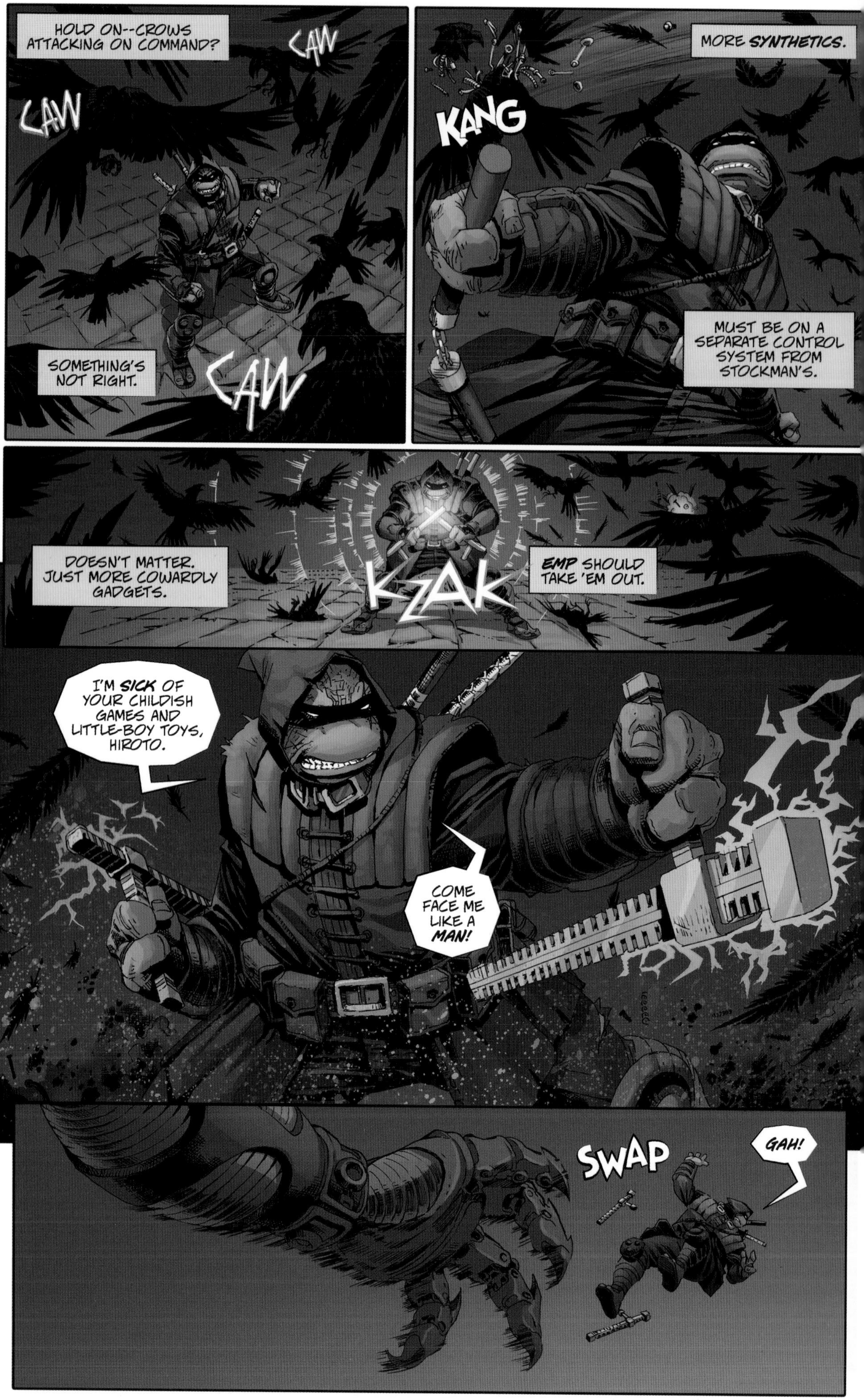

HOLD ON--CROWS ATTACKING ON COMMAND?
CAW
CAW
SOMETHING'S NOT RIGHT.
CAW
MORE SYNTHETICS.
KANG
MUST BE ON A SEPARATE CONTROL SYSTEM FROM STOCKMAN'S.
DOESN'T MATTER. JUST MORE COWARDLY GADGETS.
KZAK
EMP SHOULD TAKE 'EM OUT.
I'M SICK OF YOUR CHILDISH GAMES AND LITTLE-BOY TOYS, HIROTO.
COME FACE ME LIKE A MAN!
SWAP
GAH!

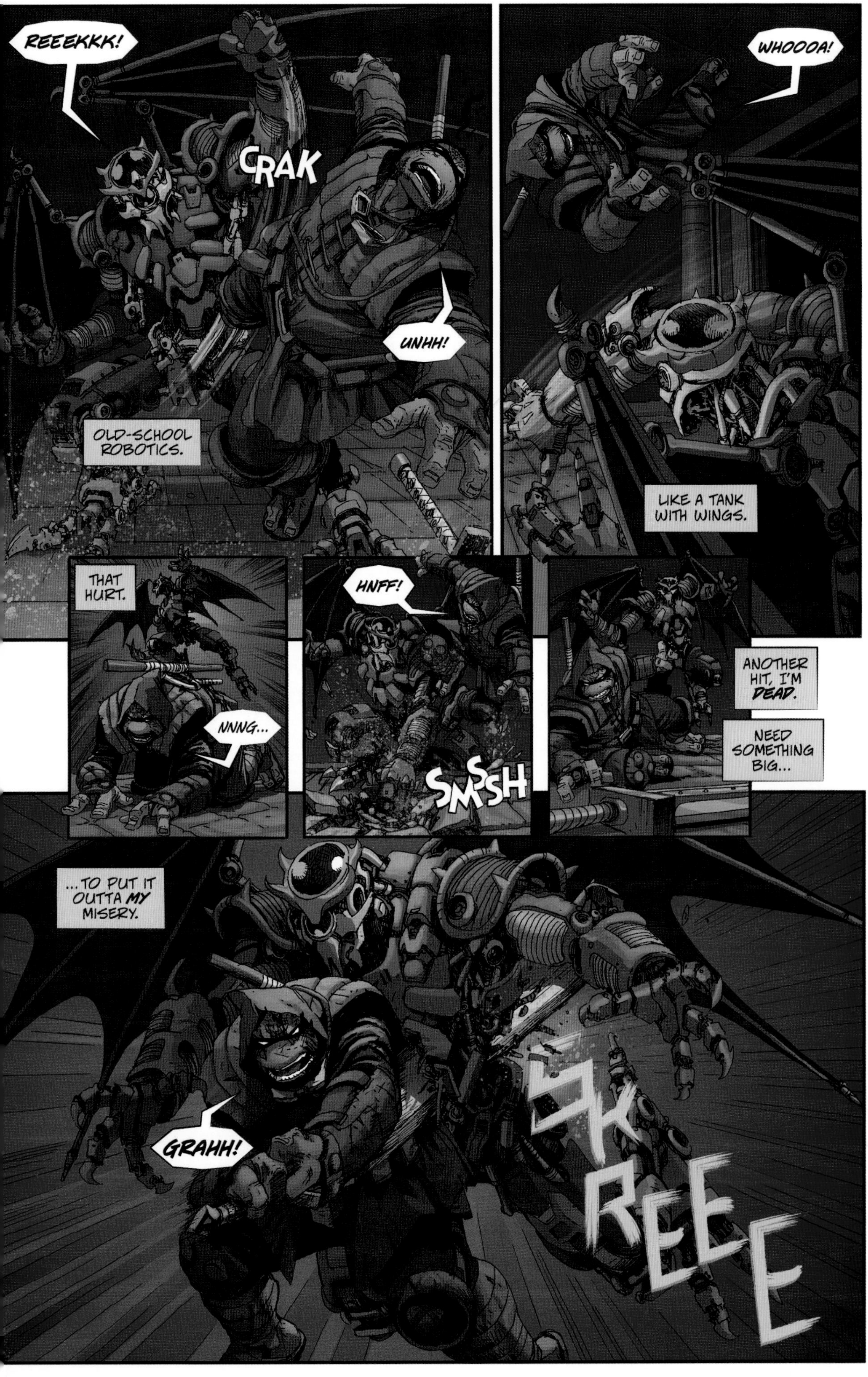
REEEKKK!
CRAK
UNHH!
OLD-SCHOOL ROBOTICS.
WHOOOA!
LIKE A TANK WITH WINGS.
THAT HURT.
NNNG...
HNFF!
SMSSH
ANOTHER HIT, I'M DEAD.
NEED SOMETHING BIG...
...TO PUT IT OUTTA MY MISERY.
GRAHH!
SKREEE

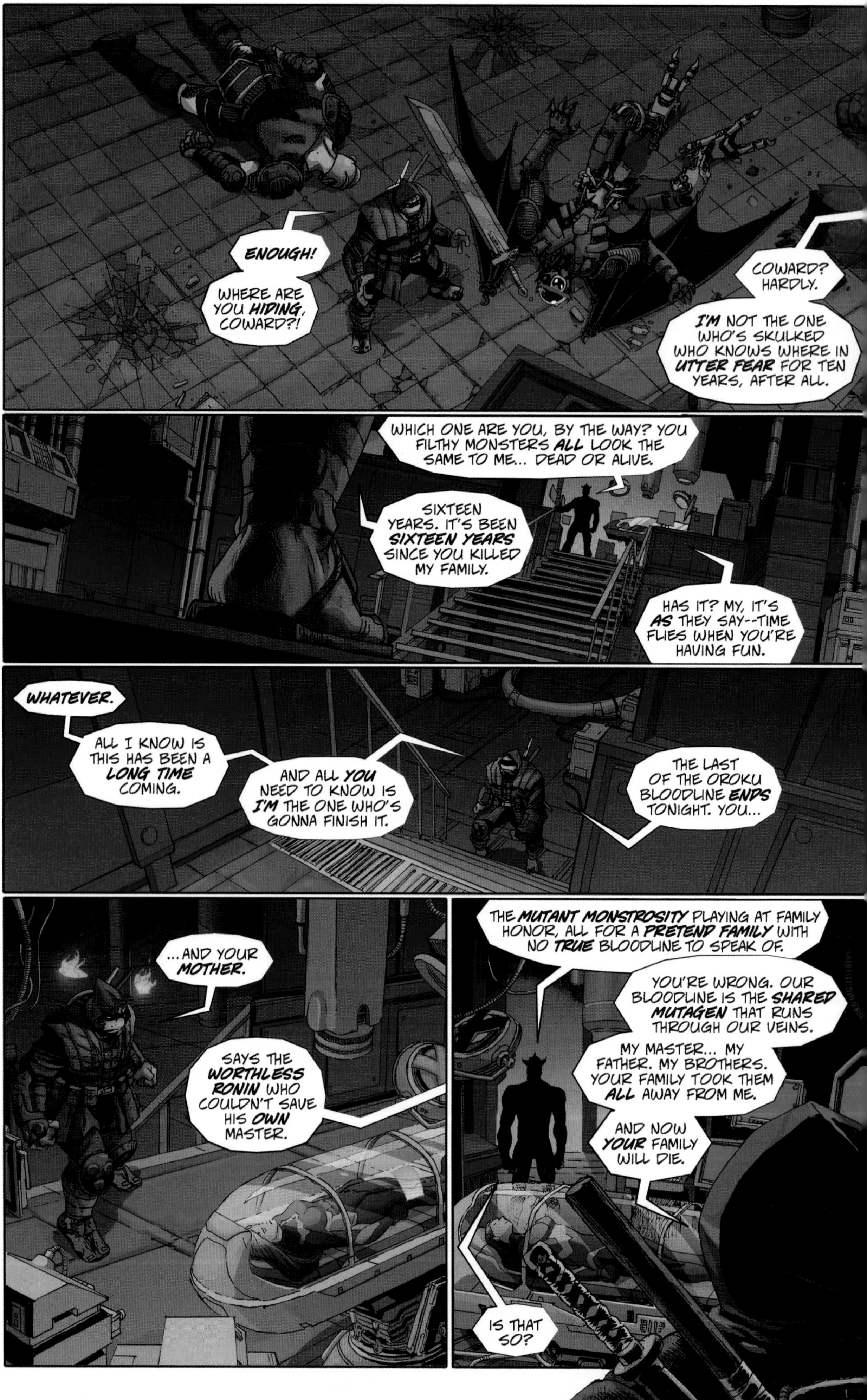
ENOUGH!
WHERE ARE YOU HIDING, COWARD?!
COWARD? HARDLY.
I'M NOT THE ONE WHO'S SKULKED WHO KNOWS WHERE IN UTTER FEAR FOR TEN YEARS, AFTER ALL.
WHICH ONE ARE YOU, BY THE WAY? YOU FILTHY MONSTERS ALL LOOK THE SAME TO ME... DEAD OR ALIVE.
SIXTEEN YEARS. IT'S BEEN SIXTEEN YEARS SINCE YOU KILLED MY FAMILY.
HAS IT? MY, IT'S AS THEY SAY--TIME FLIES WHEN YOU'RE HAVING FUN.
WHATEVER.
ALL I KNOW IS THIS HAS BEEN A LONG TIME COMING.
AND ALL YOU NEED TO KNOW IS I'M THE ONE WHO'S GONNA FINISH IT.
THE LAST OF THE OROKU BLOODLINE ENDS TONIGHT. YOU...
...AND YOUR MOTHER.
SAYS THE WORTHLESS RONIN WHO COULDN'T SAVE HIS OWN MASTER.
THE MUTANT MONSTROSITY PLAYING AT FAMILY HONOR, ALL FOR A PRETEND FAMILY WITH NO TRUE BLOODLINE TO SPEAK OF.
YOU'RE WRONG. OUR BLOODLINE IS THE SHARED MUTAGEN THAT RUNS THROUGH OUR VEINS.
MY MASTER... MY FATHER. MY BROTHERS. YOUR FAMILY TOOK THEM ALL AWAY FROM ME.
AND NOW YOUR FAMILY WILL DIE.
IS THAT SO?

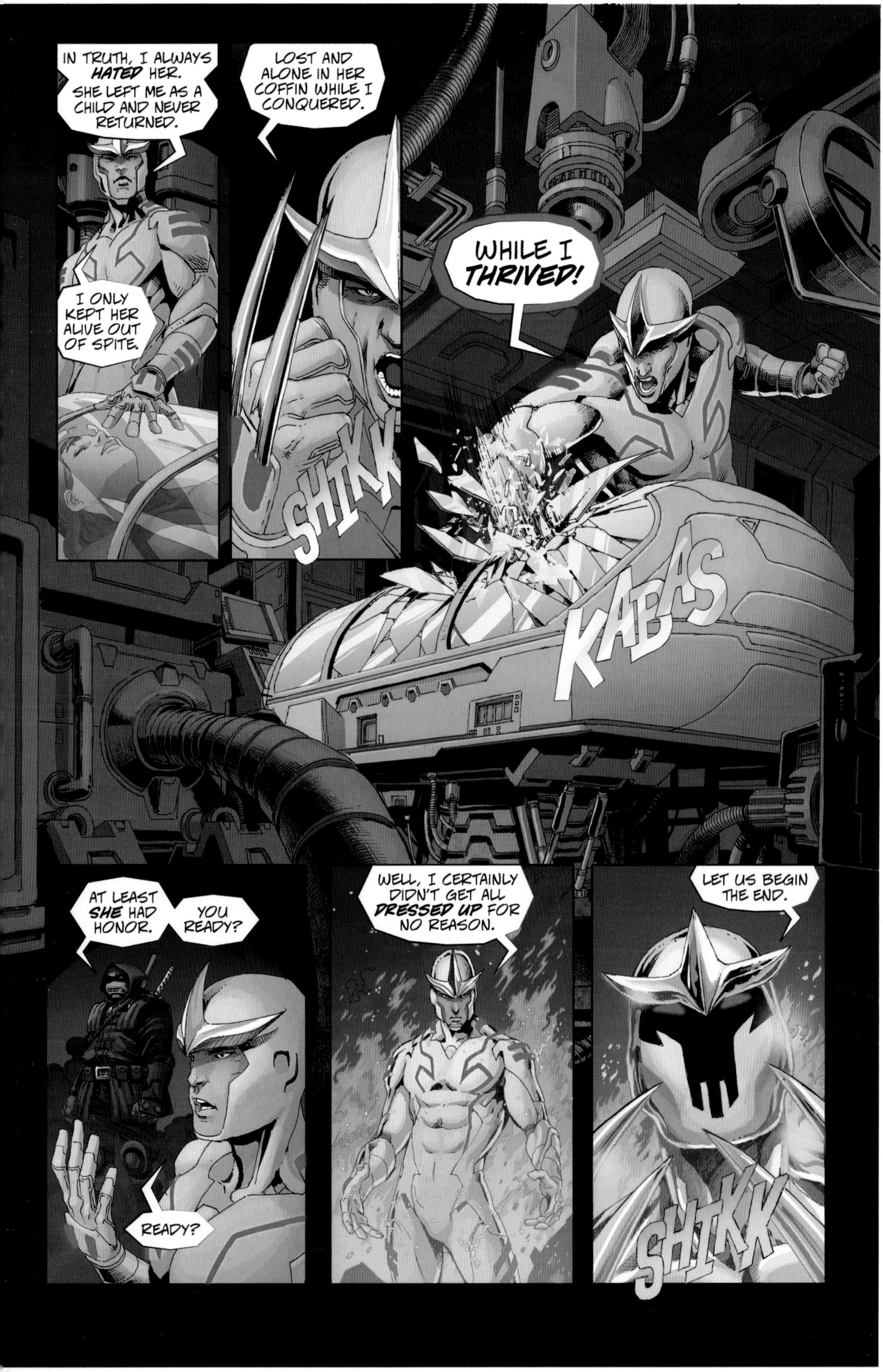
IN TRUTH, I ALWAYS HATED HER. SHE LEFT ME AS A CHILD AND NEVER RETURNED.
I ONLY KEPT HER ALIVE OUT OF SPITE.
LOST AND ALONE IN HER COFFIN WHILE I CONQUERED.
SHIKK
WHILE I THRIVED!
KABAS
AT LEAST SHE HAD HONOR.
YOU READY?
READY?
WELL, I CERTAINLY DIDN'T GET ALL DRESSED UP FOR NO REASON.
LET US BEGIN THE END.
SHIKK

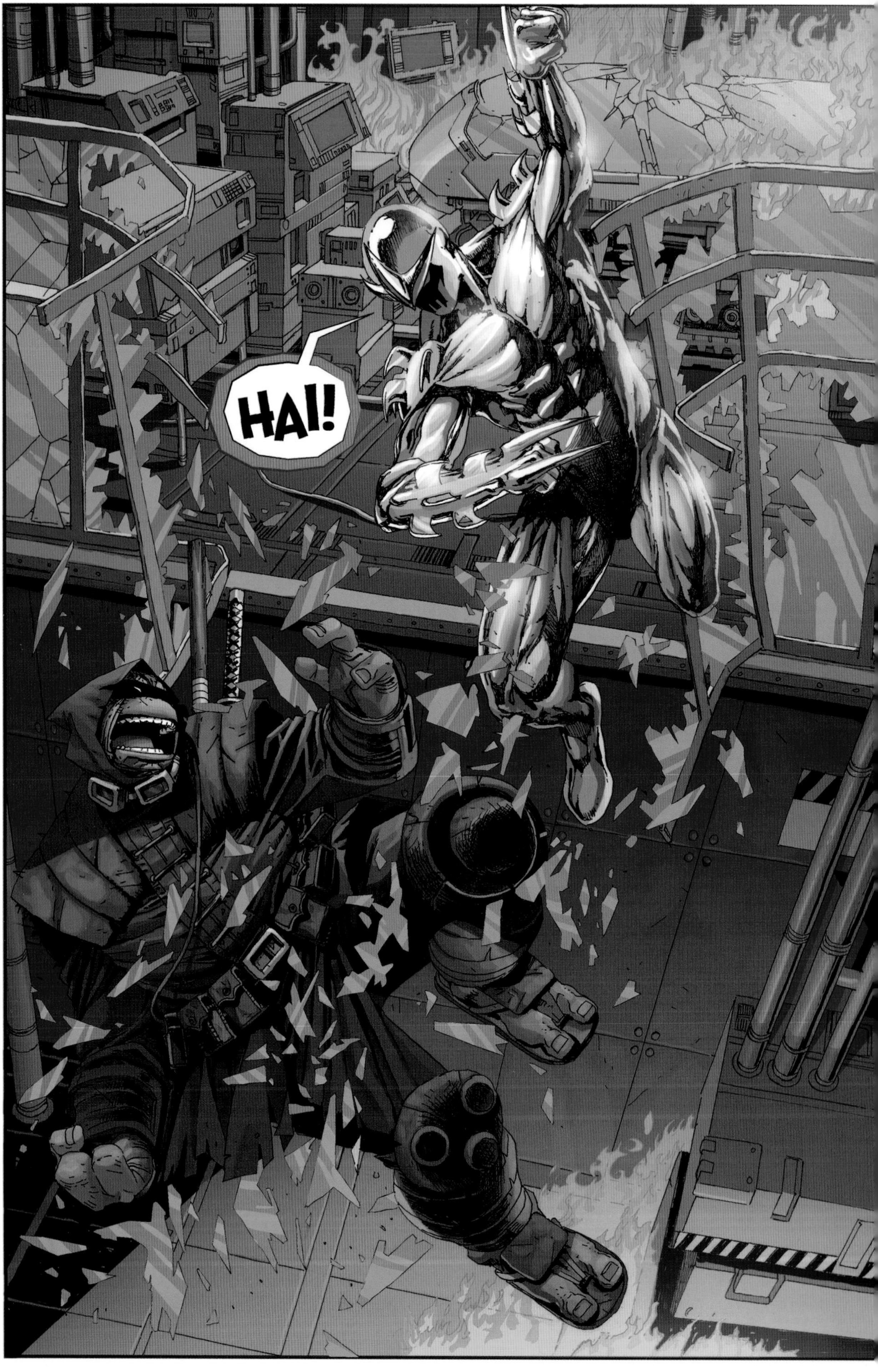
HAI!

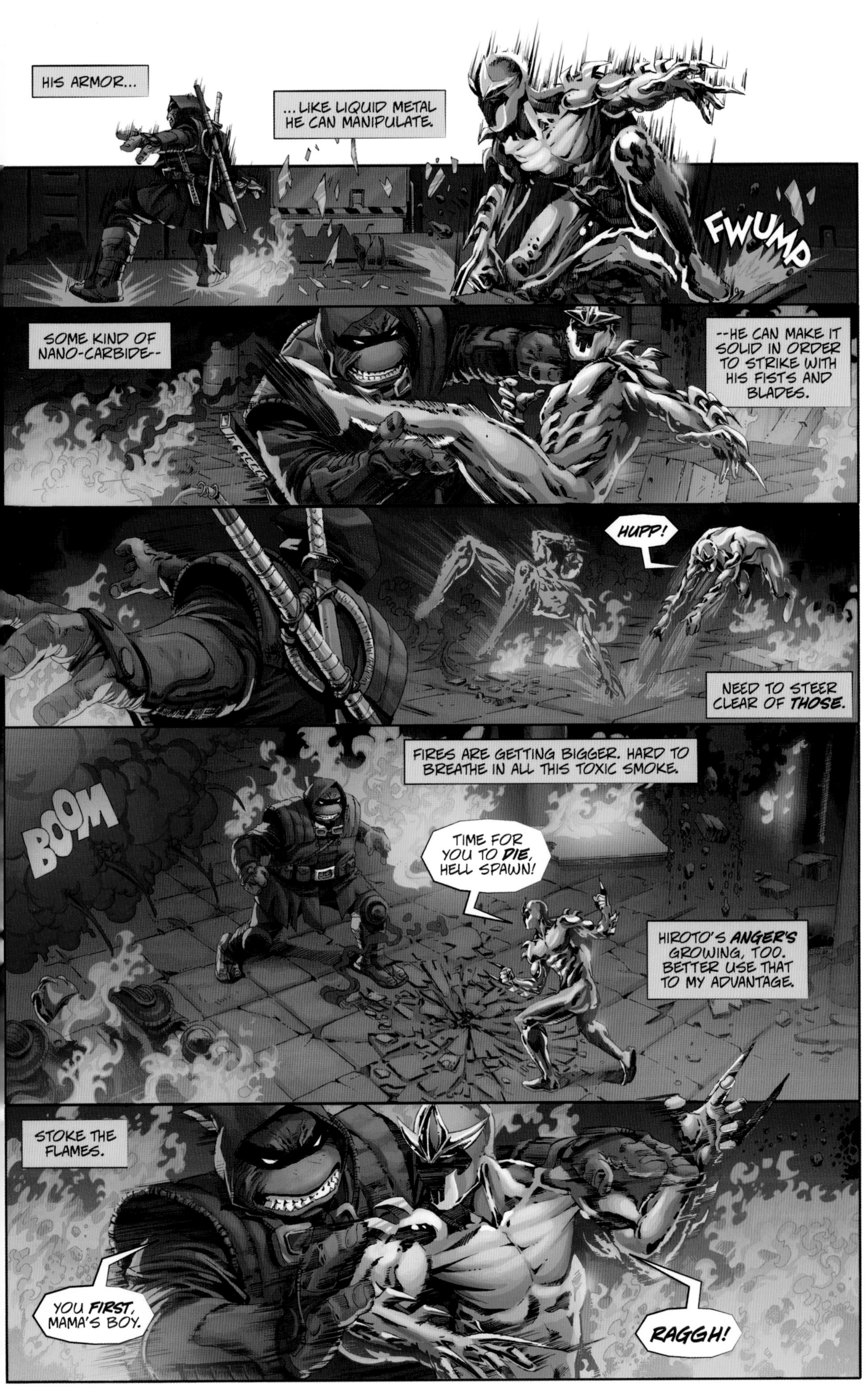
HIS ARMOR...
...LIKE LIQUID METAL HE CAN MANIPULATE.
FWUMP
SOME KIND OF NANO-CARBIDE--
--HE CAN MAKE IT SOLID IN ORDER TO STRIKE WITH HIS FISTS AND BLADES.
HUPP!
NEED TO STEER CLEAR OF THOSE.
FIRES ARE GETTING BIGGER. HARD TO BREATHE IN ALL THIS TOXIC SMOKE.
BOOM
TIME FOR YOU TO DIE, HELL SPAWN!
HIROTO'S ANGER'S GROWING, TOO. BETTER USE THAT TO MY ADVANTAGE.
STOKE THE FLAMES.
YOU FIRST, MAMA'S BOY.
RAGGH!

SHAKA BOOMM

HEY! ROCK BOTTOM'S REPORTING AN *EXPLOSION* IN HIROTO'S TOWER!

WHAT? SERIOUSLY?

LOTTA GOOD THAT DOES US IF WE ALL *DROWN* DOWN HERE.

WE GOTTA GET TO THE MAIN PUMPS DOWNTOWN-- *FAST!*

DAMMIT, SENSEI...

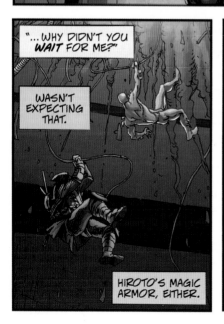

"...WHY DIDN'T YOU *WAIT* FOR ME?"

WASN'T EXPECTING THAT.

HIROTO'S MAGIC ARMOR, EITHER.

INCLINE SHOULD SLOW OUR FALL.

STILL A LONG WAY *DOWN*, THOUGH.

BEEN THERE. DONE THAT.

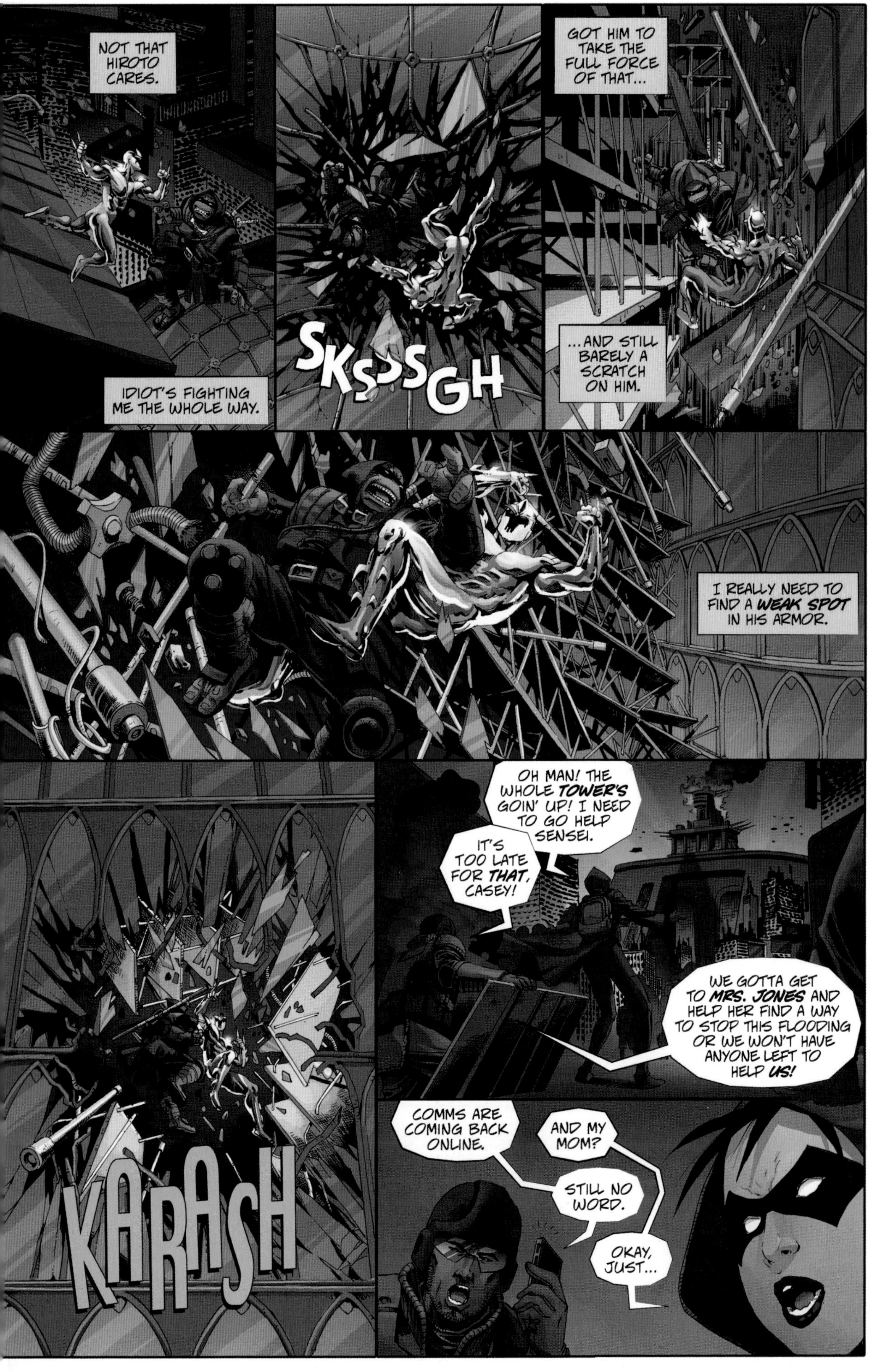
NOT THAT HIROTO CARES.
IDIOT'S FIGHTING ME THE WHOLE WAY.
SKSSSGH
GOT HIM TO TAKE THE FULL FORCE OF THAT...
...AND STILL BARELY A SCRATCH ON HIM.
I REALLY NEED TO FIND A WEAK SPOT IN HIS ARMOR.
KARASH
OH MAN! THE WHOLE TOWER'S GOIN' UP! I NEED TO GO HELP SENSEI.
IT'S TOO LATE FOR THAT, CASEY!
WE GOTTA GET TO MRS. JONES AND HELP HER FIND A WAY TO STOP THIS FLOODING OR WE WON'T HAVE ANYONE LEFT TO HELP US!
COMMS ARE COMING BACK ONLINE.
AND MY MOM?
STILL NO WORD.
OKAY, JUST...

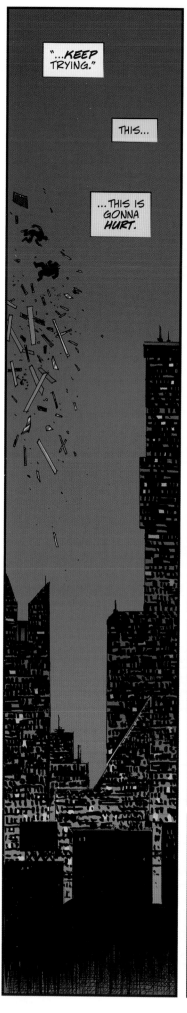

"...KEEP TRYING."

THIS...

...THIS IS GONNA HURT.

A LOT.

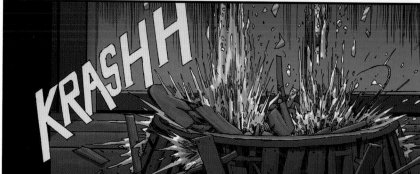

KRASHH

WHOOSH

NOTHING BROKEN... I THINK. AT LEAST NOTHING IMPORTANT.

THAT WATER TOWER WAS A GIFT.

FOR BOTH OF US, UNFORTUNATELY.

C'MON, HIROTO...

...SHOW ME A FLAW.

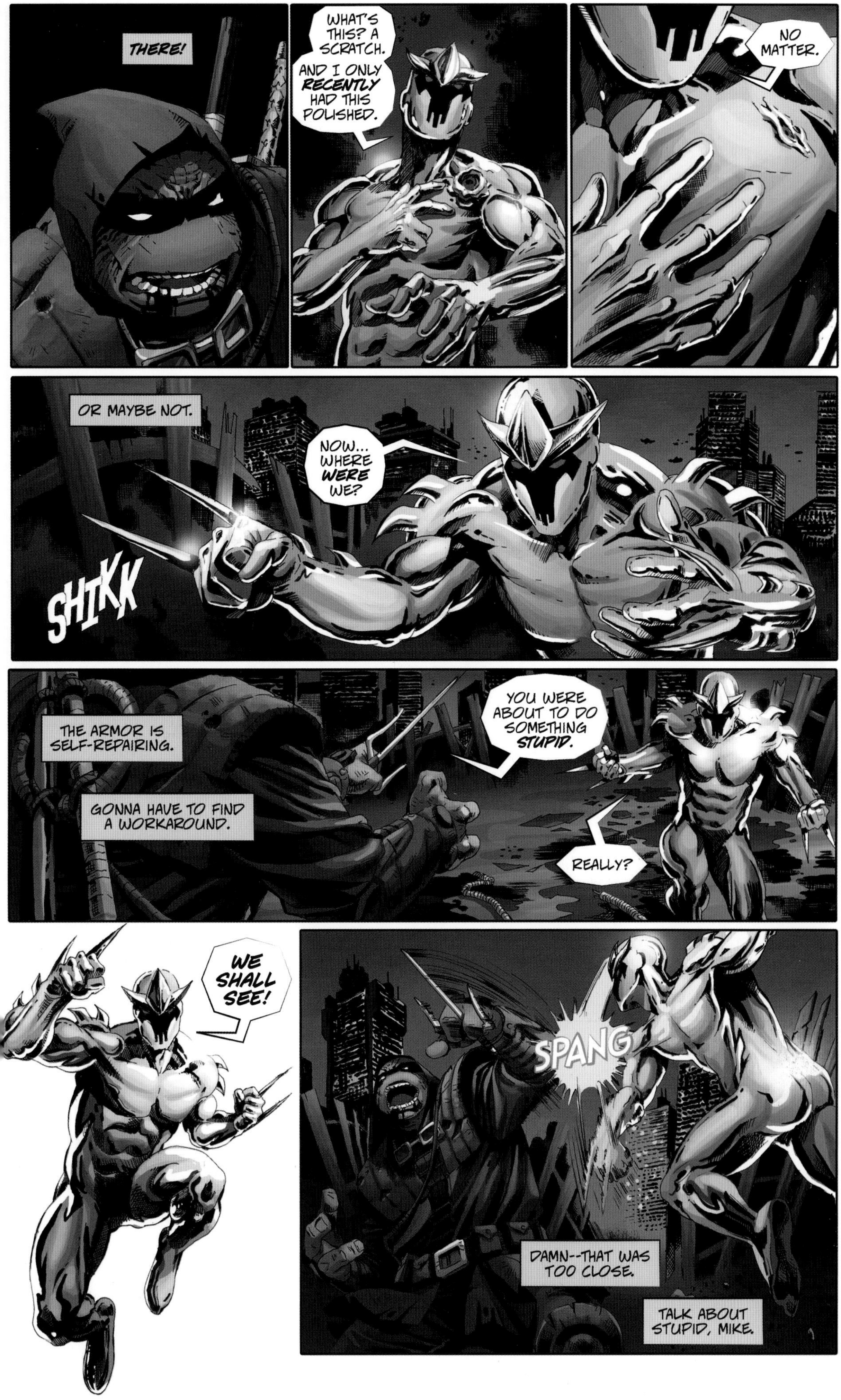
THERE!
WHAT'S THIS? A SCRATCH.
AND I ONLY RECENTLY HAD THIS POLISHED.
NO MATTER.
OR MAYBE NOT.
NOW... WHERE WERE WE?
SHIKK
THE ARMOR IS SELF-REPAIRING.
GONNA HAVE TO FIND A WORKAROUND.
YOU WERE ABOUT TO DO SOMETHING STUPID.
REALLY?
WE SHALL SEE!
SPANG
DAMN--THAT WAS TOO CLOSE.
TALK ABOUT STUPID, MIKE.

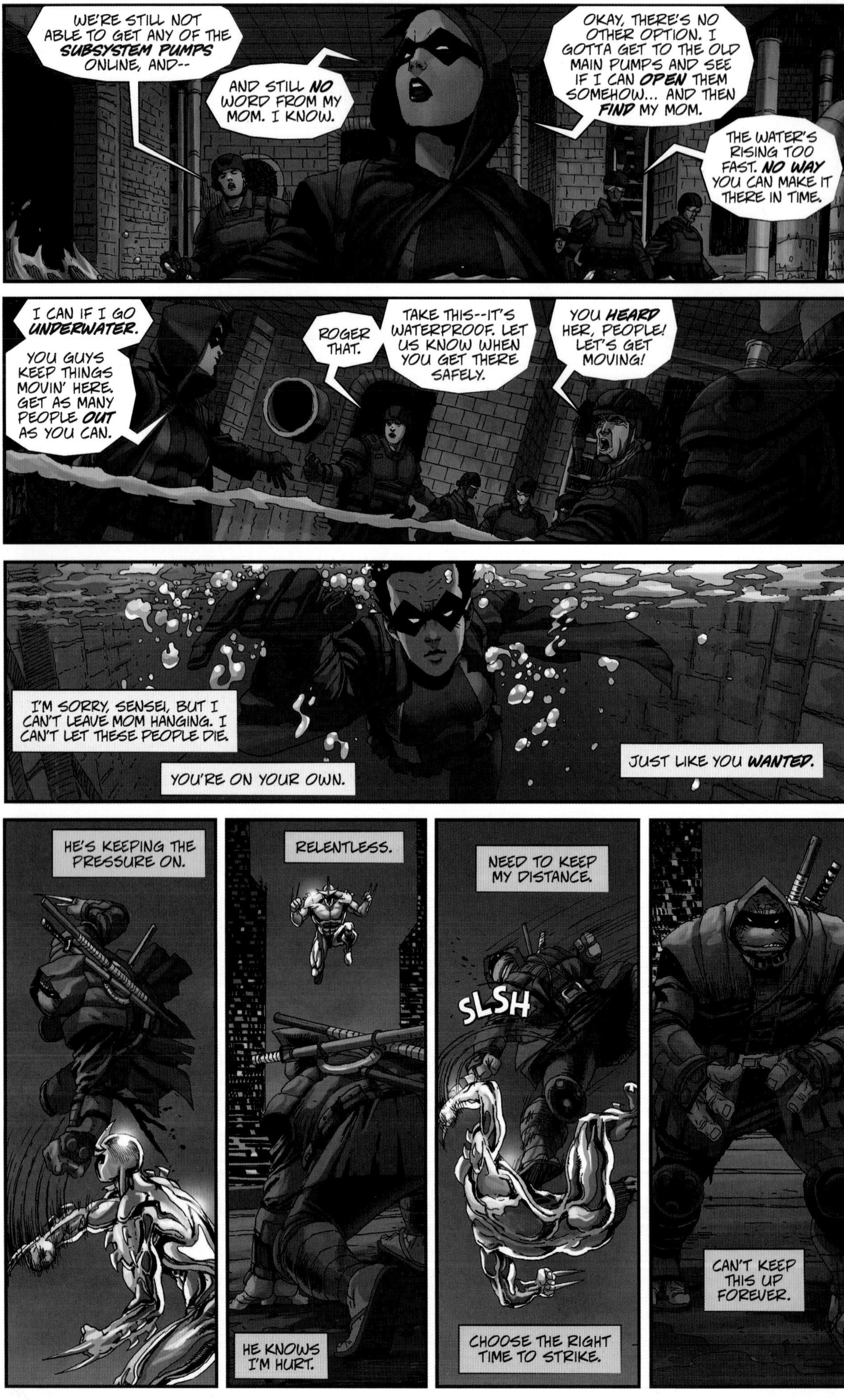

WE'RE STILL NOT ABLE TO GET ANY OF THE SUBSYSTEM PUMPS ONLINE, AND--
AND STILL NO WORD FROM MY MOM. I KNOW.
OKAY, THERE'S NO OTHER OPTION. I GOTTA GET TO THE OLD MAIN PUMPS AND SEE IF I CAN OPEN THEM SOMEHOW... AND THEN FIND MY MOM.
THE WATER'S RISING TOO FAST. NO WAY YOU CAN MAKE IT THERE IN TIME.
I CAN IF I GO UNDERWATER.
YOU GUYS KEEP THINGS MOVIN' HERE. GET AS MANY PEOPLE OUT AS YOU CAN.
ROGER THAT.
TAKE THIS--IT'S WATERPROOF. LET US KNOW WHEN YOU GET THERE SAFELY.
YOU HEARD HER, PEOPLE! LET'S GET MOVING!
I'M SORRY, SENSEI, BUT I CAN'T LEAVE MOM HANGING. I CAN'T LET THESE PEOPLE DIE.
YOU'RE ON YOUR OWN.
JUST LIKE YOU WANTED.
HE'S KEEPING THE PRESSURE ON.
RELENTLESS.
HE KNOWS I'M HURT.
NEED TO KEEP MY DISTANCE.
SLSH
CHOOSE THE RIGHT TIME TO STRIKE.
CAN'T KEEP THIS UP FOREVER.

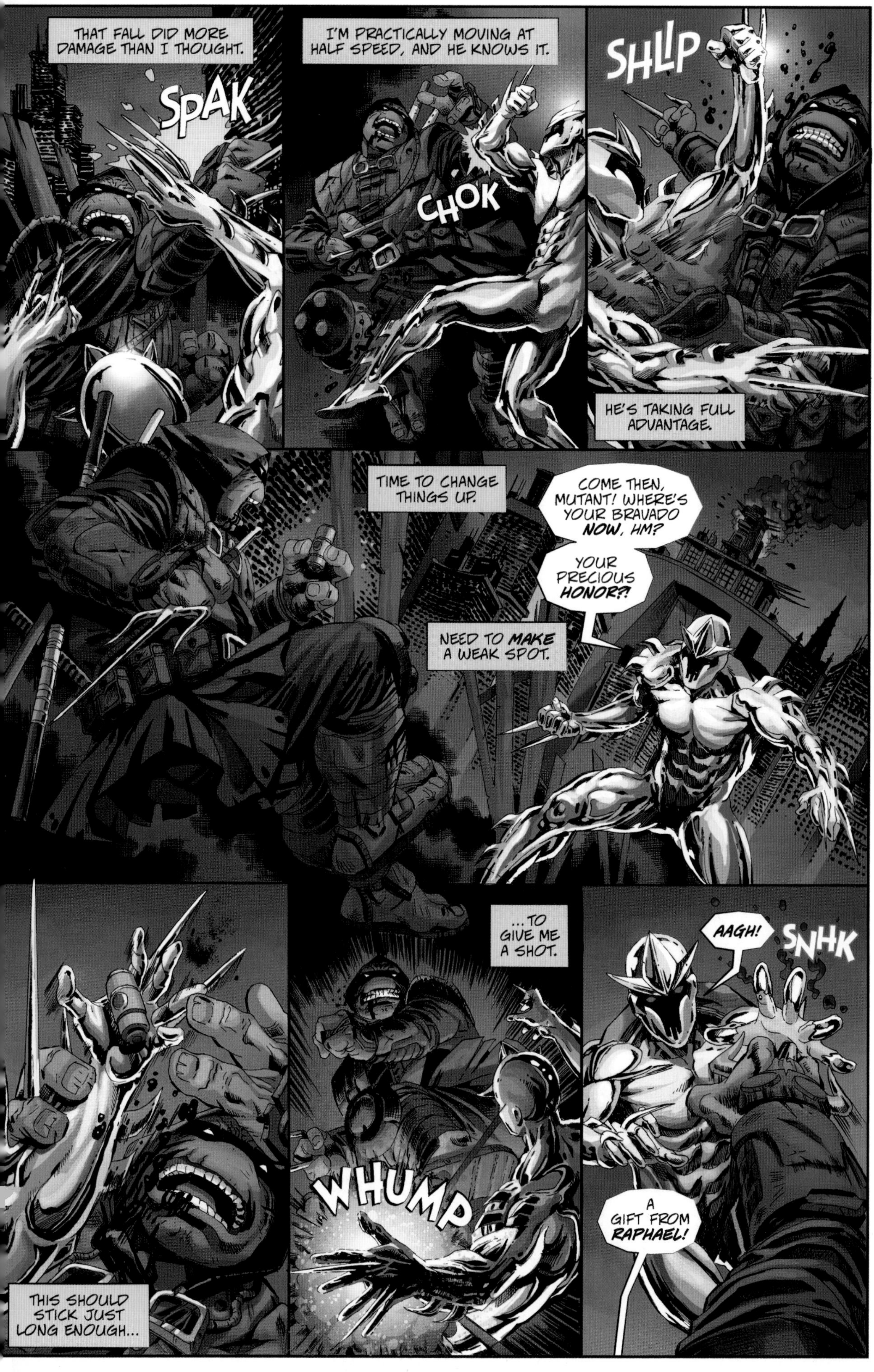
THAT FALL DID MORE DAMAGE THAN I THOUGHT.
SPAK
I'M PRACTICALLY MOVING AT HALF SPEED, AND HE KNOWS IT.
CHOK
SHLIP
HE'S TAKING FULL ADVANTAGE.
TIME TO CHANGE THINGS UP.
COME THEN, MUTANT! WHERE'S YOUR BRAVADO NOW, HM?
YOUR PRECIOUS HONOR?!
NEED TO MAKE A WEAK SPOT.
THIS SHOULD STICK JUST LONG ENOUGH...
...TO GIVE ME A SHOT.
WHUMP
AAGH!
SNHK
A GIFT FROM RAPHAEL!

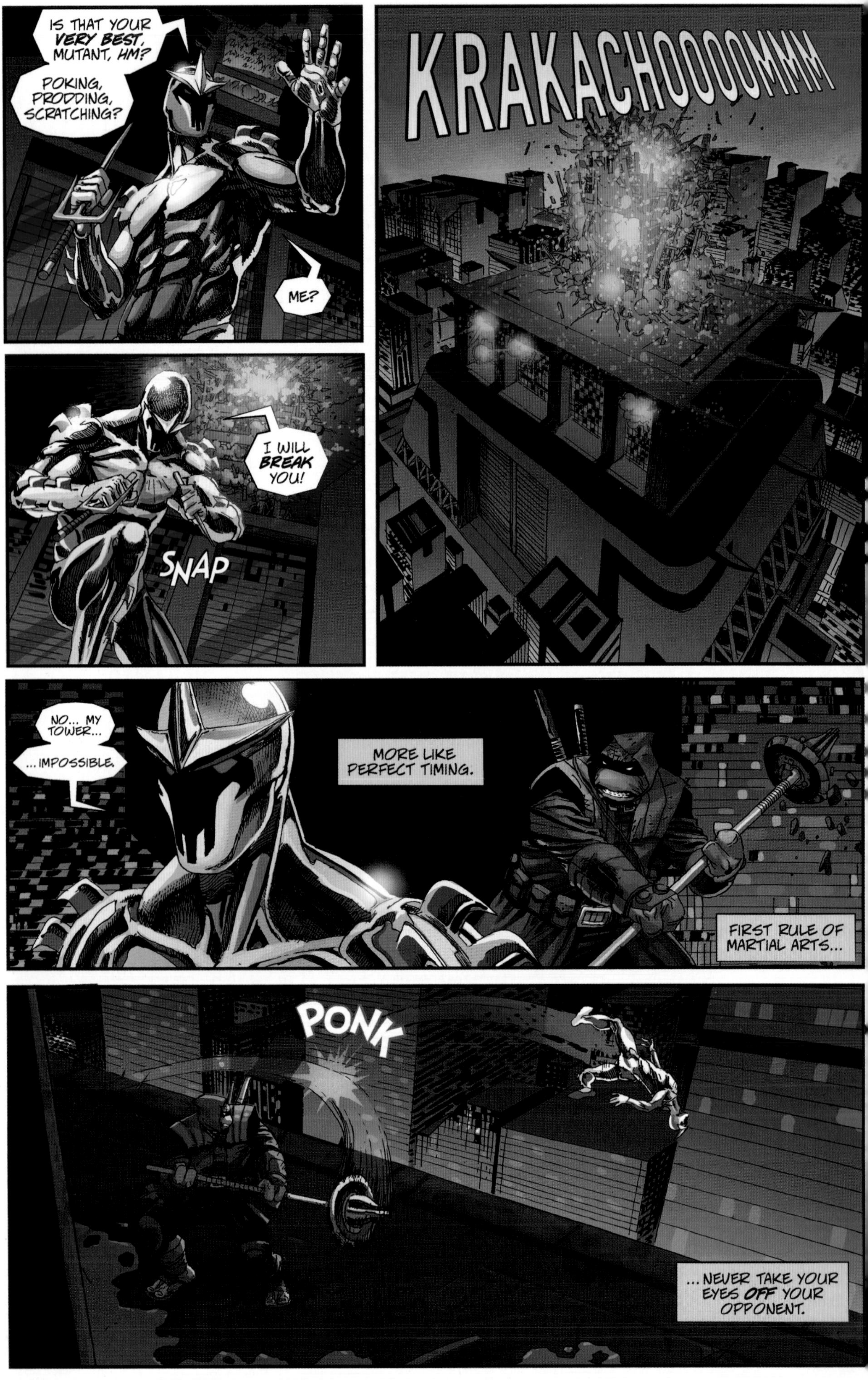
IS THAT YOUR VERY BEST, MUTANT, HM?
POKING, PRODDING, SCRATCHING?
ME?
KRAKACHOOOOOMMM
I WILL BREAK YOU!
SNAP
NO... MY TOWER...
...IMPOSSIBLE.
MORE LIKE PERFECT TIMING.
FIRST RULE OF MARTIAL ARTS...
PONK
...NEVER TAKE YOUR EYES OFF YOUR OPPONENT.

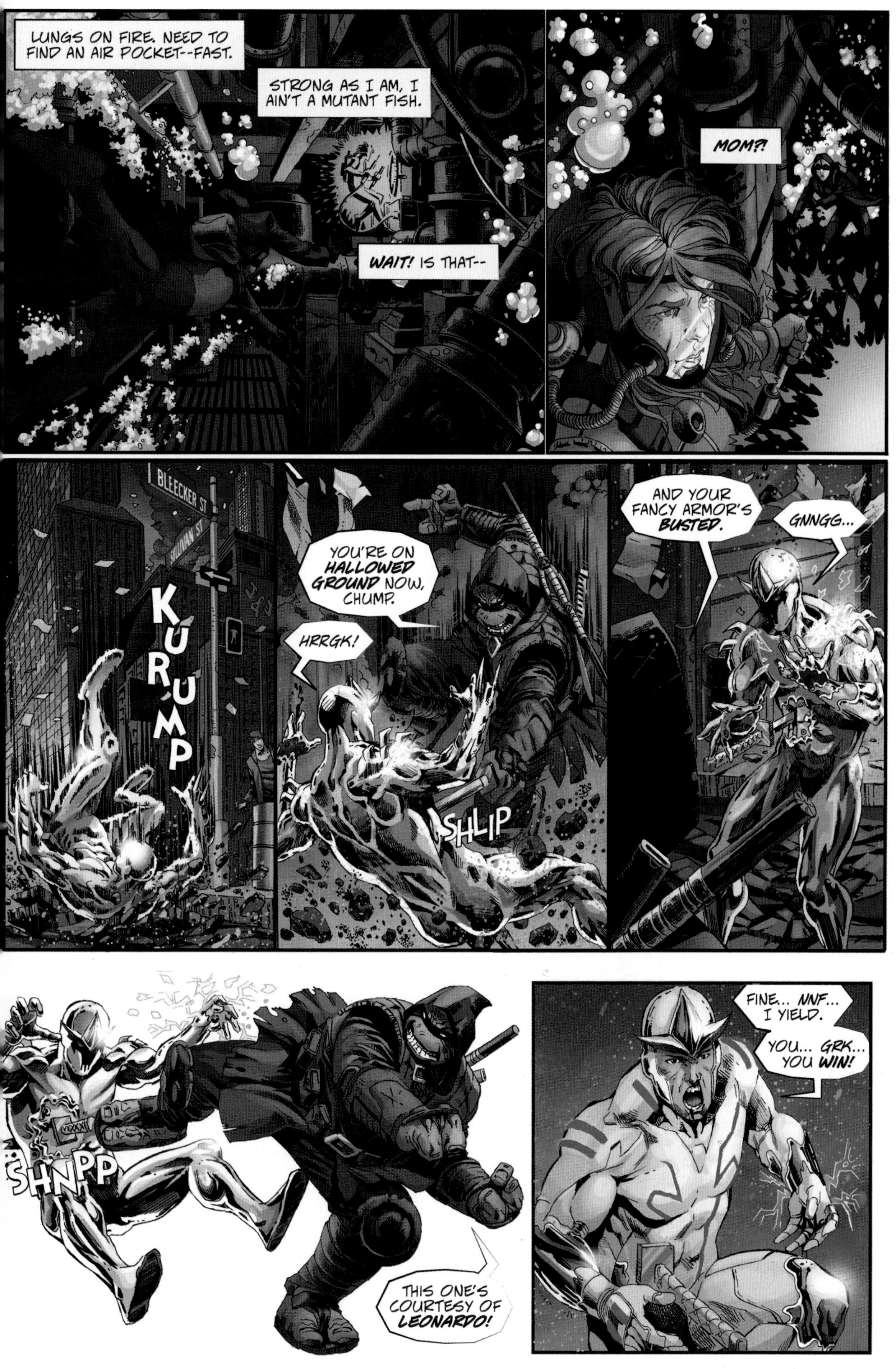
LUNGS ON FIRE. NEED TO FIND AN AIR POCKET--FAST.
STRONG AS I AM, I AIN'T A MUTANT FISH.
WAIT! IS THAT--
MOM?!
BLEECKER ST
SULLIVAN ST
KURUMP
YOU'RE ON HALLOWED GROUND NOW, CHUMP.
HRRGK!
SHLIP
AND YOUR FANCY ARMOR'S BUSTED.
GNNGG...
SHNPP
THIS ONE'S COURTESY OF LEONARDO!
FINE... NNF... I YIELD.
YOU... GRK... YOU WIN!

KABOOM
RUMBLE
SCHRAK

"YOU STILL DON'T GET IT, DO YOU, HIROTO?

THERE'S NO WIN OR LOSE TODAY.

ONLY AN *END.*

YOU'RE RIGHT.

SHIKK

THIS *IS* AN ENDING, MUTANT!

STUPID, COCKY FOOL.

GUHH...

YOURS!

OLDEST TRICK IN THE BOOK...

...AND I *FELL* FOR IT.

NEED TO REGROUP.

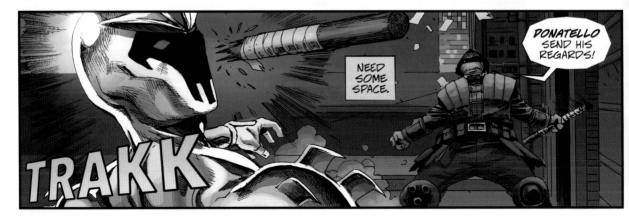

NEED SOME SPACE.

DONATELLO SEND HIS REGARDS!

TRAKK

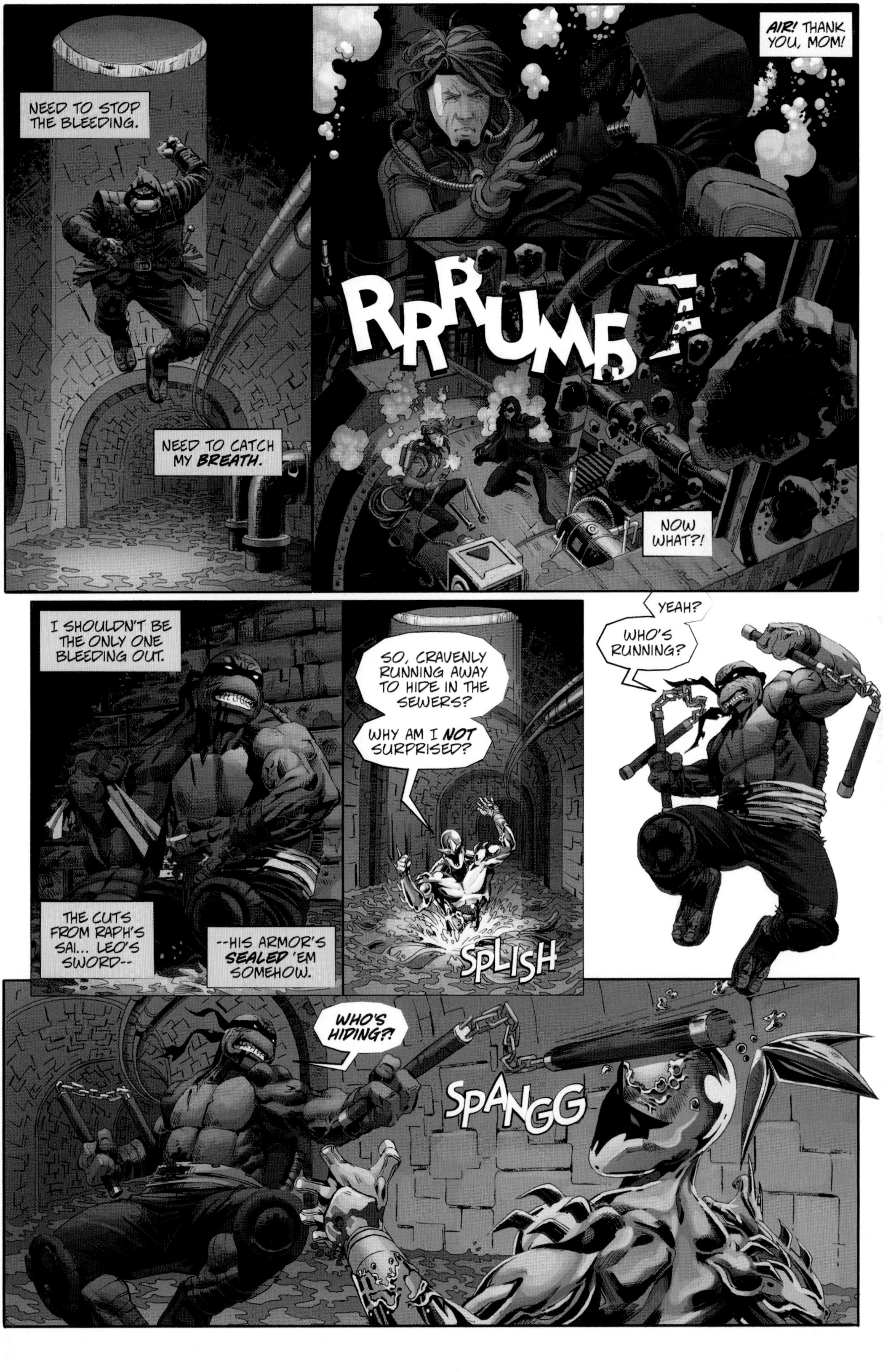

NEED TO STOP THE BLEEDING.
NEED TO CATCH MY BREATH.
AIR! THANK YOU, MOM!
RRRUMB
NOW WHAT?!
I SHOULDN'T BE THE ONLY ONE BLEEDING OUT.
THE CUTS FROM RAPH'S SAI... LEO'S SWORD--
--HIS ARMOR'S SEALED 'EM SOMEHOW.
SO, CRAVENLY RUNNING AWAY TO HIDE IN THE SEWERS?
WHY AM I NOT SURPRISED?
SPLISH
YEAH?
WHO'S RUNNING?
WHO'S HIDING?!
SPANGG

ROCKS FALLIN' EVERYWHERE.

KNCH

GOTTA PROTECT MOM--

--BUY HER MORE TIME.

WHUP

MMF!

ZIRRKK

KACHAK

WHIRRRRR

HIS ARMOR... FAILING HIM.

FWAP

GOTTA FINISH THIS--

KRAK

--BEFORE MY BODY FAILS ME.

NO!

ROARRRR

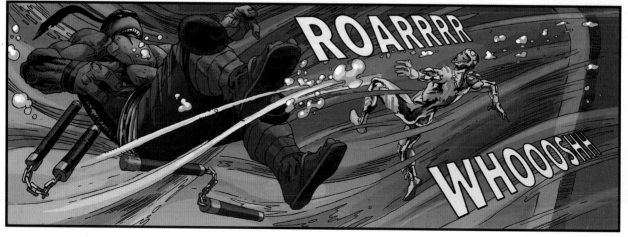

ROARRRR

WHOOOSH

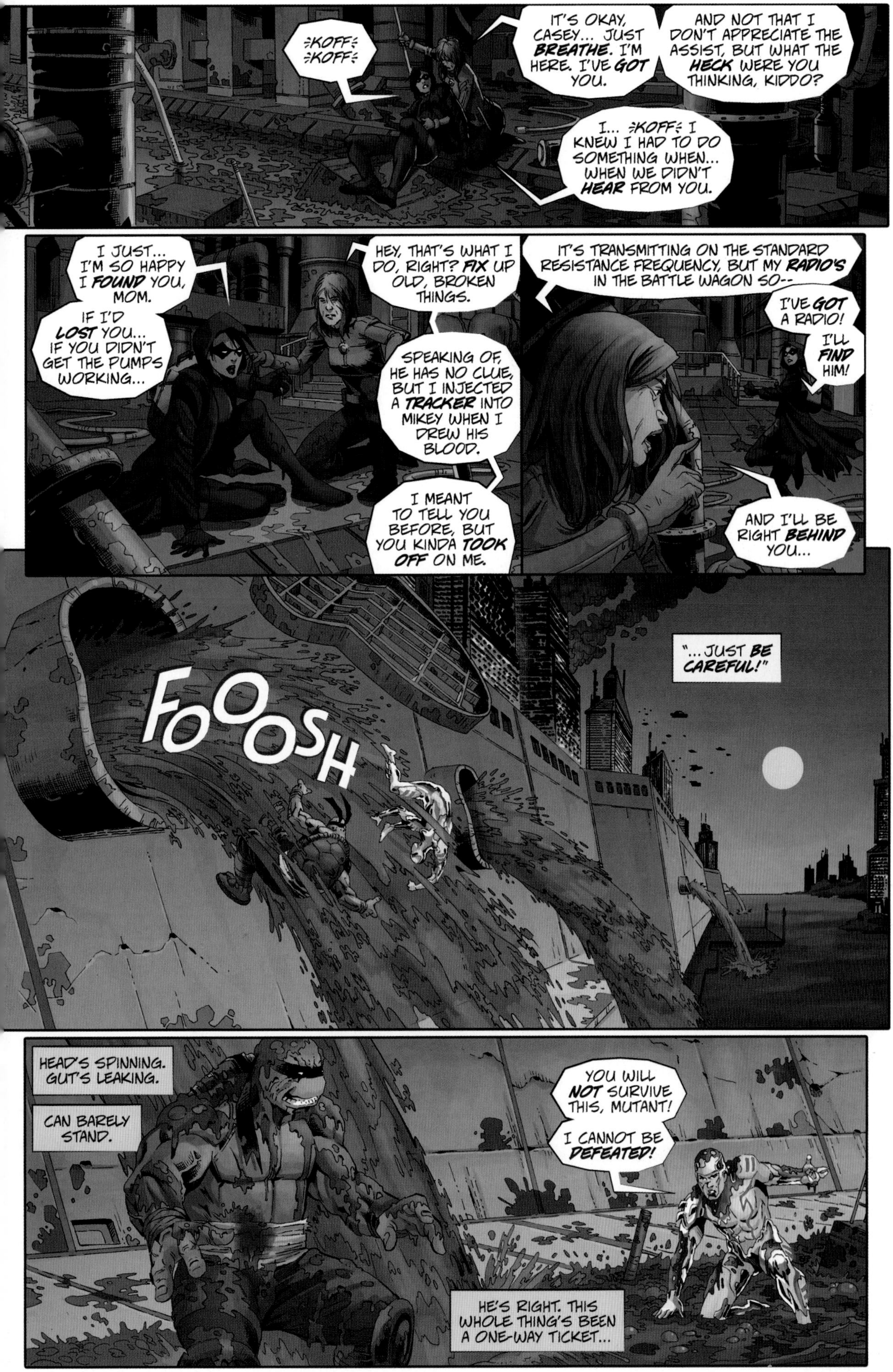

KOFF KOFF
IT'S OKAY, CASEY... JUST BREATHE. I'M HERE. I'VE GOT YOU.
AND NOT THAT I DON'T APPRECIATE THE ASSIST, BUT WHAT THE HECK WERE YOU THINKING, KIDDO?
I... KOFF I KNEW I HAD TO DO SOMETHING WHEN... WHEN WE DIDN'T HEAR FROM YOU.
I JUST... I'M SO HAPPY I FOUND YOU, MOM.
IF I'D LOST YOU... IF YOU DIDN'T GET THE PUMPS WORKING...
HEY, THAT'S WHAT I DO, RIGHT? FIX UP OLD, BROKEN THINGS.
SPEAKING OF, HE HAS NO CLUE, BUT I INJECTED A TRACKER INTO MIKEY WHEN I DREW HIS BLOOD.
I MEANT TO TELL YOU BEFORE, BUT YOU KINDA TOOK OFF ON ME.
IT'S TRANSMITTING ON THE STANDARD RESISTANCE FREQUENCY, BUT MY RADIO'S IN THE BATTLE WAGON SO--
I'VE GOT A RADIO!
I'LL FIND HIM!
AND I'LL BE RIGHT BEHIND YOU...
"...JUST BE CAREFUL!"
FOOOSH
HEAD'S SPINNING. GUT'S LEAKING.
CAN BARELY STAND.
YOU WILL NOT SURVIVE THIS, MUTANT!
I CANNOT BE DEFEATED!
HE'S RIGHT. THIS WHOLE THING'S BEEN A ONE-WAY TICKET...

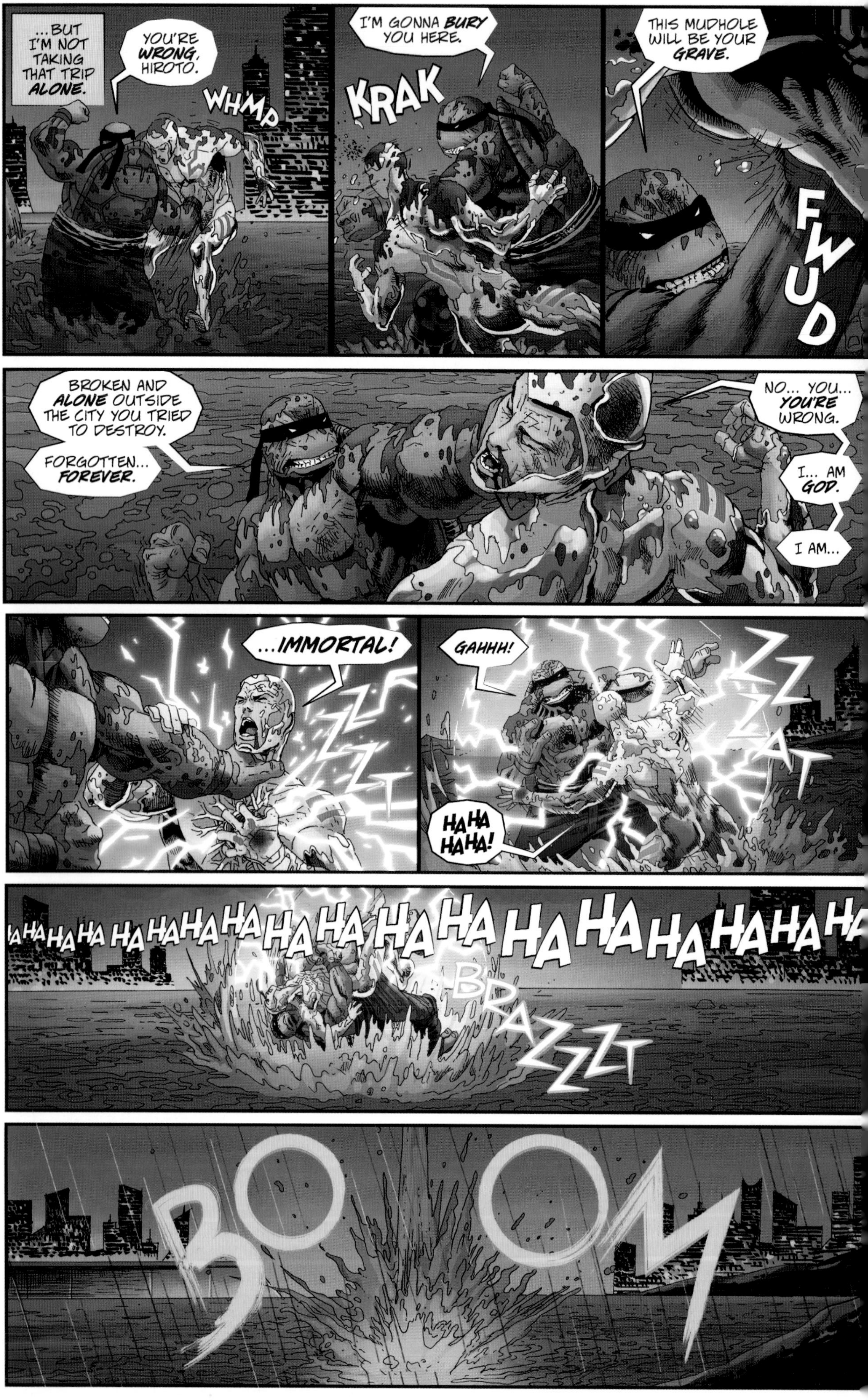
...BUT I'M NOT TAKING THAT TRIP ALONE.
YOU'RE WRONG, HIROTO.
WHMP
I'M GONNA BURY YOU HERE.
KRAK
THIS MUDHOLE WILL BE YOUR GRAVE.
FWUD
BROKEN AND ALONE OUTSIDE THE CITY YOU TRIED TO DESTROY.
FORGOTTEN... FOREVER.
NO... YOU... YOU'RE WRONG.
I... AM GOD.
I AM...
...IMMORTAL!
ZZZT
GAHHH!
ZZZAT
HAHA HAHA!
HA HA HA HA HA HA HA HA HA HA HA HA HA HA HA HA HA HA HA HA HA HA
BRAZZZZT
BOOM

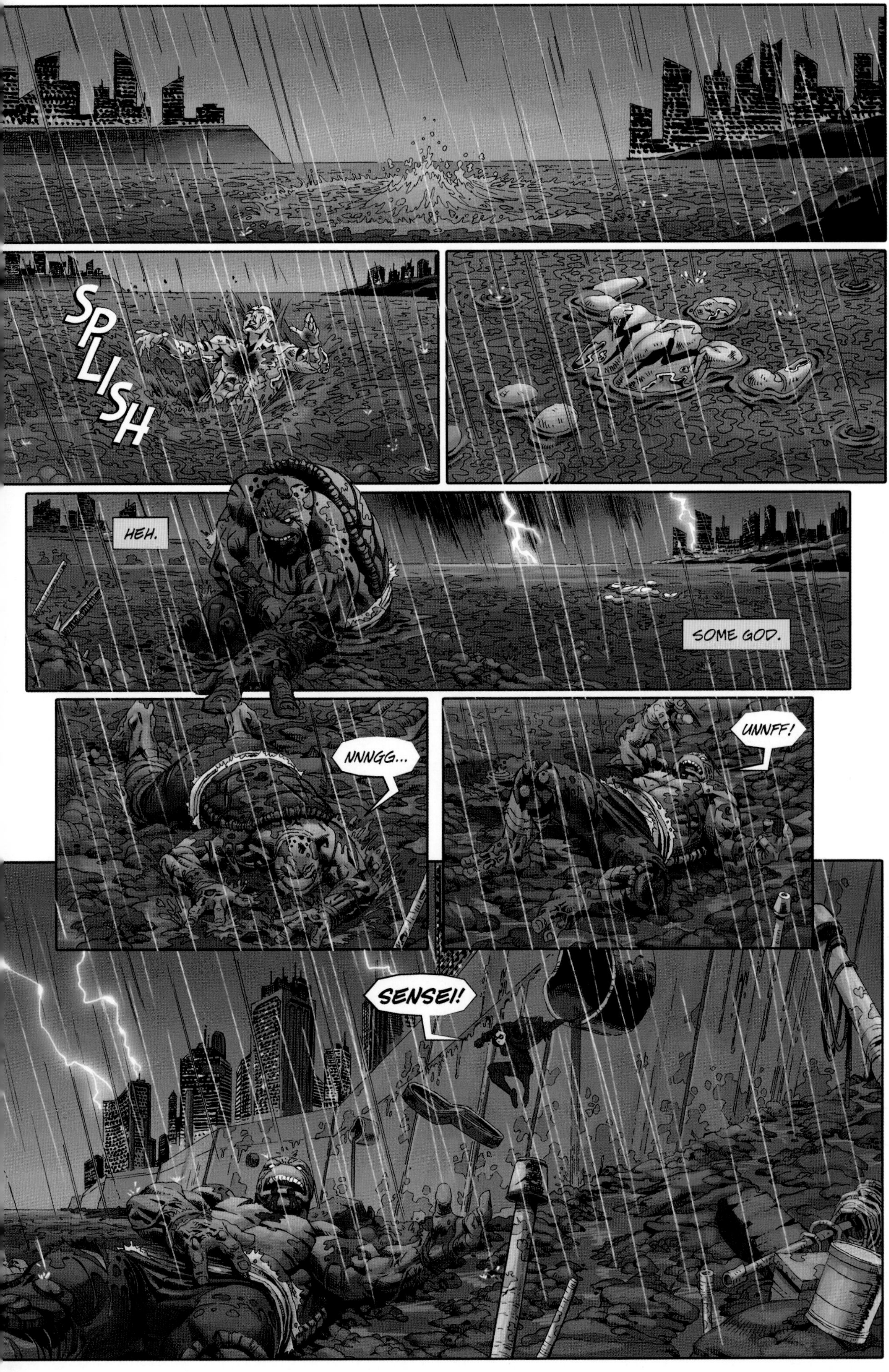
SPLISH
HEH.
SOME GOD.
NNNGG...
UNNFF!
SENSEI!

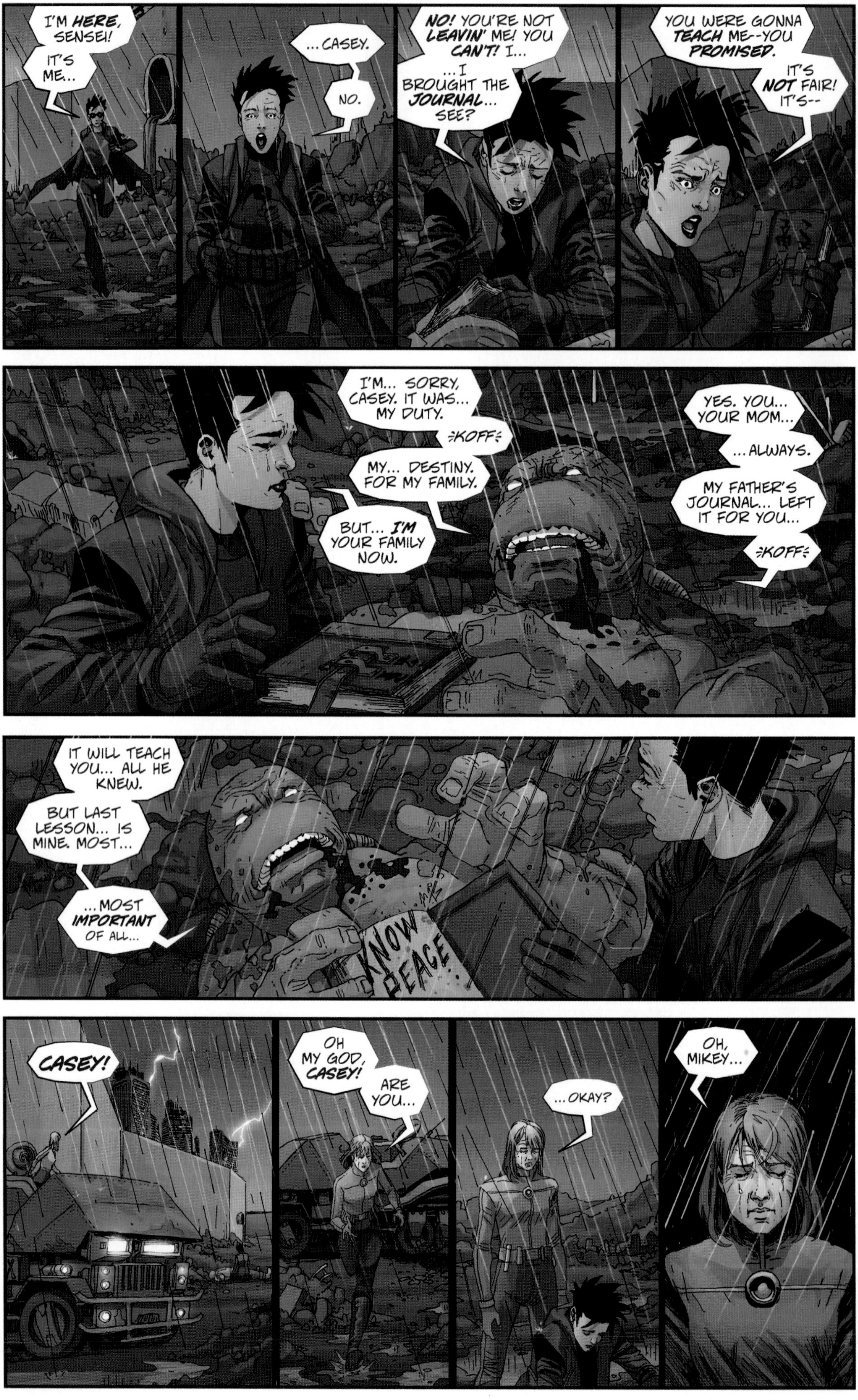
I'M HERE, SENSEI!
IT'S ME...
...CASEY.
NO.
NO! YOU'RE NOT LEAVIN' ME! YOU CAN'T! I...
...I BROUGHT THE JOURNAL... SEE?
YOU WERE GONNA TEACH ME--YOU PROMISED.
IT'S NOT FAIR! IT'S--
I'M... SORRY, CASEY. IT WAS... MY DUTY.
KOFF
MY... DESTINY. FOR MY FAMILY.
BUT... I'M YOUR FAMILY NOW.
YES. YOU... YOUR MOM...
...ALWAYS.
MY FATHER'S JOURNAL... LEFT IT FOR YOU...
KOFF
IT WILL TEACH YOU... ALL HE KNEW.
BUT LAST LESSON... IS MINE. MOST...
...MOST IMPORTANT OF ALL...
KNOW PEACE
CASEY!
OH MY GOD, CASEY!
ARE YOU...
...OKAY?
OH, MIKEY...

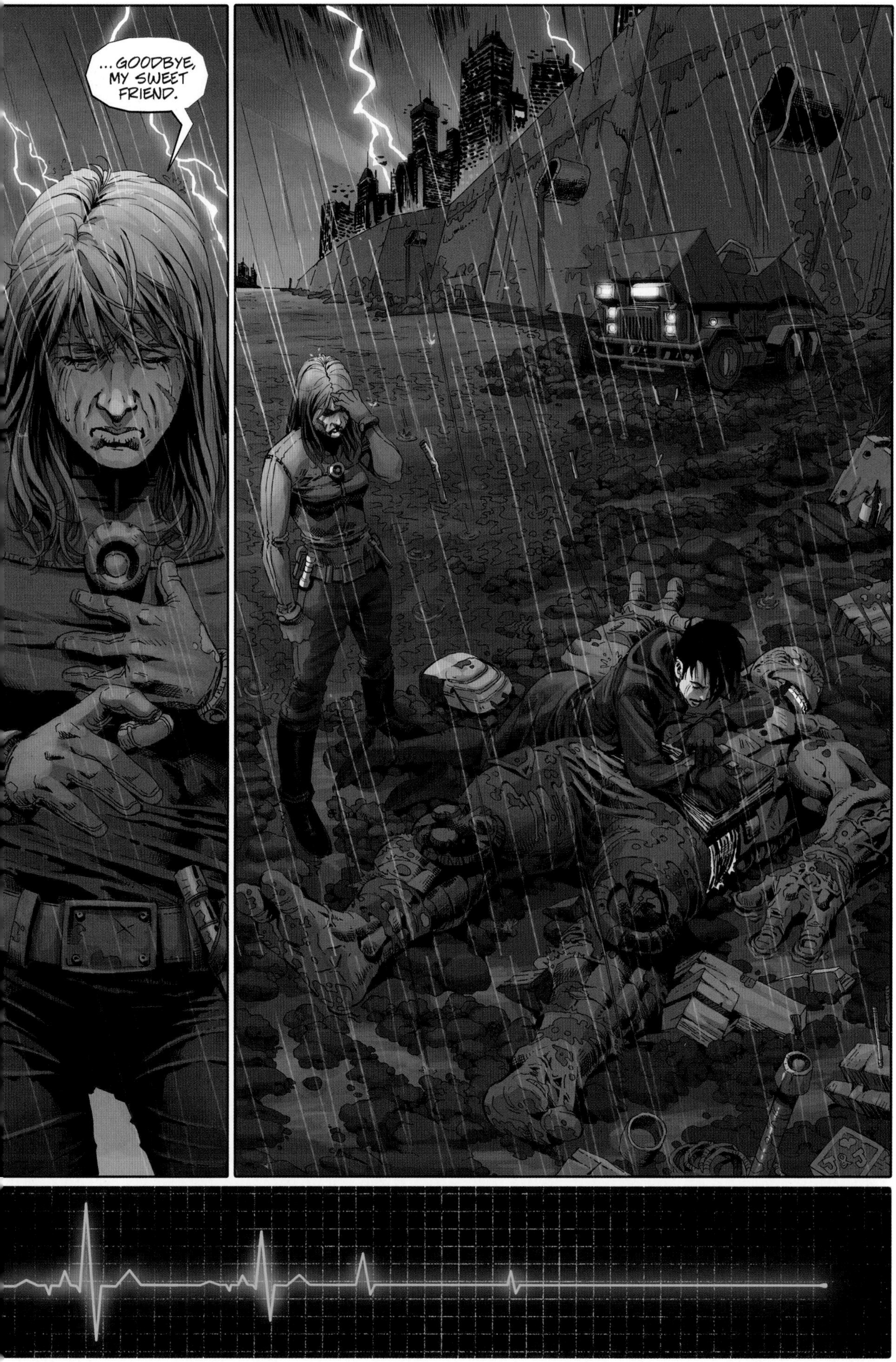
...GOODBYE, MY SWEET FRIEND.

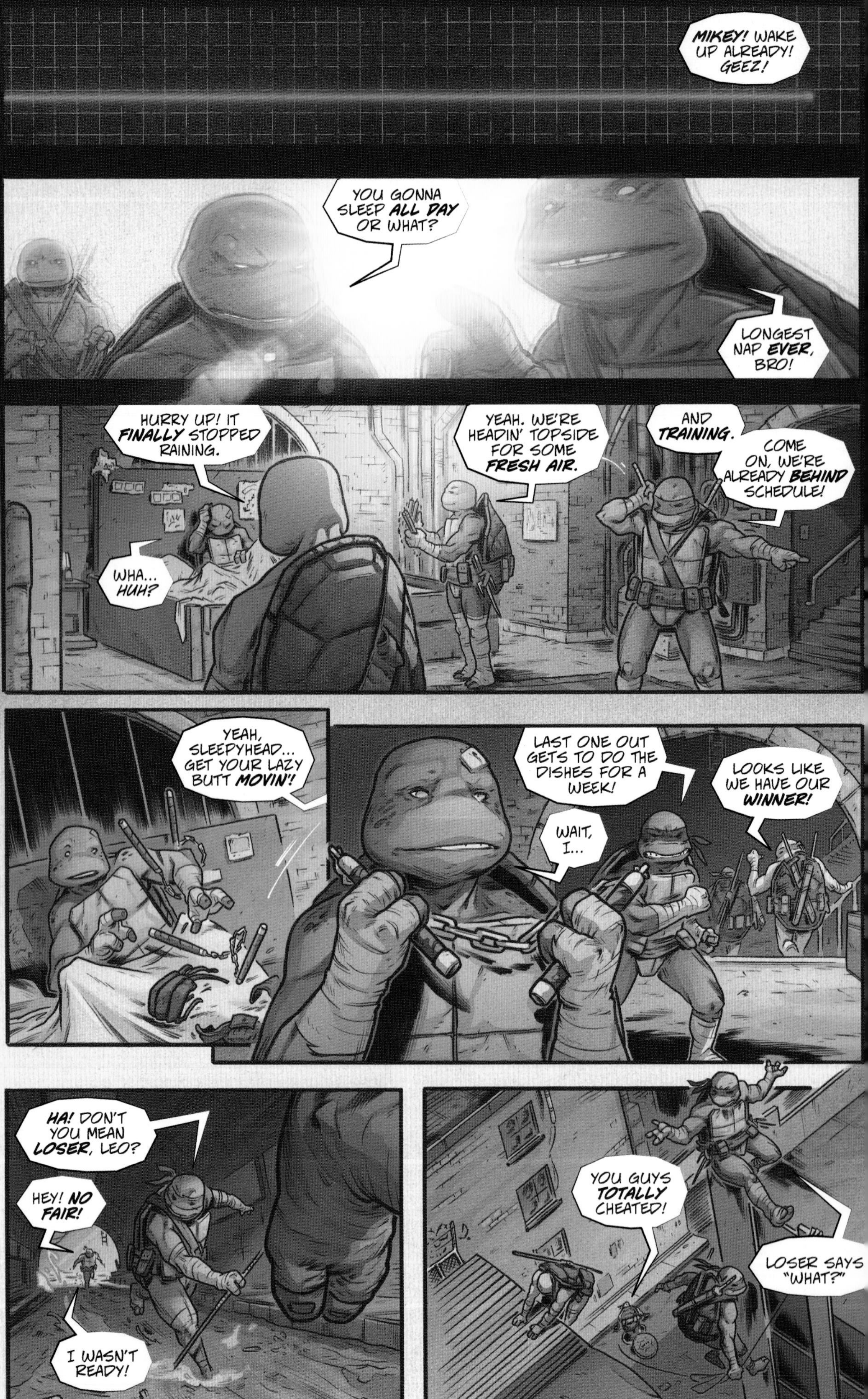
MIKEY! WAKE UP ALREADY! GEEZ!
YOU GONNA SLEEP ALL DAY OR WHAT?
LONGEST NAP EVER, BRO!
HURRY UP! IT FINALLY STOPPED RAINING.
WHA... HUH?
YEAH. WE'RE HEADIN' TOPSIDE FOR SOME FRESH AIR.
AND TRAINING.
COME ON, WE'RE ALREADY BEHIND SCHEDULE!
YEAH, SLEEPYHEAD... GET YOUR LAZY BUTT MOVIN'!
LAST ONE OUT GETS TO DO THE DISHES FOR A WEEK!
WAIT, I...
LOOKS LIKE WE HAVE OUR WINNER!
HA! DON'T YOU MEAN LOSER, LEO?
HEY! NO FAIR!
I WASN'T READY!
YOU GUYS TOTALLY CHEATED!
LOSER SAYS "WHAT?"

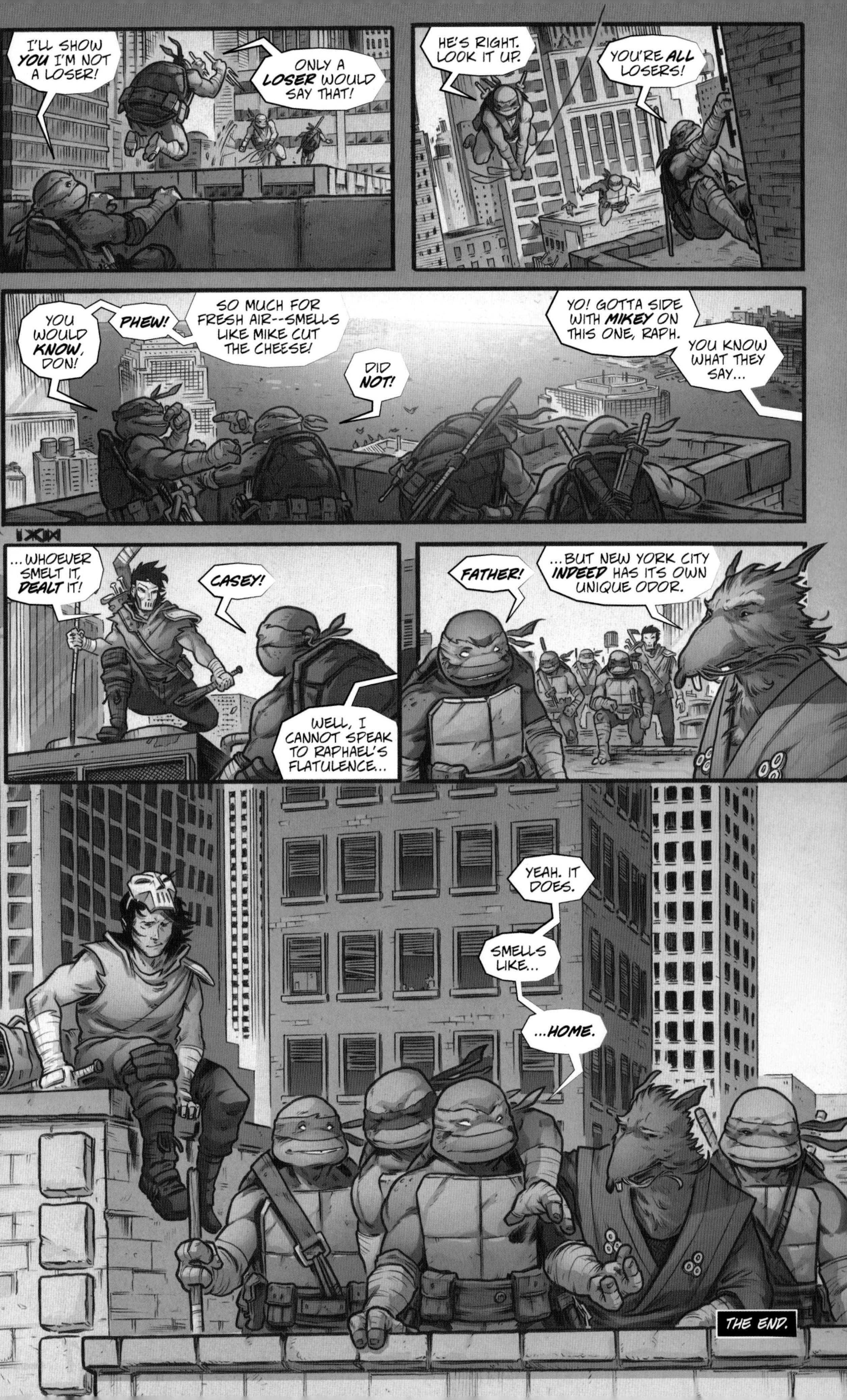

I'LL SHOW YOU I'M NOT A LOSER!
ONLY A LOSER WOULD SAY THAT!
HE'S RIGHT. LOOK IT UP.
YOU'RE ALL LOSERS!
YOU WOULD KNOW, DON!
PHEW!
SO MUCH FOR FRESH AIR--SMELLS LIKE MIKE CUT THE CHEESE!
DID NOT!
YO! GOTTA SIDE WITH MIKEY ON THIS ONE, RAPH.
YOU KNOW WHAT THEY SAY...
...WHOEVER SMELT IT, DEALT IT!
CASEY!
WELL, I CANNOT SPEAK TO RAPHAEL'S FLATULENCE...
FATHER!
...BUT NEW YORK CITY INDEED HAS ITS OWN UNIQUE ODOR.
YEAH. IT DOES.
SMELLS LIKE...
...HOME.
THE END.

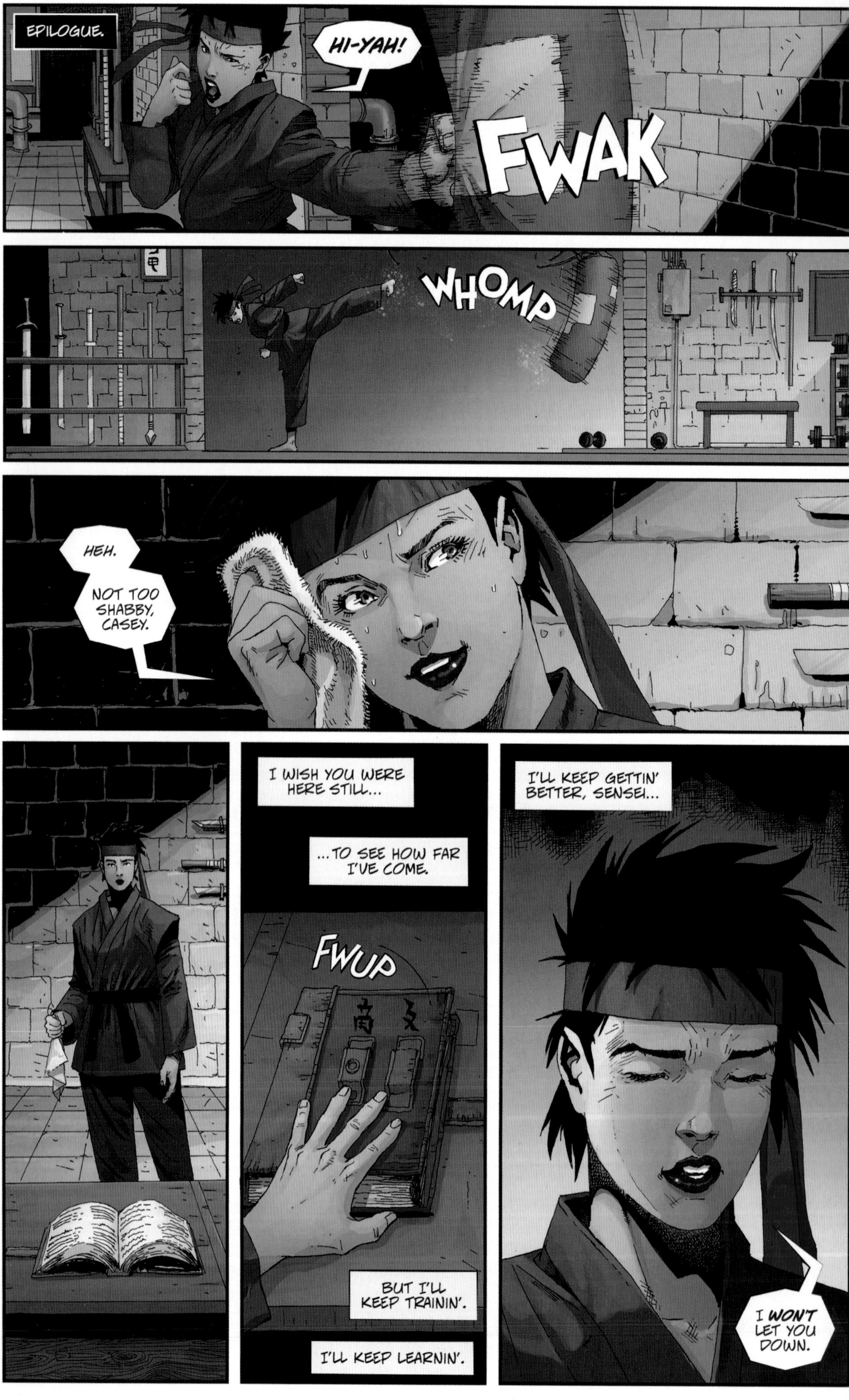
EPILOGUE.
HI-YAH!
FWAK
WHOMP
HEH.
NOT TOO SHABBY, CASEY.
I WISH YOU WERE HERE STILL...
...TO SEE HOW FAR I'VE COME.
FWUP
BUT I'LL KEEP TRAININ'.
I'LL KEEP LEARNIN'.
I'LL KEEP GETTIN' BETTER, SENSEI...
I WON'T LET YOU DOWN.

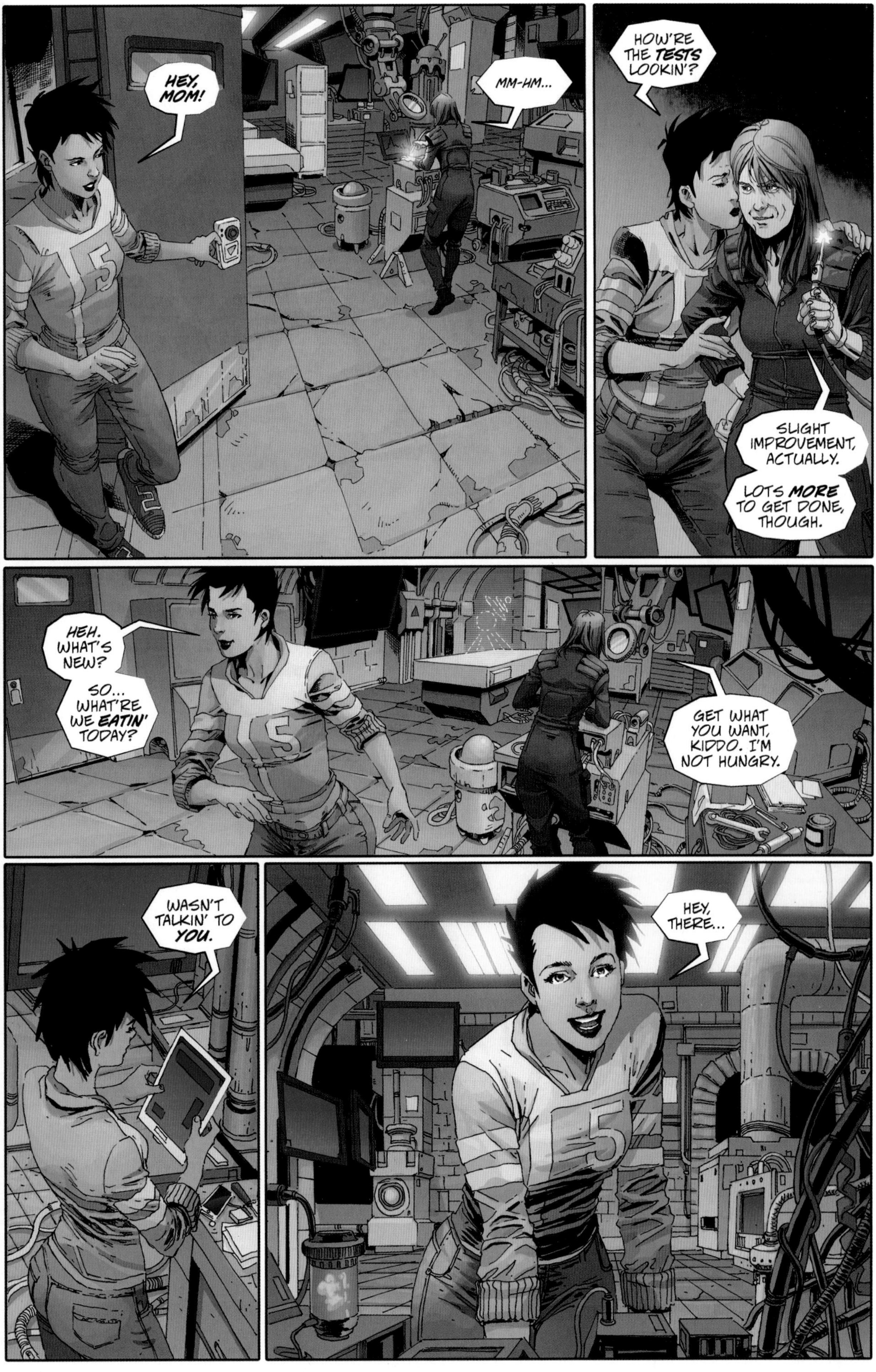
HEY, MOM!
MM-HM...
HOW'RE THE TESTS LOOKIN'?
SLIGHT IMPROVEMENT, ACTUALLY.
LOTS MORE TO GET DONE, THOUGH.
HEH. WHAT'S NEW?
SO... WHAT'RE WE EATIN' TODAY?
GET WHAT YOU WANT, KIDDO. I'M NOT HUNGRY.
WASN'T TALKIN' TO YOU.
HEY, THERE...

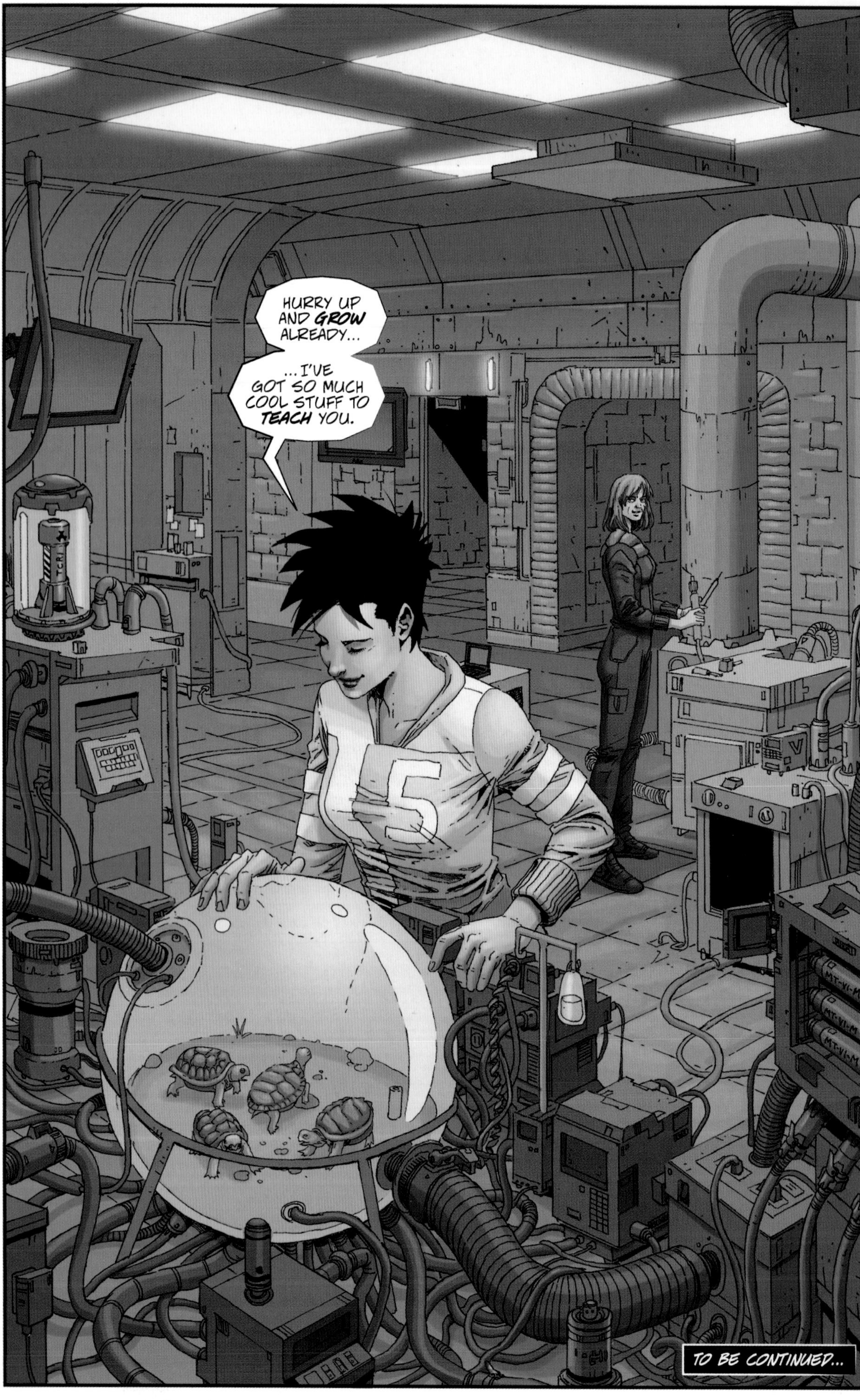
HURRY UP AND GROW ALREADY...
...I'VE GOT SO MUCH COOL STUFF TO TEACH YOU.
TO BE CONTINUED...

Afterword

I remember the peeling wallpaper of the tiny living room at 28 Union Street in Dover, New Hampshire, as Peter Laird and I took turns filling in the last black square of an organizational chart that represented the workflow of *Teenage Mutant Ninja Turtles* issue one.

It was now late spring and the 40 pages of story that we created, wrote, and drew together were completed, and we couldn't have been more thrilled. It was the longest story either of us had ever produced and good, bad or ugly, it was all ours.

With all that sweat equity, coupled with a $1,200 loan from my very supportive uncle, Quentin Eastman, the final product was sent off to a local printer. If we were in luck, we'd get it back just in time for a local comic convention our friend Ralph DeBernardo was hosting over in Portsmouth.

The stars aligned, everything arrived in time, and on May 5th, 1984, we unleashed our creation on an unsuspecting public. That was 38 years ago.

We had produced a story with a beginning, middle, and an end—an origin story (leaving the door open for more)—but we never planned a second issue. The public, however, had other plans for us.

By 1987, the dream had more than come true. We were drawing comics full-time, following in the footsteps of the creative heroes that inspired us, and things couldn't have been any better.

As we built out our characters' universe, we wondered how long this would all last. We had our beginning, lots of outrageous adventures, but what would the end look like for our creations? Their final story? What if we looked 30 years into the future and explored a story set then?

So, we wrote it down, but this time our characters had other plans for us.

Thirty-two years later, in the year 2018, the time to re-explore that idea had arrived.

The extremely gifted writer Tom Waltz, with an incredible army of talented artisans, was heading toward wrapping up ten years and one hundred issues of the IDW *TMNT* universe, and Tom and I had the same conversation Peter and I'd had all those years ago: where does it go from here?

That original draft was dusted off, and the idea of *The Last Ronin* began to take shape. The approach was completely organic, like the old days when Peter and I worked together. The final story steadily evolved through years of rewrites, designs, and layouts, including tweaking dialogue the night before it went to press in order to make it perfect.

It is one of the most challenging projects I have ever worked on, and one of the most rewarding.

Thanks doesn't say enough, Tom.

Besides the brilliant Tom Waltz, series artists Esau & Isaac Escorza and Ben Bishop, topped off with colorist Luis Antonio Delgado, are a true dream team. Without them, as well as series editor Bobby Curnow, designer Shawn Lee, and the entire IDW and Nickelodeon crews, this book would not have been possible.

I would like to dedicate this book to my awesome co-creator, Peter Laird.

As we did in 1984 with issue #1, I would also like to dedicate *The Last Ronin* to Jack Kirby and Frank Miller. The TMNT would never have been possible without you.

This one is for Courtney and Shane, with all my love and gratitude for your support.

My heartfelt thanks go out to the fans. You've given me the greatest job and the greatest life I could have never imagined. I will continue to try to earn it.

Kevin Eastman

March 2022

Art by **Kevin Eastman**

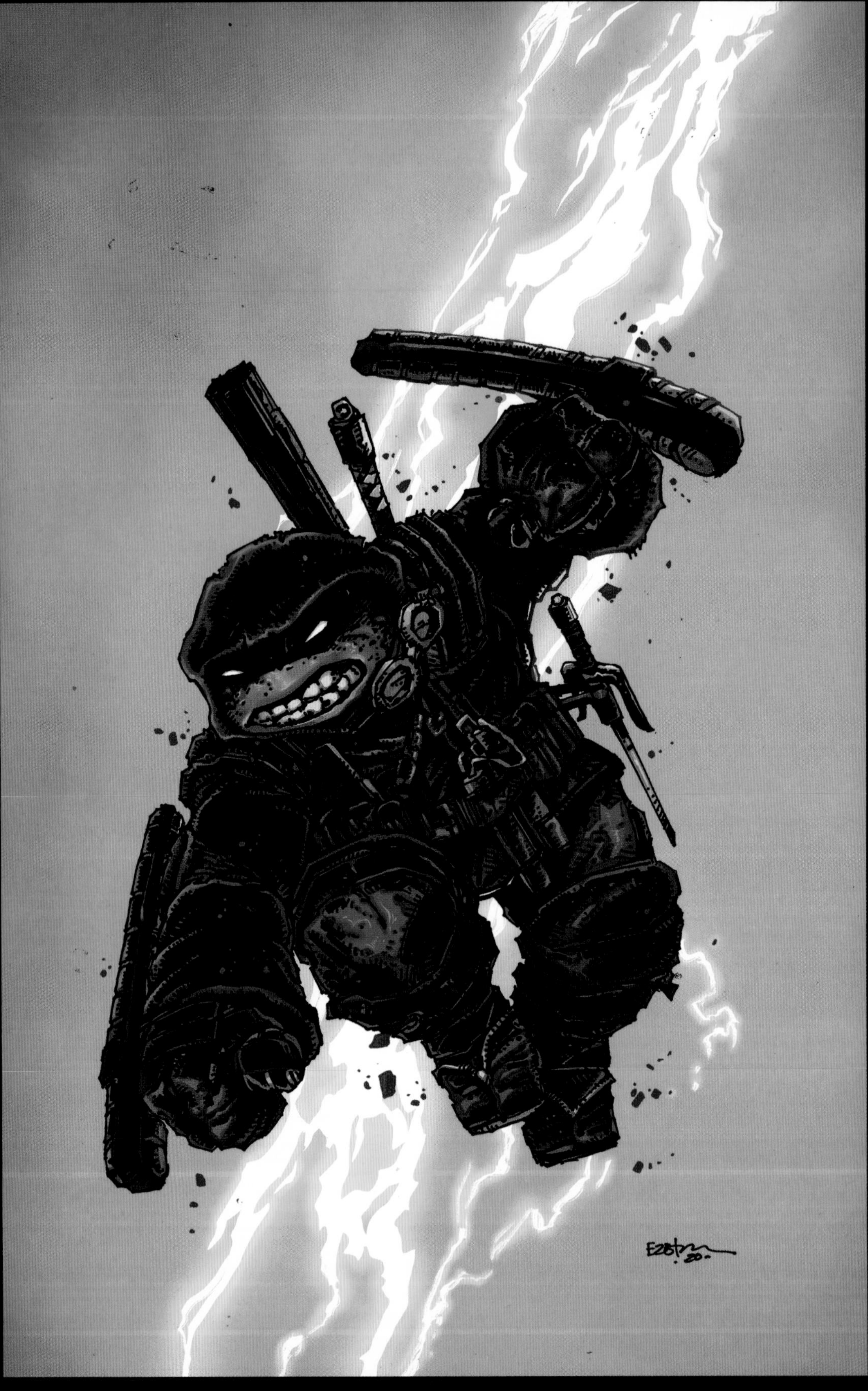

Colors by **Brittany Pezzillo**

Art by **Mateus Santolouco**

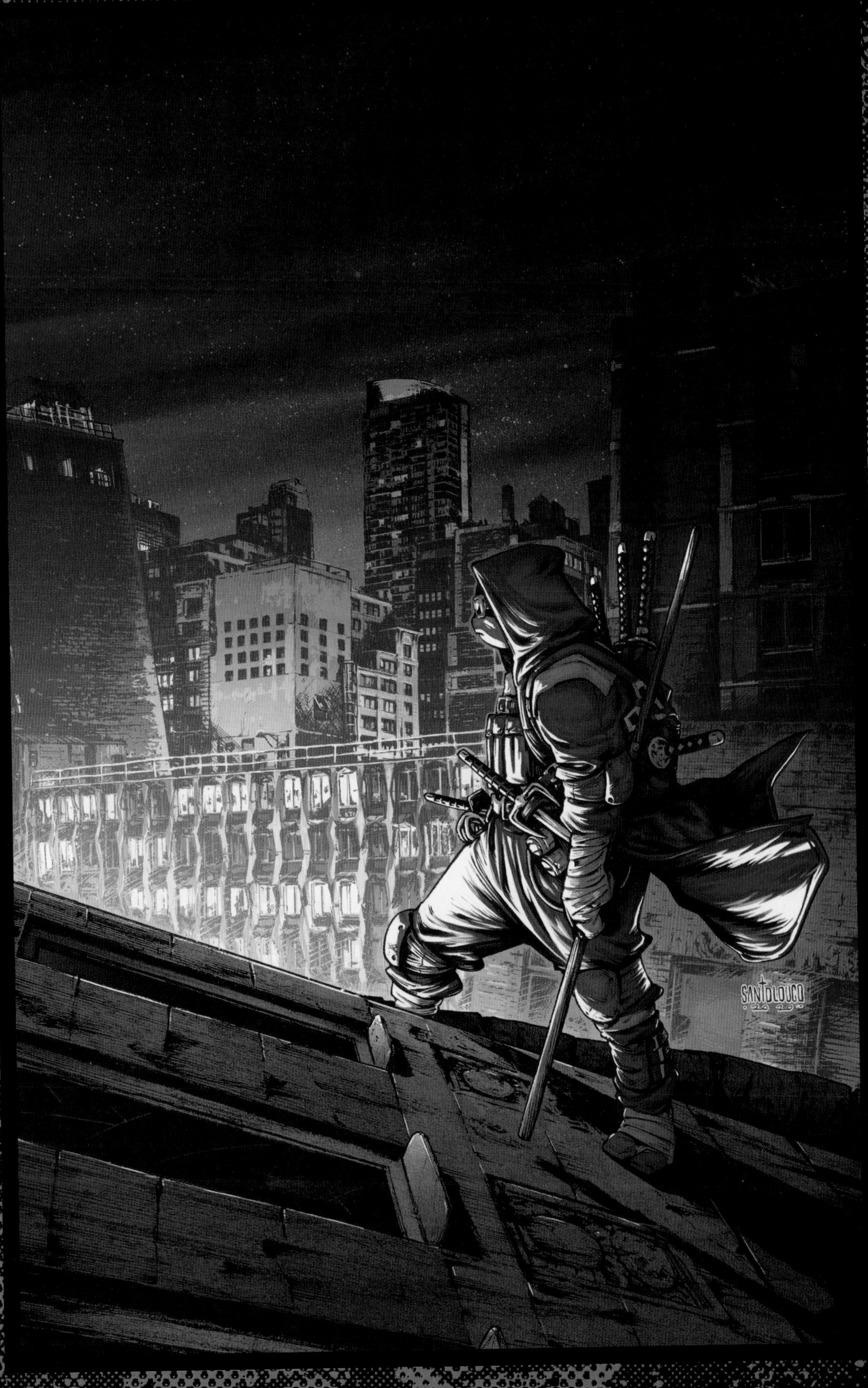
SANTOLOUCO

Art by **Esau** & **Isaac Escorza**

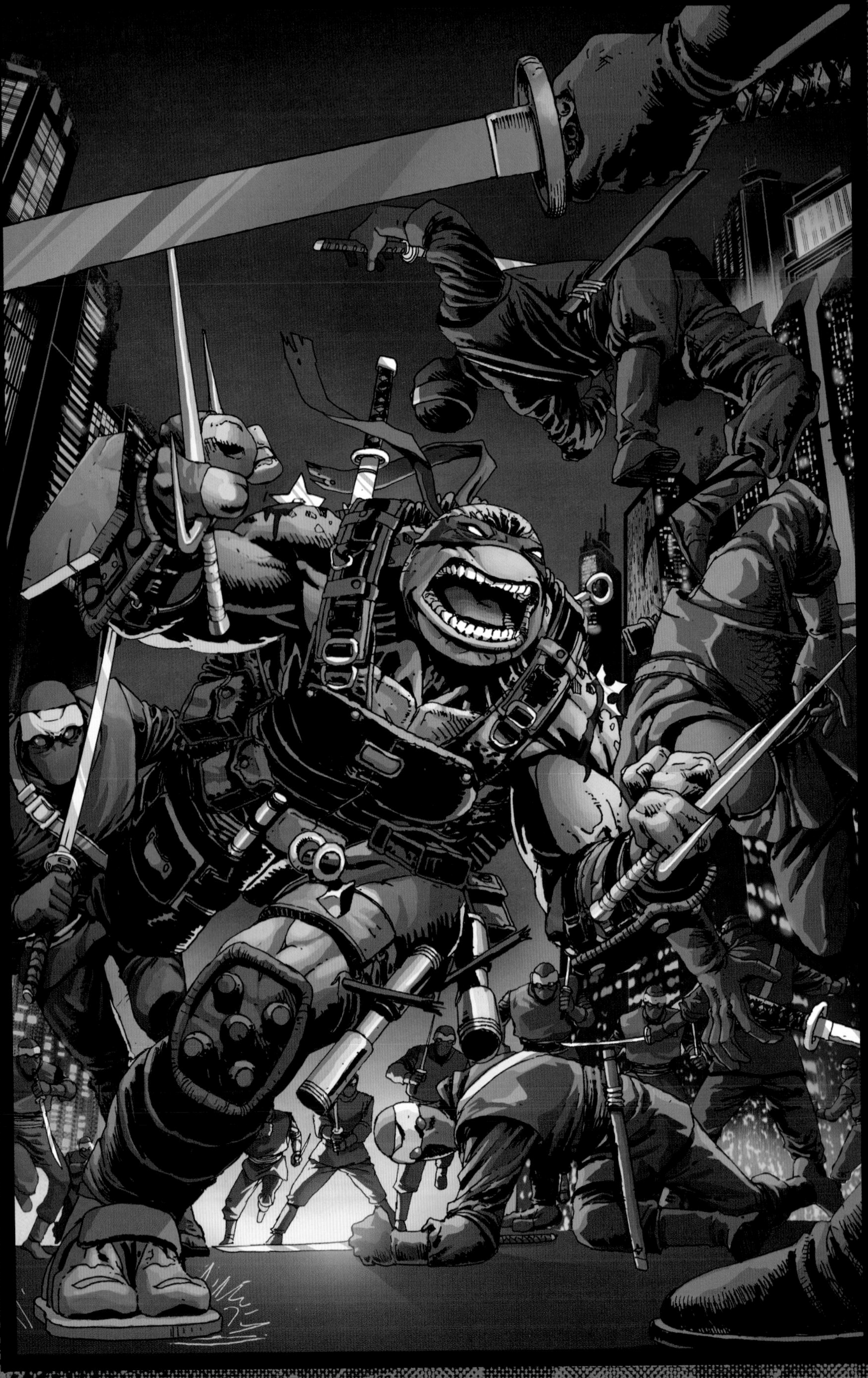

Colors by **Luis Antonio Delgado**

Art by **Sophie Campbell**

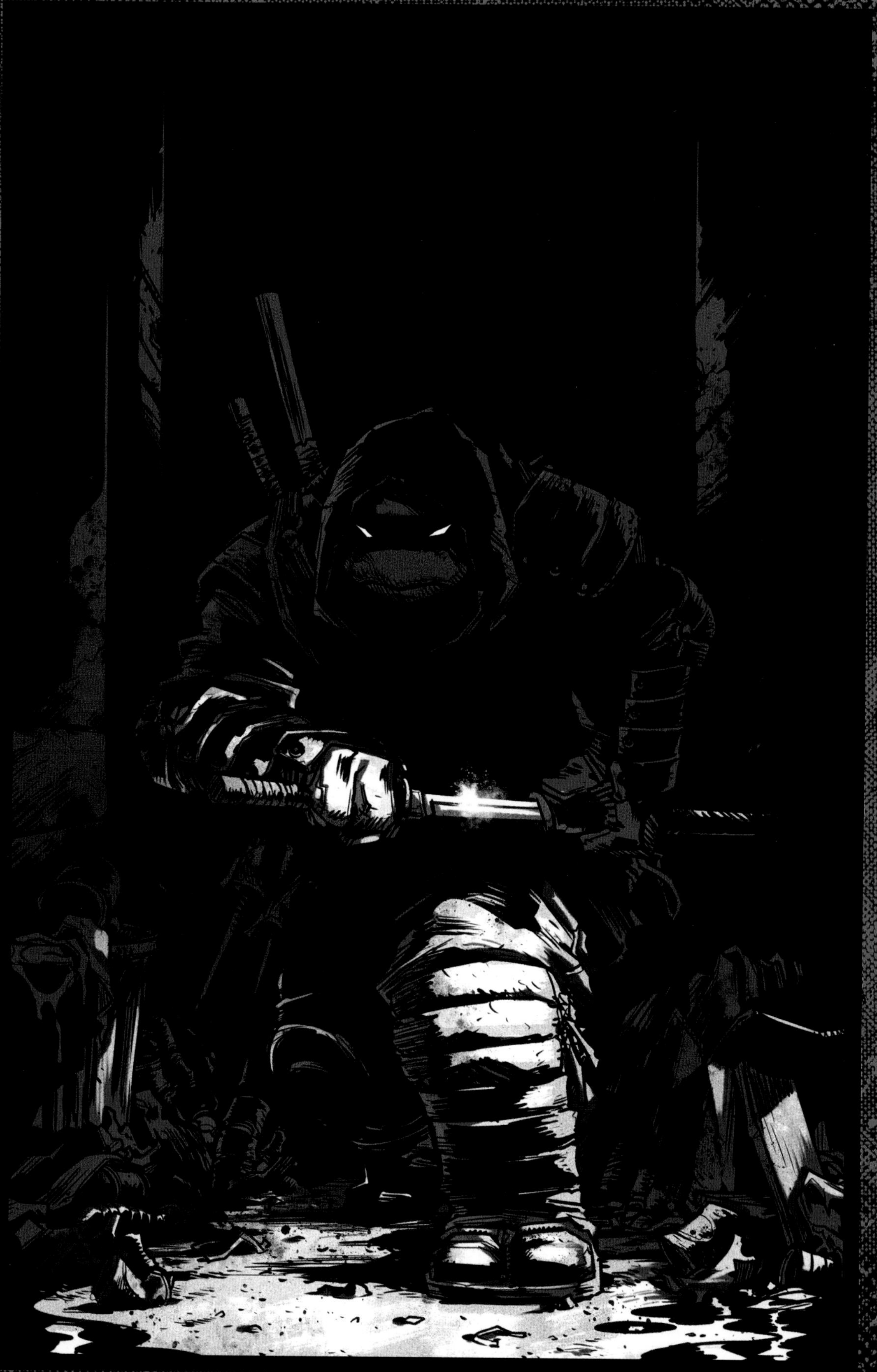

Art by **Esau** & **Isaac Escorza**

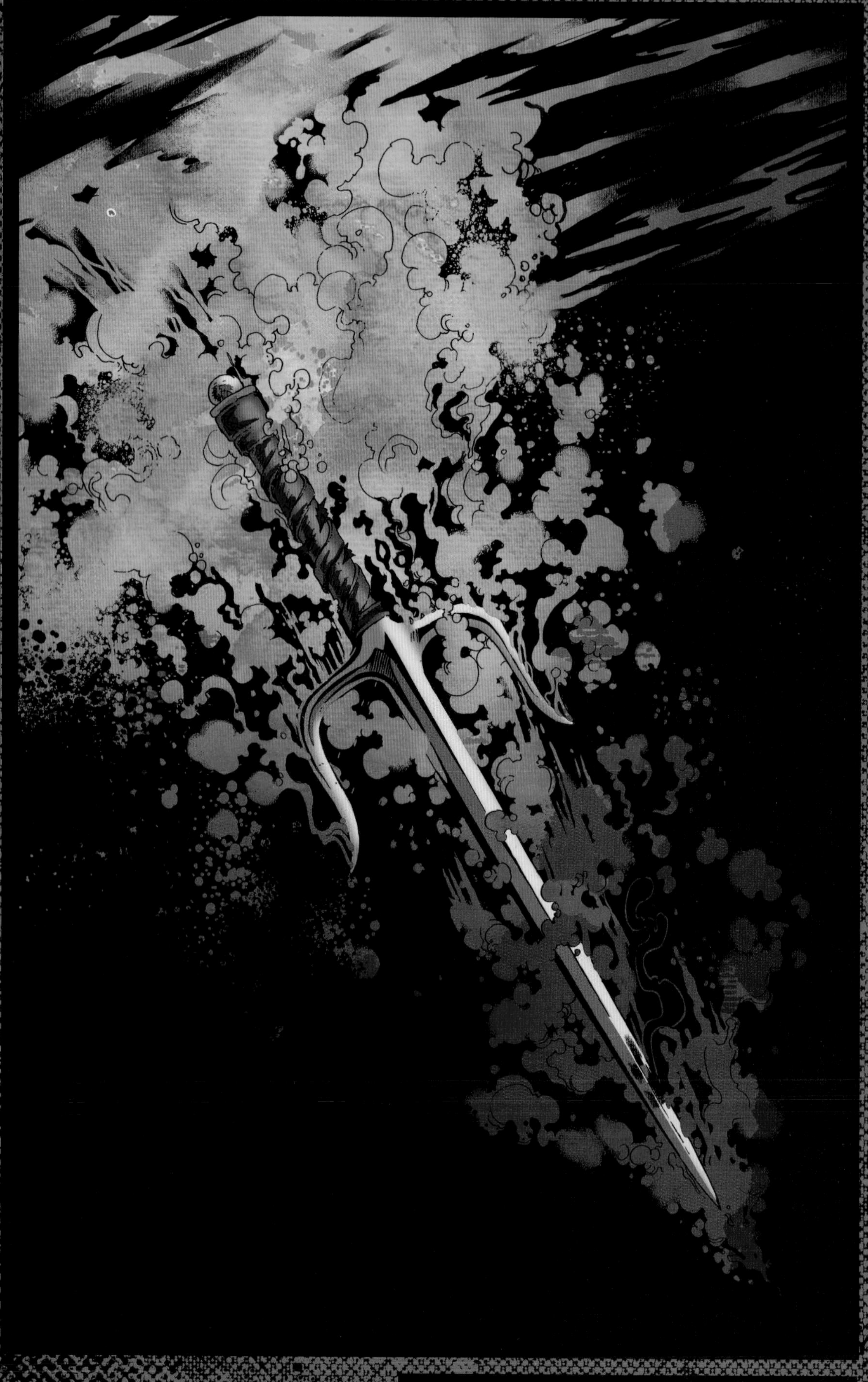

Colors by **Luis Antonio Delgado**

Art by **Esau** & **Isaac Escorza**

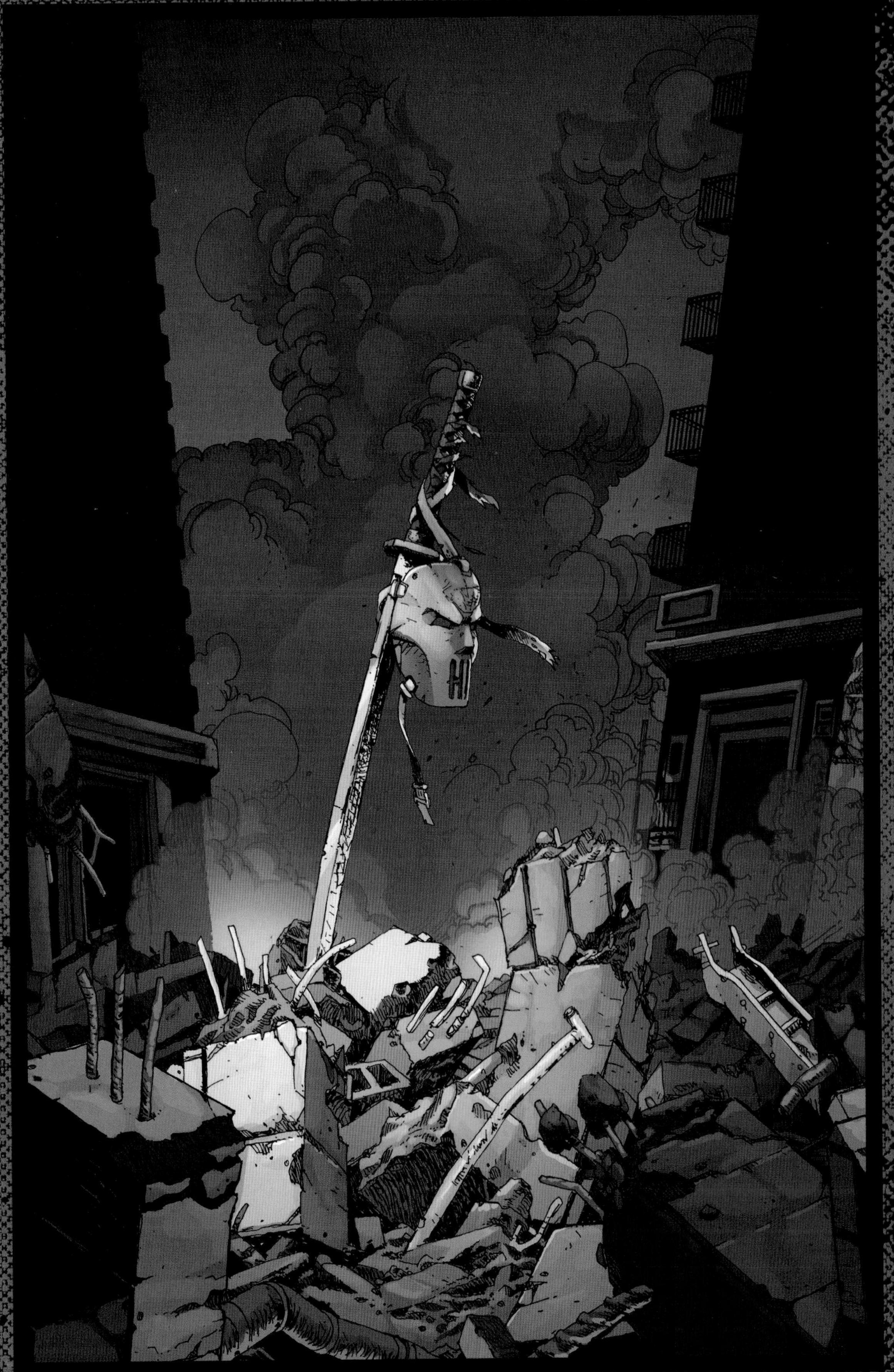

Colors by **Luis Antonio Delgado**

Art by **Esau** & **Isaac Escorza**

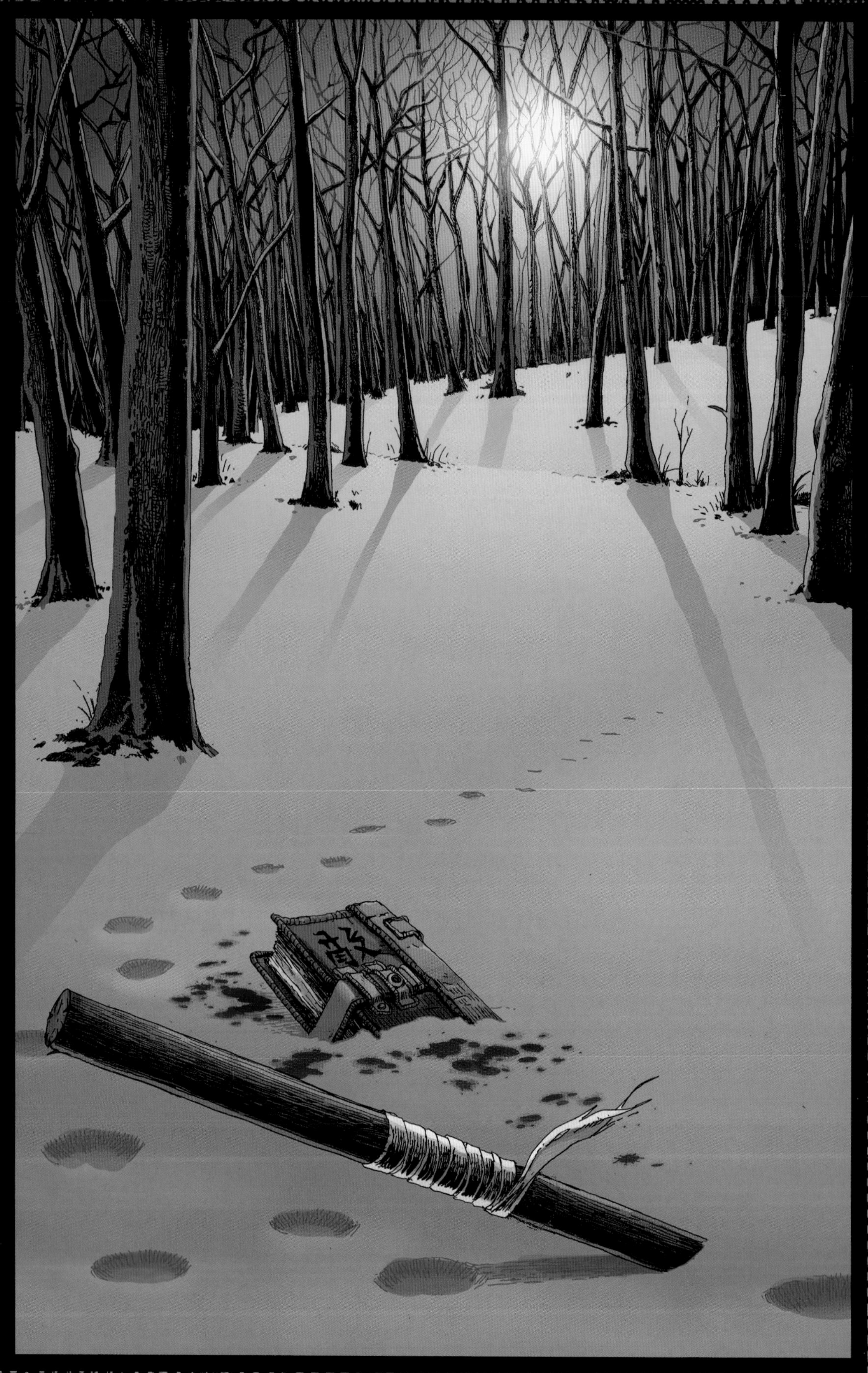

Colors by **Luis Antonio Delgado**

Art by **Freddie Williams II**

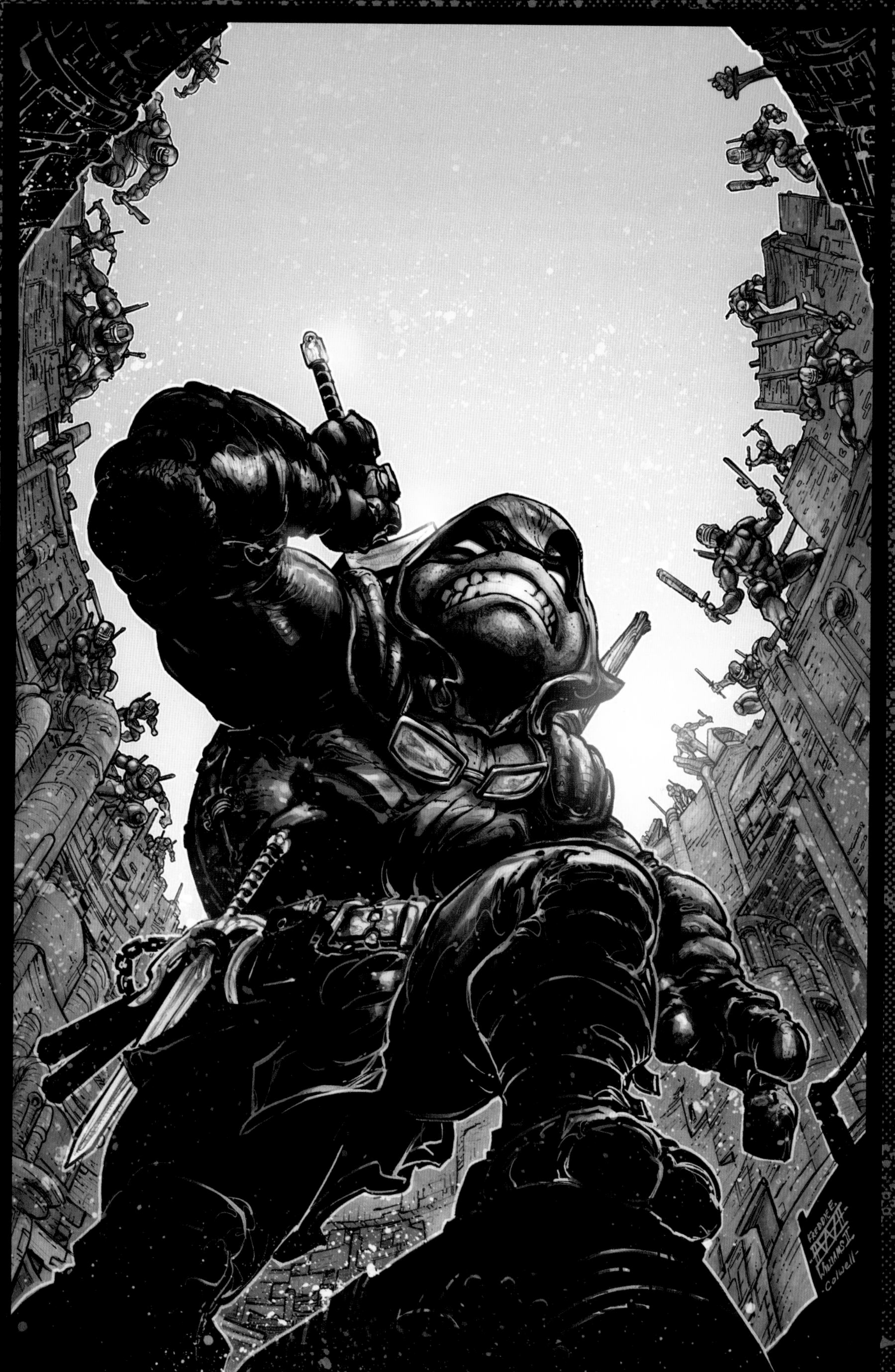

Colors by **Jeremy Colwell**

Art by **Dave Wachter**

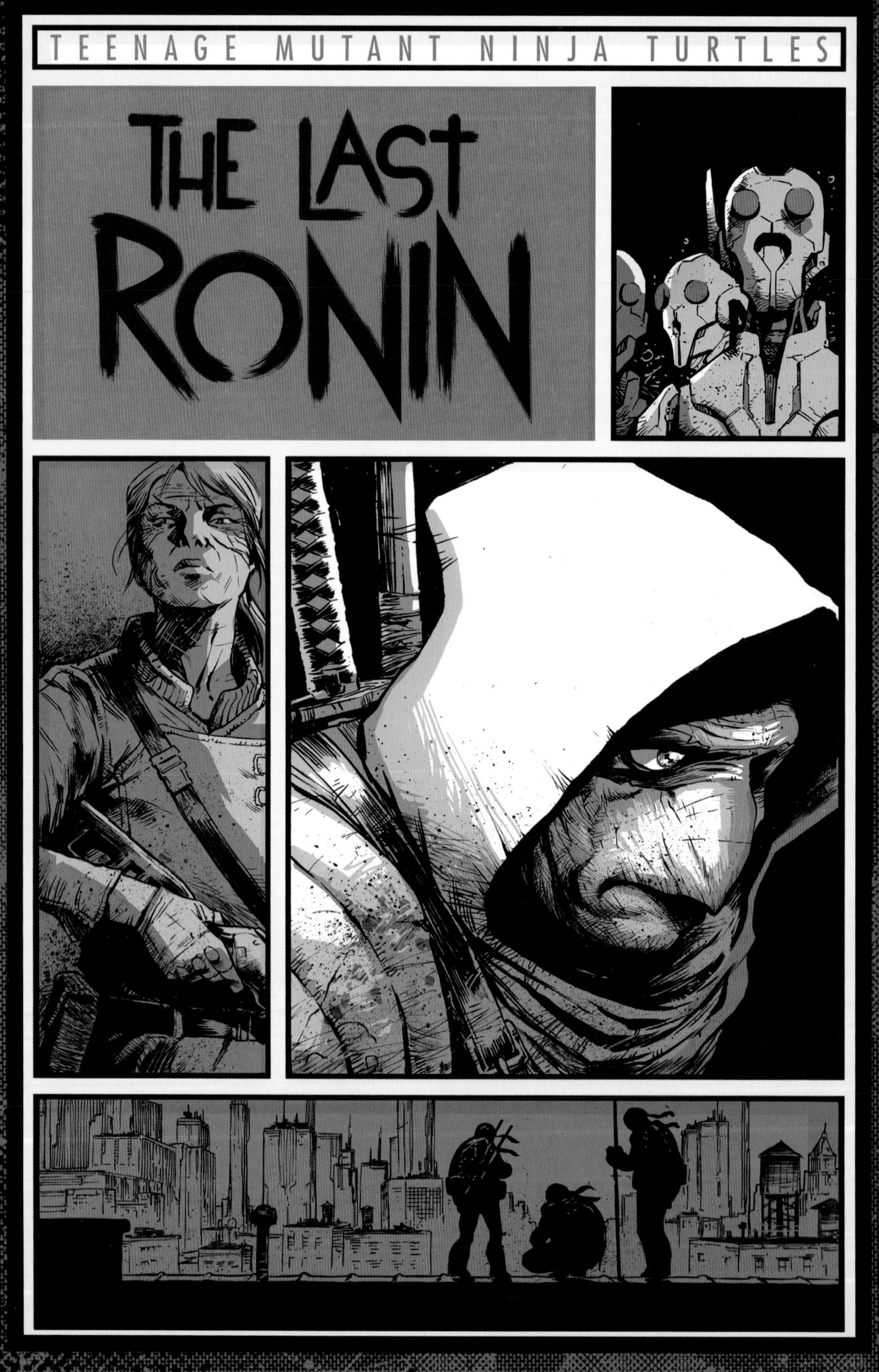
TEENAGE MUTANT NINJA TURTLES
THE LAST RONIN

Art by **Justin Roiland** & **Kevin Eastman**

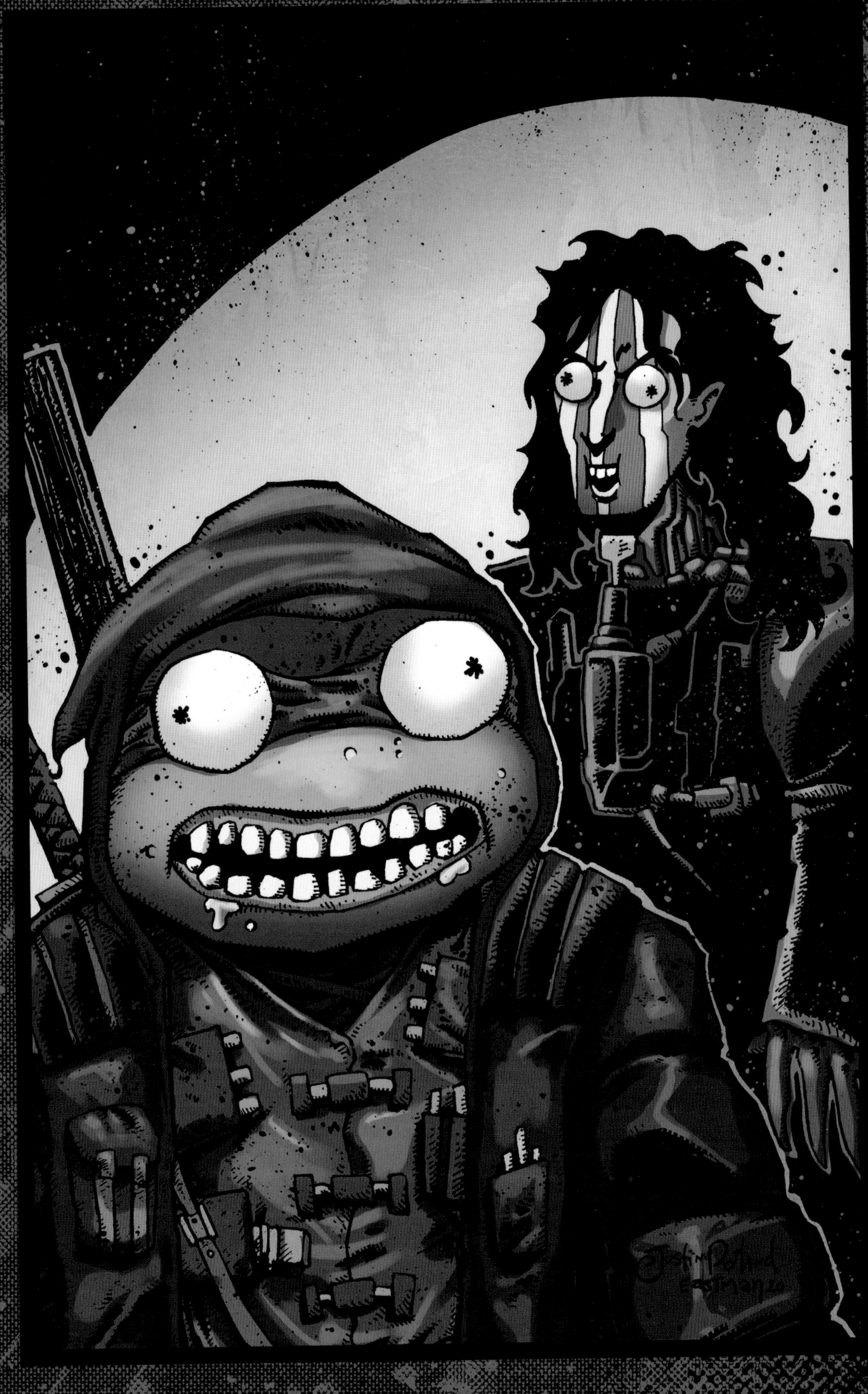

Art by **Kevin Eastman**

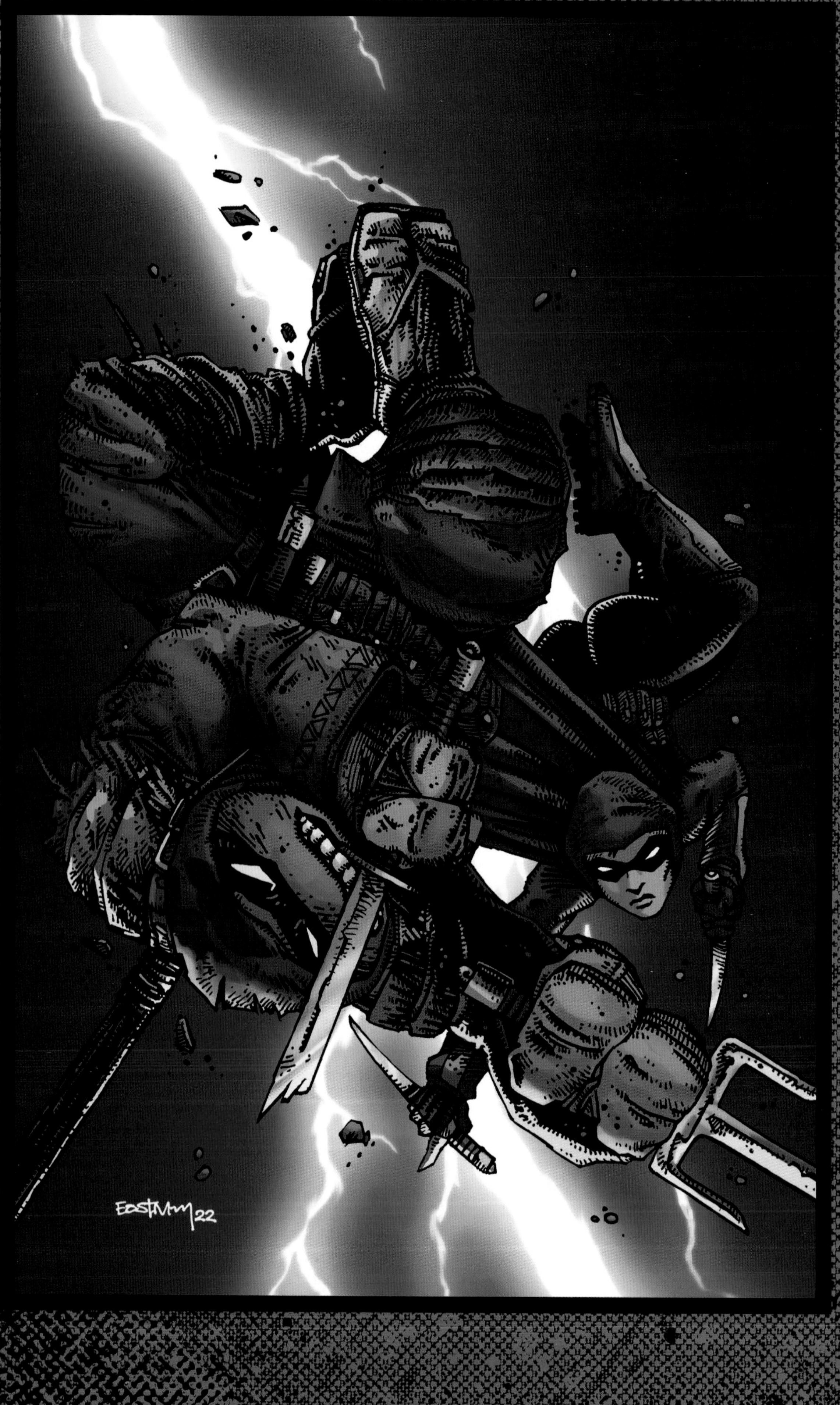

Art by **Esau** & **Isaac Escorza**

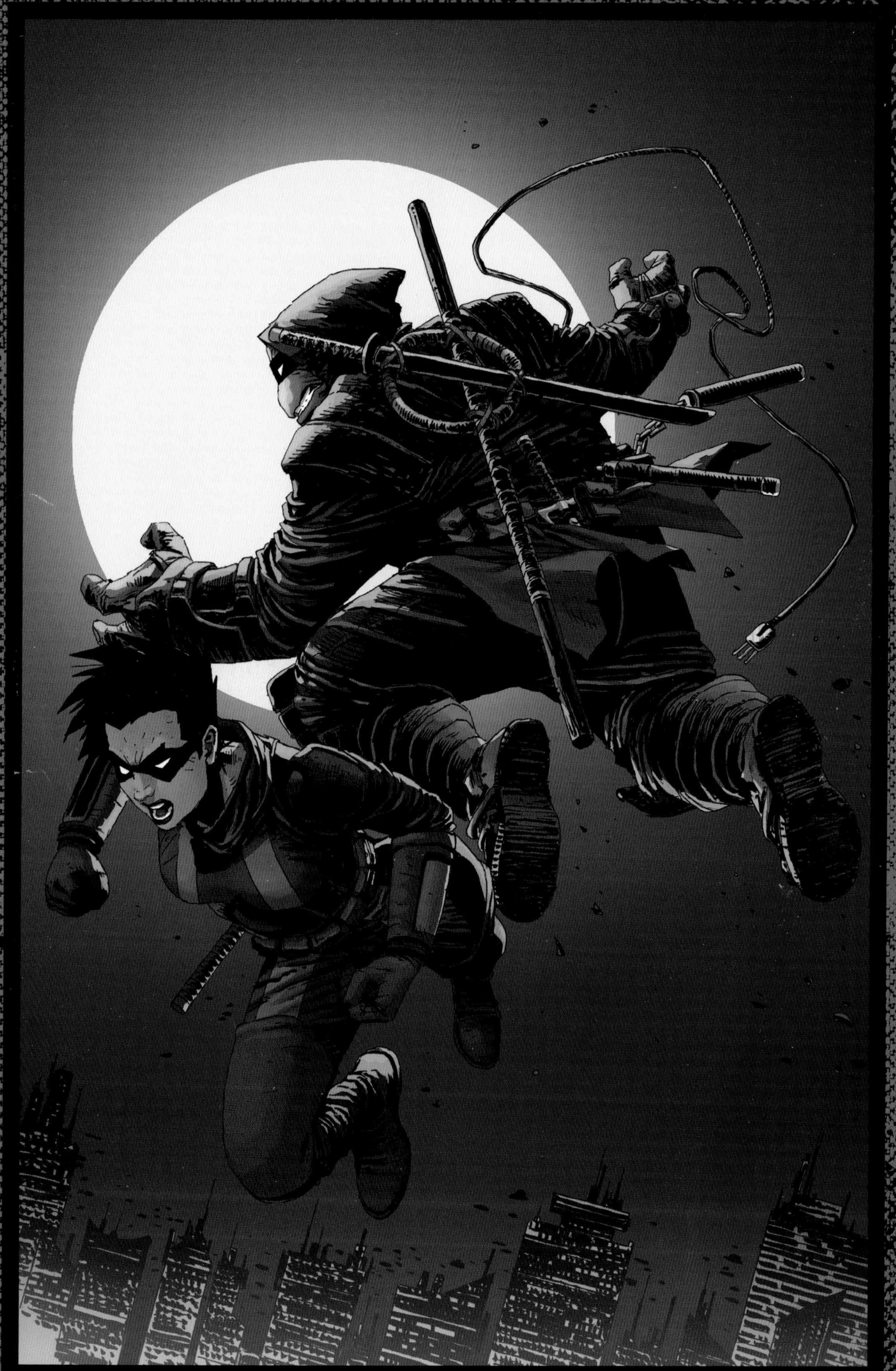

Colors by **Luis Antonio Delgado**

Art by **Ben Harvey**

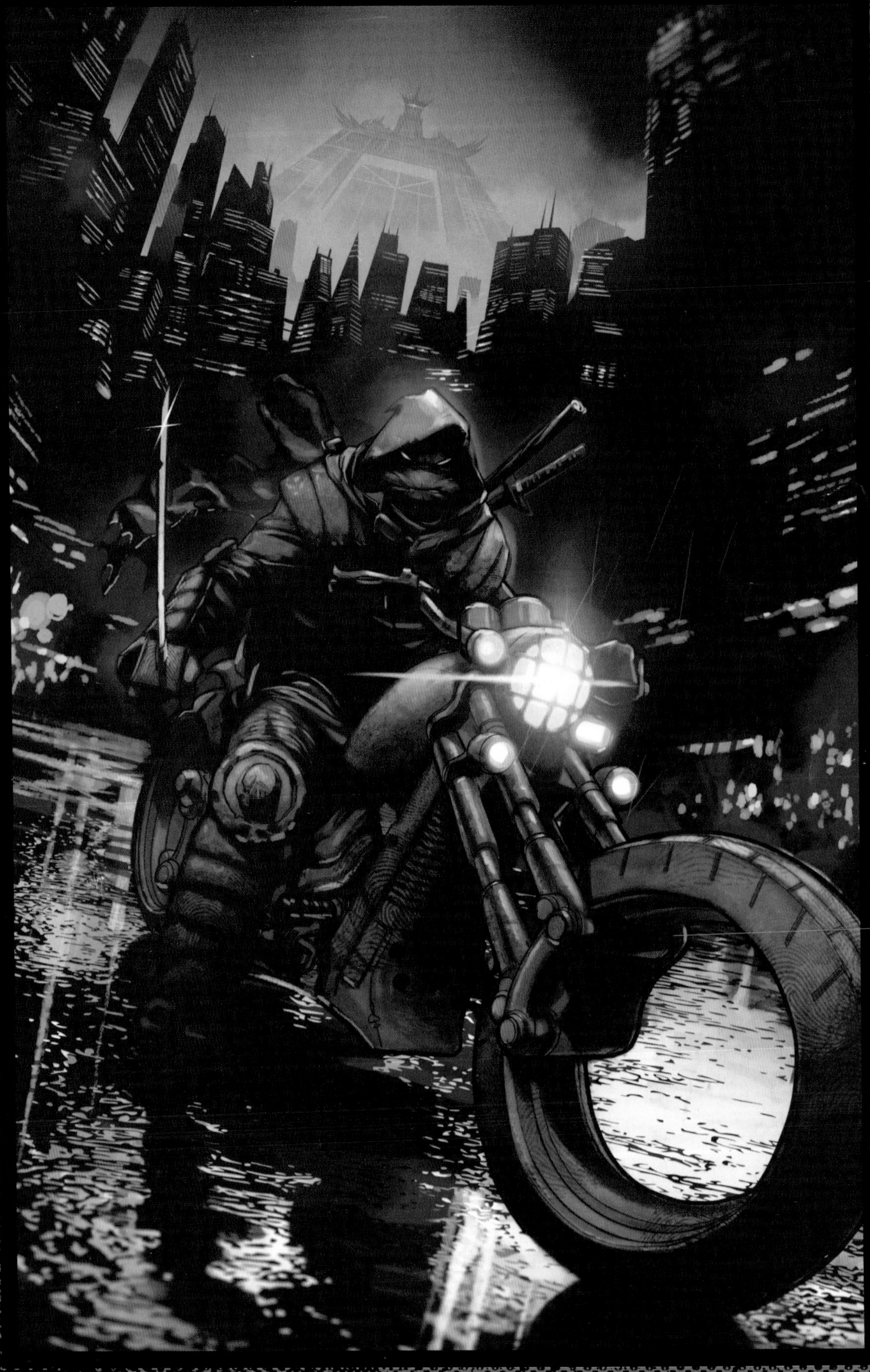

Art by **Jim Lawson**

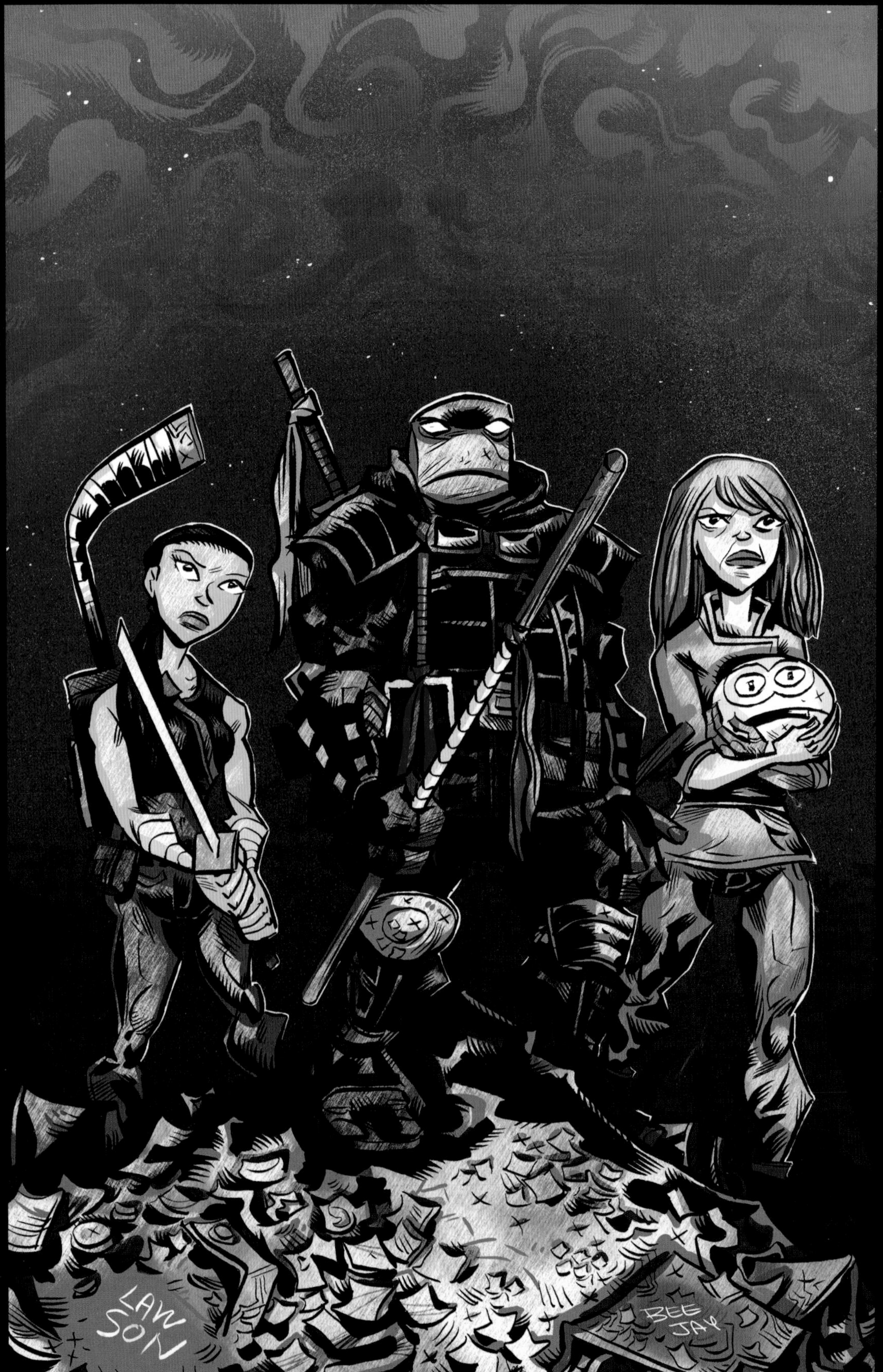
LAW SON
BEE JAY

Colors by **Beejay Hawn**